T0320047

Managing Hedge Fund Risk and Financing

Adapting to a New Era

Managing Hedge Fund Risk and Financing

Adapting to a New Era

DAVID P. BELMONT, CFA

WILEY

John Wiley & Sons (Asia) Pte. Ltd.

Other Wiley Editorial Offices

John Wiley & Sons, 111 River Street, Hoboken, NJ 07030, USA
John Wiley & Sons, The Atrium, Southern Gate, Chichester, West Sussex, P019 8SQ,
    United Kingdom
John Wiley & Sons (Canada) Ltd., 5353 Dundas Street West, Suite 400, Toronto,
    Ontario, M9B 6HB, Canada
John Wiley & Sons Australia Ltd., 42 McDougall Street, Milton, Queensland 4064, Australia
Wiley-VCH, Boschstrasse 12, D-69469 Weinheim, Germany

Library of Congress Cataloging-in-Publication Data
ISBN 978-0-470-82726-0 (Hardback)
ISBN 978-0-470-82728-4 (ePDF)
ISBN 978-0-470-82727-7 (Mobi)
ISBN 978-0-470-82729-1 (ePub)

Typeset in 10/12pt, Sabon-Roman by Thomson Digital, India
Printed in Singapore by Markono Print Media Pte Ltd
10 9 8 7 6 5 4 3 2 1

*I am grateful to Tilly, Will and Emma
for the time to write this book.
You have done without
my attention for too long.*

Contents

Contents

Acknowledgments

The recent credit crisis and its aftermath provided the content for this book. My various mentors gave me the framework for organizing that experience and distilling its lessons. My colleagues gave me a forum in which to debate and refine my ideas before writing. My wife and family gave me the time to write it.

The opportunity to publish came from Nick Wallwork at John Wiley & Sons, who plucked me from a podium in Singapore and asked me if I could convert my ideas about how risk management can be used to create shareholder value into a book. That moment led to my first book and started my publishing career.

The quality of this book has also been much improved by my editor, John Owen, who brought to it much-needed cogency and organization.

There are many more people I could thank, but time, space, and their modesty compel me to stop here.

Introduction

Managing Complexity and Uncertainty

Hedge funds and hedge fund investing is complex. Managing the risk of a hedge fund is similarly complex. At its core a hedge fund is a portfolio of securities whose future value is uncertain because of investment risk. However, the use of leverage, the operational realities of derivatives trading, the pledging of securities as collateral, and the asymmetric rights granted to investors, prime brokers, and hedge fund managers introduce funding, counterparty, and operational risk. Together these dramatically increase the complexity of the total risk management challenge for the hedge fund and the investment risks faced by investors.

Every hedge fund is unique in terms of its strategies, capabilities, investors, risk appetite, funding profile and legal structure. Collectively, however, hedge funds represent a fragile business model where investors' equity and prime broker funding should be balanced against investment risks and leverage if sustainable alpha is to be generated.

The risk profile of a given hedge fund can appear unique but thoughtful inspection reveals that hedge funds are not in fact a distinct risk species but, rather, share a common risk genus. Aspects of the risk management challenge and priorities for a given fund may be distinct but, fundamentally, hedge fund risks are more similar than they are different. Hedge funds share common vulnerabilities to investment, funding, counterparty and operational risks.

Hedge fund performance in the infamous market environment of 2008 showed that these vulnerabilities were underappreciated. Statistical risk modeling and measurement techniques which focused only on the potential returns of hedge fund investment portfolios grossly underestimated funding risk and the potential losses. Realized losses exceeded worst-case expectations of investors as a result of the impact of risks external to the investment portfolio; namely, counterparty, funding, and operational risks. In particular, assumptions about funding stability proved false when investors, prime brokers, and hedge fund managers acted to protect their interests. These hedge fund stakeholders exercised rights and forced actions which were optimal for individual investors, senior creditors and hedge-fund principals but sub-optimal for investors as a whole. To manage this risk going forward, an integrated risk management approach that combines stress and scenario testing of investment performance with worst-case investor-redemption behavior, a contraction in margin financing, and the proactive structuring of financial relationships with investors, creditors and trading counterparties should be considered.

This book presents in detail a new perspective on the risk which hedge fund investors and managers face. It proposes an integrated strategy by which hedge fund managers can structure financing and manage investment, counterparty, funding, and operational risks. These strategies can be customized to a specific hedge fund's investment strategy. The book details the construction, risk profile, and performance of all major hedge fund strategies over the past decade and specifically through the 2008 credit crisis. It summarizes the risk management lessons learned and details the minimum risk management capabilities a hedge fund should demonstrate across investment, funding, counterparty and operational risks to be prepared for the next crisis. Lastly, it recommends risk management strategies for each risk type and details ISDA, prime brokerage, fee and margin lock-up, and committed-facility lending terms that can be negotiated to manage counterparty and funding liquidity risk.

CHAPTER 1

The Quick and the Dead: Lessons Learned

THE GLOBAL CREDIT CRISIS: 2008–2010

The global economy and capital markets have gone through a number of cycles in the 80 years since the Great Depression but none of the downturns has been as dramatic and severe as the credit crisis of 2008–2010. In the span of just eight weeks beginning in September 2008, a "tsunami" swept through the financial markets. The first ripple began on September 7, 2008, when the U.S. government stepped in to prevent the collapse of two cornerstones of the U.S. economy and took control of Fannie Mae and Freddie Mac in an extraordinary Federal intervention in private enterprise.

A week later, the ripples became waves and on September 14, Lehman Brothers, a 150-year-old institution that had survived the Great Depression, capsized and became the largest company to enter bankruptcy in U.S. history. On the same day, Merrill Lynch agreed to merge with Bank of America in order to avert its own demise. Two days later, AIG, the world's largest insurer, received an US$85-billion bailout package from the U.S. Federal Reserve in order to stave off collapse.

On September 21, with the crisis deepening and just five days after the AIG bailout, Morgan Stanley and Goldman Sachs, the two leading providers of financing to the hedge fund industry, sought shelter in safe harbors and received Federal approval to become bank holding companies. This enabled both firms to gain much-needed access to the Federal Reserve's emergency-lending facilities to ensure their liquidity. The move effectively ended the era of investment banking that arose out of the Glass–Steagal Act of 1933, which separated investment banks and commercial banks following the Stock Market Crash of 1929.

Pressures in the financial markets continued to mount and on September 26, Washington Mutual became the largest bank failure in U.S. history when it was seized by Federal regulators. With confidence in the financial markets under intense pressure, the White House and Congress drafted a historic US$700-billion bank rescue plan for the financial sector on September 29. This rescue plan would eventually become known as the Troubled Assets Relief Program (TARP).

Hedge funds continued to sail in this tempest and navigate a trifecta of forces that threatened their extinction. Some of these privateers understood the limitations of their fragile craft and sought shelter, while others risked their fortunes and sought to profit from opportunities created by the distress. During this turbulent period, concern regarding the health of the hedge fund industry was widespread, as catastrophic investment perform-ance put the entire industry under unprecedented pressure. A record 1,471 individual hedge funds either failed or closed their doors during the credit crisis of 2008. A further 668 closed or failed in the first half of 2009. The difference between those that survived and those that failed is that the latter had great conviction about the future return of their investments while the former knew they could not predict the future, had prepared for uncertainty by investing in their firm's risk manage-ment, and followed their risk management discipline to get to a safe harbor until the financial tsunami passed.

Figure 1.1 shows that the rate of hedge fund failures more than doubled, from less than 7 percent in 2007 to more than 16 percent in 2008.

Figure 1.2 shows the massive contraction in assets under management of the hedge fund industry in 2008, as fund performance fell, funds failed, and investors exited hedge fund investments.

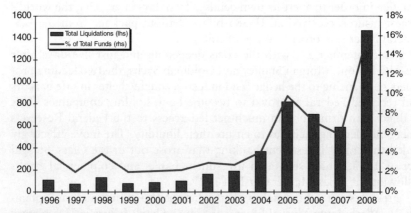

FIGURE 1.1   Hedge fund failures (1996–2009)

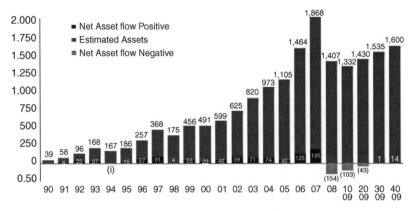

FIGURE 1.2 Estimated growth of hedge fund net assets (1990–2009)
Source: Hedge Fund Research, Inc. as of January 2010

Increased Systematic Risk

The first of the three forces threatening the performance and survival of hedge funds was systematic risk. The systematic disruption in the capital markets directly increased the volatility and risk in the markets in which most hedge funds traded. Fundamental systematic risk manifested itself in the form of market volatility and illiquidity, leading to mark-to-market losses for many hedge funds and increased demands for margin from their creditors.

As evident in Figure 1.3, the market volatility during 2008 was unprecedented, with both the frequency and size of large market price movements increasing well beyond historical norms.

The bear market that began after the market peaked in October 2007 was one of the worst bear markets since the 1920s, and second only to the

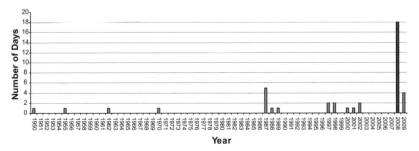

FIGURE 1.3 Day-to-day price moves greater than 5 percent (S&P Index)
Source: Bloomberg

TABLE 1.1 Largest one-day market declines in S&P 500

Date	Decline (%)
October 19, 1987	20.47
October 15, 2008	9.03
December 1, 2008	8.93
September 29, 2008	8.79
October 26, 1987	8.28
October 9, 2008	7.62
November 13, 2008	6.92
October 27, 1997	6.87
August 31, 1998	6.80
January 8, 1988	6.77

Source: Bloomberg

Stock Market Crash of 1929. From the peak of the bull market on October 9, 2007 the broader equity market, as measured by the U.S. S&P 500 index fell more than 58 percent. Over 25 percent of that decline occurred in the 13 days prior to October 16, 2008. Indeed, while all of 2008 was a lethal year for hedge funds, September and October were particularly deadly. As shown in Table 1.1, five of the largest one-day declines ever in the S&P 500 occurred in 2008, and three of those days were in September and October.

Amid one of the worst bear markets in history, volatility rose to unprecedented levels, surpassing the volatility experienced even on "Black Monday"—October 19, 1987. Figure 1.4 shows the rolling 60-day

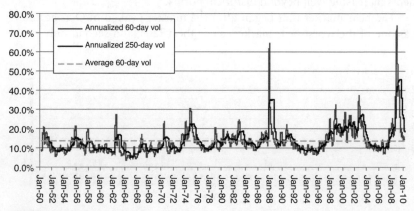

FIGURE 1.4 Standard & Poor's 500 Index rolling 60-day volatility, 1950–2010
Source: Bloomberg

volatility of the Standard & Poor's 500 Index and allows comparison of volatility levels in prior crises. The levels of volatility realized during the Credit Crisis of 2008–09 surpassed those of the "Black Monday" crisis and all prior crises by more than 15 percent.

By October 15, 2008, volatility had risen to 51.18 percent, equaling Black Monday,[1] and continued to grow higher thereafter.

The depth and breadth of the increase in volatility was unprecedented. Between January 1, 2008 and January 1, 2009, the S&P 500 Index closed up or down 5 percent or more on six separate trading days. Never before had any year had as many 5 percent moves.[2] In addition, all six of the moves occurred in the trading days in the first half of October 2008. The gauntlet that hedge funds had to run during these two weeks in 2008 was deadly.

Similarly, as shown in Figure 1.5, the CBOE Volatility Index (VIX), a benchmark market measure of volatility, also reached unprecedented levels.

The CBOE volatility index typically trades in the 10–30 range. However, in October 2008, the index was trading at over 80.

As much as inter-day volatility had increased, intra-day volatility had also increased to levels not previously seen. For the trading days comprising the first half of October 2008, the S&P 500 experienced intra-day price swings of greater than 5 percent on eight occasions. From October 1 through October 16, intra-day volatility of the S&P 500 index (as measured by the difference between the intra-day high and low) went from 2.25 percent to 10.31 percent. This succession of extremely volatile trading days had simply never happened before in the previous 46 years (see Figure 1.6). Similarly, on October 24, 2008, the CBOE Volatility Index reached an all-time intra-day high of 89.53.

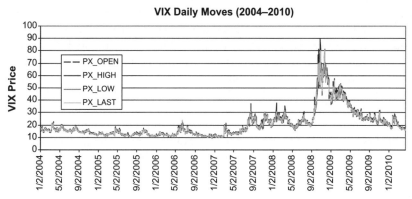

FIGURE 1.5 CBOE Volatility Index, 2004–10
Source: Bloomberg

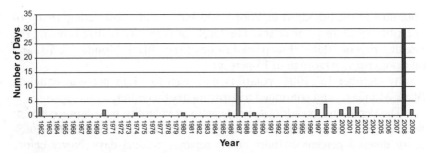

FIGURE 1.6   Standard & Poor's 500 Index intra-day price moves greater than 5 percent (1962–2009)
Source: Bloomberg

Amidst this wind shear in security valuations, the value of hedge-fund portfolios declined and prime brokers increased their margin requirements to protect themselves from losses as hedge fund defaults became increasingly likely. By increasing margin levels, prime brokers increased the collateral they held and reduced the amount of credit extended to hedge funds. The increased margin requirements caused mark-to-market losses to be realized and further drove down security values as hedge funds liquidated positions to generate cash needed to post to their prime brokers and avoid default.

Contraction of the Interbank Funding Markets

The second of the three forces threatening the performance and survival of hedge funds was the freezing of the interbank funding markets. Uncertainty regarding the solvency of major financial institutions caused a severe contraction and the eventual collapse of the interbank funding markets. This eroded the solvency of almost all hedge fund counterparties and led to the sudden failure of several major financial institutions (including Bear Stearns and Lehman Brothers). It dramatically weakened broker-dealers such as Goldman Sachs and Morgan Stanley, which had to convert to bank holding companies in order to use the Federal Reserve's emergency-lending facilities. Hedge funds sought to rapidly withdraw their assets held at these brokers as default concerns mounted, leading to the equivalent of a run on the brokers by the hedge funds. Morgan Stanley reportedly had 95 percent of its excess hedge fund equity requested to be withdrawn within one week.

Investor Redemptions

The third of the three forces threatening the performance and survival of hedge funds was the vicious cycle of de-leveraging that panicked hedge fund investors, causing them to make unrelenting demands to redeem their hedge fund shares. This in turn undermined less-liquid hedge fund investment strategies and forced hedge funds to further realize market losses by selling assets to meet investor demands or forcing them to refuse redemption requests in an effort to ride out the storm without selling assets at distressed prices. Many hedge funds were unprepared for the redemption maelstrom that engulfed them. Several have failed dramatically, while many more quietly gated their fund, slowly liquidated and ultimately shuttered their doors after suffering significant losses.

THE QUICK AND THE DEAD

Prime brokers provided much of the leverage exploited by hedge funds to generate high returns before the crisis. Essentially, prime brokers, through their margin requirements, determine how much cash a hedge fund needs to post to invest in a security. The prime brokers provide the difference between the price of the security and the margin requirement as financing (essentially a loan) to the hedge fund to finance the purchase of the security. The prime broker holds the security as collateral against the loan. As the security's value rapidly falls, the fund needs to post more cash with the prime broker in order to remain invested in the position.

In the crisis, not only were security values falling (resulting in hedge funds having to post additional cash to remain invested), but several prime brokers were also increasing their percentage of a security's value a hedge fund had to post to own the security. Sometimes this was a specific response to a decline in a particular hedge fund's creditworthiness and sometimes this margin change was applied across all funds holding a certain type of risky asset. Regardless of cause, having to post greater margin further reduced hedge funds' liquidity and available cash to meet redemptions.

Prime brokers, hedge fund managers and their investors faced a prisoner's dilemma[3] where, if the demands for cash were balanced, they could all increase the probability they would collectively emerge from the crisis while the first one to individually grab the cash would be certain to minimize their losses. In the crisis, investor cash and margin financing were like plasma in a trauma unit and there was not enough to go around. Funds had been shattered by the market crash. Investors and prime brokers needed to meet their own cash needs and had to decide which funds were too far gone to recover and which funds were likely survive if investor cash and margin financing was maintained.

So what differentiated those hedge funds that survived from those that failed? Risk management and maintaining liquidity were critical to differentiating a fund's performance in the crisis. Hedge funds that recognized the fragility of their business model; had cohesively planned their investment, funding, counterparty, and operation risk as an integrated discipline; had proactively analyzed their worst-case potential funding needs; and had structured their investor, prime brokerage and counterparty relationships to ensure that their funds could remain liquid, survived to take full advantage of the opportunities presented by the financial crises.

Funds failed or survived and thrived depending on the quality of their integrated risk management. Quantitative investment risk models using historical data failed in the face of unprecedented market volatility and a dramatic decline in trading liquidity. Not realizing that they had sailed off the map, and convinced that their historical models were right and the market was wrong, some funds followed a flawed compass and foundered on the rocks of illiquidity. Other funds mitigated losses by pragmatically jettisoning the deadweight of historical models and focusing on fundamental principles of risk management: de-lever and diversify. However, the best funds were not forced to de-lever and diversify. The best funds had the ability to maintain or increase leverage and funding liquidity because they had negotiated binding lock-ups and committed facilities with prime brokers so that margin financing remained stable. Redemptions were managed by having lengthy investor lock-ups and redemption terms that matched the liquidity of the investment portfolio with potential investor cash redemption demands. Such funds were able to maintain their liquidity and opportunistically profit from the crisis. To briefly illustrate the shortcomings of traditional risk measurement, we look at the performance of hedge funds over the period from 1999–2008.

Analysis of Hedge Fund Performance, 1999–2008

Prior performance did not predict future performance in 2008. Firstly, the crisis of 2008 was so severe that only one out of 12 hedge fund strategies— short selling—was profitable in 2008. Secondly, as shown in Table 1.2, the magnitude of the negative performance of many mainstream strategies in 2008 was so significant that it outweighed the typically positive performance of the prior two years, making the three-year average and cumulative performance of convertible bond strategies, distressed investing strategies, emerging markets strategies, fixed income arbitrage strategies and even fund of funds negative.

Traditional Hedge Fund Risk Analysis

Traditional risk analysis is based on historical data. It dramatically failed to predict the magnitude of losses hedge funds experienced in 2008 as the

TABLE 1.2 Comparison of short-term and long-term hedge fund strategy performance[4] (1999–2008)*

	2008 Return	2007 Return	Max Return (1997–2008)	Min Return (1997–2008)	Year of Max Return	Year of Min Return	Three-year Average Return (2006–2008)	Three-year Cumulative Return (2006–2008)	10-year Average (1999–2008)	10-year Cumulative (1999–2008)
Conv Bond Arb	−26.48%	3.87%	17.77%	−26.48%	2000	2008	−5.02%	−14.31%	4.75%	59.00%
CTA Global	12.78%	9.89%	14.58%	−0.35%	2002	2005	10.40%	34.55%	7.39%	104.02%
Distressed Debt	−19.40%	7.16%	27.35%	−19.40%	2003	2008	−0.93%	−2.76%	9.28%	142.93%
Emerging Markets	−30.30%	20.79%	44.59%	−30.30%	1999	2008	−1.69%	−4.97%	10.71%	176.56%
Equity Market Neutral	−7.34%	8.34%	15.44%	−7.34%	1997	2008	2.18%	6.69%	6.46%	87.06%
Event Driven	−16.20%	9.65%	22.74%	−16.20%	1999	2008	1.06%	3.23%	8.06%	117.12%
Fixed Income Arb	−16.80%	6.01%	12.62%	−16.80%	1999	2008	−1.82%	−5.35%	4.65%	57.48%
Global Macro	−2.88%	12.93%	23.91%	−2.88%	1997	2008	5.60%	17.76%	8.17%	119.24%
Long/Short Equity	−15.57%	10.53%	31.40%	−15.57%	1999	2008	0.05%	0.14%	7.00%	96.79%
Merger Arb	−1.03%	9.11%	18.11%	−1.03%	2000	2008	6.63%	21.23%	7.46%	105.33%
Relative Value	−13.70%	9.43%	17.17%	−13.70%	1999	2008	1.44%	4.39%	6.80%	93.07%
Short Selling	24.72%	7.38%	27.27%	−23.86%	2002	2003	9.04%	29.66%	3.02%	34.64%
Funds of Funds	−17.08%	10.07%	28.51%	−17.08%	1999	2008	−0.41%	−1.23%	6.22%	82.83%

* Annualized statistics are given

Source: EDHEC Risk and Asset Management Research Centre

events of that year were unprecedented. Traditional statistical analysis of historical data can dramatically underestimate the magnitude of potential losses.

The impact of this failure in risk measurement and management was that the Sharpe and Sortino Ratios for eight out of 13 strategies turned negative for the period 2006–2008. The magnitude of the failure in risk measurement is clear from an examination of the maximum monthly realized drawdown for each strategy and comparing that to the monthly historical return volatility. As shown in Table 1.3, for the period from 2006–2008, historical monthly volatility was less than the maximum drawdown for all hedge fund strategies except CTAs. In addition, the monthly 95th percentile VaR was less than the maximum drawdown by a factor of more than four times for most strategies.

The results for 1999–2008 are similar to those of 2006–2008 in that the maximum drawdown observed in 2008 was still far greater than what would have been predicted by the volatility and value at risk. This indicates that longer-term historical analysis incorporating several crisis periods was not sufficient to improve the predictive accuracy of the risk measures. The maximum drawdowns by strategy are even greater multiples of the volatility and value at risk measures than they are in the 2006–2008 period. The Sharpe and Sortino Ratios when viewed over the longer period of 1999–2008 remained positive, but were less than 1 for all but one out of 13 strategies; but even over the longer period hedge funds failed to beat U.S. Treasuries in risk adjusted performance (see Table 1.4).

Value at Risk (VaR) is but one perspective on the risk of a hedge fund; namely, investment risk. The inadequacy of traditional volatility-based VaR measures to quantify the potential worst-case loss of hedge fund investments is clear. In addition, if the crisis of 2008 demonstrated anything it was that risk is transmutable and contagious. It can expand from investment risk into funding liquidity risk, which can then convert into counterparty and operational risk. The market plunge made lenders to Lehman Brothers uncertain regarding the magnitude of losses at Lehman Brothers. This in turn increased the perceived counterparty credit risk they bore by dealing with Lehman and affected Lehman's ability to fund itself and to lend out securities to generate cash liquidity. This in turn led to Lehman's collapse and impacted the operations of all of its hedge fund clients. The crisis of 2008 was much more than a market-risk event. To avoid or even to predict the potential losses of 2008, hedge fund risk managers would have had to have run extreme tail-event scenarios where investment risk, counterparty risk, funding liquidity risk, and operational risk combined in a complex, multi-staged scenario.

TABLE 1.3 Hedge fund strategies' risks (January 2006–December 2008)

	Max Drawdown (in %)	Volatility (in %)*	Max Drawdown/ Vol	Modified VaR (in %)***	Max Drawdown/ VaR	Sharp*/***	Sortino*/***
Conv Arb	29.27%	10.32%	2.84	6.76%	4.33	-0.82	-0.58
CTA Global	5.29%	7.71%	0.69	2.73%	1.94	0.90	2.33
Distressed Securities	22.60%	7.60%	2.97	4.47%	5.06	-0.57	-0.45
Emerging Markets	34.54%	13.73%	2.52	7.85%	4.40	-0.37	-0.34
Equity Market Neutral	11.08%	4.85%	2.28	2.74%	4.04	-0.26	-0.06
Event Driven	20.07%	7.60%	2.64	4.18%	4.80	-0.31	-0.21
Fixed Income Arb	17.60%	6.87%	2.56	4.35%	4.05	-0.77	-0.47
Global Macro	7.92%	5.30%	1.49	2.13%	3.72	0.41	0.94
Long/Short Equity	21.04%	8.50%	2.48	4.65%	4.52	-0.40	-0.34
Merger Arb	5.65%	4.42%	1.28	1.80%	3.14	0.72	1.25
Relative Value	15.94%	6.56%	2.43	3.77%	4.23	-0.30	-0.14
Short Selling	14.93%	12.11%	1.23	3.73%	4.00	0.46	1.59
Funds of Funds	20.22%	7.53%	2.69	4.21%	4.80	-0.51	-0.45

* Annualized statistics are given
** The risk-free rate is the average three-month U.S. Treasury bill during the period from 2006 to 2008 (3.44%); minimum acceptable return (MAR) is fixed at 2.5%
*** Non-annualized 5%-quantiles are estimated
Source: EDHEC Risk and Asset Management Research Centre

TABLE 1.4 Hedge fund strategies' risks (1999–2008)

	Max Drawdown (in %)	Volatility (in %)*	Max Drawdown/Vol	Modified VaR (in %)***	Max Drawdown/VaR	Sharp*/**	Sortino*/**
Conv Arb	29.27%	6.74%	4.34	3.55%	8.25	0.24	0.26
CTA Global	11.68%	8.80%	1.33	3.52%	3.32	0.48	1.01
Distressed Securities	22.60%	5.88%	3.84	2.50%	9.04	1.04	1.22
Emerging Markets	34.54%	11.60%	2.98	5.05%	6.84	0.65	0.91
Equity Market Neutral	11.08%	3.17%	3.50	1.28%	8.66	1.05	0.91
Event Driven	20.07%	5.83%	3.44	2.56%	7.84	0.84	1.04
Fixed Income Arb	17.60%	4.21%	4.18	2.03%	8.67	0.36	0.33
Global Macro	7.92%	5.27%	1.50	1.56%	5.08	0.95	2.16
Long/Short Equity	21.04%	7.60%	2.77	3.14%	6.70	0.51	0.86
Merger Arb	5.65%	3.58%	1.58	1.31%	4.31	1.21	1.68
RelativeValue	15.94%	4.52%	3.53	2.08%	7.66	0.81	0.82
Short Selling	36.30%	17.74%	2.05	7.91%	4.59	-0.01	0.05
Funds of Funds	20.22%	6.18%	3.27	2.43%	8.32	0.50	0.78

* Annualized statistics are given
** The risk-free rate is the average three-month U.S. Treasury bill during the period from 1999 to 2008 (3.14%); minimum acceptable return (MAR) is fixed at 2.5%
*** Non-annualized 5%-quantiles are estimated
Source: EDHEC Risk and Asset Management Research Centre

Value of Integrated Risk Management

Prior to the crisis, the minority of hedge funds employed a dedicated risk manager. A recent PriceWaterhouseCoopers survey (see Table 1.5) indicates that only 31 percent of all hedge funds have an independent risk manager.

This in no way means that hedge funds do not practice risk management. Risk management is the complementary strand to return maximization in the double helix of investment management. It is in the DNA of all successful hedge fund managers. However, risk management has been focused on the investment portfolio and practiced in isolation from the business risks. Typically, examples of investment risk management by a hedge fund manager would be keeping investment concentrations small and proportional to his conviction and the expected return of each trade, monitoring the liquidity profile of his securities portfolio, monitoring overall leverage, and reviewing his VaR and historical stress test results to minimize the potential losses the positions in his investment portfolio could generate. The investment risks of the portfolio are typically evaluated with respect solely to the intrinsic risks of the securities in the investment portfolio, and not in the context of the funding, counterparty and operational risks of the fund and not with respect to the potential actions of various stakeholders in the fund. This focus on investment risk implicitly assumes that the significant risks in the hedge fund all emanate from the investment portfolio and that the portfolio manager has sole and exclusive rights governing the assets of the fund under all circumstances. This is an incorrect and potentially disastrous assumption.

The following fictionalized account of Icarus Capital illustrates the complexity of the risk management challenge at a hedge fund and the implications of a risk management framework that focuses exclusively on investment risks and does not consider the potential incentives and actions of hedge fund creditors and investors.

TABLE 1.5 Proportion of hedge funds with independent risk manager positions[5]

Position Established	Very Large (>$5 billion)	Large ($5B<$1 billion)	Medium (<$1 billion)	All percent
Compliance Officer	83%	71%	44%	65%
In-house Counsel	78%	56%	22%	49%
Risk Manager	37%	44%	12%	31%
Head of IT	45%	41%	32%	40%

ICARUS CAPITAL: PORTRAIT OF A FAILING FUND

By any measure, Ivan Jones was successful. He was Ivy League educated and earned an MBA from Harvard Business School in 1992. He was recruited directly from Harvard to Goldman Sachs graduate training program and had been a successful proprietary equities trader during his 10 years at the firm, rising to be the U.S. head of equities prop trading and one of the youngest partners at the firm. He had repeatedly proven his ability to take risk and use leverage, beating the S&P 500 throughout his time at the firm. For his efforts, the firm had paid him decently but not extravagantly in his view, and he had amassed a net worth in excess of $20 million.

In 2002, he decided that he needed a new challenge. He wanted to be his own boss and keep more of the profits generated by his skill and intellect. He had a great track record at the firm and knew that he deserved more than the additional deferred millions the firm was putting aside for him. He told the firm that he was quitting and starting his own hedge fund. His managers understood, as he was following a path blazed by many other former star traders at the firm. They decided that rather than lose the revenue stream he generated within the firm, they could replicate it by investing $200 million in his new fund. After all, he would still stay loyal to the firm and trade with them. The firm's prime brokerage could be of help to Ivan as well and the firm could earn additional trading and financing fees.

Ivan named his fund "Icarus Capital" and launched in early 2002 with $400 million of assets under management (AUM) provided in part from the firm, his Alma Mater's endowment, several funds of funds and investments by his friends and family. He put his entire $20 million of net worth into the fund.

For the next 58 months, he followed a disciplined equity long/short strategy. He made relative bets on the direction of the market, the performance of various industrial and market sectors, and the relative value of companies with common fundamentals. From time to time, he would take directional market bets but his instincts typically proved right. The fund achieved an impressive return of 22.83 percent annualized (as shown in Table 1.6). The returns looked a little choppy with volatility around 13.32 percent but most of the volatility appeared to be skewed to the upside and he had relatively low downside volatility (6.37 percent).

TABLE 1.6 Return analysis of Icarus Capital

Icarus Capital	
Mean	1.74%
Standard Deviation	3.84%
Annual Return	22.83%
Annual Volatility	13.32%
Skew	0.57
Kurtosis	3.78
Downside Volatility	6.37%
Max Consecutive Gain	29.27%
Max Consecutive Loss	−8.90%
% Up Months	78.57%
% Down Months	31.63%
Serial Correlation of Returns	0.08%
VaR Normal	−4.59%
VaR Adjusted	−4.87%
Expected Tail Loss	−6.38%
Maximum Drawdown	−8.90%
Best Month	12.63%
Worst Month	−5.97%

With his good performance, he'd been able to progressively attract more capital after the first year from pension-plan sponsors, endowments, and high-net-worth individuals. His prime broker had also been helpful in introducing his fund to new potential investors. In a relatively short time his AUM quickly rose to $1 billion. As the CEO and Portfolio Manager, the pressure was on him to continue to deliver results and he spent most of his time thinking about market trends, evaluating recommendations from his analysts, and scouring the market for additional opportunities.

THE ROLE OF THE CFO

He left the day-to-day running of his fund to his old friend from Harvard, Bart Stokes, whom he employed as the CFO for Icarus. Bart spent a lot of time dealing with investors, prime brokers, accountants, Operations, and IT, and managing the fund administrator and the custodian. He needed to take care of the details of running the fund so Ivan was free to focus on generating alpha. Ivan's performance was consistently good and they were all getting rich off the 20 percent performance fee they earned. Ivan and most of the staff were required to invest a portion of their compensation back into the fund. Being the CFO, Bart knew that all the staff, himself included, reinvested practically all their disposable income back into the fund. As time went on, Ivan hired four senior traders to assist him in running different aspects of the portfolio. Opportunities were getting harder to find and less rewarding. Having more senior traders to help find, evaluate and invest their investors' capital helped him sustain performance. Each trader followed a different equity related strategy while Ivan focused on equity relative value and made the day-to-day decisions regarding how much money to allocate to each trader's strategy. The four traders followed convertible-arbitrage, event driven, emerging market and activist strategies, respectively. The activist strategies focused on small capitalization companies as these required less investment to get a meaningful shareholding to influence management. The convertible-arbitrage strategy focused on sub-investment grade and non-rated convertible bonds as these were less widely covered by other hedge funds and often had greater option value that could be monetized. The emerging market strategy focused on Brazil, Russia, Chile and Indonesia as Ivan felt these commodity-exporting economies had strong potential for appreciation given Chinese and Indian demand for raw materials. The event driven strategy invested both in companies Ivan expected would merge or be taken over as well as in announced deals.

To help him manage the traders' activities, Ivan had implemented analytics and reporting similar to those he had used at Goldman. However, unlike his prior role where he had his risk taking observed and limited by Goldman's risk managers, at Icarus he was free to make his own decisions about risk taking without being second-guessed by Goldman's risk managers.

He had his daily P&L reports for each position, strategy/trader, and the portfolio as a whole. He had value at risk reports that showed him with 95 percent confidence, and how much his portfolio and even individual trade positions could lose in a day if they had been held over the past year. He had liquidation reports which showed how long it would take to sell the securities in the portfolio and move to the safety of cash, given current market volumes. He had concentration reports which showed how his portfolio was spread across individual stocks, industrial sectors, and countries. He had cash availability reports that showed him the amount of leverage each position was using and how much he had borrowed from his prime brokers and how much cash he had available. He liked to keep this cash amount at between 10–20 percent of the fund's AUM. Around these reports, Ivan had some guidelines that had served him well throughout his successful career. He did not want any one position to have the potential to reduce monthly P&L by more than 1 percent unless it was a really high-conviction trade. He didn't want any position to be more than 10 percent of the gross market value (GMV) of the portfolio unless it was an event driven deal that was sure to close or an activist position they needed to influence a company's board decisions. He did not want any position to be more than five days of trading volume unless it could be put in the side pocket of his fund as a longer-term investment. They had a weekly risk committee where Ivan, Bart, and the four traders would review the portfolio and discuss market trends and asset allocations. They also discussed exceptions to the rules that Ivan typically used to guide the fund. At the end of each meeting, Ivan would make his decisions about how much fund equity to have committed to each trader's strategy depending on how rich the opportunity set was for that strategy. Generally, Ivan controlled about 60 percent of the equity of the fund in his relative-value strategy and the other traders controlled about 10 percent each. Ivan's positions as a result tended to be substantially bigger than the others and most of the exceptions to the rules arose from his positions. His performance showed his judgment was far superior. The investors had placed their money with him; he was the founder and time had shown that he was far more often right than wrong.

P&L Correlations Increase

In July 2007, there was a jump in volatility in the market after a number of quantitative funds liquidated a large number of their positions. That was a unique month for Icarus because it was one of the few months where all of their strategies recorded a slight loss that led to negative 3.45 percent return for the month. Ivan viewed the event as an aberration caused by the actions of a few large quant funds. For August and September, the company's strategies resumed their typical pattern of low correlation of returns. Some or all strategies typically posted small gains and when performance was mixed, the gains typically outweighed the losses to result in a positive month for the fund. A closer look at July with respect to major factors such as exposures to global equity market's betas, equity volatility, credit spreads, commodity prices, and yield curve factors would have been revealing.

Performing factor analysis of the fund's returns versus those factors, Icarus would have obtained the sensitivities shown in Table 1.7.

TABLE 1.7 Factor analysis of Icarus Capital

Factor	Beta
Intercept	0
Global Equity	0.1
Yield Curve	1.3
Equity Volatility	0.01
Commodity Prices	−4.66
Credit Spreads	−8.76

Further factor analysis would have revealed that while the fund was remaining market neutral and the exposure to beta remained low, the exposure to credit spread factors via the convertible arbitrage substrategy and commodity price factors via the emerging market substrategy was increasing.

Directionally, the fund had a slight positive exposure to global equities markets, a slight long volatility exposure, and a positive yield curve exposure but a highly negative exposure to commodity price increases and credit spread increases. These exposures suggest that the fund would benefit from rising equity markets but could suffer under various "flight to quality" scenarios where equity markets fall, treasury yields fall and credit spreads rise. By simulating shocks to each factor and then applying factor sensitivities to estimate the effect of such shocks on its returns, Icarus could have simulated a distribution of returns given its factor exposures and compared this to its VaR. However, this analysis could also be taken further by applying a macro view as to the direction and magnitude of factor changes under various economic scenarios and stress events. Had the factor, stress or scenario analysis been done it would have shown Ivan Jones that despite his VaR telling him he could lose no more than 4.87 percent with a 95 percent confidence in a single month, his factor loadings were exposing Icarus to potential tail losses of 6.38 percent or more in a month and this assumed that he could liquidate their positions without a problem. Had he and his investors known this, it would have prompted him to re-evaluate the fund's positioning at the time and caused investors to consider redeeming or reducing their allocations to the fund.

MARGINS INCREASE

Simultaneously, the jump in volatility experienced in July was prompting hedge fund creditors—namely, prime brokers—to re-evaluate their margins on securities they financed for their clients. Significant losses by fixed income focused hedge funds due to MBS and ABS losses were beginning to be reported. Bear Stearns had allowed two of its fixed income focused funds to fail and the anticipated liquidation of those funds' assets was causing fixed income, and particularly structured credit, to fall and become increasingly illiquid. By the winter of 2008, prime brokers all looked at the deteriorating creditworthiness of Bear Stearns and started to contemplate the implications of a default by Bear. In March 2008, the Federal Reserve Bank of New York provided an emergency loan to try to avert a sudden collapse of Bear Stearns but the company could not be saved and was sold to JPMorgan Chase. Lastly, concerns about counterparty risk in the interbank funding markets were starting to reduce the liquidity of the rehypothecation[6] markets for lower-rated fixed income bonds, sub-investment-grade convertible bonds; and small cap and emerging market equities. In early August, Bart Stokes went to an industry dinner hosted by his prime broker to hear what their global head of fixed income research had to say about the action in the fixed income markets. Bart also wanted to canvas his peers at other hedge funds regarding the latest financing terms they had been able to negotiate with their prime brokers and make sure Icarus was getting the best deal possible. For better or worse, he was seated next to the risk manager of the prime brokerage. The risk manager said that he was concerned about the developments in the market but that the prime broker had an implicit partnership with Icarus and all their hedge fund clients. When Bart asked whether the risk manager was considering raising margins, the risk manager replied a bit obliquely that his firm would not raise margins without due notice to their clients.

The fact that the prime broker had relatively fixed upside potential if they extended leverage in riskier markets and increasing downside risk as markets grew more disrupted told Bart that while the prime broker had no incentive to force a fund to fail, the prime broker's risk was reduced if a fund de-levered. Raising margins would improve the prime broker's risk profile in turbulent markets. That was why Bart had negotiated a margin lock-up and an ISDA agreement with his prime brokers so that they could not increase margin on

Icarus without advance notice and terminating the agreements. Termination of the lock-up required 90 days' advance notice or some kind of disaster at Icarus. The ISDA could only be broken if Icarus defaulted or the AUM at Icarus fell by 15 percent or more in one month, either due to negative performance or because of fund redemptions. Additionally, there were a lot of other prime brokers pitching for his business. If this one increased margins, he would take his business elsewhere, and fast. Later in the month, Bart noticed that the cash Icarus kept on hand for margin calls and redemptions was down from 15 percent of AUM to 12 percent. He asked his staff to review the amount of margin they were posting at their prime brokers. He realized that the margin calls they routinely received from their prime brokers had indeed been increasing. He called the risk manager responsible for setting the margins at his prime broker for an explanation. How could margins be going up when he had a lock-up? The risk manager explained that while their margin formulas were static, their margins could go up and down as market variables, which were inputs to the formulas, changed. Trading volume had declined somewhat for several large positions in Icarus's portfolio. Consequently, the margin on those positions had gone up. Some of Icarus's activist-strategy positions were now more than two days of trading volume and the prime brokers were calling for more cash margin. Bart was annoyed and took a close look at his margin lock-up agreement and realized that while the margin rules were locked up, the margin level wasn't. The risk manager then asked Bart to answer some questions. He wanted to know what Icarus's performance had been over the past few weeks and whether they had received any requests for redemptions from investors. He wanted to know the liquidity profile of their securities. How much could it liquidate within one day, two days or one week? Lastly, he asked how much unencumbered cash Icarus had on hand. When Bart replied "12 percent of AUM," a considerable silence followed before the risk manager asked whether Icarus had run any stress tests on its portfolio. Bart replied that they ran VaR and it indicated they could lose 4.87 percent in a month. The risk manager told him that the prime broker's stress analysis of Icarus's portfolio indicated they could lose 15 percent or more in the extreme case that all assets became more correlated and fell by four standard deviations of their monthly volatility. When Bart expressed the view that this scenario was extremely unlikely, the risk manager replied that it was nonetheless a possibility. Furthermore, he said, the prime brokers were not in the business of taking the same risks as hedge fund investors. Both prime brokers and investors gave hedge funds money to invest but, unlike investors, prime brokers earned nothing more if the hedge fund was profitable and lost money along with investors if the fund failed. The prime broker had no upside if they took a risk with the fund and lent more money than the securities could be worth in a worst-case scenario. The call ended with the risk manager asking if he could call Bart to be kept up to date on developments at Icarus. He told Bart that he would send him the stress analysis the prime broker ran daily and be happy to meet him and walk him through it. Bart replied that he would evaluate whether he could get lower margins at another prime broker and might move his business elsewhere if this was the case. Bart then discussed the matter with Ivan. They both agreed that the cash level was a little low but would recover after August. There was often a decrease in volumes in August when traders took their summer holidays. Liquidity typically increased again in September. Then their margins would reduce again and their cash levels would recover.

REDEMPTIONS INCREASE

Icarus was able to post a modest 0.2 percent gain in September amid slightly falling markets and continued dwindling liquidity. Further credit concerns about the capitalization of financial intermediaries shrank volumes in the rehypothecation markets and this caused equities to fall further and credit spreads to widen. In October, Lehman Brothers was forced into a buyout after nearly defaulting on its obligations. Icarus experienced a large loss in October 2008, of 12.1 percent, as most of the equity strategies lost money. In particular, the convertible bond strategy suffered significantly from the decline in liquidity and the fall in prices arising from the increase in liquidity premiums. This performance was not unique to Icarus and many hedge funds that followed similar strategies suffered significant negative performance. Bart and Ivan took many calls from their investors, especially their fund of funds investors, questioning their strategy and saying this type of return volatility was not what they expected from a hedge fund. Prime brokers across Wall St., being in a unique position to see the negative performance across many hedge fund clients, and witnessing the decline in value of the security collateral backing the margin loans they had provided to hedge funds, feared that their clients would soon run out of cash and potentially default. To protect themselves and their shareholders, prime brokers began to increase their margins, requiring funds to post more cash to maintain their positions. This increase in margin for equities and convertible bonds impacted all hedge fund that were not locked up. This forced non-locked-up funds to liquidate positions, even fixed income and currency positions, to generate cash to meet their margin calls on their equity and convertible bond positions. This de-leveraging caused further declines in the securities markets. Icarus was not directly affected, however, because of its lock-up. Bart Stokes received a call from his prime broker asking if Icarus would consider slightly higher margins even though they had a margin lock-up and a tight ISDA. The unknown was whether the prime broker would send Icarus a formal termination notice and increase margins if he disagreed. Bart asked for an analysis telling him the dollar impact of the higher margins. This showed that margins would increase from about 15 percent to 20 percent on average for Icarus. This would reduce its available cash to less than 10 percent if it did not sell some positions to generate cash. Bart said he would discuss it with Ivan and get back with an answer that week.

Bart Stokes had given investors the right to withdraw their funds on a quarterly basis with 45 days' notice. The investors had primarily put their money into Icarus for diversification, capital preservation, and bond-like upside. They had been pleased when Icarus posted double-digit positive returns but had not anticipated consecutive months of double-digit negative returns and were not willing to accept that they could lose money. Each investor was wondering whether other investors would soon redeem their investment in Icarus. Perhaps they had already given notice of their intention to redeem and would get their proceeds first. The investor community had also been nervously watching the market fall and knew that prime brokers across the street had been increasing margins. They knew that if the fund defaulted, the prime brokers would liquidate the fund's assets and use the proceeds to repay the financing they had extended to the funds. Investors would then have to divide what was left over. Icarus's losses were not unique. Most hedge funds had lost money in September and November and investors began to panic. Investors wanted their money safely in cash and wanted to get their cash out of Icarus before other investors or the prime brokers did. Investors, particularly funds of funds and institutions needing to meet their own investor demands for cash and to meet cash disbursement commitments for the coming year end, submitted demands to Icarus for partial or full redemption of their interests in the fund. On November 15, Icarus received requests to redeem 50 percent of investor funds. These would have to be paid on January 1, 2009. With the increase in margins, Icarus only had 8 percent of AUM in cash. There was no way that Ivan Jones and Bart Stokes could meet investor demands for redemptions without liquidating the majority of the fund's investments amid a market that was falling rapidly. Icarus' negative October performance was followed by even more severe losses in November 2008, where it lost 16.5 percent. If it liquidated the fund's investments, this would crystallize the mark-to-market losses. Furthermore, it would have to liquidate the most liquid assets of the fund, leaving itself and other investors with only the least-liquid fund assets.

THE DECISION TO GATE THE FUND

Also, Ivan and Bart were well aware that the current 50 percent of AUM redemptions could be just the tip of the iceberg. Once the remaining investors learned that the fund had paid out 50 percent of the AUM, they would realize the fund was becoming increasingly illiquid and submit their redemption requests for the remaining fund assets. Bart, Ivan and most of the staff who had almost all of their net worth invested in the fund would be stuck with an illiquid distressed portfolio or be wiped out. Bart also told Ivan that since the early days of 2002 when they started the fund, their operating expenses had grown. There was now no way they could pay their staff salaries out of their operating fee and there would be no performance fee. The operating fee was 2 percent of a declining AUM. Given their performance, there would be no 20 percent performance fee for 2008 or indeed until they regained their high-water mark. If they paid out the redemptions, they would have to immediately lay off the majority of their staff. All of the staff, including Ivan and Bart, had come to count on the performance bonuses paid over the last five years and had incurred large mortgages and other liabilities. The staff faced personal bankruptcy. Given that honoring the initial investor redemptions would put the remaining investors in a worse-off position, having only the less-liquid assets of the fund remaining, Ivan and Bart decided to invoke the gate on their fund. This was a clause in Icarus's prospectus that allowed them to suspend redemptions for an indefinite period of time if necessary to protect all investors in the fund, but they had never expected to need to use it. This would also freeze the AUM and provide a constant operating fee, giving them time to manage downsizing of the fund. In addition, it gave them a chance of survival if the market rebounded while the gate was up. If they liquidated now, personal bankruptcy was a distinct possibility. On November 31, 2008, Icarus announced that it was "gating" the fund. By that time it had received redemption requests for a full 90 percent of the fund assets. By January 2009, Icarus had announced that it was setting up a liquidating trust that would honor investor redemptions, partially in cash where possible, and partially by granting them in shares in a trust backed by the illiquid assets of Icarus. The 2/20 percent fees would still apply. As of the end of 2009, the market had recovered significantly but Icarus was still liquidating the trust to meet investors pending redemptions. By 2010, most of the staff had left or been let go. Ivan Jones was making plans to launch a new commodity-focused fund, mostly with $20 million of investments from friends and family. He hoped to reach $100 million AUM a year from now after demonstrating successful performance.

STAKEHOLDERS' RIGHTS

As the case above illustrates, investment risk does not exist in a vacuum. The structure of the fund's financing, the incentives and rights of prime brokers, investors, and staff all have an impact on the ultimate outcome and return.

These various stakeholders in the performance of the fund each have rights they can exercise over the assets of the fund. The primary stakeholders are investors, prime brokers, and hedge fund management staff. Each has different claims on the assets of the fund and earns different returns depending on the performance of the fund. Each also has specific rights that can affect the claims of the others (see Table 1.8). In a crisis, the varying rights prompt actions by each stakeholder that are individually loss-minimizing but which have negative implications for other stakeholders and result in sub-optimal returns for all investors collectively.

Investors' Rights

Hedge fund investors vary from sophisticated and patient institutional investors such as pension funds and endowments, to less-sophisticated and potentially skittish high-net-worth individuals, to friends and family of the

TABLE 1.8 Stakeholders' rights and risks

Stakeholder	Rights	Incentives	Risks
Investors - Have an equity claim on the excess performance of the fund and a subordinated claim in the event of default.	Right to net returns of the fund Right to redeem hedge fund shares	*Upside:* Unlimited. Excess performance of the fund after management and performance fees. *Downside:* Total loss of principal	• Can force liquidation of assets, payment of liquidity premium and realization of mark-to-market losses.
Prime Broker - Custodian and provider of leverage. Receives interest payment on financing provided. Has a debtholder's senior claim on the assets of the fund in the event of default by the fund on a margin payment or securities contract.	Right to increase margin Right to recall financing Right to refuse trades Right to liquidate collateral Right to interest on funds lent to the fund	*Upside:* Limited. Fees from provision of prime brokerage custody services and interest income from margin and securities lending. *Downside:* Partial loss of principal in the event of hedge fund default and insufficient proceeds from liquidation of hedge fund collateral.	• Can force liquidation of assets, payment of liquidity premium and realization of mark-to-market losses by increasing margin • Can restrict or stop hedging or risk taking by refusing trades. • Can seize collateral if margin is not paid and liquidate.
Hedge Fund Management & Staff - Have an equity claim on the excess performance of the fund and a subordinated claim in the event of default. Have information advantage over other stakeholders and financial and human capital invested in the fund.	Right to redeem Right to leave Right to gate the fund Right to management fee and performance fee.	*Upside:* Unlimited. Excess performance of the fund plus management and performance fees *Downside:* Total loss of net worth, loss of reputation, loss of equity in management company, loss of job.	• Can force liquidation of assets, payment of liquidity premium and realization of mark-to-market losses. • Can invoke the gate, preventing investors from receiving redemptions. • Can leave, creating both reputation and operational risk for the fund.

hedge fund manager. Then, there are fund of funds managers who create portfolios of screened hedge fund investments and then provide their clients (typically institutional investors and high-net-worth individuals) with access to hedge fund-type returns for a fee. Regardless of their background, all investors want to maximize their return from the fund within the constraints of their own unique portfolio strategy. An institutional investor probably only has a portion of its investible funds with any single fund manager (typically less than 5 percent) while a friend of the fund manager may have 50–100 percent of their net worth in the fund. Similarly, staff members at the fund may have almost all their net worth invested in the fund. Consequently, each investor has a different ability to absorb losses before needing to stop losses by liquidating their investment. In addition, each investor has a different need for liquidity. In the crisis, almost all asset classes lost value and investors that relied on their investments to fund spending found that they had to choose which investments to liquidate in order to fund those expenses. Often it was not the investments that had lost the most that were liquidated first but those that at least remained liquid that were sold.

Prime Brokers' (Creditor) Rights

The prime broker provides the hedge fund manager with one of the elements required in the alchemy of alpha creation; namely, leverage. In exchange for a senior claim on specific assets of the hedge fund, the prime broker will partially fund the manager's purchase of securities. Consider the example of a fund manager who has an existing prime brokerage relationship with one of the major Wall St. brokers. On Monday, the fund manager decides that he wants to purchase 100 shares of Procter & Gamble. Assume the common shares of P&G are trading at US$10 per share. If the fund's existing portfolio at the prime broker is diversified and the incremental purchase of the P&G shares will not create a concentration in the overall portfolio at the prime broker, then the hedge fund manager may only need to post 15 percent of the overall cost of the P&G purchase (the margin) while the prime broker would lend the hedge fund 85 percent of the value of the shares in exchange for a lien on the total portfolio the hedge fund maintains at the prime broker. In this case, the hedge fund would post US$150 while the prime broker would post US$850. The prime broker would purchase the P&G shares in the market and post US$1,000-worth of P&G shares in the hedge fund's account. However, the prime broker typically retains the right to require the hedge fund to post more cash margin. Often the hedge fund must post the additional margin by the end of the business day if the prime broker makes the demand before 10 a.m. that day. If the fund does not have the cash on hand, it will need to liquidate some of its positions in order to meet the broker's call for margin. If it does not meet the margin call, the broker has the right to liquidate all assets held by the fund at the broker.

Staff Rights

The staff of a hedge fund typically have a significant portion of their own net worth invested at the fund. At the senior level, the portfolio manager, CEO, COO, and CFO may have the majority of their personal wealth invested in the fund. Further down the ranks, traders and administrative staff may have their deferred compensation invested in the fund. In some cases, staff may have their wealth invested in the fund even if they are not required to do so by their compensation plans. In a crisis, where the fund has generated a significant negative performance that destroys staff wealth along with that of other investors, staff may have an incentive to gate the fund, and thereby avoid liquidating, in a last-ditch effort to resuscitate the fund's performance, regain their high water mark, restore their wealth, and earn performance fees sufficient to keep the fund viable. This is because the staff not only have a greater share of their personal wealth in the fund, but they also have their careers and reputations at stake. Allowing investors to redeem, forces the fund to liquidate in a down market, and crystallizes losses. Redemptions and losses reduce AUM and management fees needed to keep the fund-management company viable, and make the closing of the fund—together with the loss of a significant portion of their net worth, reputation, and employment—a near certainty for staff.

Stakeholder Redemption Scenarios

To illustrate the impact of stakeholders' actions on each other, consider a pattern seen frequently in the crisis. Funds of funds provided investors in their vehicles with the ability to redeem their investments within 30 to 90 days of investors giving notice. Meanwhile, the fund of funds may have constructed a portfolio of hedge fund investments with redemption terms varying from 30 to 360 days. As markets fell, for example, in September 2008, fund of funds investors decided to stop their losses and demanded the return of an unexpectedly large portion of their invested funds. This left the fund of funds managers with sometimes as little as 30 days to find the liquidity to honor their redemption requests. Naturally, they in turn redeemed their shares in their hedge fund investments. However, in many cases they had not matched the redemption terms they had offered to their own investors to the redemption terms they had accepted when making investments into hedge funds in their fund of funds. This fundamental asset and liability mismatch at the fund of funds caused the redemption demands to fall on the hedge funds within the fund of funds that had offered the shortest notice periods to the fund of funds investors. Consequently, what began as modest redemptions at funds of funds caused those redemptions to cascade but also concentrate in the hedge funds that took fund of funds money and which offered the shortest redemption terms. To meet the tsunami of redemption requests moving towards them, these hedge funds had to start liquidating their investments, often at a loss. Furthermore, many funds had made similar investments and followed similar strategies. They owned the same positions. Meanwhile, the prime brokers saw the assets of certain hedge funds begin to fall rapidly in value as hedge fund selling began. They also learned from the monthly reporting required of their hedge fund managers that redemption requests had increased dramatically. The rapid exit of investors from hedge funds can indicate increasing risk of failure of a fund. In addition, the increase in volatility and redemptions and the rapidly falling prices prompted prime brokers to exercise their right to increase margin requirements, forcing the hedge funds to post additional cash at the prime brokers. However, unlike investors who needed to be given their cash by the end of 30 days, the prime brokers' senior demands for cash needed to be met the same day they were made. Of course, this only increased the amount of securities the hedge funds needed to liquidate and caused prices to fall further as the hedge funds sold more positions. This in turn caused the prime brokers to increase margins further. This caused further negative performance to be reported by hedge funds and increased investor desire to stop losses and redeem shares. This further aggravated the asset–liability timing mismatches present in funds of funds and hedge funds. Understanding stakeholders' claims and rights on hedge fund assets is critical to the effective risk management of the business risks in the hedge funds business model as well as the risk management of hedge fund investment portfolios. The ability of each stakeholder to create funding pressures and demand liquidity from a hedge fund can force the hedge fund manager to divest from investment strategies prematurely and force investors to realize heretofore unrealized losses. Stakeholders' claims and the ability to create funding risk must be integrated with the typical investment, counterparty, and operational risks taken at hedge funds and managed in an integrated fashion. Not surprisingly, this ability is a characteristic of a successful hedge fund.

Risk Management of Successful Hedge Funds

Since its emergence in 1949 under Alfred Winslow Jones, the hedge-fund industry has developed from an idea, through a period of trial, error, mania and crisis to a defined set of investment strategies, executed within a standard corporate structure and governed by best-practice risk management principles. Names like D. E. Shaw, Och Ziff Capital Management, Highbridge Capital, and others exemplify the new best-practice institutions. While investment risk has been the dominant focus of risk management efforts in hedge funds, best-practice hedge funds now fully integrate the management of their counterparty, funding, and operational risk with their investment risk management. These funds are able to understand the potential impact of funding, operational and counterparty risks on investment returns, and comprehensively manage all the risks inherent in their fragile business.

Integrated Hedge Fund Risk Schema

Conceptually, an integrated risk framework is straightforward. Funding, counterparty, operational and investment risks can trigger and amplify each other. Much of the time, these individual risks can be harnessed, contained, controlled and used within a hedge fund to produce alpha. However, like a nuclear reactor harnessing nuclear fission to produce energy, a hedge fund producing alpha can go into meltdown if risks are not well controlled and reach critical mass. Integrated risk management (as illustrated in Figure 1.7) is essential to balancing risk and return, and to sustaining stable, positive risk-adjusted returns.

FIGURE 1.7 Integrated hedge fund risk management

Within each risk type shown above there are common risk-management strategies and practices followed by the leading hedge fund managers. Together they represent the minimum standard of risk management a hedge fund should demonstrate. The remainder of this book explains these strategies and practices with supporting analysis and practical steps for their implementation.

CONCLUSION

A hedge fund's investment risk cannot be managed in isolation from the overall business risks. The loss-minimizing actions of prime brokers seeking to protect the money they have lent, the redemption activity of investors seeking to preserve their principal, and the incentives of staff seeking to preserve their net worth, track record, and businesses, all directly affect the ability of a fund to manage its risks in a crisis. The majority of hedge funds don't have a risk manager. Even those that do, typically divide investment-risk management assigned to the risk manager or portfolio manager from the business risk management of the fund managed by the CFO. Optimizing the management of a hedge fund's total business risks is the focus of the remainder of this book.

ENDNOTES

1. Black Monday was Monday, October 19, 1987 when the S&P 500 Index lost 20.5 percent and the Dow Jones Industrial Average lost 22.6 percent.
2. In 1987, there were only five daily moves greater or equal to 5 percent.
3. A Prisoner's Dilemma is a term common in game theory which is characterized as a situation where collective losses are minimized or collective gains are maximized through cooperation, while individual losses are minimized or individual gains are maximized by self-serving action. The name describes the situation of prisoners who, given their greater numbers, could easily overpower their guards and escape if they cooperated but who don't to do so because potential individual loss (death) if they fail is severe.
4. Véronique Le Sourd, *Hedge Fund Performance in 2008*, EDHEC Risk and Asset Management Research Center, February 2009.
5. Marlene Horwitz and Bruce Schwartz, *Global Hedge Fund Valuation and Risk Management*, PricewaterhouseCoopers, 2004.
6. The rehypothecation markets are interbank markets which provide low-cost funding collateralized by securities to brokers and banks. In stable times, the variety of collateral accepted to support a loan is wide, extending to

lower-quality securities and the discount applied to the value of the collateral is low. In distressed markets, the forms of acceptable collateral are restricted to higher-quality securities and the discount applied to the value of the collateral is high. Effectively, in a crisis it becomes very difficult to generate low-cost funding from anything but the highest-quality collateral.

CHAPTER 2

An Integrated Approach to Hedge Fund Risk Management

What differentiated many of the surviving funds from those that invoked their gates and ultimately closed? All funds practiced some form of risk management, whether they had a dedicated risk manager or not. In most cases, traders embedded risk management discipline in their investment activities. They sized their positions to ensure that the potential negative impact on their strategy was proportional to their confidence in their positions. They hedged out unintended and unrewarded risks. They monitored their position liquidity and they liquidated positions when they hit their stop-loss limits. Portfolio managers acted as risk managers at the portfolio level ensuring that capital was allocated to strategies more likely to be successful given the macro environment, and ensuring that concentrations in specific companies, sectors, countries and asset classes did not develop across strategies and that a minimum level of cash was maintained.

Funds that had a dedicated risk manager tended to have more institutionalized risk-management capabilities and formal risk-measurement systems yet still fell short of having a complete risk framework. Often, a full suite of risk analytics was available to portfolio managers, describing in great detail the potential risks of the investment portfolio. All variants of value at risk analysis, scenario analysis, concentration reports, liquidity analyses, all manner of risk adjusted performance ratios (Sharpe, Sortino, Omega, Calmar, Sterling . . .), and back-tests were available but not always used in the investment decision-making process. The limited use of risk information in investment decision-making was in part due to the fact that portfolio managers or founders of the fund had greater ownership of the fund and this limited the risk manager's effective authority. He or she typically had no power to change an investment decision or asset allocation even if there was a formal risk committee. In most cases, the portfolio manager and founders (often one and the same person) retained all final authority. Whether a formal risk committee existed or not, whether a dedicated risk system produced advanced stress analytics showing large potential losses or not, whether there was a dedicated risk manager or not, made little difference in the recent crisis as these efforts focused almost exclusively on the investment risks in the portfolio. What differentiated successful hedge funds from those that failed was partially the degree of sophistication of their risk management but, more importantly, whether the risk framework integrated other business risks like counterparty, funding and operational risks. Regardless of strategy, adequate hedge-fund risk management should include, and then integrate, a set of minimum capabilities in the areas of investment risk, funding risk, counterparty risk, and operational risk.

MINIMUM INTEGRATED RISK MANAGEMENT CAPABILITIES

The essential objective of investment risk management in a hedge fund is to skew expected returns positively by maximizing potential upside and minimizing potential downside. Minimizing the volatility of returns is not necessarily the appropriate objective as this can lead to diversifying away all potential sources of excess return. Structuring positions to take intended risks and rewarded risks, while avoiding unintended risks, is key to creating a return distribution with positive skew.

Integrated Risk Framework

It is insufficient to simply have risk systems, risk analysis and risk reports. Risk management is about optimizing risk and return, and not just about academic risk analysis. Risk analysis alone is useless unless the information provided is integrated into the investment and portfolio management decision-making process. To embed risk analysis and risk management in an organization, a risk management framework needs to be implemented. The components of an effective risk management framework are set out in Figure 2.1:

Data: Data is a vital force in most financial institutions today. Without accurate, timely, and complete data, most financial institutions would be unable to survive. In the case of a hedge fund, the necessary data for investment risk analysis includes complete position and security level data. *Position data* are all the data needed to describe the quantity of securities a hedge fund owns and how they relate to each other in a strategy. At a minimum this is the quantity and ISIN of the security.

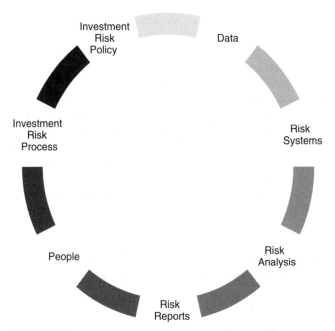

FIGURE 2.1 An effective risk management framework

Security data are all the data detailing the characteristics of the security and are based on the security identifier (i.e. ISIN, CUSIP etc.). This includes the historical volatility, daily trading volume, country of risk, industrial sector, market cap, credit rating, credit spread, issue size, CS01, DV01, OAS, maturity, and so on.

Risk systems: The risk systems employed depend on the size of the fund and its strategy. Many prime brokers offer their clients basic and intermediate risk systems, such as RiskMetrics and Imagine. These may be appropriate for strategies trading liquid securities. More specialized strategies such as distressed investing, activist, statistical arbitrage, and high-velocity strategies require unique perspectives on risk and these funds typically develop their own systems for risk management and risk analysis.

Risk analysis: This incorporates position and security level data, full stochastic and deterministic return analysis (stress and scenario analysis), funding and liquidity analysis, and credit exposure analysis.

Risk reporting: Using a risk analysis system (such as Imagine, Sophis, or Risk Metrics, for example), reports on such things as expected and potential return distributions, concentrations, liquidity, factor sensitivity, stress test results, and counterparty credit exposure are produced.

People: A dedicated risk manager and analysts implement the investment risk process, producing and analyzing risk reports to ensure that the portfolio remains within risk parameters. Exposures in excess of prescribed limits or of concern are detected and escalated.

Risk process: The process reviews risk reports and makes decisions about position sizing exposures vis-à-vis risk limits, and market outlook and events.

Exceptional positions and risk concerns are addressed by re-evaluating the initial investment thesis which gave rise to the position and determining if the return potential has reduced or become less certain. Positions with deteriorating risk-return profiles are exited or modified by implementing complementary hedges that reduce risk without eroding return.

Risk policy: This is a high-level overall plan embracing the general goals and acceptable procedures for risk taking and management set out in full in the fund's prospectus.

If any one of the above components is deficient, the entire risk framework is deficient, as each component is dependent on the other. If any one of the components is missing or incomplete, the framework will not function effectively (that is, if data are lacking, risk analysis reports will be inaccurate and lead to erroneous risk decisions being made).While it is conceptually convenient to differentiate between four broad types of risk—investment risk (also called market risk), counterparty risk, funding risk, and operational risk—these are not mutually exclusive. Risk can transmute from one form to another and sometimes with great speed. Therefore, the management of these risks should occur in an integrated risk management framework. The rest of this chapter describes the minimum integrated risk management capabilities a hedge fund should have and, for expository purposes, describes these capabilities based on the primary type of risk they manage while recognizing that these risk types overlap. Investment risk incorporates elements of counterparty risk and funding risk. Integrated risk management recognizes that risk is fungible and that each type of risk is interrelated. Investment risk primarily focuses on the impact of changes in the prices of (or rates for) securities and derivatives, the volatilities of those prices, and the correlations between securities values on the overall value of the investment portfolio. However, elements of funding risk and counterparty risk can create investment risk. For example: Security liquidity risk affects the bid or ask spread of a security's price and thereby the value of that security or derivative. This also influences the amount of financing a hedge fund can obtain to purchase that security. Liquidity risk can create investment and funding risk. Changes in the creditworthiness of a counterparty can influence the amount of collateral that needs to be posted. This can create funding risk by changing the amount of funding an entity requires. Similarly, changes in perceived creditworthiness have an impact on the value of a security or derivative issued by or indexed to that entity, creating investment risk.

Because risk can morph from one form to another, hedge fund managers should integrate the monitoring and management of risk in all its forms. Consequently, "investment risk" practices described in this chapter encompasses the credit risk associated with assets held in the portfolio and asset (or market) liquidity risk, as well as the more commonly cited investment risk factors: interest rate risk; foreign exchange rate risk; equity price risk; and commodity price risk. Counterparty risk, however, refers to the risk of non-performance by a hedge fund counterparty. This chapter includes a description of practices for monitoring counterparty credit risk. While hedge funds generally deal with counterparties with high credit quality and the credit risk of counterparties may be of less concern to hedge fund managers, Lehman Brothers and Bear Stearns did fail, creating losses and funding risk for their hedge fund clients. This underlines the importance of counterparty risk management. While investment risk is often the primary concern of hedge fund managers, funding risk can restrict their ability to finance its positions. This risk is of greater concern to hedge fund managers than to other entities given the dependence of the hedge fund business model on leverage and liquidity. There are specific techniques that should be used by hedge fund managers to manage funding liquidity risk. The use of leverage by hedge funds, amplifies investment risk inherent in the portfolio. The fact that leverage can be reduced or withdrawn makes the management of funding liquidity and leverage critical to a fund manager's ability to maintain positions until their investment thesis is realized. Leverage can be defined in relatively static financial (financial statement-based) or dynamic risk-based terms. Dynamic risk-based leverage measures provide additional information to the fund manager. Operational risks include risks relating to the failure of hedge fund staff, processes, and systems infrastructure to operate as intended. This can be the result erroneous data, crashed systems and "legal risk" of fraud or regulatory violations.

MINIMUM RISK MANAGEMENT CAPABILITIES BY RISK TYPE

Effective risk management requires that the hedge fund manager recognize and understand the source of profits and losses the fund is earning or can potentially incur (that is, the risks to which the fund is exposed). Consequently, one of the primary responsibilities of the risk management team is to identify, prioritize, quantify, and manage the sources of risk.

Investment Risk

A hedge fund manager must employ a consistent framework for measuring the risk of loss for a portfolio (and relevant subcomponents of the portfolio). To manage the risks that the hedge fund faces, its risk management team needs to produce pertinent, timely, useful, and accurate measures of investment risk. Generally, a series of expected loss estimates with defined probability of occurrence, stress test results, and scenario analyses are required. Depending on the fund's strategy or breadth of strategies, different risk analysis models may be appropriate. While the choice of framework or model for measuring risk should be left to each hedge fund manager, each model has structural limitations and these must be properly understood to ensure that models are not mis-specified and applied to portfolios for which the analysis is not robust or inappropriate. For example, measuring the degree to which the portfolio is concentrated (for example, the percentages of the portfolio allocated to the same or similar asset classes, risk factors, or geographical regions) is useful, but it is essential for the fund manager to go deeper and recognize the current and potential correlations between positions, risk factors and asset classes. For complex portfolios, many summary measures of investment risk do not reflect such correlations.

Value at Risk   A commonly cited and used potential loss model that is intended to provide a summary investment risk measure that incorporates correlations between positions is value at risk (VaR). VaR measures the maximum change in the value of the portfolio that would be expected at a specified confidence level over a specified time period. For example, if the 95 percent confidence level one-day VaR for a portfolio is $5,000,000, one would expect to gain or lose more than $5,000,000 in only five of every 100 trading days on average. The risk management team must identify the factors affecting the risk and return of the hedge fund both at the portfolio level and often at the trader and strategy level. This includes analysis of those risk factors that must be monitored, included in the investment process, and often controlled by risk limits. These risk factors are primary inputs to the VaR calculations. Commonly incorporated risk factors in VaR and other investment risk models include:

1. Prices for equities and/or equity indices
2. Level and shape of the interest rate term structure in relevant currencies
3. Foreign exchange rates
4. Commodity prices
5. Credit spreads

6. Nonlinearities (particularly the term structure of implied volatility for instruments with elements of optionality)
7. Historical volatility
8. Correlation.

In addition to the selection of risk factors, the risk manager should determine the appropriate liquidation period assumption, VaR methodology, confidence interval and data history to use in the VaR calculations.

Liquidation Period and Asset Liquidity   In choosing the liquidation period over which such potential loss estimates are calculated, the risk management team should consider "asset liquidity" (that is, the potential exposure to loss attributable to changes in the liquidity of the market in which the asset is traded) as an additional factor. Measures of asset liquidity that may be considered include:

- The number of days that would be required to liquidate and/or hedge the position in question.
- The additional value beyond that predicted based on volatility that would be lost if the asset in question were to be liquidated and/or neutralized completely within such period (that is, bid/ask spreads or lot size discounts that would need to be paid to create liquidity).

The liquidation period used in the VaR calculation is intended to reflect the time period necessary to liquidate (or hedge) the positions in the portfolio. Consequently, for highly liquid portfolios, best practice is to use standard holding periods (for example, one day, three days, five days, and 10 days in the base-case VaR calculation). In practice, many hedge funds have positions in thinly traded or illiquid instruments or have liquid positions which can turn illiquid in a market crisis. It is difficult to determine the correct liquidation/neutralization period for such securities within a VaR framework. In such cases, it is appropriate to use VaR as the base case but then employ stress tests and scenario analysis to determine the degree of holding-period risk in the hedge portfolio.

Model Selection   A VaR measure requires that a number of parameters that describe the positions in the portfolio and the characteristics of the underlying markets be input into the VaR model. In addition, users of VaR must select one of three broad standard methodologies:

- *Variance/Covariance.* This widely used VaR methodology, uses volatility (variance) and correlation (covariance) information for each position in the portfolio, and calculates the volatility estimate under the assumption that the returns for the overall portfolio will assume a normal distribution. One shortcoming of this methodology is that it does not handle optionality well. It is the least data-and-process-intensive of the VaR methodologies.

- *Historical Simulation.* This VAR methodology uses historical price data to re-price the current portfolio as if it had existed on each day over the data history. Thus a simulated daily trading P/L calculation is derived. Each day's P/L is then ranked in ascending order to create a P/L distribution. The risk estimate is drawn from a percentile of the distribution consistent with the confidence interval selected for the analysis. This VaR methodology is very process-and-data-intensive, but is considered by many to be the most intuitive and effective form of VaR. Historical simulation accounts for optionality better than Variance/Covariance.

- *Monte Carlo Simulation.* This VaR methodology uses Monte Carlo simulation to simulate a P/L distribution of the portfolio. The portfolio is re-priced across large numbers of random observations that are consistent with the volatility history of the underlying instruments. Like historical VaR, these P/L simulations are then ranked in ascending order to create a P/L distribution. The risk estimate is drawn from a percentile of the distribution consistent with the confidence level selected for the analysis. Monte Carlo VaR is typically only used for very complex portfolios, featuring abundant nonlinearities.

Each VaR method, if applied accurately and in a manner consistent with the fund's risk and capital allocation policies, can be an effective, if imperfect, means of estimating the majority of the potential investment risk distribution. However, because of the nature of hedge fund investing (hedge funds seek to generate consistent low-volatility returns by creating hedged portfolios), it is essential to complement the VaR analysis with an evaluation of the conditions under which those hedges could fail. VaR does not measure "tail risk." This requires stress and scenario analysis. While the selection of VaR methodology and liquidation period are crucial to the VaR analysis, the choice of confidence level (the probability that the change in the value of the portfolio would exceed the VaR) and time period from which the market data are drawn are equally important. The confidence level determines the percentile of the simulated P/L distribution from which the VaR estimate is drawn. The choice of time period from which the market data are drawn determines the volatility applied to the individual positions and the correlation between pairs of securities, which is in turn used in the P/L simulation. The determination of these parameters is explained further below.

Confidence Level   The choice of confidence level for a hedge fund is a business decision. It is important that the VaR results be used in decision-making for the hedge fund. For the VaR results to be of use for decision-making, they should have some information value to those making the decisions. If the confidence interval is too high (that is, 99.99 percent), the estimated loss amount can seem absurd to decision-makers and the results may be discounted entirely. If the confidence internal is too low (that is, 64 percent), the results may have no value as a control mechanism for setting limits. The limits would be broken too frequently. Depending on their risk appetite and the intended use of the VaR measure, different businesses use different confidence levels. A bank, for example, uses 99.9 percent VaR for calculating its regulatory capital and for risk control purposes. For a hedge fund, the VaR analysis is generally used more for risk-based decision-making than risk control. The appropriate confidence level is determined by the specific strategy of the hedge fund and the fund's senior management must be actively involved in its determination.

Time Period for Market Data   In selecting the time period from which volatility and correlation are drawn, two opposing issues are important. First, in a trendless market, the longer the time period used, the more representative the parameters derived from the series. Using too few historical data points leads to very uncertain VaR results (reflected by large confidence intervals around the point estimate). In addition, the longer the time series, the greater the likelihood that "fat tail" events are adequately captured and incorporated in the VaR. Second, however, using a longer time series leads to an implausible VaR estimate since it neglects the fact that data from the near past are more representative of the near future than are older data. The second issue can be partially addressed using exponential weighted data but then the weighting function itself has to be estimated.

Ultimately, the choice of time period and weighting function should be made by the risk manager and the hedge fund manager together and consider the investment process or strategy they will follow. As the VaR analysis is only of use if it contains information pertinent to the investment process, the analysis must answer critical questions about the potential loss distribution of the portfolio and match the manner in which the portfolio is managed. For example, if most investments are intended to be made, mature and be divested within a few days or less (such as in statistical arbitrage), using a short time series emphasizing the most recent data to estimate expected returns may be appropriate.[1] This version of VaR will do a decent job of estimating expected losses if the recent past is representative of the near future but it will not reflect any of the tail risk well. If used in conjunction with daily 4 and 5 standard deviation stress testing of the portfolio, it may be appropriate and sufficient. If the strategy is more focused on long-term value/overvalue and portfolio turnover is low (that is, long and short positions are put on and divested over a period of years), then using longer time series will result in a VaR with thinner tails. The VaR will do a decent job of estimating long-term expected losses but will not reflect changing economic paradigms quickly. This shortcoming can be mitigated if the VaR is complemented by scenario analysis that probes returns of the portfolio under different potential economic paradigms. Ultimately, the choice of time period should reflect the investment horizon of the fund but recognize and offset any shortcomings of the VaR methodology with robust stress and scenario analysis. In weighing their decision, the hedge fund manager and risk manager should understand that they have many other tools by which to probe the potential loss distribution of the portfolio. A hedge fund manager can use Conditional VaR[2] to strike a balance between VaR and stress testing.

Finally, VaR is a backward-looking measure in that it relies on historical data to predict future returns. If the future is fundamentally different from the past, if historical market characteristics do not extend into the future, the VaR will not be of any predictive value and alternative measures of potential losses should be used. For example, the degree of correlation between pairs of market factors is critical, because correlation has such a large impact on the VaR calculation. Most VaR models use historic correlations. However, since historic correlations are unstable (especially during periods of market stress), the hedge fund manager should employ scenario analyses and stress testing to ascertain the impact of inaccurate correlation assumptions. This is one area where the judgment of the risk manager and hedge fund manager are critical. Hedge fund managers must recognize that a single VaR number is not sufficient to capture all risks faced by the fund (that is, they do not describe the full potential loss distribution) and that successful risk management requires the risk management team to analyze both the sensitivity of the VaR to potential market conditions not represented by the VaR analysis and conduct stress and scenario analysis that offsets the weaknesses of the VaR calculations and contributes to the investment decision process.

Stress and Scenario Analysis VaR calculations are based on representative or "typical" market days. Periods of market stress or crisis—the very times of greatest risk—are often not well represented in the data used for

VaR analysis. The resulting VaR number will not capture these tail events and will underestimate the risks of severe markets. To address this shortcoming, the hedge fund manager must perform scenario analyses regularly to assess the potential loss for the current portfolio in periods of historic and potential market stress. In creating scenario analyses, account should be taken of both classic historical stress periods (for example, October 19, 1987 when the equity markets "crashed," the Asian financial crisis of 1997, and the stock market declines after March 2000 when the "dot-com" bubble burst) and the more recent credit crunch periods of October 2008 and March 2009.

Stress Testing Hedge-fund managers should stress test their portfolios by changing the parameters of the VaR model. Stress tests enable the hedge-fund manager to see what will happen to the VaR number if the actual values of market factors (prices, rates, volatilities, and so on) differ from the values used as inputs in the base-case VaR calculation. For example, if the VaR results are based on a 95 percent confidence interval (that is, 2 standard deviations of historical volatility) then a stress test based on 4 and 5 standard deviations would illuminate the tails of the potential loss distribution, complementing the VaR analysis. Among the market factors to be stressed are:

1. changes in prices
2. changes in interest rate term structures; and
3. changes in correlations between prices.

If the portfolio contains options or instruments with options characteristics, additional changes that should be considered as part of stress testing are:

1. changes in volatilities; and
2. changes in nonlinearities (for example, convexity or gamma).

Scenario Analysis Formulaically increasing standard deviations of volatility can help to probe the tail of the potential loss distribution but still assumes that the future market returns are linked to market returns of the past. Scenario analysis differs from stress testing in that its initial premise is that a new market paradigm emerges. Future market characteristics are fundamentally different from the past. The risk manager and portfolio manager then extrapolate what would be the characteristics of this new market. What would be the chain of events following some market shock? From where and to where would funds flow? What asset classes would be liquid?

What would be temporarily or permanently illiquid? What would be the policy responses from governments? What would be the market impact of those policy changes? What would be the potential changes in asset values (positive and negative) during such events and what would be the time period and sequencing? The answers to these questions are then expressed in the form of market variables and incorporated into the scenario-analysis model where the portfolio is revalued.

As market crises and paradigm shifts do not manifest themselves solely in the form of higher volatility but also as one-way or diminished trading volume, hedge fund managers also should consider including the effects of changes in the liquidity of various assets in the portfolio. For example, they should evaluate the liquidity profile to their assets in times of market stress and then express the expected liquidity under stress in the stress test by changing the holding period. A horizon of several days may reveal a chain of losses (or gains) which, in aggregate, add up to an unacceptable loss that is significantly different from the VaR results. Specific asset liquidity factors such as the number of days required to liquidate the position under normal market conditions without moving the market price, the position as a percentage of open interest, and the current bid or ask spread should be incorporated in the position-level data and used in the analytic framework. These asset liquidity factors can themselves be "stressed" to examine the impact of: (1) changes in the value that could be lost if the position in question were to be liquidated and/or neutralized completely during the standard holding period; or (2) changes in the number of days required to liquidate and/or neutralize the position in question. As discussed earlier, "breakdowns" in the correlations reflected in current market data must be of major concern to risk managers and hedge fund managers. These are the times when their carefully constructed "hedged" portfolio can break down and subject the portfolio to significant market risk. In times of market crisis, the correlations between asset prices or rates can change dramatically and unexpectedly, with the result that positions that were thought to be hedging or diversifying risk end up compounding it. While it remains difficult to hedge correlation risk, stress tests to evaluate the impact of correlation changes enable hedge fund managers to be aware of the risks involved in any asset they select should correlations change. They can then periodically evaluate if they are being sufficiently compensated for bearing that risk.

Back-testing   Concurrent with stress and scenario analysis to evaluate the shortcomings of the VaR analysis, back-testing should be performed. Back-testing is the process of relating the VaR to the actual historic P/L of the fund to see how predictive the VaR was. By comparing actual changes in the value of the portfolio to the changes generated by the VaR calculation, the hedge fund manager can gain insight into whether the VaR model is accurately measuring the fund's risk. In back-testing, it is expected that the portfolio will lose more than the VaR from time to time. For example, a 99 percent one-day VaR should be exceeded on one day in every 100 trading days on average. When the actual changes in the value of the portfolio exceed VaR, the hedge fund manager must determine the source of the discrepancy (that is, whether the VaR measure is flawed or whether this loss is simply one which was expected given the confidence level employed). Other potential sources of deviations include:

1. The VaR model or the data are flawed and did not adequately capture the sources of risk.
2. Positions changed in the portfolio between calculation and observation.
3. A change in the underlying market occurred, including changes in the volatility, correlation, or liquidity of the factors that was not present in the time series used in the VaR analysis or was outside the confidence interval used.

Relating Earnings and Risk   If back-testing is successful and the confidence in the risk measures is established, it is then possible to begin to link risk and return to create risk adjusted performance measures. There are a number of ways in which return and risk could be calculated in one risk adjusted performance measure. The Sharpe ratio is widely used by many fund managers to measure a portfolio's risk adjusted performance over a specific period. Below is the Sharpe ratio for an arbitrary portfolio calculated using the most common conventions for measuring return and risk. The numerator is the return earned on the portfolio (R_p) in excess of the risk-free rate of return (R_f) (that is, the interest rate earned on risk-free securities such as U.S. Treasury securities) over the same period. The denominator—the risk incurred—is measured as the standard deviation of the portfolio's daily return σ_P.

$$(R_p\text{-}R_f)/\sigma_P = \text{Sharpe ratio}_P$$

The Sharpe ratio is a summary risk-adjusted performance measure. The risk component of the measure used in the denominator of the Sharpe ratio is a historical measure (the standard deviation of portfolio returns). The denominator is a measure of the risk incurred in achieving the return. It characterizes the actual volatility of the return over some historical period. The numerator of the Sharpe ratio is a measure of portfolio return in excess of the risk-free rate during the period. (For example, over the past decade the Sharpe ratio for the S&P 500 has been approximately 1.2.) Investors prefer higher Sharpe ratios, since a higher ratio indicates that the portfolio earned superior returns relative to the level of risk incurred. Transparent and objective portfolio valuation is essential for accurate risk-adjusted performance measurement. It is unfortunately a frequent occurrence that illiquid positions or level-three assets are carried at cost or marked to model where the parameters are not realistic or updated frequently. This results in lower reported P&L volatility and misleadingly high Sharpe ratios.

Performance Attribution Performance attribution is important for two central reasons:

- **Risk management:** A fund that does not understand its sources of performance does not understand its risks. Does a new strategy add new risks that manifest themselves at just the wrong times, such as periods of great market stress? To answer such questions, we need to understand what drives hedge fund returns.
- **Alpha generation:** Many hedge fund managers promise positive absolute returns independent of market direction (that is, alpha). Does the hedge fund provide investment diversification with some alpha, or does it simply exaggerate market beta? The ability to distinguish between performance attributable to beta and performance from alpha is essential as alpha is what investors pay hedge funds for. Since performance attribution is important to investors, it should also be important to fund managers.

Principal Components and Factor Analysis Hedge fund managers, risk managers and investors can use factor analysis to analyze performance and risks. (For further detail on the application of factor analysis, see Chapter 3.)

However, there are two main reasons why this is not easy for investors. First, detailed factor analysis requires portfolio-level holdings and many hedge fund managers are reluctant to disclose their positions for fear of compromising their strategies. Even large institutional investors currently have difficulty obtaining this information. Second, some of the risks inherent in hedge funds arise not just from the securities they invest in but also from the strategies they employ (the timing, direction, combination, and sequence of trades). In conducting the performance attribution of hedge fund returns, it is important to allocate return not only to market factors (beta factors), but also to strategy factors. Only then is it possible to define the residual unexplained performance as alpha.

For investors to meaningfully analyze a hedge fund's ability to generate alpha, position-level return data must be analyzed. The analysis should be structured to include the following generalized steps:

1. **Organize the data:** Firstly, the data quality must be confirmed. Outliers, stale data arising from illiquidity, and identifiable data errors should be

removed from the position-level data set. Once sound return series are confirmed, the position level return data and hedge fund level return data must be categorized by hedge fund and primary strategy in order to be analyzed. Then, the data must be divided into an in-sample segment for defining the factor loadings and an out-of-sample segment for subsequent verification of the factor loadings. In broad terms, the in-sample analysis is used to reveal the significant relationships between the fund and the factors. The out-of-sample analysis is used to verify these relationships and reduce spurious results.

2. **Define lexicon of factors:** The selection process identifies a relevant set of factors for each hedge fund separately but drawn from a set of pre-defined factors. The factors are separated into Beta factors (performance attributable to market exposures), and strategy factors (performance attributable to any fund following a similar strategy). The number of selected factors should be minimized in order to increase the potential explanatory power. The inclusion of extraneous factors within a returns-based model risks the introduction of spurious results. Each beta factor must have an ex-ante economic rationale for explaining the performance characteristics common to the hedge fund population. Each strategy factor must have an ex-ante rationale for explaining the performance characteristics exclusive and common to the strategy. These strategy factors are selected to capture those sources of a hedge fund's return arising from known or conventional risk factors. The heterogeneity of hedge funds within strategy groups generally is quite high. Therefore, it should not be expected that every fund within a strategy group will have a significant exposure to each predefined factor used to model its peer group. The risk that does not stem from Beta or strategic factors is fund-specific. It reflects the idiosyncratic investments, strategies or processes of the manager and therefore performance attributable to alpha.

   ■ **Beta factors:** Hedge fund performance is shaped partially by broad, systematic factors that potentially influence many funds, as well as the idiosyncratic behavior of the fund. Most hedge funds invest in traditional asset classes such as equities, bonds, currencies and commodities or derivatives written on them. Extensive research has identified factors that drive the returns to securities within each of these asset classes. What may be surprising to some investors is that many hedge fund managers do not fully hedge their exposure to these factors. Long or short equity funds, for example, usually are biased toward following the direction of the market. Also, fixed income arbitrage funds often bet on the convergence of credit or interest rate spreads between instruments with different risk profiles. Thus, a portion of hedge fund risk arises from exposures to familiar factors that underlie conventional investments.

■ **Strategy factors:** Strategy factors include additional factors that are not already explained by beta factors but common and exclusive to funds following a defined strategy. These strategic specific sources of return arise from the manner in which a portfolio is managed. For example, one strategy of convertible bond funds is to buy convertible bonds with embedded options and then hedge the convertible bond by buying credit default swap (CDS) protection and delta hedging the option. The fund captures an arbitrage profit as the combined cost of the CDS and delta hedging the option is less than the cost of the convertible bond. However, this strategy suffered greatly in 2007 and 2008 and showed that convertible arbitrage funds share a set of common risks. Specifically, the liquidity of the convertible bond market decreased dramatically during the crisis, while that of the CDS market remained high. The effective increase in the liquidity discount applied to convertible bonds destroyed the stability of the hedge ratio between convertible bonds and credit default swaps on the same issuer. Convertible bonds fell dramatically in price while spreads on CDS did not increase proportionately, creating losses for the strategy. Strategy factors identify common sources of performance affecting all funds following that strategy. Additional examples of strategy factors include the phenomenon that many merger arbitrage deals may break at the same time when the market plummets (an event arbitrage factor) or the fact that performance of commodity trading advisors (CTAs) is due more to their collective trend-following behavior than to the commodities or currencies in which these funds are invested. Strategic factors are especially useful in modeling hedge funds within peer groups such as merger arbitrage, distressed securities and convertible arbitrage. This is because the funds within these peer groups tend to follow similar, unconventional strategies and manage a relatively homogeneous set of investments. This behavior generates commonality across the funds within each of these peer groups that does not arise from passive investing in liquid asset classes.[3]

3. **Estimate exposures:** After establishing a set of factors that are well suited to modeling the returns of a particular fund, the fund's exposures with respect to these factors should be estimated. While a variety of estimation techniques exist, it is critical to adopt the most appropriate model. The optimal statistical approach will vary depending on the precise objective of the study and the structure of the data. An obvious and

popular technique used to estimate model parameters, such as exposures, is ordinary least squares (OLS) multivariate regression but this assumes that factor exposures are constant.[4] A lack of rigid investment restrictions provides hedge fund managers with the flexibility to make rapid and significant changes in their style, sector or market bets according to their future expectations. As a result, they can be much more dynamic in their investment approach than traditional managers. A method used frequently within the regression framework to account for the dynamic behavior of hedge funds is the moving-window regression.[5] However, this comes at a cost of statistical accuracy since the estimation is performed using a smaller data sample. In addition, this method will not capture exposure changes over the shorter window. OLS multivariate regression might be the best choice for a hedge fund whose exposures vary little over time. Conversely, a moving-window regression might be selected during a period when the fund's common factor exposures have been very volatile. Ultimately, the optimal estimation method depends on the funds being studied and the objective of the study.

4. **Out-of-sample model evaluation and return replication:** The first step is to analyze the predictability of the exposure estimates. This is accomplished by first calculating a series of out-of-sample returns, as follows. Assuming monthly return data, for a given month-end return estimate the fund exposures to a set of factors using data available through the end of the previous month. These exposures are combined with the factor returns observed over the current month to compute the common factor return that can be explained by the model over the month. In particular, for month t, the replicated return is $\sum_k X_{k,t-1} f_{k,t}$, where $X_{k,t-1}$ are the fund's exposures estimated using data through the end of the previous month, $t-1$, and $f_{k,t}$ are returns to the factors over the month. There are several analyses that can be performed on these replicated common factor returns to measure particular aspects of the model's out-of-sample performance. A commonly used measure in this framework is the R^2 of the regression of the realized returns versus the replicated returns. R^2 is only a measure of the ratio of the out-of-sample return variation captured by the factors to the hedge fund's total return variation, not a measure of the model's total risk forecasting ability *per se* as fund idiosyncratic variation is not included.

5. **Estimate factor exposures:** Using the hedge funds' return history, their corresponding style classifications, and the regressions derived in the previous step, the sources of return can be estimated for an individual fund.

This process provides a robust model that can be used to analyze the sources of returns for a given fund or portfolio of hedge funds. The extent to which a given hedge fund's return variation is correlated to variations in levels of beta factors is indicative of the fund's ability to generate returns uncorrelated to the market. High correlations indicate that returns are significantly related to market factors, while low correlations indicate that they are not and the manager is likely delivering alpha. Similarly, a high correlation of fund returns to strategy factors indicates the extent to which the manager deviates from his peers. A high correlation indicates the manager is likely following a strategy consistent with his peers, while a low correlation is a possible indication of style drift. Lastly, a low correlation of the manager returns to either type of factor is a possible indication of a misspecified model or potential fraudulent returns.

Funding Risk

What caused so many hedge funds to fail and liquidate in 2008 and 2009 was a trifecta of market, credit and liquidity events. The first funds to fail were the convertible bond funds. When the fall in the equity markets caused such funds that were not fully hedged to record sharp mark-to-market losses on their positions and the collapse of Bear Stearns created counterparty risks which froze the convertible bond market, previously liquid positions became illiquid and leverage provided by prime brokers was progressively, and sometimes suddenly, withdrawn. Then investors demanded redemption of their interest in the fund, forcing the fund manager to either gate the fund or liquidate at distressed prices. When this occurs at multiple hedge funds, the liquidation of positions into the market causes a cascade in prices because of a high volume of one-way liquidation orders. Strategies for managing funding risk are discussed in depth in Chapter 5.

Liquidity Crisis Cycle   A liquidity crisis cycle can be broken down into five stages:

1. A market disruption leads to a period of higher volatility and risk aversion.
2. A rumor of loss or actual loss at a hedge fund or group of funds triggers demands for higher margin from counterparties.
3. This causes hedge funds to liquidate positions in a disorderly manner to raise cash to meet their immediate margin calls.
4. The need to pay increased demands for investor redemptions also forces liquidations but this comes after the payment of margin calls as investors are required to give 45 or more days' advance notice of their intention to redeem. Further liquidation may be required because of redemptions by investors caused by the initial and ongoing losses.

5. The hedge fund's net asset value (NAV) or assets under management (AUM) continue to drop as the market reacts to actions by the fund community. Attempts by hedge funds to sell positions in large size too quickly for the market liquidity to bear cause a further drop in prices, precipitating a further decline in the hedge fund's NAV, and leading in turn to yet a further need to liquidate to satisfy margin calls or redemptions. This downward spiral can be exacerbated if other market participants have information about the hedge fund's positions.

In such an environment, a fund without alternative sources of liquidity or additional cash to meet margin calls and redemption requests is facing a death spiral. As illustrated in Figure 2.2, the hedge fund manager faces a grim choice: a) either continue to liquidate to generate cash when each liquidation has a greater impact on the value of the remaining hedge fund position than the amount of cash raised from the liquidation; or b) gate the fund and deny redemption requests while using any available cash to meet margin calls. Gating the fund buys time and allows for a more controlled liquidation over time and may reduce losses. The action of gating the fund,

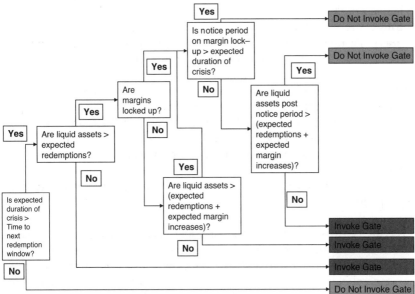

FIGURE 2.2 Hedge fund manager's crisis decision tree

however, does not typically result in the resurrection of a fund, as investor confidence is shattered.

Once losses move beyond a critical point and there is "blood in the water," the liquidity crisis at the fund becomes self-sustaining. Creditors will not risk a default by the fund and will increase margins. Similarly, investors will not risk further losses and will demand their money back. Competitors will only pay distressed prices for hedge fund assets. The best course of action is for the fund managers to ensure that they will always be able to satisfy the demands of their creditors or investors by managing their funding risk and so avoid being caught in this accelerating, downward liquidity spiral.

Measuring Funding Risk All asset managers and financial institutions face funding liquidity risk but because leverage is involved, it has proven to be the Achilles heel of hedge fund managers. This is because funding liquidity problems dramatically increase the risk of failure. Consequently, hedge fund managers should focus significant attention and resources on measuring and managing funding liquidity risk.

There are a variety of metrics hedge fund managers should use to track funding liquidity risk. Obviously, cash is king and they must monitor the liquidity available in the hedge fund by tracking its cash position (that is, cash and short-term securities issued by high credit quality entities). The adequacy of this cash to meet various demands from creditors and investors during a stressed or crisis scenario should be evaluated. Similarly, an evaluation of the adequacy of the fund's borrowing capacity (for example, its access to borrowings under margin rules or credit lines) must be included but fund managers should be aware of the reality that these rules can be changed and lines withdrawn, typically at short notice. Whether available liquidity is sufficient is a relative question. There is no dollar amount or percentage of NAV that is deemed adequate to protect the fund in all cases. Fund managers should monitor measures of relative liquidity and relate these measures (Cash or Cash + Borrowing capacity) to the need for that liquidity.

The following measures are indicators of a hedge fund's potential need for liquidity:

1. **VaR:** VaR is currently the most widely used prospective measure of investment risk. Consequently, tracking the ratio of Cash or Cash + Borrowing capacity to VaR provides the hedge fund manager with a general indication of whether the fund's liquidity relative to its need for liquidity is rising or falling but it does not inform any decision as to whether the amount is adequate.

2. **Equity or NAV:** The ratio of Cash or Cash + Borrowing capacity to the investors' equity or fund NAV provides the hedge fund manager with a general indication of whether the fund's liquidity relative to its size is rising or falling. While this ratio is very widely demanded by investors and creditors on a monthly basis and creates a means of comparing liquidity across hedge funds, it again does not inform any decision as to whether the amount is adequate. A hedge fund's need for liquidity during periods of market stress is determined by its relative performance, its investors' redemption terms, its margin agreements with its creditors, the size of the portfolio, and the characteristics of the assets it holds (in addition to its need to fund redemptions). Consequently, hedge fund managers need to have measures of potential liquidity that reflect the riskiness of the portfolio.

3. **Worst historical drawdown:** This indicator provides a measure of risk and of the amount of liquidity the hedge fund has required in the past. This measure is, however, a backward-looking measure of risk and may not be indicative of the fund's current exposure. Young hedge funds, with few years of operating history, may not actually have experienced a significant drawdown, or the drawdowns experienced to date may be insignificant compared to potential crises.

While no absolute determination about the adequacy of liquidity can be made from these measures, additional insight about funding liquidity can be gained by looking at the variability in the relative liquidity measure over time. A relative liquidity measure that varies over time is evident and consistent with "effective liquidity" (that is, the assets are liquid and the manager is willing to take advantage of that liquidity). Beyond simply monitoring liquidity, hedge fund managers must manage liquidity in several dimensions.

Adequate Management of Funding Risk   The foremost of these is the use of the hedge fund manager's experience and judgment to maintain liquidity levels that are adequate given the risk of loss and/or the likelihood of investor redemptions. They should actively manage (or monitor) the cash in margin accounts.

Again, integrated risk management of market, credit and liquidity risks should occur whereby scenarios are constructed, maintained and updated that model the impact of a confluence of such events hitting the fund. Even if current liquidity is insufficient in the face of such a scenario, the fund manager will know that he is running this risk and how much of an impact it will have on the fund if it occurs.

Also, in a crisis, uncertainty is exacerbated. Fund managers should strengthen and maintain lines of communication with their credit providers, providing them with timely summary measures of the fund's risk and liquidity. In the past crisis, the scarcest commodity (after cash) was accurate information. As a result of the heightened levels of risk aversion and turmoil in the markets, requests from creditors for "transparency" into fund operations and risk positions increased in frequency and in detail. When responses were not received in a timely fashion, creditors had to assume the fund was illiquid and acted to recover their principal before the fund collapsed. They consequently exercised their rights to withdraw financing by increasing margins and thereby exacerbated the liquidity needs of the hedge funds, sometimes creating the crisis they feared.

To maintain creditor financing during a crisis, hedge fund managers should provide detailed risk analysis and more frequent, high-level, and personal communication. This lowers the uncertainty regarding the hedge fund's creditworthiness and may prevent a decision to withdraw all financing.

Lastly, contractual rights should be negotiated at the outset of the creditor–hedge fund relationship that defines each party's ability to use unused borrowing capacity and change margin terms. Hedge fund managers should negotiate margin levels, the speed at which prime brokers can dictate an increase in margin rates, and bilateral collateral agreements, where appropriate, to further reduce the likelihood of running out of liquidity.

Leverage   Attempting to manage the risks of a hedge fund without addressing the ability of leverage to increase the likelihood of those risks occurring, and the magnitude of the loss when those risks occur, is naïve. Because of the levered nature of hedge funds, controlling leverage is necessary in order to concurrently manage risk. This is true even though leverage itself is not a precise or directly useful measure of risk. Nonetheless, leverage is critical to hedge fund managers because of the impact it can have on the three major areas of risk addressed earlier: investment risk; counterparty risk; and liquidity risk. Leverage is not an independent source of risk; rather, it is a factor that influences the rapidity with which changes in these three risk factors change the value of the portfolio.

To acquire more than a superficial understanding of leverage, it is essential to consider what leverage means—or does not mean—in the context of a hedge fund:

1. The liquidity and price volatility of the position being leveraged is relevant to assessing effective leverage. The leverage employed by a hedge fund that holds one-year Treasury bills with ten-to-one leverage may be

of less concern due to Treasury bills' low volatility and high liquidity than that employed by a hedge fund levered two-to-one and invested in sub-investment grade convertible bonds.

2. An isolated asset-based leverage number may not contain very much information and can be dangerously misleading. A risk-reducing transaction can increase asset-based leverage measures, while risk-based leverage measures are insensitive to the size of a portfolio. A very large but well-hedged portfolio may show low risk-based leverage despite being potentially illiquid.

There are several varieties of "leverage" measures used in finance. Some pertain to financial analysis of accounting statements (operational leverage) while others are used solely in the investment field. While all are ratios, leverage metrics vary depending on the financial relationship being evaluated. Leverage ratios used in investing are asset-based or risk-based.

Asset-based Leverage Measures Using borrowed money (or its equivalent) enables an investor to increase the assets controlled for a given level of equity capital. The asset-based measures of leverage seek to capture the relationship between the total assets controlled through the use of debt and equity, and the funds borrowed to invest in those assets. Asset-based measures typically relate some measure of "asset value to equity." Both returns and risk, relative to equity, are magnified through the use of traditional, asset-based leverage.

A number of widely used asset-based measures of leverage have evolved in the industry over time and are generally accepted because of their usefulness (see Table 2.1). Hedge fund managers should calculate and monitor these measures as they can contribute to an overall understanding of risk when tracked over time. In addition, creditors, counterparties and investors routinely require them as part of the due diligence and ongoing monitoring of the fund (see Appendix 1 for a sample due diligence questionnaire). Credit is provided to a hedge fund both directly (via margin financing and repurchase agreements) and indirectly (via short sales, swaps, futures, and other derivative contracts). Certain accounting measures provide information regarding how much direct or indirect credit a hedge fund is using. The most widely used and generally accepted financial statement-based measures of leverage are those that relate items from a hedge fund's balance sheet.

The most straightforward and widely used measure of leverage in finance is Gross Balance Sheet Assets to Equity. This routine measure is easily calculated from published financial statements but fails to incorporate two important elements of a hedge fund's effective leverage.

TABLE 2.1   Asset-based leverage measures

Leverage Metric	Pros	Cons
Gross Balance Sheet Assets to Equity	Unambiguous Widely applicable to variety of legal entities Easily calculated Based on audited financial statements	Not well suited to hedge-fund entities. Does not incorporate off-balance-sheet items Fails to incorporate risk-reducing effect of hedges Can understate true economic risk
Net Balance Sheet Assets to Equity	Appropriate for hedge-fund legal structure More detailed but still easily calculated Partially addresses need to incorporate risk-reducing effects of hedges	Does not reflect portfolio correlation or less direct hedges that fall outside the definition of matched book assets Does not incorporate off-balance-sheet instruments.

Firstly, the risk-reducing effect of on-balance-sheet hedges is not recognized. When a hedge is put on, the hedge is added to the balance sheet as an asset. This increases assets and thereby increases this leverage measure, even though the transaction may substantially offset the risk of another asset.

Secondly, the market value of derivative instruments is typically recorded on the balance sheet rather than the full notional amount. As illustrated in the short-option example later in this section, the value of derivative contracts can change rapidly and substantially. To the extent that the full notional amount of a long or short derivative position is not recorded as an asset or liability, this measure may understate the hedge fund's true economic risk. A more appropriate measure for measuring a hedge fund's asset-based leverage is Net Balance Sheet Assets to Equity. While this measure requires more detailed information about the positions in a hedge fund's portfolio, it does provide a partial solution to the shortcomings of the Gross Balance Sheet Assets to Equity measure by including offsets and direct hedges as reflected in matched book assets. However, two important elements of the hedge fund's effective leverage are still not incorporated.

Firstly, Net Balance Sheet Assets to Equity does not reflect portfolio correlation or less direct hedges that fall outside the tight definition of matched book assets. For example, in the case of a diversified portfolio of U.S. equities, a hedge of long S&P 500 index puts would not count as a matched asset and would increase the asset side of the balance sheet, as it would not be netted against the diversified equities component of the portfolio.

Secondly, the Net Balance Sheet Assets to Equity measure does not incorporate off-balance-sheet instruments. For example, if the diversified portfolio of long U.S. equities described in the previous paragraph were hedged with a customized portfolio swap that perfectly replicated the performance of the U.S. equities portfolio, the long side of the equity positions would still show as an asset on the balance sheet while the short position via the swap was off-balance-sheet. Because of the real economic impact off-balance-sheet transactions can have, other financial statement-based measures have been proposed to capture off-balance-sheet transactions (for example, forward contracts, swaps and other derivatives). However, it must be recognized that even these measures have shortcomings, particularly as stand-alone measures of risk to equity.

For a risk manager, the critical question is how much risk a given level of equity must support. While asset-based measures of leverage are commonly used, they are not truly comparable as the assets supported by equity can vary in their riskiness. For example, a portfolio of out-of-the-money short options with a total contract size of US$1,000 and paying a premium of US$75 and supported by US$100 of equity will initially have an asset-based leverage of 0.75. But should those options begin to go in-the-money and cost US$1,000 to close out, the asset-based leverage quickly goes to 10:1. What is the necessary amount of equity needed to support this portfolio? Is the correct measure of leverage the current 0.75 or the potential 10:1? Some sort of expected value of the assets is necessary given the dynamic nature of the assets. Consequently, risk managers and hedge fund managers need risk-based measures of leverage to capture the risk of insolvency arising from potential changes in the value of the portfolio.

Risk-based Leverage Measures   The risk-based measures relate a hedge fund's investment risk to its equity by evaluating the ratio of "risk to equity." Risk-based measures (see Table 2.2) present a measure of investment risk (usually VaR) relative to a measure of the resources available to absorb risk (cash or equity). In doing so, risk-based measures can oversimplify the risk by consolidating several dimensions of risk into a single number. While this may be attractive for investors and creditors seeking to compare leverage across funds, the result is that some of the details are lost. Consequently, the true risk of the fund may be underappreciated as the specific effect of leverage is intertwined with dimensions of market, credit, and funding risk.

For example, funding risk is often lost in both the asset-based and risk-based leverage measures. Consider two funds with identical VaR/Equity risk-based leverage. One follows a long or short equity strategy that uses US$100 million of margin financing (debt) and US$100 million of investor equity to support a portfolio of US$200 million long microcap equity positions and US$200 million short microcap equity positions. This results in 2-to-1 Gross Balance Sheet Assets to Equity leverage while investing in "low risk" strategies (for example, long/short equity strategies) using borrowed funds. The VaR is US$50 million, resulting in a VaR/Equity leverage ratio of 0.5.

A second fund uses no Net Balance Sheet Assets to Equity leverage. Its macro strategy is to buy US$100 million of U.S. Treasuries with its US$100 million of equity but to sell deep out of the money-index options for a slight premium. This fund uses no directly borrowed money but because of the risk of the sold options, generates a VaR of US$200 million and a VaR/ Equity leverage ratio of 2:1. The macro fund is high-risk but high-liquidity, while the long/short equity fund is low-risk and low-liquidity, yet each achieves a similar VaR and thereby risk-based leverage. The liquidity risk of the assets is ignored.

This comparison highlights the reason why leverage measures should not be used in isolation to evaluate risk. Risk-based leverage measures reflect the relation between the riskiness of a hedge fund's portfolio and the capacity of the fund to absorb the impact of that risk; but by using VaR and consolidating risk into a single number, they can oversimplify risk. While this is not the only measure that could be used (borrowing capacity is an alternative), the hedge fund's equity provides a useful measure of risk-taking "capacity." A hedge fund manager should utilize more comprehensive measures to evaluate leverage in the context of multiple risk dimensions. An assessment of the contribution of leverage requires additional information.

There are, however, different measures of investment risk that could be used depending on the strategy employed and the purpose of the analysis.

Volatility in value of portfolio/equity is a measure of actual performance volatility over a given horizon relative to equity. While useful, it is subject to criticism. Since it is a retrospective measure, it is less useful if the composition of the portfolio changes or if future market conditions are not like historical conditions. Moreover, it does not isolate the effect of financing on the hedge fund's risk since it includes financed assets.

VaR/equity gives a picture of the hedge fund's capacity to absorb "typical" market movements. The criticism of such a measure is that it does not reflect the risk of the fund's portfolio in extreme markets.

Scenario-based investment-risk measure/equity assesses the impact of extreme events; the leverage measure could be calculated using an investment-risk measure derived from analysis of extreme-event scenarios (or stress tests). This measure gives senior management information about the hedge fund's ability to absorb extreme market events. While these are the leverage measures most commonly used by hedge-fund managers, other

TABLE 2.2 Alternative risk-based leverage measures

Leverage Metric	Pros	Cons
Volatility in value of portfolio/equity	Objective, as it is based on realized portfolio volatility Unambiguous Easily computed	Can be misleading if portfolio composition changes or market conditions change Does not break out impact of financing on the risk profile of the fund
VaR/Equity	Comprehensive measure of market risk to equity	Does not reflect a fund's ability to absorb non-standard market scenarios
Scenario-derived investment-risk measure/equity	Flexible, in that various scenarios can be specified	Subjective, in that scenarios are hypothetical or historical Lack of probability assigned to scenario occurrence undermines usefulness

measures may be used to analyze leverage. Indeed, because of the inter-relation between investment risk, funding liquidity risk and leverage, measures of funding liquidity risk—particularly Cash + Borrowing Capacity relative to VaR—also provide the hedge-fund manager with insights the fund's leverage.

Leverage and Liquidity Liquidity is a crucial dimension influencing a hedge fund's ability to absorb the impact of extreme market events. Liquidity determines the degree to which a fund can modify its risk-based leverage, especially during periods of market stress.

Starting with the least-adverse scenario—where hedge-fund assets are fully liquid, investors are not redeeming funds, and markets are stable—a fund manager can reduce risk-based leverage in two ways:

1. While continuing with an existing investment strategy, risk-based leverage could be reduced by reducing the **size** of existing on- and off-balance-sheet positions and effectively move further towards an all-cash portfolio.
2. Reduce risk-based leverage by reducing the level of risk that is being accepted (for example, by diversifying positions, changing strategy, taking exposures through more liquid securities, or hedging risks in the portfolio).

If markets are increasingly volatile, reducing the size of positions may not be sufficient to reduce risk-based leverage. Similarly, if positions are illiquid, it will not be possible to reduce the size of positions. Lastly, if investors are redeeming their investments, it may not be possible to reduce risk-based leverage since, as positions are reduced, the equity released will be paid to investors. In the final case, the fund may be left with only illiquid positions and minimal equity, resulting in an increase in risk-based leverage.

To track the degree to which the hedge fund is able to modify its risk-based leverage, the fund manager, investors and creditors should track variations in the fund's investment-risk measure (for example, VaR) over time. The following two measures could be used to track the relationship over time between measures of investment risk and actions taken by the fund Manager to adjust leverage. Both of these measures consider a short time interval (one day, two days . . . one week); and, both assume that equity is constant:

1. Changes in portfolio investment risk: A decline in a portfolio's investment-risk measure (for example, VaR) in a period following an increase in that measure in the preceding period could be evidence of the fund manager's ability to de-lever the portfolio during a period of market stress (the investment-risk measure could be VaR or the observed volatility of the value of the portfolio during the relevant period).
2. Relationship between a change in investment risk and a subsequent change in Cash + Borrowing capacity: All other things being equal, if a fund manager is able to reduce the portfolio's asset-based leverage, the result would be an increase in cash or in borrowing capacity. Therefore, an increase in Cash + Borrowing capacity in a period following an increase in the investment-risk measure for the portfolio (for example, VaR) could be evidence of the fund manager's reacting to market stress by reducing leverage.

Although useful in this capacity, risk-based leverage measures do not convey any information about the role borrowed money plays in the risk of insolvency.

Funding Risk and Leverage In summary, no single measure captures all of the risk elements that market participants, regulators, or market observers attribute to the concept of leverage. Funding and leverage should be evaluated in the context of the fund's strategy, asset liquidity, investor stability, relationship with its prime brokers, immediate market conditions and the size of the fund.

While continuing to track and use asset-based measures of leverage, hedge fund managers should focus their attention on measures of leverage that relate the riskiness of the portfolio to the fund's capacity to absorb that risk (that is, investment risk—including the credit risk associated with assets in the portfolio—and funding-liquidity risk). Fund managers should focus on such measures because traditional financial statement-based leverage by itself does not necessarily convey risk of insolvency. To say that one hedge fund is levered 2-to-1 while another is not levered does not necessarily mean that the levered fund is more risky or more likely to encounter liquidity problems. If the levered fund were invested in government securities while the fund that is not levered is invested in equities, asset-based leverage would lead to erroneous conclusions about the risk of the two funds. In this sense, asset-based measures of leverage are arguably the most deficient since they convey the least information about the nature and risk of the assets in a portfolio.

Counterparty Risk

Counterparty credit risk should be another area of concern for hedge-fund managers.[6] Hedge funds are exposed to counterparty credit risk, which is the risk of loses arising from the failure of a counterparty to perform as expected by the contract. This is the risk that changes in the credit quality of counterparties impose a cost on the hedge fund, either in the form of replacement costs arising from non-performance on a security contract, the non-return of collateral due to counterparty default, or by forcing the fund manager to find alternative counterparties. Strategies for managing counterparty risk are detailed more fully in Chapter 6. Hedge fund managers enter into transactions with a variety of counterparties including banks, securities firms, exchanges, and other financial institutions. Counterparty risk is present to some extent in almost any dealing with a third party, including the settlement of securities and derivatives transactions, repurchase agreements, collateral arrangements, and margin accounts. It is also present in open derivatives positions where the exposure of one counterparty to another will change over the life of the contract as the contract's value fluctuates.

Hedge-fund managers should select only highly creditworthy counterparties, calculate and track counterparty risk exposures, avoid concentrations of counterparty risk with individual counterparties and, where applicable, different regions of the world. If concentrations arise, they should be diversified up to the point where the diversification begins to impose an operational or financial cost to the fund.

One of the factors that should be considered in determining how willing a fund manager should be to enter into a transaction with a specific counterparty is the loss that the fund would suffer were the counterparty to default. That, in turn, depends on the magnitude of its exposure to the counterparty, the documentation governing that relationship, and the likelihood of default (that is, the counterparty's creditworthiness).

Assessing Counterparty Exposure   An assessment of exposure to a particular counterparty should include analysis of the following elements:

1. Current replacement cost: The amount the hedge fund would lose if its counterparty was to become insolvent at the current time and the fund manager had to replace the contract in the market.
2. Potential future exposure (PFE): The exposure a fund has to loss arising from a specific counterparty failing to meet its contractual obligations on an individual securities contract can vary over time. A stochastic estimate of the expected and potential exposure that could result if the counterparty defaults at some date in the future life of the contract is necessary to quantify the risk. Most risk systems can now calculate this exposure (for example, CreditMetrics). Potential exposure is particularly applicable to derivatives transactions where exposure is reciprocal and likely to change substantially before the contract expires, such as swaps.
3. The probability of loss: When dealing with a large number of counterparties, the likelihood of a loss in the event of a default by a counterparty over a relevant time horizon can be usefully modeled and used to manage counterparty risk. Probability of loss is a function of the nature of the transaction itself (as we shall see shortly), the counterparty's current credit quality, and the length of the transaction.
4. Risk mitigation and documentation: The extent to which initial and variation margin collateral, cross-netting provisions, cross-default and set-off provisions or credit enhancement, such as two way collateral posting, reduce the magnitude of the exposure to a counterparty is an important consideration in quantifying potential loss.

All of these concepts are fully illustrated, for example, in a swap contract. Swaps are commonly traded by hedge funds and are executed with a variety of counterparties of varying creditworthiness, from banks to broker dealers to corporations. They typically have zero value at inception, and thus zero initial replacement cost, but have extended maturities that result in significant potential exposure. Risk-mitigating netting agreements, margin terms, and collateral terms are highly standardized and clearly documented under ISDA agreements.

In a swap contract, assume a hedge fund is long the receiving leg and short the paying leg. Because both legs can change in value, a swap contract can sometimes be an asset and at other times a liability depending on whether the hedge fund is owed or owes money under the contract. When the swap is an asset and the investor (hedge fund) is owed money, a default by the swap counterparty would result in a loss for the investor. When the swap is a liability, there is no counterparty exposure as no money is owed by the counterparty.

Swap trading, whether it is an interest rate swap, cross currency swap, an equity swap, or a credit default swap, is typically governed by an International Swaps Dealers Association (ISDA) Agreement, under which recovery in the event of a default by a counterparty is the market value of the swap (that is, the value of principal and payments owed).

For example, consider a five-year S&P Index Swap with the hedge fund being long the receiving leg. In a flat market, with low volatility, the swap will have nearly zero market value and thus zero replacement cost. Consequently, at inception there will be no counterparty exposure. However, the swap has a five-year maturity and market conditions can change before maturity. In an upwardly trending market with high volatility, the swap has the potential to be fairly valuable in the future, in which case the potential exposure is large and default by the counterparty could cause a substantial loss to the other party. The potential for the swap to become valuable as the market moves, the timing of those market moves, and the likelihood that the counterparty which owes money at that time defaults, all affect the value of the swap.

These factors are combined and quantified in a metric used to manage counterparty risk called the "counterparty valuation adjustment."[7] This is the price deficit of the contract based on the risk that the counterparty may default over the life of the contract. It is the difference between the actual price of the contract and the price the contract would carry if the counterparty were risk-free. The difference between these two values is the price of default risk to the counterparty. The magnitude of this difference depends on the creditworthiness of the counterparty as expressed by its CDS spread, interest rates, and the volatility of the risk factors underlying the contract.

"Wrong Way" Counterparty Risk   Hedge fund risk managers should be particularly alert to "wrong way" counterparty risk. This occurs when the likelihood of a counterparty default is correlated to the potential exposure. Imagine, for example, if a hedge fund had, presciently, bought protection against a default by Lehman Brothers in 2006 but, less impressively, bought it from Bear Stearns. When the financial crisis hit, the value of the protection on Lehman increased as Lehman's default probability increased. However, so did that of Bear Stearns, and more rapidly. Bear Stearns actually defaulted before Lehman, so the CDS would have been worthless, even though it provided protection, since payment would have been owed by Bear Stearns. Obviously, the likelihood of Bear Stearns defaulting and Lehman Brothers defaulting were correlated. The amount owed to the fund under the swap increased as Lehman Brothers' creditworthiness fell but the counterparty risk of Bear Stearns rose faster. This is an example of wrong-way risk.

Minimum Counterparty Risk Management Capabilities   Best-practice counterparty risk management includes the following items:

1. Counterparty acceptance and contracting standards
2. Credit quality monitoring
3. Counterparty exposure measurement and limits
4. Counterparty risk reporting
5. Counterparty risk mitigation and hedging

Counterparty Acceptance and Contracting Standards   Before a hedge fund initiates a transaction with a proposed counterparty, it should review all available public information—including CDS spreads, credit-agency reports, and counterparty financials—before agreeing to trade. It is also important to segregate counterparties according to legal entities and evaluate their specific creditworthiness; trading or utilizing the services of a subsidiary of a AAA-rated bank may provide little or no financial protection in the event of a default.

Furthermore, it should be assumed in general that a benefit of trading with one legal entity cannot be netted against a loss to another legal entity within the same firm unless appropriate documentation is in place. For example, if a company is owed US$10 million by the European arm of a financial institution, and owes US$10 million to the American subsidiary of the same counterparty, and the European entity defaults, it will still have an obligation to the American subsidiary.

Contracting standards refer to the types and forms of contracts that may be entered with an appropriately initiated counterparty. For example, in most derivative contracts, a standard contract such as the ISDA contract is used. Even standard contracts require customization, however. The Credit Support Annex (CSA) of the ISDA details the unilateral or bilateral collateral-posting requirements of the counterparties. It also typically contains provisions for material adverse changes (MAC) in the credit quality of the counterparties, perhaps calling for more collateral when credit ratings are downgraded or CDS spreads exceed a certain level. Finally, the CSA details rules for termination of contracts—for example, upon failure to supply collateral. ISDA Master Agreements should be established to guarantee netting across different legal entities of the same counterparty.

Counterparty Quality Monitoring   The financial status of the counterparty should be continually monitored to anticipate and detect situations where the counterparty's credit quality might deteriorate. Looking back to the credit crisis from a hedge fund perspective, this should have included monitoring the CDS spreads of banks and brokers; and ensuring that they had access to stable long-term funding and the ability to utilize the U.S. Federal Reserve, European Central Bank, Bank of Japan, Swiss National Bank or other government-supported discount-window and repo facilities in order to determine which banks and brokers were financially sound.

Counterparty Exposure Measurement and Limits   The appropriate risk-measurement approach varies by hedge fund. For a large fund trading over-the-counter derivatives with numerous financial intermediaries of varying credit quality, measuring current and potential exposure is appropriate. For a fund trading exclusively in standardized exchange-traded contracts where the exchange is the counterparty, and/or simply trading cash securities, counterparty risk measurement is less of an issue as the exchange is typically highly creditworthy and collateral is exchanged daily. However, even in this case, knowing how much excess cash was deposited in the broker's accounts and the mark-to-market value of collateral posted to exchanges daily is appropriate.

Counterparty limits may be set based on actual current exposure or potential future exposure depending on the derivative activities of the fund. Counterparty limits refer to the amount of counterparty risk that may be taken to approved counterparties with acceptably negotiated trading contracts. In most funds, counterparty limits are set on an aggregate basis by counterparty. For example, if a fund is unwilling to take more than US$100 million in counterparty risk to any one bank with an A rating, it may divide that limit among various trading activities within the fund, such as CDSs, equity swaps, variance swaps, and so on.

Counterparty authority refers to the ability of any individual trader or trading desk to enter into new transactions with a counterparty, considering the possible impact on current or future counterparty exposure. Best-practice funds use some measure of potential future exposure in setting their counterparty limits, although many focus only on current exposure. Some funds will also set portfolio concentration limits, for example, restricting an individual fund's counterparty exposure to a particular broker and enforcing a degree of risk diversification. In all cases, funds should establish exception policies to deal with situations where counterparty limits are inadvertently or deliberately breached.

Transaction approval is a verification process to ensure that, before an individual transaction is executed, all of its requirements—counterparty initiation, contract negotiation, collateral provisions, collateral collection (if applicable), and compliance with limits—have been met. Some funds do not follow such processes or, because of time constraints, apply them only to their larger transactions, allowing significant slack in the process. These are a practical consequence of the need to make real-time trading decisions, but funds should aspire to minimize these occurrences.

Counterparty Risk Reporting   Counterparty risk reporting should address counterparty risk across each fund managed by the fund manager, whether the counterparty risk is due to trading, collateral rehypothecation, or excess equity maintained at the counterparty. Aggregate mark-to-market, potential future exposures, and aggregate collateral posted (bilaterally) should be brought together in a comprehensive report showing counterparty exposure by non-netted legal entity and netted exposure. Best practice reporting highlights aggregate exposures against limits, limit violations, potentially correlated exposures, concentrations, and sensitivity of exposure to key market drivers.

Counterparty Risk Hedging and Mitigation   There are several options available to hedge funds to shape and hedge their counterparty exposures. When a fund determines that it has too much exposure to a single counterparty, and it is unable to collect collateral, it may undertake several actions. First, attempts may be made to close out some trading positions, move any excess cash with the counterparty, or initiate new trading positions that have the effect of reducing the risk. Second, the fund may attempt to novate a contract or have it intermediated and given up to a more creditworthy broker—that is, to reassign the contract to a different counterparty for some consideration. Third, a fund may try to "collapse" a trade, if it finds it has identical and offsetting trades to two different counterparties. All of these options, however, typically require counterparty agreement.

Barring these shaping strategies, the other risk management strategy is to obtain default insurance for the expected loss to a defaulting counterparty. As a general statement, if a counterparty is a financial institution, a hedge fund should be able to hedge its counterparty exposure. Buying a credit default swap is essentially buying the rights to a contingent payment triggered by a counterparty credit event and made by another, third-party, derivatives-trading counterparty.

Using a CDS to hedge counterparty exposure presents certain effectiveness challenges and incurs transaction costs. In most derivative trading situations, the actual exposure is variable, making it difficult to hedge 100 percent of the exposure at all times without frequent hedge adjustments and payment of bid/ask spreads. Second, in CDS markets, the payment-triggering event may not correspond exactly to a counterparty's default event. For example, when Takefuji,[8] a Japanese consumer-finance company, went into restructuring in 2010, CDS protection owners had to wait several days before the event was classified as a default event in CDSs and synthetic collateralized-debt obligations (CDOs). Third, as we learned in 2008, CDS protection can become extremely expensive when needed and CDS counterparties can be subject to their own performance risk, as Lehman Brothers' counterparties discovered.

Operational Risk

Operational risk is a risk category consisting of all non-investment, credit, and liquidity risks associated with hedge fund investing. It is the risk of loss caused by deficiencies in internal controls, business processes, or information systems and may be the result of internal or external events. The classic operational risks faced by all financial institutions include risks arising from such things as data entry or reconciliation errors, fraud, system failures and errors in valuation or risk measurement models. However, for hedge funds these risks cause them to fail much more frequently. Studies have shown that between 40 percent and 60 percent of hedge fund failures are attributable to poor management of operational risk.[9]

The primary reason for this is that hedge funds are not as mature in their processes and management of operational risk. Perhaps because hedge funds typically start up as an organization built around implementing the portfolio manager's investment strategy, and initial hires all tend to be front office staff, their investment and focus on operational processes is limited. In addition, most funds initially outsource most of the administrative, legal, and/or regulatory compliance functions. This leaves them vulnerable to deficiencies in administration and back office functions and controls, to internal and external fraud, and to business interruptions from system failures and ineffective disaster recovery procedures.

Vulnerability to these events can increase depending on the fund's investment strategy, the size of the organization, and the degree of institutionalization of the core processes of the fund.

Investment Strategy   Strategies that require investments in structured derivatives, private placements, or distressed securities require a higher degree of operational sophistication than those that utilize vanilla derivatives and exchange traded equities. This is primarily due to the fact that valuation of less liquid structured securities is complex and ultimately somewhat subjective.

Valuation is critical to all funds but especially to those that offer short investor lock-ups and monthly or quarterly redemptions. Valuation is critical because assigned values must be able to be realized in the event that all eligible investors redeem their investments simultaneously. Also, management and incentive fees are paid and redemptions are made on both realized and unrealized gains. Pricing is often determined by the fund manager in small funds and by a valuation committee in institutionalized funds.

The ability of a manager to subjectively assign a value to an investment can lead to operational risk. Valuations should be transparent and investment-fund portfolios should be priced in accordance with the Generally Accepted Accounting Principles (GAAP) and reviewed periodically by independent parties. Under GAAP, investments should be reported on the fund's books at "fair value," which is defined as the price at which an asset or liability could be exchanged between two knowledgeable and unrelated parties. Consequently, liquidity premiums and discounts should be factored into a fund's valuations.

The fair value for exchange traded securities is evident by the prices published by the exchange and received by the fund when it buys and sells securities on the exchange. When a fund holds unlisted securities, operational risk is increased. Over-the-counter (OTC) or non-listed investments may include distressed debt, convertible debt, bank loans, corporate bonds, swaps, OTC derivatives, and private or restricted equity positions.

Non-listed or OTC securities trade "by appointment" in negotiated markets. These securities are inherently more risky because of the lack of price transparency and the higher degree of subjectivity in the valuation assigned. Liquidity is also a major factor that can influence the realized price of a security and create dramatic differences between the assigned price and the realized price. Liquidity manifests itself in the form of bid/offer spreads and bloc-size discounts, making it difficult to determine the realizable price for a security. Non-listed securities typically have their value assigned by the manager and are based on any number of pricing practices, which can be subject to error depending on the source, amount and timeliness of the pricing data, the liquidity of the instrument and, most importantly, the size of the position. Multiple managers often assign significantly different prices to similar positions.

In cases where a model is used, the validity of the model and its inputs are crucial. Input errors and a lack of knowledge of the assumptions that underlie the model by operations staff using it increase the risk of a flawed valuation. Other firms rely solely on indicative quotes from a single broker that typically sold the security to the fund initially. This is considered preferable to disclosing their positions to other market participants. However, relying solely on the counterparty's mark also creates a conflict of interest.

Private equity or direct lending are also common assets found on hedge-fund balance sheets and especially in their side pockets. They too, however, are difficult to value. Private equity is typically carried at cost, but GAAP rules require that market data be incorporated into its fair valuation. Private equity can therefore be marked up or down if there is a market event that supports the change in valuation. While private investments are often segregated into side pockets, where incentive fees are not charged until the investment value is realized, this is not always the case. For direct loans, the valuation is based on a combination of the receipt and discounting of interest payments, the creditworthiness of the obligor, and the value of any underlying collateral.

Restricted securities such as PIPES (Private Investments in Public Equity Securities) also create price subjectivity. Accounting guidelines direct that these securities be valued at a discount to market prices of their underlying publicly listed securities. Many managers, however, price their PIPES without a discount or apply the discount subjectively.

However, in case after case of funds failing as a result of operational risk, intentional or unintentional errors in valuation have played a role. In the case of Amaranth, where the fund had a concentrated position[10] in natural gas futures contracts (at one point in 2006 it owned 40 percent of the outstanding natural-gas contracts trading on the NYMEX and more on the ICE[11]), ineffective pricing failed to consider the liquidity discount buyers would require if Amaranth were to sell such positions.

In the case of GLG Partners, the fund registered a monthly loss in May 2005 of 14.5 percent arising from flaws in its valuations of credit default swaps and collateralized-debt obligations after Ford and General Motors were downgraded. In a letter to investors, GLG stated that the fund's losses were due to a flaw in its CDO pricing models, which failed to account for volatility in the automotive sector resulting from the downgrades. When the CDOs were marked to market rather than market to model, the losses were apparent.[12]

In other cases, the lack of independent review of hedge fund valuations enabled outright fraud to be perpetrated. In February 2005, the U.S. Securities and Exchange Commission (SEC) charged the principals of Global Money Management with defrauding investors of over US$100 million. The SEC contended that no independent audit of the hedge fund's performance or financials ever occurred and this enabled the principals to use the funds provided by investors for their personal use. Frauds by KL Investments and Bayou Group were similarly enabled by a lack of independent oversight of valuations and financials.

Independent oversight of valuations cannot fully prevent fraud. Beacon Hill is a case in point where overvaluations of mortgage-backed securities (MBS) held in three feeder funds (Bristol, Safeharbor, and Milestone) were used to offset losses the fund incurred from a large short position in 10-year U.S. Treasuries. After suffering losses as a result of falling interest rates, the value of MBS in the feeder funds were overstated by as much as 54 percent and not picked up by auditors until several months later.[13]

Size of Organization The size of the fund management company is correlated to the degree of operational risk at the fund. Management companies can be small start-ups, medium-sized managers with a few years of track record, or large institutional fund managers. Operational risk is higher for smaller organizations that may have less segregation of duties, where the manager may have significant influence over valuations, and where the trade management and accounting systems may not be well developed, compliance policies may be ill-defined or non-existent, and back office staff may be very junior and of poor quality.

Degree of Institutionalization Even a large fund, if it is still in start-up mode, may incur increased operational risk as it implements new operating policies and hires new employees who have yet to become acquainted with new roles and systems. A new portfolio manager who had previously led a proprietary trading desk at an investment bank and was supported by a strong middle and back office and benefited from a host of corporate services, will have a steep management and administrative learning curve as his new hedge fund implements his strategy. The portfolio manager should also establish compensation and human-resource policies, manage legal and accounting issues, and other administrative functions.

Similarly, the learning curve for his newly hired organization will be almost vertical as it settles its first trades.

The more institutionalized the fund, the more established these central operational capabilities are and the more focused the portfolio manager can be on core investment process and strategy.

Operational Risk Management While the appropriate techniques and practices to deal with operational risks are the same techniques and practices used by larger and public financial entities, hedge funds have little incentive to incur the cost of such control-oriented investments unless pushed to do so by investors. The fact is that such investments in stern control staff, seemingly bureaucratic procedures, and expensive systems infrastructure comes out of the management fee. The short-run value of implementing such controls as random spot checks on prices; dual or triple sign-off on pricing decisions; investing in scalable automated trading and general ledger systems with built-in control procedures; maintaining centralized pricing data sets; developing contingency plans and maintaining redundant systems in preparation for failures in the fund's core systems, or for responding to the failure of a third-party service provider can seem low. Start-up and smaller hedge funds have limited ability to spread these fixed costs which directly reduce the short-run returns to the principals.

For operational risk management to be significantly improved, potential investors will need to know and be given evidence of operational controls that are most relevant to the individual fund's idiosyncrasies as a prerequisite to investing in the fund. Expecting a fund to attain a standard of operational control that is ill-suited to its size or investment strategy will be wasteful; but requiring a credit relative-value fund, for example, to discuss the main assumptions and weaknesses of its CDO pricing model, whether it uses any stale data in its valuations, how frequently it checks model prices against dealer quotes, and how it factors market liquidity into its valuations is appropriate.

THE IMPORTANCE OF INTEGRATED RISK MANAGEMENT: LEHMAN BROTHERS INTERNATIONAL (LBIE)

Lehman Brothers International is a good case study of how operational, counterparty, and market risks can combine to create losses for hedge funds. In particular, the hedge funds that had the operational capability to know rapidly what their exposures were to LBIE and to take proactive action to withdraw excess funds, to find alternative sources of short security positions and leverage, to know the extent to which their securities were rehypothecated, to cancel trading agreements and to novate portfolios to new prime brokers before Lehman collapsed avoided the losses and the protracted recovery procedures that followed.

Lehman Brothers was founded in Montgomery, Alabama, by German immigrants Henry, Emanuel and Mayer Lehman in 1850—and prospered over the following decades as the U.S. economy grew. The collapse of the U.S. housing market ultimately brought Lehman Brothers to its knees, as its headlong rush into the subprime mortgage market proved to be a disastrous step. In 2007, Lehman underwrote more mortgage-backed securities than any other firm, accumulating an US$85-billion portfolio, or four times its shareholders' equity.

As the credit crisis erupted in August 2007 with the failure of two Bear Stearns hedge funds, Lehman's stock fell sharply. In the fourth quarter of 2007, Lehman's stock rebounded, as global equity markets reached new highs and prices for fixed income assets staged a temporary rebound. However, the firm did not take the opportunity to trim its massive mortgage portfolio and, as subsequent events proved, this was to be its last chance.

In 2007 Lehman's high degree of leverage—the ratio of total assets to shareholder equity—was 31 and its huge portfolio of mortgage securities made it increasingly vulnerable to deteriorating market conditions. On March 17, 2008, following the near-collapse of Bear Stearns—the second-largest underwriter of mortgage-backed securities—Lehman shares fell by as much as 48 percent on concern it would be the next Wall Street firm to fail. Confidence in the company returned to some extent in April, after it raised US$4 billion through an issue of preferred stock that was convertible into Lehman shares at a 32 percent premium to its price at the time.

On June 9, Lehman announced a second quarter loss of US$2.8 billion, its first loss since being spun off by American Express, and reported that it had raised another US$6 billion from investors. The firm also said that it had boosted its liquidity pool to an estimated US$45 billion, decreased gross assets by US$147 billion, reduced its exposure to residential and commercial mortgages by 20 percent, and cut down leverage from a factor of 32 to about 25.

However, these measures were perceived as being too little, too late. Over the summer, Lehman's management made unsuccessful overtures to a number of potential partners. The stock plunged 77 percent in the first week of September 2008, amid plummeting equity markets worldwide. Hopes that the Korea Development Bank would take a stake in Lehman were dashed on September 9, as the state-owned South Korean bank put talks on hold.

The news was a deathblow to Lehman, and led to a 45 percent plunge in the stock and a 66 percent spike in credit default swaps on the company's debt. Its hedge-fund clients began pulling out, while its short-term creditors cut credit lines. On September 10, Lehman pre-announced dismal fiscal third-quarter results that underscored the fragility of its financial position. The firm reported a loss of US$3.9 billion, including a write-down of US$5.6 billion. The same day, Moody's Investor Service announced that it was reviewing Lehman's credit ratings, and also said that Lehman would have to sell a majority stake to a strategic partner in order to avoid a rating downgrade. These developments led to a 42 percent plunge in the stock on September 11. Last-ditch efforts over the weekend of September 13 between

Lehman, Barclays PLC and Bank of America, aimed at facilitating a take-over of Lehman, were unsuccessful.

At dawn on Monday, September 15, 2008, Wall Street's fourth-largest investment bank filed for bankruptcy, ending a run on the bank and resulting in panicked hedge fund managers becoming common creditors of the shuttered investment bank. At the time, Lehman had 25,000 employees worldwide and US$639 billion in assets and US$619 billion in debt. On paper, the value of its assets far surpassed those of previous bankrupt giants such as WorldCom and Enron. Lehman's bankruptcy filing was the largest in history.[14]

The prime brokerage industry's hierarchy was scattered to the wind. Bear Sterns was bought by J.P. Morgan, Merrill Lynch merged with Bank of America, and Lehman's brokerage divisions were divided geographically between Barclays Capital and Japanese investment bank Nomura.

According to some estimates, some hedge funds had as much as 20–70 percent of their assets held by Lehman Brothers and its various affiliates and subsidiaries. Many funds also had margin-lending agreements with Lehman Brothers International, a Financial Services Authority (FSA)-regulated entity in the United Kingdom, which entered administration by PriceWater-houseCoopers. For hedge funds that were solely reliant on Lehman for prime-brokerage services, the announcement was a death blow. In 2008, the US$1.9 trillion hedge fund industry was staggering toward the end of its worst year in two decades. After being down 4.7 percent through August 2008, hedge funds lost another 5.3 percent on average in September 2008.[15]

Hedge Fund Failures

As the list of funds trapped in the Lehman morass kept growing, certain common themes emerged.

First, as Lehman Brothers, Inc.'s bankruptcy in the U.S. and the FSA-approved administration of Lehman Brothers International in the U.K. continued, many hedge funds discovered that they were now general, rather than secured, creditors of Lehman Brothers. Clients of Lehman Brothers International (LBIE), Lehman's U.K.-domiciled brokerage arm, had much greater difficulty getting their security and cash collateral returned even if they had fully repaid all their loans to Lehman. This was because assets held at LBIE were not segregated into separate customer accounts and LBIE could not find and identify their specific collateral.

Many U.S. fund managers had preferred to deal with Lehman's international entity than with the U.S. broker dealer, which was constrained by U.S. regulations with regard to the leverage it could offer. Lehman's London-based prime brokerage had about 3,500 active clients, including hedge funds that owned about US$45 billion in securities and an additional US$20 billion in short positions, or bets that prices would fall.[16]

Many ambitious and overconfident hedge fund managers wanted the maximum leverage possible and that could only be provided outside of the U.S. regulatory regime. Even more prudent managers preferred to deal with the Lehman's international arm simply to avoid the cap and have the option to use higher leverage if needed. It was a rare hedge fund manager who valued the greater bankruptcy protection provided by U.S. regulations that required client assets to be segregated from those of the broker and preferred having the U.S. entity as his counterparty.

Second, in the case of those hedge funds that had margin-lending agreements with Lehman Brothers, the recovery of assets was further complicated by the fact that many of the assets that funds invested with Lehman Brothers had been rehypothecated. These funds had pledged securities as collateral against loans given to the fund, resulting in Lehman Brothers having the "right to use" those assets and lend them to other investors, thereby terminating the hedge fund's proprietary rights in those assets. Lehman routinely used that right and lent the securities to other investors who wanted to go short or used the securities as its own collateral to generate low-cost secured financing in the shadow banking market to fund its own operations. When LBIE filed for bankruptcy, that collateral became ensnared in the extremely complex web of transactions frozen in stasis due to the bankruptcy. This included US$8 billion in cash that Lehman's parent company allegedly withdrew from its European unit before the collapse.[17]

Even if the assets could ultimately be retrieved, hedge fund managers lost the ability to trade out of those assets and stop losses as well as losing a key source of liquidity to meet rising margin calls at other prime brokers and redemption requests from investors. Consequently, many hedge funds either closed or had their performance negatively impacted by the Lehman default.[18]

Ironically, some of the additional margin calls came from Lehman itself. While hedge funds were largely unable to access their Lehman accounts, the value of the securities continued to fluctuate along with the markets. Just as when mortgage lenders failed homeowners still had to pay their mortgages in order to retain ownership of their homes, so Lehman clients were required to put up more collateral when the value of those securities dropped if they wanted to continue to own their positions.

Lessons Learned

The collapse of Lehman Brothers provides a case study in risk management for hedge funds and their investors. Many investors' funds were, or still are, caught in the Lehman Brothers bankruptcy; for those fortunate enough not to have been entangled, there are several lessons to be learned.

Stability: Banks Not Brokers Many of the credit bubble's excesses can be traced to the "shadow banking" sector, which is essentially the intersection between commercial banking and investment banking business models. Commercial banking and investment banking each have funding models that suit their asset risk profile. Commercial banks make relatively illiquid loans, but they have privileged access to relatively resilient core deposit funding. Investment banks hold inventories of relatively liquid securities, which enable them to use extremely efficient, short-term, low-cost funding (such as the overnight "repo" markets).

Shadow banks, however, took illiquid credit and interest rate risk (like commercial banks), but funded themselves principally through the wholesale markets (like investment banks). Big brokerage firms like Goldman Sachs, Lehman Brothers, Bear Sterns, Morgan Stanley and Merrill Lynch were the biggest players in the shadow bank network. Because of long-recognized regulatory loopholes, shadow banks were also frequently able to operate with significantly lower capital requirements than commercial bank competitors. With both capital and funding advantages in hand, shadow banks grew to some 60 percent of the U.S. credit system. Unfortunately, they proved to be extraordinarily fragile; both the asset and liability components of their business models suffered as the credit cycle turned.

While this system became a huge and vital source of money to fuel the U.S. economy, the subprime mortgage crisis and ensuing credit crunch exposed a major flaw. Unlike regulated banks, which can borrow directly from the government and have federally insured customer deposits, the shadow system didn't have reliable access to short-term borrowing during times of stress. Furthermore, while acting like banks, these shadow entities weren't subject to the same supervision, so they did not hold as much capital to cushion against potential losses. When subprime mortgage losses started to erode their highly leverage balance sheets, their sources of short-term financing dried up. Lehman failed; Bear Sterns and Merrill Lynch were forced to merge with stronger regulated banks, J.P. Morgan and Bank of America, respectively.

These events underscore the importance to hedge funds and their investors of scrutinizing the strength of counterparty balance sheets. The prime brokerages which form part of investment banks, which themselves are part of a universal banking model, are at an advantage as they have the balance sheets and multiple sources of funding to generate greater confidence.

As a direct result of the failure of Lehman Brothers, there has been a significant shift of hedge-fund assets away from prime brokers that did not previously adopt a banking business model. In July 2009's Global Custodian annual survey, hedge funds reported that they had reduced their balances with firms that had previously followed the broker model. Significantly, 43.6 percent of hedge funds polled said that they had reduced their balances with Goldman Sachs, while an incredible 70.2 percent of respondents admitted to doing so at Morgan Stanley. The average reduction across all custodians in the survey was 25.4 percent. The studies also showed that true banks had increased market share, with Deutsche Bank and Credit Suisse replacing Morgan Stanley and Lehman Brothers as the top two.

Multiple Primes   In the aftermath of Lehman's demise, while individual prime brokers have benefited, the biggest single winner over the past 12 months has been the multi-prime model itself. The economic situation has affected the prime brokerage industry in that hedge funds are now more concerned about their credit exposure, and are making sure they have contingencies at least in the supply of the services they demand. Many investors also refuse to invest with hedge funds unless they have at least two prime brokers.

The use of multiple prime brokers is nothing new among the largest hedge funds, many of which had relationships with as many as 10 providers as they shopped around for the best liquidity in their stock loans, and chose banks that provided them with an increasingly wide range of investment strategies to support the hedge funds' evolution.

The Tabb Group's *Hedge Funds 2008: Perspectives on Prime Brokerage, Volatility and Expansion* reports that small and medium-sized funds adopted a multi-broker model as they attempted to diversify their counterparty risk and reduce the potential impact of a single broker failing, and to broaden their access to sources of financing and stock loans. The Tabb Group's research found that the average number of prime brokers used was three, as this allowed hedge funds to diversify their exposures and gave them leverage when negotiating fees for securities lending and other services.

Collateral Protection   The delays, and in some cases total failure, experienced by hedge funds in obtaining from Lehman collateral initially posted as margin on trades that were subsequently terminated when Lehman declared bankruptcy has increased their demands for collateral management solutions. In particular, they want to maintain greater control over their collateral, ensure its speedy return when owed, and reduce their counterparties' ability to rehypothecate the collateral beyond certain limits. In addition, the funds are looking for greater segregation and control over their assets.

Rehypothecation Limits and the Need for Speed   The collapse of Lehman Brothers underscored the risks of rehypothecation and violated portfolio managers' assumptions that collateral would be speedily returned once the decision has been made to pull assets from prime brokers or banks they perceive as risky.

Consequently, hedge funds are seeking to limit the right of the prime broker to "re-use" clients' assets for its own purposes and ensure their speedy return on demand. Some hedge funds have already renegotiated the terms of their existing prime brokerage agreements, having reviewed them through the post-Lehman lens. Among the terms that are becoming standard are:

Rehypothecation limits: A key issue is the common market practice of rehypothecation (the right of a prime broker to re-use clients' assets for its own purposes). When assets are rehypothecated, hedge funds lose title to them and are left with a contractual right to their redelivery. Upon a prime broker insolvency, hedge funds may be left as general unsecured creditors in respect of the rehypothecated assets, depending on the jurisdiction[19] prime brokers are typically not required to provide regular reports showing which assets have been rehypothecated and a broker is not required to maintain physical possession and control of securities it borrows under an agreement that satisfies the requirements of Exchange Act Rule 15c3-3(b)(3). This leaves hedge funds unable to monitor or manage this aspect of prime-broker credit risk.

Consequently, hedge funds have sought to limit the extent to which counterparties can rehypothecate their collateral to 140 percent of their debit (amount borrowed). This amount is based on the U.S. Exchange Act Rule 15c3-3. Under this rule a broker (i) is required to maintain physical possession and control[20] of fully paid securities and securities (excess margin securities) *only* with a value in excess of 140 percent of the customer's debit balance (the Fully Paid/Excess Margin Security Requirement), (ii) may treat as its own property and sell, lend, rehypothecate and otherwise use for permitted purposes, including margin lending, property of a customer with a value up to 140 percent of such debit balance.

Committed timing of collateral return: Hedge funds are seeking mechanisms that will permit the early release of segregated assets upon prime-broker insolvency. The speedy return of collateral is increasingly being required in certain prime brokerage agreements. The speed of the return of the collateral varies by type. Typically, return of cash collateral is required within 24 hours of request, securities collateral that has not been rehypothecated within 36 hours, and securities that have been rehypothecated within "commercially reasonable" time. These requirements are critical, for instance, if a prime broker has been permitted to use group entities as sub-custodians and subsequently becomes insolvent. In the likely event of the sub-custodians also being subject to insolvency proceedings in a different jurisdiction, it may be difficult for the insolvent prime broker to retrieve client assets from them; even if it succeeds in doing so, it may not retrieve the full amount. The use of client omnibus accounts and the existence of security interest provisions in favor not only of the prime broker but also of the prime broker's affiliates may cause similar issues relating to shortfalls and delays in return. However, if non-compliance with timing commitments for the return of collateral is the result of a default event, brokers will do their utmost to ensure that they can comply and will restrict their rehypothecation activities and retain better control of client assets.

Segregation of Assets   One of the central lessons from Lehman is that the level of protection provided by the segregation of assets and the speed with which assets can be returned to hedge funds are critical. The ability to rapidly identify and discriminate between hedge fund assets and the general assets and liabilities of a defaulted prime broker enables a hedge fund to more rapidly recover its assets and resume normal operations after a prime broker defaults.

There is a growing perception that the U.S. regulatory regime provides greater protection to prime-brokerage clients than the U.K. The U.S. SEC Customer Protection Rules and the SIPC Trustee regime were drafted primarily to protect the customers of a broker in the event of default, while the U.K. insolvency regime is cited as protecting the interest of creditors as a whole over the customers of the insolvent prime broker. Hedge funds can choose between counterparties who are subject to and benefit from different regulatory regimes. Consequently, the LBIE experience has created a preference among hedge fund managers for U.S.-regulated counterparties because of the U.S. requirement that brokers maintain customer assets in clearly segregated accounts. This ensures rapid sorting and return of assets in the event that a U.S. broker defaults.

By way of counterargument, U.K. prime brokers quote the FSA Client Asset and Client Money Rules. The U.K. Financial Services Authority aims to protect hedge fund assets ("client money") from the claims of creditors in the event of a counterparty's insolvency and to prevent firms using client funds to finance their business. This protection is provided by the FSA's Default Regulations, which set out how client money should be handled and establish a procedure for distributing the client money of a firm that has become insolvent. These requirements create a statutory trust, under which a firm must keep all client money separate from its own (unless otherwise agreed with the client) and which "ring-fences" this client money from the claims of the general creditors of the firm should it fail. They point out that, even where U.S. prime brokers are used, non-U.S. assets may be held by U.K. affiliates in any case.

Two-way event of default rights Simply put, hedge funds are increasingly seeking to have the non-return or delayed return of collateral by the prime broker legally considered a default and have such provisions included in the documents governing the trading and prime-broking relationship. The ability of the fund to put the financial institution in public "default" is a powerful motivator and helps to ensure that funds are returned promptly when demanded. Previously, the default provisions were only one-way in that only the lender (the prime broker) could put the borrower (the hedge fund) in default.

Third-party Custodian Agreements: One innovation to result from the increased focus on counterparty risk since the Lehman collapse is the use of tri-party relationships with bank custodians. A tri-party custody agreement allows hedge funds to hold their long positions with a custody bank and their shorts with a prime broker. This not only ensures that the assets are segregated in the event of a default by the prime broker, but typically also result in the assets being held at a AAA+ credit-rated institution.

By ensuring cash is deposited with a AAA-rated custodian, hedge funds enable prime brokers to continue to transact with hedge-fund managers, while reassuring their investors that their cash is better protected. Many AAA-rated custodians have put in place legal agreements and the necessary operational procedures to allow hedge fund managers to post cash for the benefit of their prime broker or brokers. In addition, many AAA-rated custodians are also offering hedge fund managers and their institutional investors the further reassurance of custody services for the buy-and-hold assets in their long books. Under this offering, securities and other assets are no longer kept by the prime brokers but are, instead, placed in the custody of the AAA-rated custodians.

Having learned from the Lehman bankruptcy that even unencumbered securities are at risk of being caught up in an insolvency process, institutional investors are reassured that long assets are held by a third-party custodian.

Potential Liabilities: Conflicts of Interest, Gross Negligence and Redemptions

If a hedge fund manager had known of the problems facing Lehman yet, out of self-interest, had failed to act, he could well have been accused by investors of gross negligence. Consequently, many larger managers have established procedures under the governing documents to resolve conflicts of interest that usually require the approval of an independent advisory committee. In addition, these committees can rapidly be consulted and ratify a non-investment-related decision.

Redemptions The timing of Lehman's bankruptcy on September 15 created substantial redemption risk for both redeeming investors and non-redeeming investors. September 30, 2008 marked the end of the quarter and many funds were facing redemption requests. The question for investors is whether the fund manager complied with redemption requests rather than gating the fund and, if so, on what basis the manager arrived at the value of the fund given that collateral was tied up in the Lehman bankruptcy and the amount and timing of payment of any claim were unknown. Redeeming investors may have received more than they were entitled to, relative to their investment in the fund. If so, they may face the unhappy prospect of having to repay a portion of their redeemed capital. Non-redeeming investors should be vigilant to ensure that they were treated fairly in valuation matters—both quantitatively and qualitatively.

Lehman Postscript

Lehman's collapse roiled global financial markets for weeks, given the size of the company and its status as a major international player. Lehman's collapse was a seminal event that greatly intensified the 2008 crisis and contributed to the erosion of almost US$10 trillion in market capitalization from global equity markets in October 2008, the biggest monthly decline on record at the time.

Many questioned the U.S. government's decision to let Lehman fail, as compared to its tacit support for Bear Stearns (which was acquired by JPMorgan Chase) in March 2008. Lehman's bankruptcy led to more than US$46 billion of its market value being wiped out. Its collapse also served as the catalyst for the purchase of Merrill Lynch by Bank of America in an emergency deal that was also announced on September 15.

CONCLUSION

Investment risk management is a core capability of all hedge funds that deliver on their capital preservation commitment to investors. The crisis of 2008 demonstrated that expertise in managing investment risk is not enough: minimum competency in the areas of funding, counterparty, and operational risk management are also essential. These risk management capabilities should be developed and integrated into a cohesive framework customized to take account of the primary risks of a given hedge fund.

ENDNOTES

1. A short time series will potentially result in a VaR based on a fat-tailed distribution.
2. Conditional VaR is performed by assessing the likelihood (at a specific confidence level) that a specific loss will exceed the value at risk. Mathematically speaking, CVaR is derived by taking a weighted average between the value at risk and losses exceeding the value at risk. The size of losses exceeding the value at risk is often based on stress and scenario tests. Note the problem with relying solely on the VaR model is that the scope of risk assessed is limited, since the tail end of the distribution of loss is not typically assessed. Therefore, if losses are incurred, the amount of the losses will be substantial in value.
3. Alvarez, Miguel, and Michael Levinson 2006. *Hedge Fund Risk Modeling*, MSCI Barra.
4. This technique is used frequently because its implementation is straightforward and it is easy to understand. However, a critical assumption necessary to obtain robust exposures from regression estimation is that they remain constant over the estimation period. Consequently, it will be difficult to capture a hedge fund's typically diverse and dynamic behavior using a model based solely on regression estimation.
5. This method involves using a shorter and more recent data window to estimate the regression parameters. Discarding past data in this manner will allow the model to capture recent changes in the exposures more rapidly. The downside is that the use of a shorter data window may produce noisy estimates and inferior forecasts.
6. A change in the credit quality of issuers of securities that affects the value of the portfolio through a change in the price of those securities is incorporated into "investment risk."
7. Potential exposure is also referred to as "Potential Future Exposure (PFE)" and "Counterparty Valuation Adjustment (CVA)."
8. On September 28, 2010, Takefuji filed a petition for commencement of a corporate re-organization under the Japanese Corporate Reorganization Act, effectively putting itself into bankruptcy
9. Indeed, a study carried out by Feffer and Kundro (2003) indicated that 50 percent of hedge fund failure can be attributed to poor operational controls and procedures.
10. The fact that the concentration was allowed to occur in the first place was another operational failure of Amaranth to adhere to its stated risk management guidelines for diversification.
11. U.S. Senate 2007, *Excessive Speculation in the Natural Gas Market*, Report of the Permanent Subcommittee on Investigations.
12. Failure to test the pricing model in advance to determine its accuracy under prospective stress scenarios was also a cause.
13. It is rare that large operational losses arise from a single cause. In the case of Beacon Hill and Amaranth, concentrated positions were first taken which

deviated from the funds' stated investment and risk management principles. These in turn led to large losses.

14. Even hedge funds that were not prime-brokered at Lehman suffered. PWC reported that Lehman's bankruptcy produced more than 141,000 failed trades.

15. According to the Global Hedge Fund Index compiled by Hedge Fund Research Inc.

16. "Lehman's Hedge Fund Clients Face Margin Calls on Frozen Assets," Tom Cahill, Bloomberg, October 15.

17. "PricewaterhouseCoopers, Lehman's bankruptcy administrator in the U.K., where its European prime brokerage was based, doesn't know how much money is at stake. PWC said last month it's trying to recoup about $8 billion in cash that Lehman's parent company allegedly withdrew from its European unit before the collapse." Bloomberg, October 1.

18. London-based MKM Longboat Capital Advisors LLP closed its $1.5 billion Multi-Strategy fund in part because of assets stuck at Lehman, according to an investor letter. Chicago-based Oak Group, with US$25 million of assets, relied on the Lehman's prime brokerage in London. "We're probably going out of business and liquidate, game over," it said. "We've lost 70 percent of our assets." New Jersey-based LibertyView Capital Management Inc. owned by Lehman's Neuberger Berman unit, told investors on September 26, 2008, that it had suspended "until further notice" attempts to calculate the value of its funds. LibertyView was not included in the September 29, 2008, sale of Neuberger to Bain Capital LLC and Hellman & Friedman LLC.

While clients yanked about 50 percent of Lehman's prime brokerage assets in the week before the bankruptcy, many transfers were delayed, resulting in complications for other managers with a smaller percentage of assets in Lehman limbo. These included Harbinger Capital Partners, Amber Capital LP, Diamondback Capital and Bay Harbour Management LLC, RAB Capital plc, GLG Partners Inc, and Newport Global Advisors LP.

Pride Revelation Fund, one of dozens of hedge funds in Hong Kong that used Lehman as their sole prime broker, could not even shut down because they did not know what assets they had left in order to determine the amounts to disburse to investors to liquidate the fund.

19. If a U.S. prime broker (or other broker or dealer) becomes insolvent, the rights of its customers are governed by a combination of Securities and Exchange Commission rules and regulations (including Exchange Act Rules 15c3–2 and 15c3–3), the U.S. Bankruptcy Code, the Securities Investor Protection Act (SIPA) and relevant state law, including the UCC.

20. Physical possession and control may be, and typically is, maintained through third parties such as a clearing corporation or other subsidiary organization of a national securities exchange or registered national securities association, another broker or dealer in compliance with Regulation T, or a bank.

CHAPTER **3**

A Survey of Hedge Fund Strategies and Risks

HEDGE FUND STRATEGIES

Classifying hedge fund strategies and understanding the risks of each is a useful conceptual exercise and a means of organizing a wide array of information into a coherent mental framework. However, the reality is that few hedge funds perfectly follow a pure single strategy. Any investor who has reviewed a hedge fund's prospectus will have noted the significant latitude fund managers reserve for themselves when they describe their investment and portfolio construction guidelines. The reality today is that the typical hedge fund, if it is not a self-professed "multi strategy" fund, is at least a hybrid of several archetypal strategies. In the end, fitting a hedge fund into a specific and well-defined strategy is like trying to fit a unicorn into a scientific genus and species. Consequently, any real-world classification of fund strategies is subjective and imperfect. This chapter provides a classification and description of the risk of distinct archetypal hedge fund strategies.

Table 3.1 divides the hedge fund universe into event driven, relative-value, and opportunistic strategies. The directionality[1] (that is, sensitivity to market increases or decreases) of each strategy group decreases from left to right.

Opportunistic Strategies

As the name indicates, these strategies seek to profit from fundamental themes, inefficiencies and dislocations in the financial markets at a macro, market-sector, stock-specific, factor, or exchange level. Depending on their conviction about the fundamental themes influencing the market or their market sector, opportunistic funds may go directionally long or short the market as whole.

TABLE 3.1 Hedge fund strategies

Opportunistic	Event Driven	Relative Value
Macro	Risk Arbitrage	Convertible Bond Arbitrage
Long/Short	Distressed Securities	Equity Market-neutral
Emerging Markets	Activist Strategies	Statistical Arbitrage
Sector-focused Funds		Fundamental Arbitrage
		Capital Structure Arbitrage
		Fixed Income Arbitrage
		High Velocity Trading

Macro Strategies Macro funds seek to capitalize on shifts in the global economy. They operate in very liquid and efficient markets such as fixed income, foreign exchange (FX), and equity index futures and have extremely wide investment latitude. They seek to make their money by anticipating systematic price change early and not necessarily by exploiting market inefficiencies. For example, macro funds in 2009 took thematic exposures to commodity currencies and sovereign debt. The typical macro fund shorted U.S. dollars and OECD currencies and debt, and went long FX and sovereign debt of commodity-based economies in anticipation that demand for commodities would continue to create trade surpluses in commodity-exporting countries and therefore strong commodity currencies and sovereign debt; while fiscal deficits would grow in the OECD, weakening those currencies and debt securities.

Equity Long/Short Strategies Different from macro but still opportunistic, long/short funds seek to develop, through in-depth research, information advantages vis-à-vis other investors and identify over- and undervalued securities. They may seek to profit from themes at an industrial or country-sector level. Sub-strategies of long/short funds are funds that focus on one geographic or industry sector.

Emerging Market Strategies Emerging market investing is no longer an emerging discipline. "Developing"[2] and "frontier-market"[3] investing are more precise terms for describing the discipline but the term "emerging markets" is used here for expediency and recognition.

Historically, developing countries have suffered from volatile international capital flows. By upgrading their financial systems they have decreased this vulnerability while creating investment opportunities for hedge funds. Increasing wealth and domestic bank lending have enabled domestic credit supply to increasingly substitute for international credit supply, which has historically been withdrawn in crises. In addition, as domestic corporate champions have grown they have increasingly accessed the international bond and equity market, which provides more stable financing than domestic or international bank lending, and in so doing have created opportunities in internationally tradable securities. In addition, local bond and equity issuance is growing, creating further investment opportunities.

While the developed markets have been mired in the credit crisis, stock and bond markets have flourished in many developing countries. A good measure of this is the ratio of bank credit to the size of domestic bond markets. In Asia and Latin America, domestic bond issuance (including government bonds) has outpaced both international issuance and bank borrowing by firms in the last decade. In Eastern Europe, market development has lagged Asia, in part because the region followed the Western European model of corporate finance dominated by bank lending. Additionally, E.U. expansion gave firms in the East easy access to developed financial markets, reducing the need to build domestic stock and bond markets. In Africa, the adoption of modern stock exchanges has been gathering pace over the past five years, a transition that has been accelerated by the global economic downturn.

Hedge funds investing in developing markets apply heterogeneous and increasingly sophisticated versions of alternative investment strategies previously deployed exclusively in developed markets. The common factor here is that effective alpha generation in developing markets requires deep specific knowledge of the progressively sophisticated regulations, market structure, political economy, and investors in the local market. In addition, the ability to go short a security, to purchase and trade derivatives, to obtain leverage and to transfer funds in and out of the country freely are often prerequisites for deploying traditional hedge fund strategies in developing markets.

Frontier markets are increasingly open markets that often lack the ability to go short onshore, have lower market capitalization, lower liquidity, less-developed derivatives markets, and more capital account controls compared to developing markets. The frontier equity markets are typically pursued by investors seeking high, long-term returns and low correlations with other markets.

In addition, developing and frontier market hedge funds seek to profit from the more rapid but more volatile growth of emerging market economies compared to developed economies and the fact that many companies in these countries are not as well researched as their developed country peers. By researching these markets, they seek to gain an information advantage.

Sector-focused Strategies Like emerging market funds, sector-focused funds seek to specialize in one part of the markets, capitalize on a thematic trend in that sector and profit from an informational advantage in that market. Common-sector foci are technology, financials, energy, healthcare and biotech. For example, in 2010 healthcare-focused funds were in vogue because of the changing healthcare regulatory framework in the United States Hedge funds that are focused on healthcare are going long and short stocks and, to a lesser extent, bonds of companies expected to benefit from these anticipated reforms. In addition, sector-focused funds, through their "superior" information and knowledge of the sector, seek to pick over- and undervalued securities in the sector to go long or short. An example of an informational advantage for a healthcare-focused fund might come from tracking Food and Drug Administration test results for drugs in development by micro cap biotech firms, a segment of the market not well covered by most investors.

Event Driven Strategies

Event driven strategies are strategies where the underlying investment opportunity and risk are associated with a corporate event. The securities prices of the companies involved in these events are more influenced by the idiosyncratic outcomes relating to the particular event than to the change in value of the general debt or equity markets. Practitioners of event driven strategies rely on fundamental research that extends beyond a valuation of the securities of a single company to researching issues affecting an industry that is undergoing restructure, identifying potential distressed, target and/or acquiring companies, and assessing the legal and structural issues likely to be encountered as events unfold to restructure the industry.

In risk arbitrage, this event is typically a merger or corporate action. In distressed investing, the events surround the failure, restructuring, or recovery of a company in distress. In activist investing, the hedge fund, through its equity or debt ownership of the company, seeks to directly instigate the event or influence its timing and nature to create shareholder value.

The goal of event driven investing is to profit when the price of a security changes to reflect more accurately the likelihood and potential impact of an event. As event driven strategies seek to profit from valuation disparities created by corporate events, their performance is less correlated with the performance of the overall stock market. That said, distressed and activist investing are not truly arbitrages as they typically have a long bias, while risk arbitrage is more market neutral.

Risk Arbitrage Strategies   Also known as "merger arbitrage," risk arbitrage involves a wager on a proposed corporate deal being accepted by regulators and shareholders. The corporate deal could be a merger, tender offer, liqui-dation, spin-off, or corporate reorganization. The securities used to imple-ment the strategy are typically common stocks, preferred stocks, bonds and equity options.

A portfolio manager utilizing this strategy simultaneously invests in long and short positions in the companies involved. In a merger or acqui-sition where stock is swapped, the portfolio manager is typically long the stock of the company being acquired and short the stock of the acquiring company. When the acquisition is paid for in cash, the portfolio manager seeks to capture the difference between the tender price and the price at which the company's stock is trading.

Distressed Investing Strategies   In essence, distressed security investing in-volves being net long low-investment grade credit. The portfolio manager following this strategy invests across the capital structure, typically in the debt and/or equity of companies in financial distress or bankruptcy. Securi-ties of such companies trade at substantial discounts to par. By taking posi-tions in different parts of the capital structure of the distressed company, portfolio managers seek to profit from two types of mis-pricings.

Firstly, the difference between the market price for the distressed secu-rity and the intrinsic value of the security is a source of profit. The intrinsic value is the actual value represented by the cash flows likely to accrue to the security. Intrinsic value consists of both expected interest on debt plus the share of the enterprise value of the distressed company expected to accrue to the security holder after restructuring.

Secondly, changes in the relative value of securities are a source of profit in distressed investing. Relative value strategy is the differential in value of one class of security relative to other securities in the capital structure of the same company. While a company is restructuring, the prices of securities of different seniority can become mis-priced. This is an opportunity for capital structure arbitrage. The portfolio manager following the distressed-investing strategy purchases the undervalued security and sells short the overpriced security.

Activist Strategies   Activist investing is when a portfolio manager acquires an influential stake in a company's securities and then uses that stake to actively influence the outcome of events. The portfolio manager does not assume a passive position when voting on corporate actions but, instead, seeks to instigate and then direct the resolution of corporate events such as spin-offs, restructurings, mergers or acquisitions that result in either the creation of shareholder value or the direction of a greater share of enterprise value to the holders of certain securities in the capital structure.

Relative Value Strategies

Relative value strategies seek to profit from mis-pricings of related securities. Relative value mis-pricings may be identified based on a theoretical arbitrage-free formula, statistical analysis of historical relationships, or fundamental analysis. These strategies are engineered to profit when a particular set of securities return to or move to their historical or theoretical correct comparative-value relationship. Such strategies seek to have little or no exposure to the underlying equity or bond markets. They tend to be market- or beta-neutral.

Convertible Bond Arbitrage Strategies   Convertible bond arbitrage is about exploiting market inefficiencies in the pricing of convertible bonds vis-à-vis their hedges. Portfolio managers seek to buy securities which are convertible into equity and then hedge out the market risks for less than the cost of the convertible security itself, resulting in a profit. Portfolio managers following these strategies use convertible bonds, warrants, convertible preferred shares, common stock, CDS, corporate bonds, interest rate futures and swaps, and equity options to construct their portfolios.

The value of the convertible bond is based on the bond value and the optionality in the convertible bond. The value of the option to convert the bond into equity is driven primarily by the expected volatility of the underlying stock. Unlike many other relative-value strategies, convertible arbitrages tend to be more certain because of the legal contractual formulae embedded in the convertible-bond documentation that specifies exactly how one convertible bond can be converted into equity.

Typical convertible arbitrage trades are:

1. Going long a convertible bond and shorting the underlying stock to isolate the value of the embedded option (delta hedging).
2. Going long a convertible and buying protection from default by shorting a corporate bond of similar tenor by the same issuer or buying credit default swap protection.
3. Arbitraging volatility by being long a portfolio of convertible bonds where the value of the embedded options implies a low expected volatility and short equity-index options with higher implied volatility.
4. Arbitraging price inefficiencies between complex convertible securities such as convertible bonds and convertible preferred stocks with callable, puttable or conversion options.

In theory, convertible arbitrage should be market-neutral but, in practice, portfolio managers may hedge imperfectly and retain some residual long delta exposure.

Equity Market Neutral Strategies Equity market neutral strategies seek to profit from equity market inefficiencies while being beta- and/or currency-neutral. This can be achieved either through statistical analysis or fundamental analysis.

Statistical Arbitrage Strategies Portfolio managers following statistical equity market neutral strategies use quantitative analysis of historical data to identify opportunities. Statistical arbitrage studies the historical relationship between different securities, such as stocks, commodities, futures, and options, and trades those positions that deviate significantly from past relationships. The portfolio managers seek to identify typically small but statistically significant return opportunities across a population of stocks that are fundamentally similar in some aspect. Then, they seek to exploit anomalous, statistical relationships between the securities in the population.

Statistical arbitrage strategies tend to use significant leverage to increase profits, but also increase losses, and can force the closing of positions when the value of the fund falls below the level required to maintain its margin. This method may fail if historical relationships are distorted by forced selling because of redemptions.

These portfolio managers first hypothesize the existence of a systematic fundamental relationship between security prices and a set of accounting or economic factors. These may be anything from inventory-turnover ratios to GDP. Analysts then back-test this hypothesis and use factor analysis to refine the relationship and develop a valuation model. Once a historically profitable relationship has been identified and back-tested, the model is implemented and directs the construction of the portfolio, though the portfolio manager may override the model from time to time. Potential sources of alpha are doubled in that stocks that are undervalued according to the model are purchased long and stocks that are overvalued according to the model are shorted. The intent is to be long and short highly diversified and equal beta-weighted portfolios of stocks on each side of the portfolio.

As markets are constantly changing, it is essential that the factors that unify a group are continually re-tested as they may not continue to do so. Statistical arbitrage managers must determine when and if to drop stocks from the group and add new ones. Similarly, they should continually review the factors thought to unify a group of stocks. The portfolio manager should vigilantly re-test the model to keep it up to date and dynamic.

A typical trade is implemented around the concept of mean reversion. Valuation of similar stocks within a group tends to revert to the mean valuation of the group. Stocks with valuations above the mean of the group are sold short. Stocks with valuations below the mean are bought and held long. The expectation is that both sides will converge to the mean of the group.

Fundamental Arbitrage Strategies As with statistical arbitrage, managers of fundamental equity long/short portfolios seek to profit from relationships between security prices but the investment process is based more on individual judgment. In contrast to statistical arbitrage, with fundamental arbitrage portfolio managers derive their investment strategies through fundamental security analysis rather than historical analysis. Fundamental arbitrage is one of the oldest hedge fund strategies and is akin in its fundamental valuation discipline to value-and-growth investing, but portfolio managers can also express their views by going short. Like statistical arbitrageurs, they too construct portfolios where the potential sources of alpha are doubled in that stocks that are undervalued are purchased long and stocks that are overvalued are shorted. While the intent is to be market-neutral and highly diversified, fundamental arbitrageurs typically are somewhat concentrated in their highest-conviction positions and rarely achieve complete diversification or equal beta-weighted portfolios.

Capital Structure Arbitrage Strategies Capital structure arbitrage seeks to profit from the relative mis-pricings of securities of different seniority (typically debt and equity) issued by the same company. Because of differences in market infrastructure and market participants, inefficiencies between the debt and equity markets can develop. Equities are typically exchange-cleared, while debt is traded over the counter. Retail investors are much more active in the equity markets than in the debt markets, which tend to be dominated by institutional investors. This can lead to differences between the market price of a company's debt and equity securities and their fundamental value. A portfolio manager following this strategy constructs his portfolio by buying the security in the capital structure he believes to be undervalued and short selling the security he believes is overvalued and then waiting for the fundamental value relationship to re-assert itself in the market.

However, given the low short-run stability and highly idiosyncratic nature of the relationship between debt and equity prices of the same issuer, portfolios of capital structure arbitrage positions should be diversified in order to generate low-volatility and low-market-correlated returns.

Fixed Income Arbitrage Strategies Fixed income arbitrage seeks to profit from mis-pricings in the global fixed income markets. Portfolio managers following this strategy construct portfolios of offsetting long and short positions in similar fixed income securities that are mathematically, fundamentally or historically related but temporarily mis-priced relative to one another. The arbitrage opportunity may develop out of market events, investor preferences, incompletely expressed economic expectations, exogenous shocks to fixed income supply and demand, or structural inefficiencies in the fixed income markets.

Typical fixed income arbitrage trades are:

- Yield curve arbitrage and spread trading.
- Arbitrage of on-the-run vs. off-the-run bonds (fixed income supply and demand-driven trade).
- Arbitrage between similar bonds in the same capital structure (for example, Government bonds vs. Agencies).
- Arbitrage between exchange traded fixed income futures and options and the physical underlying bonds.
- Arbitrage between corporate bonds and credit default swaps.
- Arbitrage between implied volatility of options embedded in asset-backed securities (ABS) and the swaptions and interest rate futures markets.
- Speculating on the TED[4] spread by being long (short) T-bill futures and short (long) Eurodollar futures.

High-velocity Trading Strategies High-velocity or algorithmic strategies seek to profit from very short (intra-day) price anomalies and short-term market trends, and by providing liquidity (making markets) in certain markets. These highly quantitative strategies require intensive high-speed computing power, direct low-latency execution ability, real-time market price feeds, and substantial leverage in order to identify opportunities and generate a profit. A portfolio manager following such a strategy will mine historical market data to derive a series of trading rules describing a certain market dynamic, pattern or behavior. A computerized trading algorithm is then developed around this relationship. The performance of the program is then evaluated by using live market data but no principal to see what the simulated performance would be. If the performance is stable and persistent, the program goes live. A portfolio manager may build multiple programs to construct an intra-day portfolio of 1) offsetting long and short positions in similar securities that are mathematically related but temporarily mispriced relative to one another; 2) positions in highly liquid securities expected to appreciate in value during the day (based on observed price momentum in similar securities) and/or; 3) positions accumulated in the process of making markets in options or futures and hedging with the cheapest cost hedging instrument.

Typical high-velocity trading strategies are:

- Momentum: "Momentum" traders look to find stocks that are moving significantly in the short term in one direction on high volume. They then try to jump on board to ride the market's momentum to a desired profit before the direction changes.
- Trend following: "Trend Following" traders aim to identify long-term market trends and then take benefit from temporary market deviations from those trends.
- Market making: Providing liquidity for a price in options markets and hedging exposure more cheaply with futures, and vice versa.

HEDGE FUND INVESTMENT RISKS

Each of the strategies we've looked at faces significant and differentiated risks. Certain risks are common across the strategies; some are endemic to the hedge fund business model; others are unique to certain strategies. Furthermore, each risk has varying probabilities of occurrence depending on the strategy. Lastly, each risk has a different potential loss depending on the strategy. Some risks may be frequent but small in their impact, while others can be infrequent but have disastrous consequences. Any risk-management framework developed and applied to a hedge fund must be customized to the specific strategy it pursues and focus on managing the most probable and significant risk it faces.

For explanatory purposes, the following section categorizes risks based on their sources. Risks categorized as investment risks originate from the investment portfolio and are generally germane to the securities owned by the hedge fund. Counterparty, funding and operational risks arise in large part, though not solely, from the hedge fund business model.

Types of Investment Risk

Hedge funds face a wide array of investment risks. Some are specific to certain strategies while other are simply more pronounced in certain strategies.

Idiosyncratic Risk: In portfolio theory, price changes due to the unique circumstances of a specific security, as opposed to the overall market, are described as "idiosyncratic," "unsystematic" or "specific" risk. Most commonly in the context of hedge funds, it is called "alpha," the letter assigned to idiosyncratic risk in the capital asset pricing model (CAPM). This risk can be virtually eliminated from a portfolio through diversification.

Idiosyncratic risk is the source of return that hedge funds seek to isolate and maximize through asset allocation, portfolio concentration, informational advantages, efficient hedging, leverage and other techniques to create a portfolio with returns uncorrelated to other asset classes.

Examples of idiosyncratic risk include:

- Event risk: A change in the price of a security as a result of a takeover, merger, acquisition, capital raising or other corporate event
- Deal break risk: A change in the price of a security arising from the cancellation of an expected takeover merger, acquisition, capital raising or other corporate event.
- Fraud risk: A change in the price of a security caused by the revelation of a falsehood, corruption or misdeed.
- Liquidity premiums: Excess returns paid to holders of illiquid securities.
- Distressed securities: Securities whose value depends on the resolution of company-specific events.

Systematic Risk: In portfolio theory, systematic risk is the risk of loss to a diversified securities portfolio that cannot be further reduced through additional diversification. Real-life examples of systematic risk are changes in policy interest rates, recessions, depressions, and wars. They affect the entire market and cannot be avoided through diversification. Systematic risk is sometimes also called "market risk," "aggregate risk," "undiversifiable risk," or "beta." It is the risk associated with the variability of overall aggregate market returns and the one that hedge funds most typically seek to minimize or avoid entirely.

In the capital asset pricing model, the rate of return required for an asset in market equilibrium depends on the idiosyncratic and systematic risk associated with returns on the asset; that is, on the covariance of the returns on the asset and the aggregate returns to the market (beta).

Given a diversified portfolio of assets, each individual security's idiosyncratic risk is diversified away, leaving only systematic risk exposure. The returns of any one security in relation to the portfolio returns are small and uncorrelated. Hence, the contribution of idiosyncratic risk to the riskiness of the diversified portfolio as a whole is negligible, leaving only systematic risk.

Systematic risk is manifested in the following interrelated risk factors:

1. Equity Risk Premium:[5] The equity risk premium is the excess return the overall stock market provides over the risk-free rate. The risk-free rate in the market is often quoted as the rate on longer-term government bonds, which are considered risk free because of the low chance that the government will default on its loans. On the other hand, an investment in stocks is

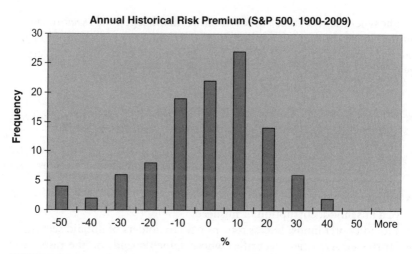

FIGURE 3.1 Volatility of the equity risk premium

far less guaranteed, as companies and economies regularly suffer recessions and depressions attendant on economic cycles. The equity risk premium theoretically compensates investors for taking on the relatively higher risk of the equity market by paying a higher return in the long run. The size of the premium will vary as the risk in the stock market as a whole changes; investing at high-risk periods is, theoretically, compensated in general with a higher equity premium. The justification for the equity premium is based on the risk–return tradeoff, in which a rational investor would require a higher rate of return in order to make riskier investments.

Figure 3.1 shows the annual equity risk premium of the S&P 500 since 1900. While the median of the distribution is positive, one standard deviation is 18.85. Equity risk premiums and, by extension, systematic risk levels, are not stable. Furthermore, the distribution is leptokurtotic, meaning that large negative events are more likely than large positive events.

2. Interest Rates: Central banks and market forces change the risk-free interest rate routinely, depending on monetary-policy objectives and economic cycles. There is no way to diversify away the impact of a change in the level of interest rates, though it can be hedged. A change in the level of interest rates affects the cost of borrowing for every economic entity. This can increase or decrease the earnings of a company and thereby the returns to holders of securities issued by that company. Furthermore, interest rates are recognized as a component of systematic risk in the forward-looking assumptions about the future level of the risk-free rates which underlie almost all models used to determine the fundamental

values of almost all securities. The risk-free return is used to represent the opportunity cost of undertaking a risky investment. However, the mis-named "risk-free rate" is, in fact, not risk free. It is risky because it changes and affects the value of securities, especially bonds, and cannot be diversified away.

3. Inflation: The level of inflation affects the *real* return on all assets. The prices of certain asset classes, such as fixed income securities, are nega-tively correlated to inflation, while returns of "real assets" such as com-modities and real estate are less sensitive. Stocks have varying inflation sensitivities as companies in different economic sectors may be price-makers, able to pass along increases in the cost of their goods while other firms may be price-takers, unable to pass along prices without decreasing demand. From an investor's perspective, the impact of inflation cannot be fully diversified away and can only be hedged.

4. Foreign Exchange: The level of foreign exchange rates affects the home currency return earned by domestic investors on foreign currency denominated investments. Government policy actions have an impact on foreign exchange rates. Foreign exchange risk cannot be fully diversified away and can only be hedged. Determinants of foreign exchange levels include:

- Differentials in interest rates and inflation: Interest rates, inflation and exchange rates are all highly correlated. By manipulating in-terest rates, central banks exert influence over both inflation and exchange rates, and changing interest rates affect inflation and currency values. Higher interest rates offer lenders in an economy a higher return relative to other countries. Therefore, higher inter-est rates attract foreign capital and cause the exchange rate to rise. The impact of higher interest rates is mitigated, however, if infla-tion in the country is much higher than elsewhere, or if additional factors serve to drive the currency down. The opposite relation-ship exists for decreasing interest rates; that is, lower interest rates tend to decrease exchange rates.

- Current account deficits: The current account is the balance of trade between a country and its trading partners, reflecting all payments between countries for goods, services, interest and divi-dends. A deficit in the current account shows the country is spend-ing more on foreign trade than it is earning, and that it is borrowing capital from foreign sources to make up the deficit. In other words, the country requires more foreign currency than it receives through sales of exports, and it supplies more of its own currency than foreigners demand for its products. The excess de-mand for foreign currency lowers the country's exchange rate until domestic goods and services are cheap enough for foreigners, and foreign assets are too expensive to generate sales for domestic interests.

■ Terms of trade: A ratio comparing export prices to import prices, the terms of trade is related to current accounts and the balance of payments. If the price of a country's exports rises by a greater rate than that of its imports, its terms of trade have improved. Increasing terms of trade indicate greater demand for the country's exports. This, in turn, results in rising revenues from exports, which provides increased demand for the country's currency (and an increase in its value). If the price of exports rises by a smaller rate than that of its imports, the currency's value will decrease in relation to its trading partners.

5. Sovereign risk: Actions of sovereign governments change the returns to investors holding all securities issued in a given country. Sometimes these actions can be gradual and positive. In other cases, they can be sudden and negative. Foreign investors inevitably seek out politically stable countries with strong economic performance in which to invest their capital. A government fostering such positive attributes will draw investment funds away from other countries perceived to have more political and economic risk. Political turmoil, for example, can cause a loss of confidence in a currency and a movement of capital to the currencies of more stable countries, with a dramatic impact on the return to investors in the suddenly less-stable country. Potentially unstable countries will engage in large-scale deficit financing to pay for public sector projects and provide government funding. While such activity stimulates the domestic economy, nations with large public deficits and debts become increasingly less attractive to foreign investors, since a large public debt encourages inflation, and if inflation is high, the debt will be serviced and ultimately paid off with cheaper real dollars in the future. In a public debt inflationary spiral, a government may print money to pay part of a large debt, but increasing the money supply inevitably causes greater inflation. Moreover, if a government is not able to service its deficit through domestic means (selling domestic bonds, increasing the money supply), then it must increase the supply of securities for sale to foreigners, thereby lowering their prices. Finally, a large debt may prove worrisome to foreigners if they believe the country risks defaulting on its obligations. Foreigners will be less willing to own securities denominated in that currency if the risk of default is great. For this reason, the country's creditworthiness or sovereign risk is a crucial determinant of its exchange rate. The ultimate sovereign risk occurs when a government becomes unwilling or unable to meet its loan obligations, or reneges on loans it guarantees. Examples of sovereign risk include North Korea (which in 1987

defaulted on some of its loans), Russia (in the 1998 financial crisis, Russia defaulted on its internal debt (GKOs), but did not default on its external Eurobonds), and Argentina (in its economic crisis of 2002, Argentina defaulted on US$1 billion of debt owed to the World Bank). Such unilateral sovereign actions affect the value of all securities in those countries as the national cost of capital increases dramatically. Sovereign risk cannot be fully diversified or hedged.

Basis Risk: This is the potential loss arising from the relationship between the prices of related securities deviating from their zero arbitrage values. It is the difference between the change in value of a security's position whose price is to be hedged and the change in value of the position(s) (typically a derivative) used to construct the hedge.

An example of basis risk in finance is the risk associated with imperfect hedging using futures.

This occurs when the spot prices of an underlying asset and the futures price do not converge on the future expiration date. The amount by which the two quantities differ measures the value of the basis risk.

That is,

$$\text{Basis} = \text{Spot price of hedged asset} - \text{Futures price of contract}$$

Distinct types of basis risk include calendar basis (a mismatch between the expiration date of the futures and the actual selling date of the asset). Location basis is the difference between location of the asset being hedged and the location for physical delivery to meet a futures contract on that asset, at expiration.

Transitory changes in market structure caused by exogenous events often create deviations in the basis between two related types of securities. Consequently, the basis is not always stable. Deviations in basis create investment opportunities and risks for hedge funds. Speculation on the direction of the basis between two related securities is the foundation for most mean-reversion strategies. Consequently, basis risk is present in most mean-reversion strategies.

For example, many hedge funds active in fixed-income arbitrage (and particularly credit arbitrage) were hurt by deviations in the bond vs. CDS basis in 2007 and 2008. Given the greater liquidity of the CDS market, bid/ask spreads on five-year CDS contracts and those of five-year bonds of the same underlying issuer deviated substantially. The same was true for the convertible bond arbitrageurs in 2008 when restrictions on short selling were imposed and the rehypothecation market for all but the top quality convertible bonds dried up. These two factors limited the ability of convertible bond holders to hedge options embedded in certain bonds and liquidate positions without having to pay substantial liquidity premiums, respectively.

Concentration Risk: This is the potential loss arising from the synchronous movement of security values as a result of a correlation of risk factors or a correlation of sources of returns. In portfolio management, concentration risk denotes the overall spread of risk of a hedge fund's securities across its total portfolio holdings. Concentration risk can be measured along many portfolio vectors but is commonly evaluated with respect to security type, asset class, industrial sector, geography/region, or underlying risk factors.

In the case of individual securities, this risk is calculated using a concentration ratio which explains what percentage of the fund's gross market value each security or security strategy represents. For example, a fund that has five strategies of equal gross market value would have a concentration ratio of .2; if it had three, it would be .333, and so on.

In the case of individual risk factors, this risk is calculated using a concentration ratio which explains what percentage of the fund's total risk each risk factor represents. For example, a fund that has five risk factors (Equity Beta, FX, Interest Rate, Credit Spreads, and Commodity Index Volatility) of equal risk contribution would have a concentration ratio of .2; if it had three, it would be .333, and so on.

Various other factors enter into this equation in real-world applications, where securities are not evenly distributed. A fund with 10 positions, valued at US$1,000,000 apiece would have a concentration ratio of .10; but if nine of the positions were for US$111,111 each, and the last was for US$9,000,000, the concentration risk would be considerably higher (0.90). Also, security positions weighted towards specific economic sectors or geographic regions would create a higher concentration ratio than a set of evenly distributed securities because the evenly spread securities would serve to offset the risk of an economic downturn in any one specific industry damaging the fund's performance.

Hedge funds typically construct concentrated portfolios by investing most heavily in positions, strategies, asset classes, or investment themes in which they have the greatest conviction in an effort to maximize alpha. They then seek to hedge out any residual systematic risk, as much as it is cost efficient to do so.

The difficulty in this strategy is that the fund may fail to identify and hedge out "hidden" concentrations and risk factors. Because securities prices are determined by the trading activity of all market participants, correlations across securities prices are only stable when trading activity by all market participants is unchanged. The reality, however, is that activity by market participants is constantly changing and securities that were once uncorrelated become increasingly correlated. When this occurs, previously hidden risk factors manifest themselves in the price of a security. If this occurs across multiple securities or asset classes, concentrations of these hidden factors can form in the portfolio. Subsequently, a further change in investor sentiment or trading activity can create simultaneous movements in securities prices in the portfolio.

Evaluating the presence of "hidden factor" concentration in the portfolio requires constant measurement of the correlation and components of returns of securities and strategies in the portfolio. If the correlation of P&L of distinct and previously uncorrelated strategies in the portfolio increases, then performance attribution and a principal-components analysis should be conducted on the portfolio to identify the source of the correlation. Then, the portfolio should be reconstructed to optimize the diversification of risk factors in order to eliminate any unintended concentration.

Credit Risk In this book, credit risk is considered an investment risk as hedge funds typically buy and sell securities whose values depend in part on credit risk. Hedge funds seek to exploit various forms of credit risk to generate returns. These types of credit risk are a) credit spread risk b) default risk c) correlation of default risk d) recovery rate risk and e) prepayment risk. Securities traded to profit from changes in credit risks are investment grade corporate bonds, distressed and high yield bonds, CDOs and CLOs, mortgage-backed securities, asset-backed securities, and convertible bonds.

1. *Credit Spread Risk:* The credit spread is the yield spread, or difference in yield between different securities, arising from different credit quality. The credit spread reflects the additional net yield an investor can earn from a security with more credit risk relative to one with less credit risk. The credit spread of a particular security is often quoted in relation to the yield on a credit risk-free benchmark security or reference rate such as U.S. Treasury bonds.

There are several measures of credit spread, including Z-spread and option-adjusted spread. The magnitude of each spread represents the riskiness of a specific security. Hedge funds may be long or short securities with credit spread risk. Changes in these spreads can create changes in the value of a hedge fund portfolio and, consequently, gains and losses for hedge fund investors.

Z-spread: Hedge funds are always looking for arbitrage opportunities and use the Z-spread to identify differences in a bond's intrinsic value and its market price. The Z-spread of a bond or asset swap is the number of basis points needed to apply to a series of zero coupon rates such that the present value of the bond, accounting for accrued interest, equals the sum of all future cash flows discounted using the adjusted zero-coupon rate. Each cash flow is discounted using its maturity and the spot rate for that maturity term, so each cash flow has its own zero-coupon rate. The spread is calculated iteratively and provides a more accurate reflection of value than other measures as it uses the entire yield curve to value the cash flows. The difference between the intrinsic values calculated using the Z-spread and market prices can arise because the market price incorporates additional factors such as liquidity and credit risk. The Z-spread quantifies the impact of these additional factors.

Option Adjusted Spread (OAS): This is a method used in calculating the relative value of a fixed income security containing an embedded option, such as a borrower's option to prepay a loan, or a convertible bond issuer's option to convert his bond to equity. OAS models, taking into account the effects of prepayments under various interest-rate scenarios, attempt to estimate the future value of a security. The methodology makes it easier to work out a side-by-side comparison of two different bonds, one of which has a call option (or prepayment option) and one that does not. The callable bond often has a higher yield to compensate for the early redemption feature. OAS is widely used in pricing mortgage-backed securities, structured notes, and convertible bonds.

Hedge funds following convertible arbitrage strategies, MBS arbitrage, and various other fixed-income arbitrage strategies use OAS analysis to identify undervalued bonds that can be efficiently hedged to capture arbitrage profits. It is the stability of the relationship between the value of the fixed-income instrument and its hedge (that is, basis risks) that is the primary risk in these arbitrage strategies.

2. *Default Risk*: Default occurs when a debtor fails to meet legal obligations (has not made a scheduled payment, or has violated a loan covenant) under a debt contract. A default is the failure to pay back a loan. This can occur with all debt obligations, including bonds, mortgage-backed securities, CDOs, bank loans, and promissory notes. All hedge funds investing in these securities are generally exposed to default risk and manage their exposure to such risk.

Default may occur if the debtor is either unwilling or unable to pay their debt. "Insolvency" is a special case of default where a debtor is unable, rather than simply unwilling, to pay their debts.

Types of default: Default can be of two types: debt service default and technical default. Debt service default occurs when the borrower has not made a scheduled payment of interest or principal. Technical default happens when an affirmative or a negative covenant is violated.

Affirmative covenants are clauses in debt contracts that require firms to maintain certain levels of capital or financial ratios. The most commonly violated restrictions in affirmative covenants are tangible net worth, working capital/short-term liquidity, and debt-service coverage.

Negative covenants are clauses in debt contracts that limit or prohibit corporate actions (for example, sale of assets, payment of dividends) that could impair the position of creditors. Negative covenants may be continuous or incurrence-based. Violations of negative covenants are rare compared to violations of affirmative covenants.

With most debt (including corporate debt, mortgages and bank loans) a covenant is included in the debt contract which states that the total amount owed becomes immediately payable on the first instance of a default of payment. Generally, if the debtor defaults on any debt to the lender, a cross-default covenant in the debt contract states that that particular debt is also in default.

In corporate finance, upon an uncured default, the holders of the debt will usually initiate proceedings (file a petition of involuntary bankruptcy) to foreclose on any collateral securing the debt. "Bankruptcy" is a legal finding that imposes court supervision over the financial affairs of those who are insolvent or in default. Even if the debt is not secured by collateral, debt holders may still sue for bankruptcy, to ensure that the corporation's assets are used to repay the debt.

There are several financial models for analyzing default risk. These include the Jarrow-Turnbull model, Edward Altman's Z-score model, or the structural model of default by Robert C. Merton (Merton Model).

3. *Default Correlation Risk:* Hedge funds following fixed income relative-value strategies go long and short securities with varying levels of default risk. In addition, hedge funds invest in securitized credit-risky products such as CDOs. They also go long and short different tranches of these securities based on their view of default correlation.

Default correlation is the likelihood of a contagion effect occurring within a tranche of a CDO and actual defaults being higher than expected. For example, if all the companies in a CDO are in the banking industry, and one begins to fail and therefore is unable meet its creditors' demands; there is a greater-than-random chance that a common factor in the banking industry is causing banks to falter. Therefore, if one bank fails, the probability of another failing increases. Default correlation risk is the risk of change in default correlation or the risk that realized default correlation differs from expected levels.

Hedge funds use varying methods to determine default correlation. Some use the correlation of equity prices, some use correlation of

CDS spreads, and some use historical default correlation based on rating-agency studies. However, as the credit crisis has amply demonstrated, there are also major problems in measuring and even thinking about default correlation. The thorniest problem is quantification. Deriving default correlation from market prices has proven flawed because of the market's risk appetite driving down credit spreads below levels sufficient to compensate for expected default, the multiplicity of factors (not least liquidity) that is also reflected in credit spreads and equity prices, and that when looking at historical rates of default, it is impossible to distinguish default correlation from changing default probability.

4. Recovery Rate Risk: This is the change in expected or recovery rates. The recovery rate is the amount that a creditor would receive in final satisfaction of the claims on a defaulted credit. This is typically expressed as a percentage of the debt's par value. An alternative definition commonly in the reduced-form models is to state recovery as a percentage of market value.

Recovery rate risk is relevant to credit risk arbitrage hedge funds trading bonds as opposed to CDS, CDX/CDOs or CDX/CDO tranches and other credit-risky strategies, as the recovery rate is an input into the value of the securities in their portfolio. Changes in expected recovery rates change the value of their securities.

5. Prepayment Risk: This is the risk associated with the unscheduled early return of principal on a fixed income security. Some fixed income securities have embedded call options which may be exercised by the issuer. Changes in prepayment rates can affect the value of ABS and MBS as they change the magnitude and timing of expected cash flows to the holder.

In the case of MBS and ABS, the yield to maturity of such securities cannot be known for certain at the time of purchase since the timing and amount of the cash flows are not known. For example, when principal is returned early, future interest payments will not be paid on that part of the principal. If the bond was purchased at a premium (a price greater than 100), the bond's yield will be less than was estimated at the time of purchase.

Generally, for a bond with an embedded call option, the higher its interest rate relative to current interest rates, the higher the prepayment risk. This is because the opportunity cost of not refinancing the obligation by the borrower at the lower current interest grows as the difference between the bond's interest rate and the current interest rate grows.

For example, on a mortgage-backed security, the higher the interest rate relative to current interest rates, the higher the probability that the underlying mortgages will be refinanced. Investors who pay a premium for a callable bond with a high interest rate take on prepayment risk. In addition to being highly correlated with falling interest rates, mortgage prepayments are highly correlated with rising home values, as these provide an incentive for borrowers to trade up in homes or use cash-out refinances, which both lead to mortgage prepayments.

For hedge funds investing in mortgage- and asset-backed securities, changes in prepayment rates is a significant risk.

Portfolio Liquidity Risk

Portfolio liquidity risk (also termed "asset liquidity risk") is the risk that the securities in the hedge fund's portfolio cannot be sold for a fungible cash amount equal to their intrinsic value because of a lack of liquidity in the market.

Causes of Portfolio Liquidity Risk   This risk arises from situations in which a hedge fund interested in selling an asset cannot do so because it cannot find a buyer in the market that wants to trade that asset or trade it in the size the seller requires to generate more fungible cash.

The risk typically does not manifest itself as a drop in the price of an asset to zero. If that were to occur, the market would be saying that the asset was worthless but not necessarily illiquid. As trading in a security declines, this risk manifests itself through decreasing daily trading volumes; reduced frequency and widening dispersion of indicative and executable market quotes; stale indicative quotes (that is, quotes that are posted but do not change); and/or widening bid/offer spreads.

Portfolio liquidity risk tends to compound other risks in the portfolio. For example, if a hedge fund has a position in an illiquid asset, its limited ability to liquidate that position at short notice will compound its investment risk. Similarly, if a fund has a position in a security with increasing default correlation risk, the inability to liquidate the position increases the fund's investment risk.

Even if an illiquid position can be hedged against market risk, it may still expose the firm to liquidity risk. Suppose a firm has offsetting cash flows as a result of going long and short with two different securities with two different counterparties but does not wish to hold both positions to maturity. If the long security is more liquid than the short, the firm may be able to exit the long position, but not be able to liquidate its short exposure simultaneously at an offsetting value. In such a case, it will have to pay a liquidity premium or be "naked short" until such time it can liquidate the short. Here, liquidity risk is compounding market risk.

Measures of Portfolio Liquidity

- **Bid/offer Spread** The bid/offer spread is used by market participants as a measure of asset liquidity. A trader willing to buy an illiquid asset from a hedge fund must be able to hold that asset in inventory until such time as it can be sold, or to maturity. The bid/ask spread is composed of inventory costs, operational costs, and administrative and processing costs, as well as the compensation required for the possibility of trading with a more informed trader. To compare the liquidity of different products, the ratio of the spread to the product's mid-price can be used. The smaller the ratio, the more liquid the asset is.

  A portfolio liquidity analysis based on bid/ask spreads should also consider the size of the position being sold compared to the market depth. The market depth is a measure of the amount of an asset or lot size that can be bought and sold at various bid/ask spreads. As the lot size increases, the bid/ask spread may widen, causing slippage and driving down the executable price. Flow traders at brokerages consider the effect of executing a large order on the market and adjust the bid/ask spread accordingly. A flow trader needs to be able to sell whatever securities he buys in short order. If he buys a large position in a specific security, and then sells it in smaller lot sizes to a variety of buyers, he may temporarily satisfy all the buying interest in that security for several weeks or it may, in fact, take him several weeks to sell the position to prospective buyers at current prices. He should not pay more for the security than it could lose over several weeks, or more than he would have to offer it at to generate buyer interest and get it off his books. Using his knowledge of buying and selling interest in the security, the flow trader will quote a bid/ask spread that ensures he can clear his inventory. Consequently, bid/ask spreads are indicators of liquidity and illiquid securities tend to be more volatile than liquid securities.

- **Immediacy (or "Days to Liquidate")** Immediacy refers to the time needed to trade a certain amount of an asset at a prescribed cost. The most common measure of immediacy is a "days to liquidate" measure. It is an estimate of the number of trading days that would be needed to sell a position typically without moving the market price down. It can also be adapted to measure "days to liquidate" assuming a certain percentage of market value might be lost in generating buyer interest.

  To determine portfolio level immediacy or "days to liquidate," security level immediacy measures are aggregated. Aggregated measures can be expressed as weighted average days to liquidate by weighting each security's days to liquidate by the percentage of total portfolio value it represents, as follows:

$$\text{Portfolio Days to Liquidate} = \sum w_i{}^*TS_i$$

where the summation is taken over the time to liquidate each security (TS_i) and multiplied by the respective market value weight (w_i) of each security in the portfolio.

Alternatively, the percentage of the total portfolio value that can be liquidated within a static number of days can be calculated (that is, 1, 5, 10, or 15 trading days).

- **Resilience** Resilience is another measure of liquidity that measures the speed with which prices return to former levels after a large transaction. Unlike the other measures, resilience can only be determined using historical analysis over a period of time. It is also limited by the fact that volumes traded by all market participants are only known for exchange-traded products. Not all exchanges share this data. For OTC products, a hedge fund is typically only aware of its own transactions.

Managing Liquidity Risk Liquidity adjusted value at risk incorporates exogenous liquidity risk into VaR and can be defined as:

$$\text{VaR} + \sum (\text{ELC})$$

where ELC is the exogenous liquidity cost for each security in the portfolio. The ELC is the worst expected half-spread (that is, "mid to ask" or "mid to bid") at a particular confidence level drawn from a distribution of historical bid/ask spreads.

Another adjustment is to consider VaR, stress and scenario tests over the period of time needed to liquidate the portfolio. Holding periods in the risk assessment are adjusted by the length of time required to unwind the positions. Simulation results are then calculated over this time period.

BUSINESS RISK MANAGEMENT STRATEGIES

The previous section looked at the investment risks that hedge funds face. These arise from the securities in its portfolio. Other risks faced by hedge funds arise in large part from the hedge-fund business model which, by its very nature, is fragile because the vast majority of its operations are outsourced and because of its dependency on third parties for funding (see Figure 3.2).

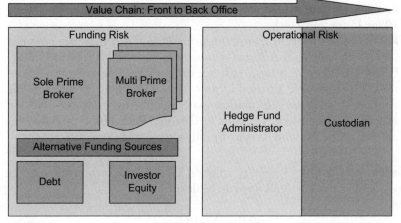

FIGURE 3.2   Sources of funding and operational risk in hedge funds

Operational Risk

An operational risk is the risk of loss resulting from inadequate or failed internal processes, people and systems, data, or from external events which preclude a firm from executing its business model as intended. The hedge fund industry is neither static nor homogenous. Operational pressures are constantly changing as the industry reaches upstream to large institutional investors such as pension funds, trades with numerous mammoth financial institutions, and responds to divergent and changing regulatory environments. As such, operational risk is a multifaceted concept and challenging to manage, both for hedge fund managers and their investors.

Capco, a global business and technology consulting firm and an early specialist in back office and risk management services to the financial industry, reports that operational risk is the sole cause of almost half of all hedge-fund failures and a contributory factor in many more.[6] Market complexity and a business model that is dependent on outsourced service providers, however, is only part of the reason for this. Higher transaction volumes, complexity of transactions, use of leverage, financial incentives that create conflicts of interest with investors, potentially fewer control staff and operations leading to incomplete segregation of duties, and inadequate checks and balances—all contribute to hedge-fund failure.

Another Capco study[7] highlights the importance of operational risk management within hedge funds. A key finding of the study was that operational risk greatly exceeds the risk related to the investment strategy, with at least 56 percent of hedge fund collapses (that is, funds that have ceased operations with or without returning the capital to their shareholders) being directly related to a failure of one or several operational processes. Some studies estimate that operational risks contribute to 80 percent of hedge fund failures.[8]

The types of operational risks underlying hedge fund failures identified in the Capco study are shown in Table 3.2.

Operational risks include fraud, fines imposed for unintended regulatory or legal violations such as insider trading, and losses arising from environmental risks, systems failures, and data errors. Style drift, or trading outside of the stated mandate, is both an operational and investment risk.

For investors, fraud is a major concern. A recent CastleHall study outlines the scope of operational failures that resulted from fraud and/or malfeasance by documenting some 327 cases with a combined financial impact of approximately US$80 billion.[9]

While responsibility for operational risk may lie with the COO and CFO, few hedge funds actually dedicate resources directly to managing operational risk. While investment risks like credit and market risks are managed by the fund's front office, operational risk is rarely coordinated centrally nor actively managed. Responsibility for various operational risks is typically dispersed between the hedge fund and its service providers, with the IT team expected to manage risks of system failure and flawed or

TABLE 3.2 Sources of operational failures at hedge funds

Operational Risk Type	% of All Operational Risk Fund Failures
Misrepresentation	41%
Misappropriation of Funds/Fraud	30%
Trading Outside Mandate	14%
Other	9%
Inadequate Technology Processes	6%

Source: Capco, 2002

missing data. Similarly, the HR head is expected to take care of personnel risks by performing background checks on new hires. The CFO and COO staff are expected to ensure that key controls are implemented. These controls include the segregation of the execution and reconciliation of trades; the requirement for dual signatories for any movement of investor funds out of the accounts; and ensuring that all financial representations made by the fund are made in accordance with GAAP rules. The hedge fund administrator and the prime broker are expected to manage all trade settlement procedures and raise any non-reconciling items. Lastly, the custodian is responsible for the safekeeping of securities and for managing all corporate actions.

However, the frequency of operational risk events and the subsequent losses involved has made investors increasingly intolerant of the lack of attention to such matters by hedge funds. The recent headlines surrounding the US$50-billion Bernard Madoff Ponzi scheme were dramatic but hardly surprising, as these events were part of an accelerating pattern of operational failures over the past 10 years.[10] As a result, end investors and fund of funds managers are performing more rigorous due diligence of hedge funds and will not invest unless they are satisfied that operational risk is well managed.

Investors now demand much greater detail on a host of operational matters ranging from legal and compliance issues to information technology, cash management and valuation. Only those funds that make the due-diligence process run as smoothly as possible for investors are likely to attract capital. Those that fall short of investors' expectations in these areas will not receive investment dollars.

Instead of outsourcing operational due diligence to funds of funds and consultants, investors are exerting greater control over the process and the scope and depth of operational issues evaluated in a due diligence review are becoming more exhaustive and frequent. This creates a greater demand for, and strain upon, the hedge funds' resources. Inevitably this will result in higher costs and lower profit margins for hedge-fund management companies, though perhaps not in lower performance for the funds themselves.

Operational Risk Management Strategies

In the context of hedge funds, the following operational risks are most common:

1. Model Risk: Potential loss due to mis-specification, unintended response, or stale model parameters. This risk is most significant for

statistical arbitrage, quantitative funds, credit arbitrage, and fixed income arbitrage funds.

2. System Failure: The potential loss due to the sudden failure of a trading, settlement, risk management or signal-generating system. All funds are vulnerable to this risk but it is an especially significant risk for statistical arbitrage funds, high-velocity trading strategies, and market making strategies.

3. Legal Risk: Potential loss due to unexpected legal outcome or unintended violation of the law. All funds are potentially exposed to this risk but it is most significant for distressed-debt, and fixed income arbitrage strategies in which tax laws play an important role; activist funds; and, to some extent, event driven funds.

4. Regulatory Compliance Risk: The potential loss arising from unintended regulatory violations. All funds are exposed to regulatory risk to some extent, though international and emerging market funds are more exposed as they must comply with a wider array of regulatory regimes. The most significant regulatory compliance risk in a hedge fund is insider trading.

5. Fraud Risk: The potential loss due to theft, corruption, conspiracy, embezzlement, money laundering, bribery and extortion. At a hedge fund, fraud typically involves expropriating assets for personal gain or falsifying performance, for example. While all funds are potentially exposed, those that 1) do not disclose full information to investors; 2) lack a third-party administrator/custodian; 3) do not employ a recognized audit firm are more vulnerable to this risk.

6. Third Party Failure: The potential loss caused by the failure of a third party to fulfill their service-level agreement. All funds that employ a third party administrator or custodian are vulnerable.

7. Data Errors: The potential loss arising from mis-specified, wrong or missing data. While all funds are vulnerable to some extent, this risk is most significant for statistical arbitrage and quantitative funds, which are reliant on accurate analysis to generate investment ideas and alpha.

To manage these common operational risks, a hedge fund should build a cohesive management strategy incorporating clear lines of responsibility. To the extent practicable, operational functions, including reporting, compensation and decision-making authority, should be independent of portfolio management. Investors will assess the experience and training of a hedge fund's operational staff in the critical areas of expertise—and, in particular, the strength and independence of its leadership, typically either a chief financial officer or chief operating officer.

Therefore, having an experienced CFO or COO who is able to ensure that the investment mandate is complied with is of the utmost importance. The CFO/COO should also ensure that adequate numbers and sufficiently experienced operations and settlement staff are employed relative to the complexity and size of the fund. Managers who trade in complex OTC derivative instruments will need to ensure that there are sufficient back-office staff to review long-form confirmations. Firms which trade in heavy volumes should invest in third party trade capture and order management systems which feed straight into the account systems to minimize manual intervention. Even where middle and/or back office functions have been outsourced, there should be operations staff who have responsibility for overseeing and assisting the service-provider's work.

From a hedge fund manager's or COO's perspective, an effective operational risk management strategy should address all of the following significant operational risks:

Model Risk   The scope of risk arising from model use will depend on the nature of the strategy, the complexity of the mandate, and the types of models used. Some hedge funds employ quantitative models extensively and in a variety of ways. Models may be used to predict potential investment performance, to make investment decisions, to attribute performance, to value investments, or to manage risks. Other funds use models to determine a quantitative strategy that directs the fund's investment process, while others use models solely as decision support tools.

Models can be imprecise. Their underlying assumptions may fail to hold. Their explanatory power can decline over time and their central insight can become commonplace. They can fail to capture the dynamic nature of management's decisions. Models can rely upon false or incomplete assumptions or incorrect data, and their application can be inappropriate. Moreover, fund managers can materially alter models, causing unintended exposures in an investor's portfolio.

Robust models should reflect the relevant factors for the investment strategy over a wide range of potential market conditions and use the best available data. A model's assumptions should be consistent with the relevant market environment and back-tested to ensure that they remain relevant expressions of market reality.

Model risk exposure primarily arises from three sources: (1) the control environment of the model, (2) the model itself, and 3) competitors using the same model.

Control Environment   Model risk can arise when a poor model control environment causes inaccurate forecasts. While hedge fund managers and model developers appreciate the creativity that can result from a relatively relaxed work environment, model development must become formal and supported by detailed documentation in order to mitigate any inherent risk. The key to success is to attain quality control, and replicable processes and documentation without becoming excessively repetitive or rigid to the extent where they handicap a fund manager's ability to monetize an opportunity or stifle innovation. Current industry standard practices are to limit model access to designated users and have comprehensively documented up-to-date application procedures. A model's key assumptions, contractual inputs and behavior assumptions are reviewed on at least a monthly basis by the fund's investment management committee.

The Model Itself   In addition, in a poor control environment, the model itself creates risk if it is mis-specified and then used to inform trading strategies. To prevent this, a validation process is typically employed to review the assumptions and implementation of any model used for trading decisions or by auditors to value positions. The absence of computational errors is clearly a requirement for a valid valuation methodology. The idea, however, that a review of the model assumptions per se can give reassurance as to the correct mark to market result is much more difficult to justify. It can be totally valid or invalid to reject a model because it allows for negative rates, because it does not allow for stochastic volatility or because it neglects the stochastic nature of discounting depending on whether it is used for arbitrage or for valuation. From a valuation perspective, if the market is happy to trade particular products with imperfect model prices, requiring that a product should be marked to market using a more sophisticated model (that is, a model which makes more realistic assumptions but which produces prices at which securities cannot be liquidated), this can be equally misguided if the market has not embraced the "superior" approach. However, where the model is used to profit from arbitrage opportunities by identifying under- and overvalued assets, then the superior approach should be adopted and the arbitrage exploited, as long as liquidity is not a concern.[11]

Competitors' Models   To avoid losses that arise from the model, it is important to know how that model compares to the competition in the market. However, to know this requires solid knowledge about the transaction prices and the nature of actual market transactions so that the model which determined the price can be reverse engineered. Without this market intelligence, the task of managing model risk is extremely difficult.

No matter how good or convincing a theoretical model might be, a hedge fund should worry if it consistently beats all competitors in a competitive-tender situation. This would indicate that the market thinks the fund is paying too much because other firms are using a different model. In this respect, contacts with brokers, traders or risk managers at other firms can provide what is possibly the most effective early-alert system.

Another possible cause for concern is the sudden occurrence of large notional trades for which it is difficult to establish a clear rationale on the basis of customer-driven demand. The motivation behind these trades could be the very actions of arbitrageurs who have identified particular types of transaction for which common market assumptions or practices cannot be justified. This may indicate that the model is becoming out of date. Historically, examples of such trades have been, for instance, LIBOR-in-arrears swaps, forward-starting swaptions, CMS caps, and so on.

System Failure Operational losses from system failures are often caused by a lack of automation in connecting front and back office functions; system limitations; insufficient scalability of systems; computer viruses; and inadequate disaster recovery plans. The most serious system failures at hedge funds result in the inability of the fund to know the correct valuation of its positions, what its available cash position is and with which counterparty it resides. This can lead to the full collapse of the fund.

There are times when a fund may be following its own policies consistently and accurately, but a flaw in the valuation procedures or processes cause a systemic mis-marking of the book. This is most common in cases where a fund is trading instruments that cannot be handled by its regular processing systems and some kind of workaround is devised which later proves to be flawed.

Issues that may occur are not limited to incorrect pricing. Entire positions can be incorrectly captured on the fund's books and records. Exotic derivatives positions may be simplified in order for them to be entered into record-keeping systems, which can then result in risk systems being unable to evaluate the risk correctly. Sometimes total positions are completely excluded in error. Mortgages, bank loans, OTC derivatives, convertible bonds, and non-dollar instruments of all kinds can be prone to these kinds of issues if underlying systems do not fully support them.

The most effective way to ensure that systems remain robust is to develop an IT systems-architecture plan early in the fund's life and then invest continuously in modular and extensible front and middle office infrastructure. As the firm grows, testing the integration of in-house systems against third party systems helps to ensure that data flows seamlessly across the organization and retains its integrity.

Legal Risk For hedge funds not directly involved in distressed debt or activist strategies, it is sufficient to maintain a close relationship with one of the major law firms specializing in hedge funds in order to manage legal risk. However, for activist and distressed debt funds, hiring an in-house counsel to coordinate the work of external lawyers and to set strategy for managing the fund's legal risk is best practice.

Regulatory Compliance Risk   Institutionalized hedge funds have defined best practice in the area of managing regulatory compliance risk. For most large hedge funds, the dedicated management team includes a compliance officer to drive regulatory compliance. Most also have developed processes to stay abreast with the changing regulatory and compliance landscape in conjunction with their auditors and legal counselors.

With respect to complying with insider trading laws in various jurisdictions, only the fund's management can mitigate this risk, which should be done as follows:

Policies and Procedures: Firms should recognize their responsibility to control access to, and reduce the risk of misuse of, inside information, and should establish policies and procedures addressing such issues as the handling of price sensitive information, addressing inquiries from the media, appointing a senior person to oversee the controls and procedures, and controlling information handled by staff.

Awareness and Training: Firms should train and otherwise assist staff to understand the importance of keeping information secret and the liabilities for improper disclosure. Among other practices, firms should consider providing training, updating staff as new rules come into effect, and testing staff awareness and understanding periodically.

"Need to Know" and Other Information Controls: Firms should take steps to limit the number of persons with access to inside information. Where practicable, they should consider separating dealing teams from other parts of the business, disclosing inside information only on a need-to-know basis. Firms may choose to implement policies regarding the secure disposal and use of confidential documents (including using code names, implementing clear-desk policies, and establishing procedures for working offsite).

Passing Price Sensitive Information to Third Parties: Firms should take reasonable care to ensure that third parties are aware of their obligations regarding the use and control of the inside information they receive. Galleon was a classic case of insider trading compounded by the passing of price sensitive information in exchange for compensation. Also, where price sensitive information must be shared, hedge funds should consider providing the information to third parties as late in the process as possible, explaining the responsibilities and ensuring that the third parties have procedures in place to protect the information.

IT Security: Hedge funds should address the security of, and access to, inside information on IT systems, create IT file audit trails, and implement controls to limit access to systems and information. They may also consider requiring IT personnel to comply with all insider trading policies and procedures and employing "ethical hackers" to test security against data theft.

Personal Dealing Policies: Firms should establish policies for trading in personal accounts, which may include trading as power of attorney, through discretionary accounts, and by immediate family members. They should consider making specific references in the policies to derivatives and related products, and to the civil and criminal penalties for dealing or enabling dealing on the basis of inside information. Hedge funds should determine which employees are covered by these policies and ensure that those employees understand exactly what is entailed. They should be given regular training in what they can and what they can't do and be asked to attest to the fact that they understand the policy.

At a minimum, the personal trading policy should do the following:

- Define "covered persons" and "covered securities" as they apply to the firm. Adopt, implement and monitor pre-clearance procedures for trading.
- Create a list of restricted securities within the firm's portfolio which details those securities in which employees are prevented from trading.
- Require employees to provide monthly and quarterly brokerage statements.
- Require employees to report their holdings periodically.
- Require new employees to report holdings within 10 business days of opening the position.
- Require employees to report any outside business activities in which they participate.
- Complete checks to make sure that employees are not front-running or tailgating[12] trades made in the fund's portfolio.

Fraud Risk Separation of duties and independence in mark-to-market has long been a fundamental principle of control in financial institutions, but is still applied inconsistently in the hedge fund industry. Robust internal controls and procedures should be in place over each stage of the trading cycle: trade authorization, execution, confirmation, settlement, reconciliation, and accounting. A breakdown in this separation of duties seems to have been a factor in almost every fraud-related fund failure. Adequate segregation of duties between those who are authorized to trade and those who are responsible for recording trade activity must be established to prevent unrecorded trading losses. The movement of funds by wire transfers or otherwise should be tightly controlled, with multiple signatories required to authorize the movement of funds. In short, independence and separation of duties means that the person who performs checks or approves valuations should not receive incentives or inducements based directly on the performance of the investment being valued, and should not report to managers who do. The trader or portfolio manager should never perform final valuations (it often makes sense, however, for the trader or manager to do their own valuation as a "reasonableness check" on an independent process but, wherever possible, an independent third party should check these valuations). Wherever possible, a fund manager should keep financial/accounting staff independent of the portfolio management team to prepare and validate marks to market.

In most cases, these staff will report to the CFO or the COO of the fund-management company, and should be compensated based on the overall profitability results of the management company rather than on the performance of any of the investment vehicles managed by the firm. In some cases, fund administrators will perform this role for a fund manager. Some valuation services will also prepare marks on an outsourced basis. Many funds will also employ an auditor to test the valuations used for financial statements to investors. A fund manager should always use an external third party to verify that portfolio valuations are accurate before they are reported to investors. This would be in addition to the fund auditor, who often will examine valuations less frequently and after they have been reported.

Occasionally a valuation problem will be part of a deliberate attempt to inflate the value of a fund, either to hide unrealized losses and report stronger performance, or to cover up broader theft and fraud. This appears to have been true, for example, in the case involving the failure of the Manhattan Fund.[13] In other cases, asset valuations may be manipulated to smooth mark to market losses and enhance the fund's performance by dampening volatility.[14]

Some securities frequently traded by hedge funds can be extremely difficult to value. Even when prices are readily available, some positions may still require adjustment anyway: for example, positions that comprise a large proportion of a single issue should be discounted to reflect the likelihood that they cannot be liquidated without a significant market impact. Also, if a security is held in a large enough quantity where public disclosure (that is, Schedule 13D in the United States) is required, an adjustment may need to be made if all or part of the position cannot be sold anonymously. Occasionally, positions will simply be mis-marked, and may cause a sudden and unexpected impact to fund valuation when the marks are corrected or the position is reversed. There can also be a significant variation depending on which "correct" price is being used—the bid, offer, or mid-point—especially when it comes to thinly traded or illiquid instruments where bid/offer spreads can be sizeable.

Third party failure Because of the enormous reliance that hedge funds have on third party prime brokers, custodians, and administrators, the proper selection of these key business partners is a key part of avoiding losses. The selection process for choosing these key business partners should focus on identifying the best partner in relation to the fund's strategy and business model.

Failure to appoint well-known, proven and independent service providers may introduce operational weakness to a fund.

Operational Risk Criteria for Choosing Prime Brokers Prime brokers provide many important services, including brokerage, securities lending, financing, and back office support (including clearing and settling trades). Prime brokers and other trading counterparties should have the resources and expertise necessary to handle the fund's investments.

The choice between using a single broker or multiple brokers is a difficult one for a fund manager. Larger hedge funds may have multiple brokers, while smaller and newer funds are unlikely to have more than one. The trade-off is one between operational simplicity and diversification of the risk of failure of a third party service provider. A single broker allows for centralized trading and settlement, enabling a fund to outsource more of the back office activities. However, reliance on a single prime broker is imprudent once a fund grows to a size where it can afford to maintain middle and back offices. All prime brokers should be high-quality financial institutions. As soon as a fund is large enough, it should move to the multi-broker model.

The choice of prime brokers should be guided by aligning the fund manager's needs to the prime broker's capabilities. Balance sheet strength, financing flexibility, and robust operational infrastructure are the key decision criteria in choosing the right mix of prime brokers. However, in order to maintain flexibility, it is necessary to set up a structure that allows for ease of data aggregation and asset transfer between brokers.

Balance sheet strength: A strong balance sheet increases the probability that the prime broker will remain creditworthy through a market crisis and able to maintain services to the hedge fund. It also provides the fund greater confidence in the safety of its collateral and reduces the risk of impairment.

Financing flexibility: Favorable financing terms (overnight and term financing at market rates are typical prerequisites) and an ability to provide various margining methodologies such as Regulation T, Portfolio

Margining, Rules-based House Margins, and Stress/Scenario-based House Margins are of varying importance depending on the fund's strategy. The ability to trade away from the prime broker but give up the trade to the prime broker for effective collateral management in a multi-prime setup is also important.

Geographic presence: Depending on the fund's strategy, operational risk can be mitigated by using one set of data infrastructure to trade in multiple geographies. A prime broker's capabilities across markets and geographies on a common infrastructure can reduce operational risk for a globally active fund. In addition, a fund with a wide geographic footprint and experience in providing guidance on legal requirements and market access in multiple markets reduces the fund's operational risk.

Product coverage: A prime broker with a broad range of product coverage tradable on a robust common infrastructure can reduce a hedge fund's exposure to operational risk.

Execution platform: A prime broker with straight through processing capabilities and direct market access coupled with a robust infrastructure and management information systems can greatly reduce operational risk. This is particularly true of hedge fund utilizing high-velocity trading strategies.

Operational Criteria for Choosing a Hedge Fund Administrator Given the increased use of multiple prime brokers by hedge funds, the capabilities of a central administrator become more important for managing the flow of information. The third party administrator plays an extremely important role in protecting investors' assets by calculating the net asset value of the fund independently of the manager.

Valuation is ultimately at the core of any investment. It is the key to deciding whether to make an investment and to calculate returns from that investment over time. The increasing complexity and diversity of fund portfolios and the increasing allocation to complex investments has resulted in a significant increase in efforts to formulate tools and processes for valuing them accurately.

Hedge fund asset valuation is critical to investor trust yet varies by hedge fund strategy, by the types of underlying investments and by the corresponding procedures required to establish accurate, fair net asset values. The complexity of security types can range from U.S.-listed, actively traded equities (easiest to value) to non-U.S., privately placed securities (which entail foreign currency conversion as well as valuation issues), and complex OTC derivative instruments. U.S.-listed securities are typically valued at the last sale price (or offer price for longs, bid price for shorts, or the bid/ask spread midpoint) on the primary exchange on which the security is traded.

Their valuation is readily available and easily verifiable through a number of publicly available sources. From this baseline, there is a spectrum of securities and valuation methodologies with decreasing objectivity and increasing complexity. Valuation methodologies include dealer quotes (either direct or through aggregators), valuation services, models and, finally, good-faith estimates by the fund manager.

The dependency on the third party administrator is more pressing for funds that follow strategies using assets that are difficult to value daily, as illustrated in Table 3.3.

Valuation can become a particular problem in unstable markets. Assets that are valued on a mark to model approach may not be saleable at anywhere near the valuation in a market liquidity crisis. On the other hand, mark to market valuations in such a crisis may dramatically underestimate the value of performing assets if looked at from a cash-generation perspective. The accuracy and appropriateness of valuation often has a profound impact on the ultimate portfolio returns reported to investors, as well as the fees paid to the manager. The choice of a stable and sophisticated third-party administrator is essential to avoid conflicts of interest and ensure the operational integrity of the fund, especially in a market crisis.

Outsourcing the middle office functions to administrators can enable fund managers to have access to best-in-class systems without having to develop their own. However, to gain this benefit, it is essential to choose third-party administrators with adequate capital resources to invest in IT systems, and high-caliber staff able to fully re-price all the securities in the portfolio.[15]

Trade application support: Administrators must be able to provide stable, round-the-clock trade support capabilities across multiple geographies and delivered via competent, experienced staff. This capability is critical to the hedge fund. Any inability to trade because of an inability to access trade applications is an operational risk and exposes the fund to potential loss. In addition, the administrator must demonstrate a robust crisis-management plan and the ability to deploy a back-up capability in the event the primary systems fail.

Portfolio accounting: The administrator should be able to demonstrate robust systems to track a wide range of investment instruments and currencies, and provide daily accounting and statutory reporting services. This is essential for the hedge fund to detect potential fraud or trade errors in a timely fashion. In addition, the administrative systems should be capable of processing complex or new types of derivative instruments. The complexity of derivative exposures has been exploited by fraudsters such as Liam Neeson and Jerome Kerviel to hide losses.

Cash and position reconciliation: Standardized processes to manage reconciliation with multiple parties and resolve breaks before NAV

TABLE 3.3 Instruments and strategies with potential valuation issues

High Yield/ Distressed Debt	Fixed Income Arbitrage	Emerging Markets	Convertible Bond Arbitrage	Global Macro	Activist Funds
Bank Debt	Bonds with Embedded Options	Bank Loans	Credit Derivatives	Inflation linked Bonds	Control Positions
Convertible Bonds	Collateralized Debt Obligations	Brady Bonds	Non rated Convertible Bonds	OTC Commodity Contracts	SPACs
Covenant Lite Bank Loans	Collateralized Mortgage Obligations	Emerging Market Listed Futures	Options on Bonds	Swaps and Options on Swaps	
Debtor in Possession Loans	Convertible Bonds	Emerging Market Listed Options	Restricted Convertible Bonds		
Distressed Bonds	Credit Derivatives	Emerging Market Convertible Bonds	Rights and Warrants		
High Yield Bonds	Exotic Interest Rate Options	Illiquid Stocks	Sub investment grade Convertible Bonds		
Increasing Rate Notes	Interest Rate Forwards	Local Bank Certificates of Deposit			
Junior Debt	Mortgage Backed Securities	Local Currency Corporate Bonds			

(continued)

TABLE 3.3 (Continued)

High Yield/ Distressed Debt	Fixed Income Arbitrage	Emerging Markets	Convertible Bond Arbitrage	Global Macro	Activist Funds
Letters of Credit	Options on Bonds	Non-deliverable Forwards in Non-convertible Currencies			
Mezzanine Debt	Swaps and Options on Swaps	Stock and Index Warrants			
Pay in Kind Securities	When Issued Securities	Structured Swaps			
Secured/Unsecured Debt					
Senior Debt					
Split Coupon Securities					
Step-up/Step-down Coupon Securities					
Subordinated Debt					
Swaps and Options on Swaps					
Trade Claims					

calculation are essential to mitigate the risk of loss due to settlement failures or failed trades. The ability to provide these services during local business hours (that is, "Follow the Sun" processing) enables hedge funds to leverage time-zone advantages when trading in multiple geographies.

Data Errors   Hedge funds rely most on accurate data at both position and security levels. Historical data at these levels are essential for managing investment risk. Common causes of operational losses from data errors are poor data sources; unreliable information; untimely data; and inaccessible data. In developing a strong management information system (MIS), it is essential to:

- Maintain consistency and integration of data across systems. Create a data steward which can enforce quality standards (particularly identification and naming standards and format consistency).
- Establish a model that enables the integration of data across the fund and can grow as new strategies are added.
- Standardize and reuse accurate data, focusing on data that are critical across departments and applications. Examples of such data are security data (security ID, security name, unitized security risk factor sensitivities such as DV01, CS01 etc.); position data (quantity owned, long/short, account/fund and so on), portfolio data (strategy ID, core position and hedges), and so on.
- Establish data management policies and procedures from the beginning and apply them across all departments.

The trading, documenting, settling, accounting, and reporting of investment securities is a complex discipline that requires precision in all its details, guided by a strong ethic of fiduciary responsibility. Hedge fund managers typically devote the majority of their time to generating alpha and not to managing the operations of their firms. While having appropriate IT resources and third party administrative assistance can help, it cannot remove this inherent operational risk entirely.

Funding Liquidity Risk

Funding liquidity risk, like operational risk, is endemic to the hedge fund business model but it is fundamentally different. Hedge funds use leverage to amplify investment returns by borrowing money to invest in securities to augment the equity provided by investors. The borrowed money should be paid back at a fixed rate of interest. Any return on securities investments greater than this fixed rate accrues to equity investors in the fund. This is a core part of the business model and the fund's ability to generate excess returns uncorrelated with market return. However, the use of leverage is also the primary source of funding liquidity risk—the risk that liabilities cannot be met when they fall due or can only be met at an uneconomic price. In addition to leverage, the potential variability in portfolio liquidity, the potential for investor redemptions to accelerate in a crisis and the ability of prime brokers to increase their margin requirements all contribute to this risk.

Funding liquidity risk is an asset liability management problem. The liquidity, tenor, currency and amount of assets and liabilities on a hedge fund's balance sheet need to be optimized so that the fund has flexibility in its sources and uses of cash without creating a cash drag on the performance of the fund.

A fund might lose liquidity if its credit rating falls as a result of a rumor of fraud or insider trading. Liquidity may fall after a period of poor performance following a rush of redemptions. A fund is also exposed to liquidity risk if markets on which it depends for funding are subject to a loss of liquidity, such as the repo market.

In 2007–2008, the collapse of Bear Stearns and Lehman Brothers, along with the dramatic rise in uncertainty regarding the creditworthiness of many other financial institutions, caused the interbank lending markets to seize up and liquidity in the markets to fall dramatically. With financial institutions having difficulty funding themselves, and previously liquid markets evaporating, the market withdrew funding extended to counterparties, including hedge funds. When financing could not be rolled over, many funds had to sell positions at a loss in order to generate cash to repay margin loans and to meet other cash obligations. In this case, funding liquidity risk compounded market risk.

Funding liquidity risk is at its most insidious when it compounds other risks. Like the Horsemen of the Apocalypse, it never rides alone and can compound credit risk. Suppose a hedge fund has offsetting cash flows with two different counterparties on a given day (for example, it has a repo transaction with one broker which it has offset with another; that is, a back-to-backed repo transaction). If the counterparty to which the fund has lent the security fails to return it and then is late in paying its equivalent "buy-in" amount, the hedge fund will have to raise or draw on another source of cash to buy the security in the market to make good on its repayment of the security to another lender. Should it be unable to do so, it too will default.

In developing a risk management strategy, the liquidity and leverage of a hedge fund, including the impact of redemptions, the ability to liquidate assets, the impact of leverage on the portfolio, the availability of financing, and the potential impact of extreme events should be assessed. Each potential source of funding liquidity risk needs to be evaluated in regard to its probability of occurrence, singly and in concert with other risks to the investment portfolio, and its potential to create substantial losses to the fund. This will enable the fund manager to prioritize the risk management initiatives.

Redemptions Another source of funding liquidity risk can be a large increase in what are effectively cash liabilities. Both investor redemptions and margin increases must be met with cash or near-cash securities. Investors typically will want their payments in cash, while prime brokers may accept near-cash securities such as Treasury bills and notes as payments (though haircuts—discounts to market value—are typically applied). Unexpectedly frequent or large demands for cash payments can be highly disruptive to a hedge fund's investment strategy and can lead to its collapse.

A hedge fund's investor liquidity terms should match or be greater than the worst-case liquidity of the fund's investments. A fund investing to capitalize on long-term demographic themes, for example, should have long-term investor lock-ups (that is, three years initially, with annual redemptions thereafter but requiring 180 days' advance notice) to ensure that the fund can stay invested in the positions until the investment thesis has time to gestate and mature.

Other appropriate terms may include "gate" provisions that limit the amount investors can redeem at any given time. The investment terms of most hedge funds allow for the suspension of redemptions in extreme situations. In addition, the ability to differentiate between the claims investors may have on liquid and illiquid assets in the portfolio can provide fund managers with additional flexibility in a crisis; namely, the ability to put assets into "side-pockets" and structure the timing of investors' claims to those assets to best match the expected monetization of the investment thesis.

Hedge funds should consider the risk posed by the behavior of all investors in the fund, and even in the same fund family, which may adversely affect the stability of the business. Funds of funds have become notorious among hedge fund managers for their own poor asset liability management which, in 2008 and 2009, created losses for many funds they invested in. Many had given their investors the ability to redeem with as little as 30 days' notice but had invested in hedge funds with much longer investor lock-ups. When they were faced with large investor redemptions on short notice, they withdrew their investments in hedge funds that offered the most generous redemption terms. Hedge funds with the shortest investor-redemption terms and large investments from funds of funds effectively became the ATMs for the fund of funds industry. In addition, ongoing uncertainty regarding the level of such redemptions caused fund of funds managers to submit large redemption requests in advance to hedge funds with longer lock-up terms in case they needed to exercise those rights over the coming months. This then caused the hedge funds that received redemption notices to move to cash by selling assets in a down market and de-leveraging in anticipation of having to honor these redemption requests which, in many cases, ultimately did not materialize. Many high-net-worth investors and family offices acted similarly. Pension funds and endowment money proved slightly more patient.

The lesson learned was that in dislocated markets, investors may exhibit herding behavior by simultaneously seeking to redeem from a fund or range of funds. This may require a hedge fund to liquidate assets at an inopportune time, at a significant loss, or to suspend investors' redemption rights, gate the fund, pay investors with securities or to restructure the fund into a liquidating trust with multiple share classes that better match the liquidity of the fund's assets.

Margin Rate Increases, Liquidity and Leverage   Hedge funds obtain leverage through the use of derivatives, repo financing, and margin financing from prime brokers. Providers of leverage are comfortable extending financing because the amount of the loan to the fund is less than the liquidation value of the securities used as collateral for the loan. For example, to buy a security position worth US$10 million, a typical hedge fund would be required to post US$2 million in cash, while the prime broker puts the security into the account, effectively lending the fund US$8 million. However, the prime broker has the right to liquidate the US$10 million security if the hedge fund fails to maintain the cash margin in its account. If, say, the security drops in market value to US$9 million, US$1 million is deducted from the cash excess in the fund's prime-brokerage account and a US$1 million margin call is made on the hedge fund. If the hedge fund defaults on the margin payment, the broker has the immediate right to sell the collateral and recoup its principal.

In times of market stability, prime brokers are willing to accept less collateral against their lending. A hedge fund might be able to purchase the US$10 million security by posting only US$1 million margin, rather than US$2 million. However, the opposite is also true. If markets become increasingly volatile or illiquid, the prime broker can change the margin requirement on that same transaction to US$5 million. This would require the fund to post an additional US$3 million cash margin to maintain its US$10 million security position.

Leverage magnifies hedge fund investment risks and can exacerbate liquidity problems in market downturns. Given this, leverage is an inverse measure of the cushion of safety a manager has to ride out market volatility;

the higher the initial leverage, the shorter a hedge fund's staying power in an increasingly volatile market. Leverage also complicates the cash management of a hedge fund because of the manifold obligations to multiple creditors, counterparties and investors, and it can increase the risk to a fund from the actions of these parties. In particular, dependence on leverage creates the risk that the fund will be unable to meet its obligations should access to margin financing become limited as a result of broader market conditions.

In 2008–2009, the severe downturn in the global markets, the dramatic increase in volatility, the poor performance of many hedge fund strategies and the concomitant high level of redemptions from hedge fund investors, and the high funding costs reduced prime brokers' appetite to extend credit to hedge funds. Margin rates were increased and significantly increased the demands for cash from hedge funds, forcing many to de-lever and liquidate positions at a loss.

Hedge fund managers that have survived the credit crisis managed their funding liquidity risk well and were well aware of the risks that leverage posed to their investment strategies. Many survived the credit crisis because they used leverage judiciously, maintained high levels of unencumbered cash to meet unexpected demands in the form of margin calls or redemption requests or, where necessary, chose to gate their fund. In addition, many had negotiated margin lock-up agreements during the "Goldilocks" period before the crisis, thus ensuring they retained buying power for a period during the crisis. New hedge fund managers should clearly understand the restrictions on the continued availability of financing and alternatives available to replace existing leverage financing in case of market dislocation or problems with an existing leverage provider.

Margin Lock-ups   In the most basic terms, a margin lock-up or a "term commitment" is a credit facility extended by a prime broker to a hedge fund or other institutional client (See Chapter 5 for a complete discussion of lock-ups). There are several significant parts in a margin lock-up that can minimize the disruption to a hedge fund's investment strategy during a time of market stress and help the fund manage its funding-liquidity risk:

- Margin levels: Margin lock-ups prevent the prime broker from changing margin methodologies and collateral requirements for the term of the lock-up. This ensures relatively predictable and stable margins and thus helps in the process of managing funding liquidity.
- Obligation to clear trades: It is essential that the lock-up includes an obligation to continue clearing trades and to allow for collateral to be substituted for other collateral of similar risks. A prime brokerage arrangement is a demand facility, and the prime broker can normally

decide to stop clearing a hedge fund's trades at any time and for any reason. This is potentially highly disruptive, and could result in significant losses for a fund. If clearing trades is covered by the margin lock-up and the lock-up grants the fund the right to substitute security collateral with other collateral of the same value and similar risk at a constant margin rate, the fund can expect to continue to trade during the notice period without significant disruption to liquidity or trading. A sufficiently long notice period allows time for the fund to make alternative arrangements with other counterparties.

■ Termination events: Termination events can be very contentious in a margin lock-up negotiation. The termination events give the prime broker the right to terminate the lock-up without having to allow the notice period to expire. Such events include NAV triggers, where the lock-up can be terminated if performance declines more than 15 percent in a month or if more than 15 percent of investor funds are redeemed in a month. While such termination events are not unreasonable, they should be made objectively and not be unilateral judgments by the prime broker.

Measuring and Managing Funding Liquidity Risk Margin lock-ups and redemption terms that match the tenor of the hedge fund's investment portfolio are two of the four cornerstones of a funding liquidity risk framework (the other two being maintaining sufficient unencumbered cash and the judicious use of leverage). Certain techniques of asset liability management can be applied to assessing liquidity risk, and determining how much unencumbered cash to maintain and the prudent levels of leverage to use.

Anticipating Liquidity Stress Periods A simple test for liquidity risk is to look at future net cash flows on a day-by-day basis. The first step in this is to map each contractual future cash flow into and out of the fund's accounts into discrete 24-hour periods. Such transactions would include settlement and reset dates on all swaps transactions,[16] interest payments on fixed-income investments, options maturity and expiry or roll dates,[17] known dividend payments,[18] fees on stock borrows, certain corporate actions, certain investor redemptions, and so on. Any day that has a sizeable negative net cash flow is of immediate concern. The second step is to superimpose contingent cash flows onto this cash flow ladder. Any day that has a potential net negative cash flow arising from contingent obligations is also of concern.

Table 3.4 shows a sample cash flow map for a US$1-billion hedge fund trading bonds and equities via both swap and cash. It also trades OTC and exchange traded derivatives. These securities are cross-margined by their prime broker. Though the model extends over a three-month period, the

TABLE 3.4 Cash flow map

Assumptions

AUM	1,000,000,000	997,300,000	996,801,350	994,309,347	993,414,468
Performance	−0.270%	−0.050%	−0.250%	−0.090%	−0.380%
Margin Rate	30%	34%	30%	32%	35%
Unencumbered cash (% of AUM)	20%	20%	20%	20%	20%
Leverage (Gross)	4.17	3.68	4,17	3.91	3.57
Margin Posted	240,000,000	271,265,600	239,232,324	254,543,193	278,156,051
DAV (Minimum 3 months or 66 Business Days)	1	2	3	4	5
CONTRACTUAL CASH FLOWS					
Swaps Settlements (Initial Margin Inflows and Outflows)	(−118,750,000)	(−131,995,588)	(−139,552,189)	79,234,026	(−191,587,076)
Swap Resets	(−11,250,000)	64,897,831	44,856,061	(−16,312,888)	(−21,287,453)
Option Settlements					
Repo Settlements	2,666,666	1,466,619	(−498,400)	4,893,866	2,980,242
Stock Borrows	3,333,332	34,318,853	(−24,587,766)	9,243,971	17,668,585
Dividend (inflows)					
Interest (Inflows) from Debt Investments					0
Corporate Actions	8,333,333				
Investor Redemptions (30 Days' Notice)					
Investor Subscriptions					

(*continued*)

TABLE 3.4 (*Continued*)

Assumptions					
Certain Total Inflows/Outflows	(−115,666,669)	(−31,312,286)	(−119,782,294)	77,058,975	(−192,225,702)
Unencumbered Cash Available	200,000,000	199,460,000	199,360,270	198,861,869	198,682,894
Certain Cash (Surplus/Deficit)	84,333,331	168,147,714	79,577,976	275,920,845	6,457,192
CONTINGENT CASH FLOWS					
Investor Redemptions					
Investor Subscriptions					
Cash Securities Variation Margin		(−31,265,600)	32,033,276	(−15,310,869)	(−23,612,858)
Certain & Contingent Cash (Surplus/Deficit)	84,333,331	136,882,114	111,611,252	260,609,976	(−17,155,666)

table uses just five business days as an example. Daily performance is randomized but positively skewed in the model. The average margin rate for the fund is also randomized between a minimum of 30 percent (base margin rate) and a maximum of 35 percent as volatility, directionality, concentration and liquidity of the fund's positions will affect the average margin rate required. It assumes the fund maintains 20 percent of assets under management (AUM) in unencumbered cash daily.

In this scenario, on Day 5 unencumbered cash is reduced to only US$6.5 million because of the need to pay on settlement of several large losing swap positions, and after a week of slightly negative performance. This is acceptable but, under the contingent cash flows, should the prime-broker margins increase to the top of their range, the fund may have to pay a US$23.6-million margin call. To do so, it will have to pay the remaining US$6.5 million cash to the broker and liquidate positions to generate US$17.2 million of margin reduction. The potential liquidity gap is $17.2 million.

Recognizing that such a scenario is possible, the fund manager may want to de-lever somewhat over the coming week to generate slightly more excess cash to mitigate the potential liquidity gap. The advantage to evaluating his options before the cash is needed is that he can choose what positions to exit over a longer time period and better maximize his trading gains rather than take the chance that he may have to liquidate more on the fifth day when markets could be less favorable. This is where funding liquidity risk and portfolio liquidity risk intersect. The portfolio must be sufficiently liquid to generate the necessary cash to fill the liquidity gap.

At a minimum, knowing that such a cash shortfall is possible and that a selective liquidation of positions may be necessary on the fifth day, the risk manager should evaluate portfolio liquidity to ensure that sufficiently liquid positions are available to be exited without moving the market.

Figure 3.3 shows the liquidity profile of a hedge fund portfolio. On the vertical axis is the percentage of the gross market value of the portfolio that can be liquidated. On the horizontal axis is the number of days in the liquidation period. Maintaining the daily liquidity profile of the fund and evaluating it against potential cash needs is essential to managing any potential cash shortfall.

Assuming the portfolio is sufficiently liquid, the risk manager and the portfolio manager should agree which positions would be liquidated if it becomes necessary to do so by evaluating the liquidity of each position and risk factors specific to each position.

Scenario analysis-based contingency plans   As a static measure of liquidity risk, the liquidity gap gives no indication of how the gap would change under alternative conditions. Consequently, liquidity gap should be evaluated

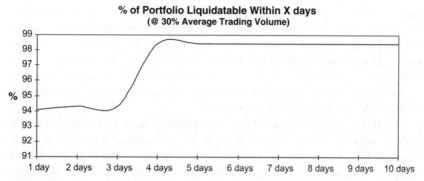

FIGURE 3.3   Portfolio liquidity

prospectively through the use of scenario analysis and that analysis should quantify the liquidity risk sensitivity and inform contingency plans. A hedge fund should undertake a contingency funding analysis that incorporates events that could rapidly affect the fund's liquidity, including a sudden inability to recall collateral from a prime broker, increasing collateral requirements and margin rates, the sudden redemption of a large group of investors, the collapse of a funding provider or an increase in other restrictive terms associated with secured borrowings.

Aside from performance and margin levels, investor redemptions and subscriptions are the other major variables affecting funding liquidity. While investors will give advance notice of redemptions and subscriptions, submitting a redemption notice is sometimes used by investors as a free option, enabling them to have the right but not the obligation to redeem or subscribe on the appointed date. Consequently, the actual number of redemptions and subscriptions cannot be known with certainty until the day they are due and the cash is wired in or out.

Table 3.5 extends the analysis to the week before the expiry of the redemption window and incorporates redemptions and subscriptions into the funding analysis. It assumes that US$140 million of subscriptions are certain and that no subscriptions are unlikely to be funded or contingent. Against this inflow, there are US$20 million of potential investor redemptions. Assuming stable performance and broker margins near the top of the range, there should be no shortfall in unencumbered cash at month-end when subscriptions and redemptions must be funded. The investment strategy should not therefore need to be disrupted.

Such an analysis then becomes the backbone of a process for liquidity stress testing whereby the contractual and contingent cash flows are

TABLE 3.5 Cash flow map (including redemptions and subscriptions)

Assumptions

AUM	984,270,505	983,483,089	984,663,269	983,383,206	986,235,018
Performance	−0.080%	0.120%	−0.130%	0.290%	0.320%
Margin Rate	32%	33%	35%	35%	34%
Unencumbered cash (% of AUM)	20%	20%	20%	20%	20%
Leverage (Gross)	3.91	3.79	3.57	3.57	3.68
Margin Posted	251,973,249	259,639,535	275,705,715	275,347,298	268,255,925
DAY (Minimum 3 months or 66 Business Days)	19	20	21	22	23
CONTRACTUAL CASH FLOWS					
Swaps Settlements (Initial Margin Inflows and Outflows)	205,312,676	73,761,232	15,824,945	40,037,745	65,265,553
Swap Resets	(−32,296,376)	(−55,879,721)	63,299,782	13,697,123	(−50,036,924)
Option Settlements				(−1,101,390,19)	(−2,830,494,50)
Repo Settlements	(−4,306,182)	4,693,896	4,219,985	5,619,332	(−5,221,244)
Stock Borrows	8,074,094	10,728,907	3,938,654	33,505,272	26,106,222
Dividend (Inflows)		111,759,442			
Interest (Inflows) from Debt Investments				29,501,496	
Corporate Actions			(−7,033,309)		

(continued)

TABLE 3.5 (Continued)

Assumptions					
Investor Redemptions (30 Days' Notice)					0
Investor Subscriptions					140,000,000
Certain Total Inflows/Outflows	176,784,211	145,063,756	80,250,057	121,259,577	173,283,112
Unencumbered Cash Available	196,854,101	196,696,618	196,932,654	196,676,641	197,247,004
Certain Cash (Surplus/Deficit)	373,638,312	341,760,373	277,182,711	317,936,219	370,530,116
CONTINGENT CASH FLOWS					
Investor Redemptions					(−20,000,000)
Investor Subscriptions					0
Cash Securities Variation Margin	(−15,440,836)	(−7,666,286)	(−16,066,180)	358,417	7,091,373
Certain & Contingent Cash (Surplus/Deficit)	358,197,476	334,094,087	261,116,531	318,294,636	357,621,489

supplemented with stress-testing regimes that incorporate multiple scenarios for market movements and redemptions over a given period of time.

Pertinent liquidity stress scenarios incorporate reduced performance, increased margins, increased and accelerated investor redemptions, and delayed and decreased subscriptions. Appropriate funding liquidity stress procedures should include:

- Map net cash flows on a day-to-day basis over a 90-day horizon.[19] This should be repeated iteratively but with varying degrees of leverage.
- Then assume a sudden and significant increase in market volatility and a related decline in market liquidity and that an important counterparty, such as a prime broker, significantly increases margin requirements.
- Then assume that, in addition, investor redemptions increase and subscriptions decline dramatically or cease.
- Lastly, assume in addition that, a counterparty fails and collateral and cash held at that counterparty are inaccessible.

This gives the risk manager, portfolio manager and CFO of the fund a tool to assess day-to-day cash flows under various scenarios and set aside sufficient unencumbered cash reserves to keep the fund solvent and avoid forced liquidation of invested positions assuming a target level of leverage.

Alternatively, such a model can also be used to determine a prudent degree of leverage given a fixed amount of unencumbered cash. It gives the fund insight into the funding risk different degrees of leverage can create in the event of market disruptions and increased margins from prime brokers.

Table 3.6 illustrates a funding liquidity stress test for our illustrative fund.

In this iteration, markets fall throughout the week, with margins progressively increasing as volatility and liquidity deteriorate. Swap settlements and resets become increasingly negative, with a few positive cash flows as the long biased positions dominate. Unencumbered cash is adequate in the first days of the week but progressively declines as the fund AUM declines. On the fifth day, certain swap settlements will overwhelm available unencumbered cash. Additionally, depending on how high and how fast prime broker margins increase, US$38 million of additional cash may be needed. To meet this cash requirement, the fund will have to exit positions at a loss. This can start a vicious cycle of negative performance, driving panicking investors towards redemption.

Table 3.7 shows the week up to and including the first redemption window. The crisis has continued throughout the month. The fund has lost over

TABLE 3.6 Funding liquidity stress test

SCENARIO: Market Crash w/Redemptions and Increased Margins

Assumptions					
AUM	1,000,000,000	980,100,000	980,384,080	961,266,398	942,041,070
Performance	−1.990%	0.080%	−2.000%	−2.000%	−4.910%
Margin Rate	32%	34%	35%	37%	39%
Unencumbered Cash (% of AUM)	20%	20%	20%	20%	20%
Leverage (Gross)	3.91	3.72	3.54	3.37	3.21
Margin Posted	256,000,000	263,450,880	276,844,723	234,873,220	293,134,543
DAY (Minimum 3 months or 66 Business Days)	1	2	3	4	5
CONTRACTUAL CASH FLOWS					
Swaps Settlements (Initial Margin Inflows and Outflows)	(112,500,000)	(53,599,219)	(95,919,787)	(113,852,616)	(172,562,940)
Swap Resets	(12,890,625)	(8,750,893)	6,255,638	(36,977,773)	(47,227,752)
Option Settlements					
Repo Settlements	(3,125,000)	(1,093,862)	(1)	(2,335,439)	4,843,871
Stock Borrows	(16,875,000)	(1,239,710)	(4,587,469)	32,436,642	(2,906,324)
Dividend (Inflows)					
Interest (Inflows) from Debt Investments					0

Corporate Actions	(−19,531,250)				
Investor Redemptions (30 Days' Notice)					
Investor Subscriptions					
Certain Total Inflows/Outflows	(−164,921,875)	(−64,683,683)	(−94,251,619)	(−120,729,187)	(−217,853,145)
Unencumbered Cash Available	200,000,000	196,020,000	196,176,816	192,253,280	188,408,214
Certain Cash (Surplus/Deficit)	35,078,125	131,336,317	101,925,197	71,524,093	(−29,444,931)
CONTINGENT CASH FLOWS					
Investor Redemptions					
Investor Subscriptions					
Cash Securities Variation Margin		(−7,450,830)	(−13,393,843)	(−8,028,497)	(−8,261,323)
Certain & Contingent Cash (Surplus/Deficit)	35,078,125	123,885,437	88,531,355	63,495,596	(−37,706,254)

TABLE 3.7 Funding liquidity stress test with redemptions

SCENARIO: Market Crash w/Redemptions and Increased Margins

Assumptions

AUM	613,742,120	594,777,489	583,417,239	566,439,797	543,272,409
Performance	−3.090%	−1.910%	−2.910%	−4.090%	−4.090%
Margin Rate	50%	50%	50%	50%	50%
Unencumbered Cash (% of AUM)	20%	20%	20%	20%	20%
Leverage (Gross)	2.50	2.50	2.50	2.50	2.50
Margin Posted	245,496,848	237,910,995	233,366,895	226,575,919	217,308,964
DAY (Minimum 3 months or 66 Business Days)	19	20	21	22	23
CONTRACTUAL CASH FLOWS					
Swaps Settlements (Initial Margin Inflows and Outflows)	0	(−9,813,829)	(−73,510,572)	(−15,293,875)	(−39,523,068)
Swap Resets	(−9,206,132)	(−13,382,493)	(−16,627,391)	3,823,469	(−17,113,081)
Option Settlements				1,416,098.49	(−782,313.27)
Repo Settlements	(−2,209,472)	(−2,408,849)	729,272	56,644	2,444,726
Stock Borrows	11,323,542	1,843,809	3,675,529	(−1,387,778)	(−9,778,903)
Dividend (Inflows)		44,608,312			
Interest (Inflows) from Debt Investments				0	

Corporate Actions			(−2,917,086)		(−20,000,000)
Investor Redemptions (30 Days' Notice)					0
Investor Subscriptions	(−92,061)	20,846,950			
Certain Total Inflows/Outflows			(−88,650,249)	(−11,385,441)	(−84,752,639)
Unencumbered Cash Available	122,748,424	118,955,498	116,683,448	113,287,959	108,654,482
Certain Cash (Surplus/Deficit)	122,656,363	139,802,448	28,033,198	101,902,518	23,901,842
CONTINGENT CASH FLOWS					
Investor Redemptions					(−210,000,000)
Investor Subscriptions					10,000,000
Cash Securities Variation Margin	12,948,091	7,585,853	4,544,100	6,790,977	9,266,955
Certain & Contingent Cash (Surplus/Deficit)	135,604,454	147,388,300	32,577,298	108,693,495	(−166,831,203)

45 percent of its AUM and prime brokers have now increased margins to 50 percent. Unencumbered cash has withered to US$109 million as AUM has declined. Investors have put in US$230 million-worth of redemption requests but have stated they may not redeem if the market starts to recover. A few potential investors have said they might start to average in and subscribe for US$10 million if they sense a bottom.

After meeting swap settlement obligations and other investment-related outflows, the fund will only have available cash to pay US$43 million of redemptions if required. Even if only a few investors have stated they are certain they will redeem US$20 million, the fund will be left with US$24 million of unencumbered cash. Of the remaining US$210 million of redemptions, if only US$23 million additional redemptions are demanded, the fund's unencumbered cash will be exhausted. Any amount over that will force the fund to liquidate positions at a loss. If there are no more sufficiently liquid security positions, the fund manager will be forced to gate the fund.

Analyses such as these cannot easily take into account all contingent cash flows, such as cash flows from derivatives or mortgage-backed securities, but they do help to reduce the degree of uncertainty regarding cash needs. If a hedge fund's cash flows are largely contingent and unpredictable, liquidity risk may be assessed using more complex forms of scenario analysis using Monte Carlo analysis to randomize the timing and magnitude of contingent cash flows.

Because hedge fund balance sheets differ so significantly from one fund to the next, there is little standardization in how such analyses are implemented. There are common elements to any measurement of funding liquidity risk, as shown above. The appropriate stress test should be prescribed by the risk manager drawing on his experience and knowledge of the specific terms in the hedge fund's governing documents with investors and counterparties.

To manage funding liquidity risk, it is important to:

- Diversify investors: Investors have different tolerances for periods of market stress and poor performance. Having a diversity of investors decreases the likelihood that a catastrophic withdrawal will disrupt the investment strategy of the fund or force the manager to gate the fund.
- Diversify funding providers: Liquidity providers to hedge funds are primarily prime brokers.
- Maintain sufficient unencumbered cash: Cash reserves ensure the fund's flexibility to meet various cash demands without having to rapidly liquidate the fund's security positions in a down market. Sufficient cash is that which ensures the fund's solvency in an extreme stress scenario.

TABLE 3.8 Generalized investor redemption term preference, by investor type

Investor Type	Investment Lock-up Terms (Days)						
	0–90	90–180	180–360	360–720	720–1,080	1,080+	Total
Pension Fund	0%	0%	25%	25%	25%	25%	100%
Endowment	0%	0%	0%	25%	25%	50%	100%
Sovereign Wealth Fund	0%	0%	0%	25%	25%	50%	100%
High-net-worth Individuals	5%	10%	25%	25%	20%	15%	100%
Fund of Funds	25%	25%	35%	15%	0%	0%	100%
Principals & Staff	0%	0%	25%	25%	25%	25%	100%

Diversifying the Investor Base   Hedge fund investors typically fall into the following types: endowments, pension funds, sovereign wealth funds, high-net-worth individuals, funds of funds, and principals of the fund itself. While each investor has different liquidity preferences, the general liquidity preferences by investor class are as set out in Table 3.8.

From a fund manager's perspective, optimal investor liquidity terms vary depending on the fund strategy. The minimum time legally required between investors' notice of redemption and cash payment of redemptions should equal or exceed the expected liquidation period of the hedge fund's assets. If this is not the case, then the fund runs the risk of having to liquidate its assets at below market rates (in essence, paying for liquidity), or gating the fund if investor redemptions are high. The liquidity profile of hedge fund assets varies depending on strategy, with distressed debt funds requiring the longest investor lock-up periods and high-velocity statistical arbitrage funds and CTAs the shortest.

Strategy aside, if the objective is simply to have a diversified investor base, the profile of a fund's investors might look as shown in Table 3.9.

TABLE 3.9 Ideal investor mix and maximum individual investment type

Investor class	% of fund AUM	Max. investor size as % of AUM
Pension Fund	20%	10%
Endowment	20%	10%
Sovereign Wealth Fund	20%	10%
High-net-worth Individuals	25%	5%
Fund of Funds	20%	10%
Principals & Staff	15%	10%

Diversifying Prime Brokers Prime brokers may withdraw financing by increasing margin rates, by ceasing or diminishing the amount of credit provided without changing margin rates, or simply by increasing the cost of that funding. An increase in margin rates may be caused by:

1. Deterioration in the fund's credit: The prime broker may perceive the fund as being a greater credit risk after a period of negative performance, reduced holdings of unencumbered cash, an increase in investor redemptions, or a regulatory sanction or investigation of the fund.
2. Decrease in quality of collateral: A prime broker may perceive the quality of the fund's collateral as deteriorating if the collateral posted becomes more concentrated in a specific issuer, industrial sector, less-liquid securities, or more-volatile securities, for example. Additionally, the collateral portfolio as a whole may become more directional and exposed to systematic risk. All of the above can arise out of conscious trading by the fund or simply because of changes in the relative market value of positions in the portfolio through time.
3. Deterioration in the broker's credit: Brokers earn their interest margin through the process of credit intermediation between the funding rates charged to the fund and the broker's cost of funding. If the broker should experience an increase in its cost of funds and is unable to pass that cost on to the fund, it may choose to withdraw funding rather than accept a decreased or negative interest margin.

If several prime brokers are providing liquidity and only one increases its costs of supplying liquidity, the impact of this on the fund will be reduced. When a hedge fund is growing and generating a stable performance, it may wish to establish durable, evergreen (that is, always available) liquidity lines of credit or committed financing facilities from its prime broker. The prime broker should have an appropriately high credit rating to increase the chances that the resources will be there when needed.

CONCLUSION

In this chapter, we defined the primary hedge fund strategies, discussed their differences and similarities, and developed a framework for categorizing them based on their unique characteristics. We also presented an integrated risk management model which defined in detail the risk types present in various hedge fund strategies, and presented a menu of basic strategies for analyzing, measuring and controlling each of those risks.

What follows in the next chapter is a discussion of the relative prioritization of risks within each hedge fund strategy as a function of their frequency of occurrence and ability to generate losses. We then review the statistical properties of hedge fund returns by strategy through the credit crisis of 2008. Together, this information can be used to establish a bespoke risk management strategy for a specific hedge fund based on its primary risks, its performance in the credit crisis, and given its strategy and unique operational set up.

ENDNOTES

1. "Directionality" means the extent to which the fund seeks to profit from the direction of the market overall. Equity Long short managers, for example, tend to be long biased and profit when the market rises, while convertible arbitrage funds are often fully hedged, have no directionality, and are indifferent to the direction of the market.
2. The IMF uses a flexible classification system for determining a country's "development" which considers (1) per-capita income level, (2) export diversification and (3) degree of integration into the global financial system. See "Q. How does the WEO categorize advanced versus emerging and developing economies?". International Monetary Fund. http://www.imf.org/external/pubs/ft/weo/faq.htm#q4b
3. The implication of a country being labeled as "frontier" is that, over time, the market will become more liquid and exhibit similar risk-and-return characteristics as the larger, more liquid, developed, emerging markets.
4. The TED spread is the difference between the interest rates on interbank loans and short-term U.S. government debt ("T-bills"). TED is an acronym formed from T-Bill and ED, the ticker symbol for the Eurodollar futures contract.
5. Dr. Robert Shiller, *Stock Market Data Used in Irrational Exuberance*, Princeton University Press, 2000, 2005, updated by Robert Shiller. Source: http://aida.econ.yale.edu/~shiller/data.htm.
6. "Understanding and Mitigating Operational Risk in Hedge Fund Investments." A Capco White Paper, March 2005
7. Capco Research and Working Paper, "Understanding and Mitigating Operational Risk in Hedge Fund Investments," 2002
8. Giraud, Jean-René. "The Management of Hedge Funds' Operational Risks." EDHEC Risk And Asset Management Research Center, April 2004.
9. *From Manhattan to Madoff: The Causes and Lessons of Hedge Fund Operational Failure*. CastleHall, 2009
10. The insider trading charges being leveled against Galleon Capital's Raj Rajaratnam in early 2010 and the SEC/FBI raids on hedge funds involved in "expert networks" demonstrate the increase in enforcement of insider trading rules.
11. Another source of danger for model-driven funds is the existence of market abnormalities and regulatory constraints that might force the liquidation of positions before they can be shown to be "right." Poor liquidity, often compounded

by the ability of the market to guess the position of a large relative value player, also contributes to the difficulties of model-driven funds. Consider, for instance, the case of a credit arbitrage fund that, on the basis of a perfectly sound model, concluded that traded bond vs. CDS basis was high, and entered large mean-reversion trade to exploit this anomaly. If the market became aware of these positions, and if, perhaps because of the poor liquidity mentioned above, the fund had to try to unwind these positions before it reverted to the mean, the latter could experience a very painful short squeeze.

12. Front-running and tailgating is the practice of buying or selling securities for an individual's personal account before executing a larger order for a client that will likely cause the price to move in one's favor.

13. The Manhattan Fund was founded by Michael Berger in 1996. Berger raised US$600 million over four years from investors who, like him, wanted to take out a sort of "insurance" against a market downturn. The problem, of course, was that this market downturn didn't come soon enough for Berger and his investors.

   The cost of maintaining short positions accumulated. As losses mounted, Berger began to cook the books by submitting fake holdings data to his administrator. That administrator trusted Berger's data since they purportedly came directly from the fund's introducing broker—a small Ohio firm that in turn used Bear Stearns as its prime broker. However, the Manhattan Fund accounted for a significant portion of the introducing broker's revenue—leading some to believe that it was too quick to acquiesce to Berger's demands. One of those demands was to accept the holding data submitted by Berger.

   For a colorful and complete telling of the Manhattan Fund story, see "Does Regulation Prevent Fraud? The Case of Manhattan Hedge Fund" by Chidem Kurdas.

14. Many funds publicize their Sharpe ratios, and dampening volatility can both falsely influence the Sharpe ratio, as well as incorrectly imply higher returns.

15. From a hedge fund investor's perspective, a full-service fund administrator that prepares a complete set of accounting records is preferable to an administrator that only reviews the fund's own accounting records (known as "NAV Lite") and does not re-price all the securities in the portfolio.

16. Swap settlement dates are generally two business days from trade date, provided that is also a New York and or London business day. If not, the settlement rolls to the next New York business day.

17. Where the maturity date of the option is known (that is, the option is European) and the expiry date of the option if it is exchange traded.

18. Dividends can be declared at any time and are typically paid one week to one month after announcement. While payments tend to occur on the last day of the week, payments can be scheduled to occur at any time.

19. The time horizon should be equal to or greater than the time from the start of the crisis to the trough and incorporate at least one investor redemption window. The three-month assumption used here is reasonable for many historical market crises and most fund redemption windows but will not necessarily be long enough to encompass all crises and fund redemption windows.

CHAPTER 4

Analysis of the Risk/Return Profile of Hedge Fund Strategies

In Chapter 3, we surveyed the primary hedge fund strategies and described their implementation. In addition, we presented an integrated risk management model, developed a detailed lexicon of hedge fund risk types, and the primary strategies and techniques for managing these risks. The following chapter goes deeper into the specific risks of each strategy by prioritizing each risk type according to its frequency of occurrence and magnitude of potential loss. Real-life examples are presented and discussed.

The performance of each strategy as represented by industry standard hedge fund return indices is statistically analyzed to characterize each strategy's performance over time, with particular focus on the recent credit crisis in 2008.

Collectively, the information in Chapters 3 and 4 can be used to customize a hedge fund risk management strategy to an individual fund's specific risks.

OPPORTUNISTIC STRATEGIES

As the name indicates, such strategies seek to profit opportunistically from fundamental themes, inefficiencies and dislocations in the financial markets at a macro, market sector, stock specific, factor, or even exchange level. Depending on their conviction about the fundamental themes influencing the market or their market sector, opportunistic funds may go significantly long or short the market as a whole, creating directionality in their returns. Under this category, we will discuss global macro, equity long/short, emerging-markets, and sector focused strategies.

Global Macro Strategies

The global macro approach to investing attempts to exploit anticipated macroeconomic events, perceived global macroeconomic dislocations[1] or trends and generate outsized positive returns by making leveraged bets on price movements in equity, currency, interest rate, and commodity markets. Global macro portfolios can hold long and short positions in world capital markets for stocks, bonds, currencies, futures, and their derivatives. Macro funds implement positions that incur broad exposure to equity markets, sovereign and corporate fixed income market term structures, and currencies. Term structure exposures arise from exposure to U.S., U.K., and Japanese yield curves and positions intended to profit from yield curve parallel shifts, steepening, flattening, and/or twisting. Currency exposures are primarily to European, U.K. and Japanese currencies. All positions are intended to be opportunistically timed to benefit from global economic trends and sovereign macroeconomic policy changes.

Risks of Macro Strategies Figure 4.1 describes the relative significance and frequency of risks faced by managers following a global macro strategy. Among the risks confronting these funds, systematic risk has the highest potential negative impact on returns because of the nature and size of their exposures. However, the frequency of macro hedge funds incurring significant drawdowns from sovereign risk events is relatively low, as the skill of macro managers generally lies in timing their exposures in such a way as to profit from upside opportunities while avoiding downside risks. That said, macro funds were hit hard in the 1990s by the U.S. rate increases in 1994

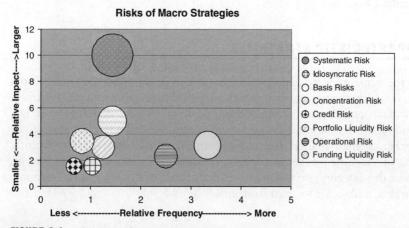

FIGURE 4.1 The risks of macro strategies

and the Russian credit crisis of 1998, where they experienced double-digit drawdowns. They were able to generally avoid fallout from the Asian crisis in 1997, the dot-com bubble of 2000–01, September 11, 2001, and the credit crisis of 2007–08.

The second most important risk these funds face is basis risk arising from their significant exploitation of relative value opportunities, where two similar assets are paired on the long and short sides to exploit perceived relative mis-pricings. Examples include U.S. mortgage agency versus U.S. Treasury-basis trades, asset swap spread narrowing, U.K. Gilts versus U.K. inflation-linked bonds, crude oil futures versus natural gas futures, the Euro versus the U.S. dollar, or East European equities versus U.S. equities. The risk is that the two assets do not converge in value as expected but diverge further, with the long asset falling in value while the short asset rises in value, creating losses on both sides of the trade. The frequency of dramatic changes in basis is low but significant anomalies can occur and persist because of changes in market structure, particularly changes in liquidity due to a sudden change in the willingness of market participants and investors to make a two-way market.

The most infamous case of basis risk torpedoing a global macro fund to date is when Long-Term Capital Management (LTCM) lost US$4.6 billion in September 1998 (see Appendix 2). LTCM had consistently profited from mis-pricings between different sovereign bonds. For example, it would sell U.S. Treasury securities and buy Italian bond futures. The idea behind the trade was that because Italian bond futures had a less liquid market, in the short term they would have a higher return than U.S. bonds, but in the long term, the prices would converge. To exploit this opportunity, LTCM used significant leverage, which was readily provided by its brokers since the Italian and U.S. bonds backing the loan where of high quality and the correlation historically stable.

However, when Russia defaulted on its debt on August 17, 1998, nervous investors fled to higher quality securities, selling their non-U.S. Treasury debt and buying U.S. Treasuries. The price of U.S. Treasuries began to increase because there were many buyers, and the price of non-U.S. bonds began to decrease because there were many sellers. This caused the difference between the prices of U.S. Treasuries and other bonds to increase, contrary to LTCM's expectations.

The third most significant risk is operational risk, which is elevated because of the significant use of derivatives and then multiplied by the global nature of the macro investments. A truly global macro strategy is exposed to operational risk if its infrastructure is not fully automated, has systems limitations, is not globally scalable, and relies on inaccurate, stale, or incomplete data. Many global macro managers have come from either a larger hedge fund or an institution with a huge infrastructure.

One global fund had a steady track record of over 20 percent per annum for many years, with a quadrupling of assets under management in the two years preceding its blowup. The growth led the manager to expand into new markets and strategies. However, his new investments could not be supported by the existing risk management system. The results were returns below and more volatile than those of his peers and those promised to investors. This then led to a 90 percent decline in assets in less than a year.

The final important risk facing macro funds is funding liquidity risk, which arises from their reliance on higher leverage to produce significant returns from small security mis-pricings. In particular, they make extensive use of the low margin charged and high leverage provided by futures exchanges, futures commodity merchants, and the very low haircuts applied to G-10 debt by brokerage repo desks to lever up their trades. While large changes in these margin levels are infrequent, they can lead to significant losses if the fund is forced to liquidate positions in a crisis because of a margin increase.

Despite these risks, the investment benefits of the macro hedge-fund strategy are evident when compared to the performance of passive indices. Figure 4.2 shows the annual performance of the Eurekahedge[2] Macro Fund Index in comparison to the Standard & Poor's 500 Index. Note the ability of the macro fund index to outperform the S&P 500 in years when the S&P 500 return was negative.

Performance of Macro Strategies   From January 2000 to January 2010, global macro hedge funds have posted an average annualized return of 10.56 percent, with an annualized standard deviation of 4.5 percent. The cumulative return of the Macro Hedge Index over the 10-year period was

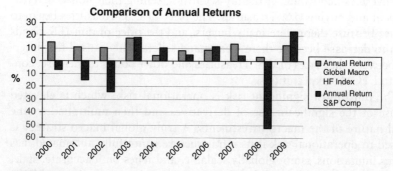

FIGURE 4.2   Eurekahedge Global Macro Index annual returns vs. S&P 500
Source: Eureka Hedge, Shiller

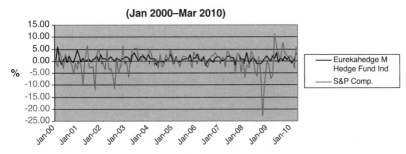

FIGURE 4.3 Eurekahedge Global Macro Index monthly returns vs. S&P 500
Source: Eureka Hedge, Shiller

105.6 percent, while the return of the S&P was −25.2 percent,[3] which demonstrates the skill of macro-fund managers in timing their moves and their ability to change exposures opportunistically. The macro funds outperformed primarily because they avoided significant drawdowns during the dot-com crash, 9/11, and the credit crisis of 2008. Furthermore, the returns generated by the S&P 500 index for the same period were more than five times more volatile. The standard deviation of S&P 500 returns was 22.85 percent for the same period.

This lower annual volatility and ability to avoid negative significant annual returns draws develops from the lower volatility of monthly returns, as shown in Figure 4.3.

The returns from global macro funds also exhibited one of the lowest correlations to the S&P 500 monthly returns (0.25) of any hedge fund strategy evaluated in this book. Since 2000, macro funds have returned a positive performance in every year, while the S&P posted negative returns in four out of the 10 years. The distribution of monthly returns is positively skewed (0.58) while that of the S&P 500 is significantly negatively skewed (−1.4) for the same time period. Kurtosis is low compared to the S&P for the same period (1.2 vs. 5.6), indicating more consistent monthly returns.

Equity Long/Short Strategies

Long/short equity hedge funds usually hold a combination of long and short positions in equities, while maintaining an overall long or short bias with respect to the market.[4] Managers seek to exploit investment opportunities by using leverage, selling short, and hedging market risks. Typically, a manager will hold a set of core long equity positions and hedge these with short sales of other stocks or short futures or hedge with options on a related stock index. There are many difficulties with managing long/short funds. The major difficulty is that to make money the hedge fund must successfully predict which stocks will perform better. Most investors grossly underestimate the difficulty of this task. It requires making intelligent use of the available information, but this is not enough—it also requires making better use of the available information than large numbers of capable investors and then having sufficient conviction in the rigor of the analysis to use significant leverage to take large positions in those securities. Additional difficulties include estimating and hedging the risks to which a portfolio is exposed, and the requirement to manage unsuccessful positions in an active manner.

The mandate to short specific stocks gives the manager access to sources of alpha that a long-only manager, by definition, cannot exploit. Firstly, skill in stock selection enables managers to identify and go long securities of companies expected to outperform their peers while going short securities of companies expected to underperform. This enables a potential doubling of alpha from one primary investment insight while neutralizing some of the market risk (though doubling the stock specific risk). Secondly, by lending out the stock and going short, the manager gains access to another source of return by earning interest on the short while collecting the short rebate.

Equity long/short is by far the most common strategy in the hedge fund industry but also one of the most heterogeneous. Funds may often have a regional focus. They also tend to concentrate their exposures to a greater extent than conventional funds, either to a preferred industrial sector or fundamental equity style (value, growth, size, or momentum). The positions held by these hedge funds can be extremely dynamic, since their mandates provide a great deal of flexibility to change the portfolio dynamically as investment opportunities arise. Consequently, their market and factor exposures can vary substantially depending upon the manager's outlook and strategy, and on immediate market conditions. For example, a typical U.S. hedge fund may have been concentrated in technology stocks with a momentum tilt during the 2000–01 tech bubble. However, during the subsequent technology bust, this hedge fund may have switched holdings to value or large cap stocks.

Risks of Equity Long/Short Strategies Figure 4.4 describes the relative significance and frequency of risks faced by managers following an equity long/short strategy. Concentration and idiosyncratic risks are linked and together have the greatest potential impact. Many of the risks associated with a long/short strategy revolve around the manager's ability to pick the "right" stocks to buy long and sell short to profit from idiosyncratic risk and then concentrating the fund's exposure through leverage on the highest-conviction positions. Generally, there are many more long positions than short positions, resulting in the short side being more concentrated.

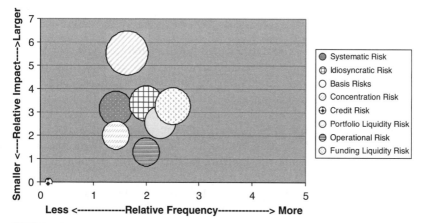

FIGURE 4.4 Risks of long/short strategies

The frequency with which these concentrated stock picks on the long and short side result in losses depends on the manager's skill. However, more concentrated exposure on the short side has the potential to be more problematic because of the potential for losses on the short side to be unlimited.

For example, if the fund is of the view that the price of a specific U.S. equity is overvalued based on the poor quality of its earnings and wishes to take advantage of a price decline, going short allows the fund to profit from this expectation, with the fund manager borrowing a specific number of shares of the company's stock from the prime broker and then selling the stock short (say at US$100 per share). If the fund manager has made the right call and the price declines, he will then repurchase the stock at the lower price (say US$80 per share). The manager uses these shares to repay the prime broker, while keeping the difference (a profit of US$20 per share). But what if the stock rallies and the short position move in the "wrong" direction? The short positions in the fund carry asymmetric risk compared to long positions, since profit on a short position is limited to the difference between the price at which the stock was sold and zero, but the loss on the same short position is potentially infinite. In comparison, the maximum potential loss on a long position is the investment itself.

Some of the key concentration risks are related with the "short leg" of the long/short strategy. Short positions that are losing money grow to become an increasingly large part of the portfolio, and their price can increase without limit. Furthermore, short positions can be subject to short "squeezing" and the risk of the lender "recalling" the borrowed stock as well as increased borrowing costs. Concentrated short positions require much focused active management in order for their risks to be managed.

VOLKSWAGEN SHORT SQUEEZE

In early October 2008, about 100 hedge funds shared the view that Volkswagen shares were overvalued on a fundamental basis and were ripe to fall. At that time, VW's stock was trading around €200 per share. Funds rumored to have this short position included many of leaders of the long/short equity community such as Odey Asset Management LLC, SAC Capital Advisors LLC, Glenview Capital, Marshall Wace, Tiger Asia, Perry Capital and Highside Capital. To these managers, there was simply no reason for VW shares to keep going up, and the funds bet on it by shorting huge amounts of VW stock, borrowing it from existing owners and selling it into circulation, waiting for the price drop they considered inevitable. It is estimated that the total short positions in VW equaled more than 13 percent of VW's outstanding shares.

On October 26, 2008, Porsche Automobil Holding SE (Porsche), a European public company and German automobile manufacturer, announced that it owned directly, or had the right under cash settled options to purchase, 74.1 percent of Volkswagen's stock. VW's stock price immediately rose on the announcement. Because the German State of Lower Saxony controlled more than 20 percent of VW, only about six percent of VW shares were available for purchase on the open market to cover the hedge fund's short positions. A dramatic "short squeeze" ensued as hedge funds scrambled to cover their short positions. VW's stock price soared from around €200 to more than €1,000 per share at the height of the squeeze on October 28, 2008. VW temporarily surpassed ExxonMobil to become the biggest company by stock market value. Some fund managers were reportedly in tears as they realized the scale of their losses—estimated to be as high as €30 billion.

While many managers employ position limits to control concentrated stock specific risk, these limits tend to be high and still allow for up to 20 percent of the fund's assets to be invested in securities of a common issuer. In addition, concentrations in particular sectors, countries, or investment themes on both the long and short sides can create further concentrations.

A secondary material risk for this strategy is linked to the potential for concentrated idiosyncratic risk. The liquidity of the portfolio has a direct impact on the fund manager's ability to manage its risk dynamically. Generally, the more concentrated a position, the larger it is. The larger the position, the less liquid it tends to be. The manager's ability to enter/exit a position with minimal market impact directly affects profitability. This risk can be magnified if a manager provides fund investors with generous liquidity terms and receives significant redemptions of fund assets in a short period. The liquidity of a manager's underlying securities can also have an impact on friction or trading costs and affect net returns. Generally, portfolio liquidity risk is infrequent but, as in the Volkswagen case above, it can have significant impact.

Thirdly, basis risk[5] is present but generally of lesser potential impact. The impact is reduced by the tendency of long/short equity managers to use, and for prime brokers to provide, less leverage for positions or portfolios with volatile basis relationships between long and short positions. Fundamental long/short equity also tends to run, on average, between one and three times leverage, with strategies involving less basis risk tending to utilize higher levels of leverage. Importantly, strategies involving less basis risk will tend to call for more leverage in order to generate returns.

Lastly, the frequency and impact of systematic risk is lower than for macro strategies because many equity long/short managers follow the discipline of full or partial hedging of market risk. The potential negative impact on returns from systematic risk varies depending on the nature and size of a given fund's exposures. Long/short equity managers do not typically manage a market-neutral portfolio and are therefore exposed to a certain degree of market exposure (long or short), depending on the portfolio's net exposure at a given time. This exposure also varies depending on the long equity portfolio's beta relative to that of the short equity portfolio. Long/short equity managers often measure the beta-adjusted net exposure to help gauge the level of market risk.

In general, U.S. equity long/short funds are exposed to systematic risks similar to those of the Russell 3000 Index. Stock momentum, size, volatility, whether the stock is a growth or value stock as well as dividend yield, earnings yield, earnings variability, leverage and liquidity are all sources of systematic risk in such strategies. A fund's industry and regional preferences may also affect its systematic risk exposure. For example, a European long/short equity fund's systematic risks would be better represented by the standard MSCI Europe Index.

The benefits and risks of equity long/short strategies manifest themselves in the annual returns of the Eurekahedge Global Long/Short hedge-fund index, as shown in Figure 4.5.

Performance of Equity Long/Short Strategies   From January 2000 to January 2010, equity long/short hedge funds have posted an average annualized return of 10.15 percent, with an annualized standard deviation of 12.7 percent. Cumulative return of the Equity Long/Short Hedge Fund Index over

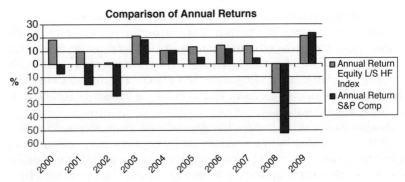

FIGURE 4.5 Eurekahedge Equity Long/Short Hedge Fund Index annual returns vs. S&P 500
Source: Eureka Hedge, Shiller

the 10-year period was 101.5 percent, while the return of the S&P was −25.2 percent.[6] Demonstrating their managers' timing and judgment, the funds outperformed primarily because they exceeded S&P 500 returns in most years and avoided significant drawdowns during the dot-com crash and following 9/11. However, like most of the strategies discussed in this book, they were unable to avoid drawdowns during the credit crisis of 2008, though their losses were less than half that of the S&P 500. Furthermore, the returns generated by the S&P 500 index for the same period were almost twice as volatile.

A comparison of monthly returns, as shown in Figure 4.6, shows the higher correlation of equity long/short strategies to the broader equity market.

Compared to other hedge fund strategies, the returns of equity long/short funds returns exhibited a higher correlation to the S&P monthly

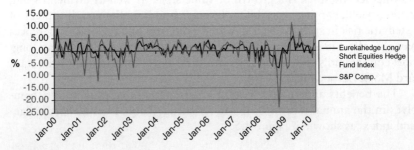

FIGURE 4.6 Eurekahedge Equity Long/Short Hedge Fund Index monthly returns vs. S&P 500 (January 2000–January 2010)
Source: Eureka Hedge, Shiller

returns (0.67) and the overall equity market. Since 2000, macro funds have returned a positive performance in nine out of the 10 years, while the S&P posted negative returns in four of those years. However, the distribution of monthly returns is slightly negatively skewed (−0.28) while that of the S&P 500 is significantly so (−1.4) for the same period. Kurtosis is lower than for the S&P for the same period (2.1 vs. 5.6), indicating more consistent returns and fewer outliers in the return distribution.

Sector-focused Equity Long/Short Strategies

Sector-focused equity long/short funds are funds that exploit opportunities in one sector only. Common sector foci are technology, healthcare/biotech, financials, media, telecom, and energy/commodities.

The risks attaching to these funds are very similar to equity long/short funds as a whole, with the exception of concentration risk. The potential impact of concentration risk is higher because all positions are in a specific industrial sector, increasing the magnitude of potential losses in the event of a sector-specific disruption.

When the dot-com bubble burst, tech-focused funds suffered. Similarly, in the credit crisis, funds focused on the financial sector floundered, despite their mandated ability to go short and, in part, due to the temporary banning of shorting of selected financial sector stocks in the U.S. The ban was imposed by the Securities and Exchange Commission on September 18, 2008 in an effort to take some downward pressure off the financial sector stocks that were considered most vulnerable in the credit crisis. The ban was originally designed to expire on October 2 but was extended to at least three business days beyond the passage of the US$700 billion government bailout package on October 9, 2008.

While it is difficult to determine the exact impact short-selling had, several financial sector focused funds, including Second Curve Capital, suffered large drawdowns during October 2008. In 2006, the New York-based fund had been a standout performer, with one of its three investment portfolios posting an eye-popping 68 percent gain and rising to over US$800 million in AUM. But by 2007, the air started coming out of Brown's fund fast, as several big long positions on subprime lenders fell dramatically. Second Curve's three investment portfolios were down an average of 40 percent by July 2007. With their long positions in financial stocks falling and a relative inability to go short financials, the fund lost over 50 percent in 2008 and its AUM dropped to less than US$200 million.

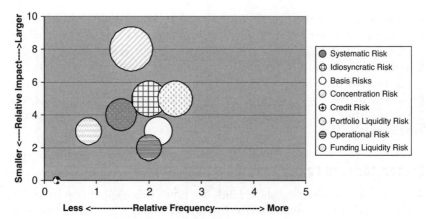

FIGURE 4.7   Risks of sector-focused long/short strategies

As the case of Second Curve shows, sector-focused long/short funds face greater sector concentration risks because of their focus on a narrow economic sector. Figure 4.7 summarizes the risks of sector-focused long/short strategies. They are similar to those of broader long/short strategies with the exception that concentration risk is typically greater.

Emerging Market Strategies

Funds within this category invest in equity, debt, foreign exchange, and derivative securities of "developing" and "frontier" sovereign governments and corporations. These securities may be listed in the domestic market or internationally. Hedge funds investing in developing markets extend increasingly sophisticated versions of alternative investment strategies previously deployed in only developed markets, the commonality being that effective alpha generation in developing markets requires specific knowledge of the progressively sophisticated regulations, market structure, political economy, and investors in the local market. In addition, the ability to go short a security, purchase and trade derivatives, obtain leverage and freely transfer funds in and out of the country are often prerequisites for deploying traditional strategies in developing markets.

Many frontier markets do not allow short selling and do not offer derivative securities. Consequently, the ability to hedge and form precise alpha-generating strategies is limited and frontier funds typically hold only long positions or have a long bias toward emerging market beta. Within developing markets, funds most often follow long/short equity strategies,

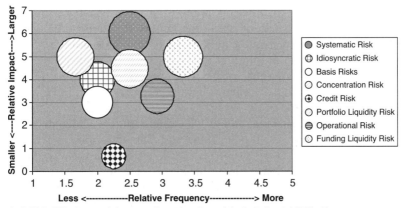

FIGURE 4.8 Risks of emerging market strategies[7]

interest rate relative value strategies, credit relative value strategies and macro strategies with a regional focus.

Risks of Emerging Market Strategies   The risks inherent in emerging market strategies are illustrated in Figure 4.8.

Systematic risk exposure is high because of long-biased directional exposure to emerging market (EM) equity indices and emerging market bonds. In addition, contagion effects triggered by global capital flows in market crises have tended historically to increase correlation and undermine even the most effectively hedged strategies. The returns of emerging market hedge funds are more volatile than for many other strategies because emerging markets themselves tend to be more volatile than developed markets while market sophistication often limits the tools available to hedge emerging market risk. While international banks will write variance and volatility swaps, sovereign credit default swaps or deep out-of-the-money puts on the major developing country indices, it has proven difficult to roll these tail-event hedges in the midst of a crisis. Often, the most liquid and persistent market for hedging is the international currency market. Despite typically hedging out their currency risks, emerging market hedge funds cannot fully avoid being fundamentally long emerging market sovereign risk and, therefore, being highly exposed to systematic risk. Consequently, systematic risk is the most significant risk in an emerging market strategy.

To mitigate risks, emerging market hedge funds attempt to diversify idiosyncratic risk but this has not always proven to be highly effective in crisis periods. Ensuring a sufficient supply of attractive shares remains a key challenge for the growth of equity markets in developing counties. A common problem is that many sectors of the economy do not have listed companies, so investors are limited in their access. In smaller emerging market economies, the number of firms of a size large enough to merit listing on the stock exchange remains limited. Countries such as Hungary and Ecuador have between 30–40 listed companies, compared to nearly 500 in Brazil, 2,000 in China, and 5,000 in India. In the major developing markets such as Brazil, Russia, India and China, although the number of firms listed on these countries' stock exchanges is substantial, many of them have low float ratios. This makes their stock less attractive because investors hold a minority interest only and are more vulnerable to manipulation by controlling shareholders. Many large firms are formerly state-owned, and governments retain majority shares. Others are controlled by founding families.

Achieving diversification in the domestic bond markets is also challenging. Not only are there relatively few domestic corporate bond issuers, but the price relationship between publicly and privately issued bonds is complex. A well-developed market for government debt provides a benchmark yield curve for private sector bonds, yet corporate bonds may be unattractive in a market saturated with government debt, which is widely regarded as carrying a lower default risk.

Diversification is also difficult to achieve across developing and frontier emerging markets. Foreign investors are an important source of liquidity, but are volatile, with funds flowing in and out in response to changes in conditions in OECD economies. Therefore, unless the majority of demand for domestic bonds and equities comes from domestic sources, increased risk aversion by foreign investors can undermine intra-market and inter-market diversification. Intra-market correlation can be higher in emerging markets than in developed markets, leading to inadvertent concentrations and higher idiosyncratic risk arising from sudden changes in correlations. In addition, increasing inter-market correlations (regional contagion) have been evident in most, if not all, emerging market crises. Typically, problems in one country form the epicenter of a shock that ripples outward to that country's trading partners before diminishing in magnitude. For diversification to be effective in an emerging markets portfolio, it should be across geographic regions and trading blocs.

Portfolio liquidity risks can be significant in emerging market hedge funds, as they invest in developing and frontier markets with less depth than many developed markets. In their search for undiscovered, under-researched, undervalued and yet-to-be-exploited inefficiencies, emerging market managers may buy less-liquid securities, becoming effectively liquidity providers in many emerging markets and consequently being long liquidity. However, capital flows into and out of emerging markets are cyclical and sometimes reverse violently, especially in frontier markets. Emerging market hedge funds typically are long liquidity and bear significant portfolio liquidity risks because of the transient nature of foreign funding.

In addition, EM hedge funds face higher funding liquidity risk. Prime brokers' margins incorporate functions that increase margins dynamically as market characteristics change. These characteristics include stock liquidity, credit spreads, and sovereign credit ratings. Regardless of whether a hedge fund has its margin rules locked up, the margin rates on EM securities themselves typically are not fixed. Margins on emerging market assets can rapidly increase as a function of those rules since, in a crisis, liquidity becomes one way, credit spreads on debt widen, and EM sovereigns are downgraded. Prime brokers also have the right to withdraw all financing for any country where they feel their legal ability to obtain a secured interest in an EM asset pledged as collateral by a hedge fund client is undermined. Regime changes or anti-foreign sentiment can result in foreign claims on assets in emerging markets being weakened. In such cases, a prime broker may choose to withdraw financing of assets in those countries entirely. Lastly, a prime broker will withdraw financing on any security which they cannot value transparently on a daily basis.

Another materially heightened risk is operational risk, where geographical distance makes the monitoring of investments more difficult. The subsequent need to rely on domestic brokers and custodians in multiple emerging markets, the challenges presented for valuing certain assets, and the complexities (sometimes vagaries) of local regulations and regulators all compound operational risk.

Performance of Emerging Market Strategies   Despite the credit crisis of 2008 being mostly a developed economy phenomenon, hedge funds with an emerging market focus could not deliver, on average, positive returns in 2008. The performance of emerging market strategies compared to the MSCI Emerging Markets Index is shown in Figure 4.9.

From January 2000 to January 2010, emerging market hedge funds posted an average annualized return of 16.23 percent, with an equally high annualized standard deviation of 16.31 percent. The cumulative return of the Emerging Market Hedge Fund Index over the 10-year period was 162.25 percent, while the return of the MSCI EM Index was 93.3 percent.[8] Emerging market funds outperformed primarily because they were able to preserve capital when EM markets fell. Drawdowns on EM funds were not as significant as those on the MSCI Emerging Market index during the

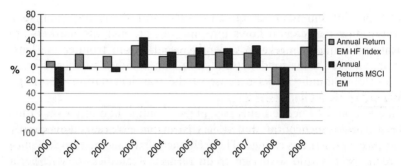

FIGURE 4.9   Eurekahedge Emerging Markets Index annual returns vs. MSCI
Emerging Markets Index
Source: Eureka Hedge, Bloomberg

dot-com crash, 9/11, and the credit crisis of 2008. Furthermore, the returns
generated by the MSCI Emerging Markets index for the same period were
almost two-and-a-half times as volatile.

These characteristics persist when monthly returns are examined, as
shown in Figure 4.10.

Compared to other strategies, the returns of emerging market hedge
funds exhibited a very high correlation to their benchmark, MSCI EM
Index monthly returns (0.90) and the overall equity market. Since 2000,
emerging market funds have returned a positive performance in nine out of
the 10 years, while the MSCI EM index has posted negative returns in four
out of those years. The distribution of monthly returns is slightly negatively
skewed (−0.87) but better than that of the MSCI EM index (−0.99) for

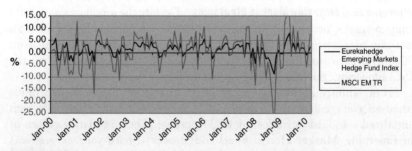

FIGURE 4.10   Eurekahedge Emerging Market Hedge Fund Index monthly returns
vs. MSCI Emerging Markets Index (January 2000–January 2010)
Source: Eureka Hedge, Shiller

the same period. Furthermore, kurtosis is lower (1.53 vs. 2.55), which is consistent with the observation that EM managers were able to mitigate losses in the significant market crises of the past decade.

EVENT DRIVEN STRATEGIES

Event driven strategies are strategies where the underlying investment opportunity and risk are associated with a corporate event. The securities prices of the companies involved in these events are more influenced by the idiosyncratic outcomes relating to the particular event than to the change in value of the general debt or equity markets. Practitioners of event driven strategies rely on fundamental research that extends beyond valuation of the securities of a single company to issues that affect a restructuring industry, the identification of potential distressed, target and/or acquiring companies, and an assessment of the legal and structural issues likely to be encountered as events unfold. Such strategies incorporate an analysis of risk-arbitrage, distressed, and activist strategies.

Risk Arbitrage Strategies

Risk arbitrage funds (also known as "merger arbitrage funds") profit from managing the spread that can be extracted from unconsummated merger and acquisition deals. In stock-swap mergers, the portfolio manager typically goes long the equity of the company targeted for acquisition (the target) and simultaneously goes short the equity of the company making the acquisition (the acquirer). In cash tender offers, the portfolio manager only has to go long the stock of the target to capture the premium.

The investment cycle starts when a company releases an announcement to the news services or the news services report a rumor announcing that an acquirer wishes to buy the stock of a target. This is often followed by a same-day conference call, stating whether the bid is 1) friendly or hostile; 2) a definitive cash agreement (having board approval), a letter of intent, or proposal; 3) for cash or stock, or a combination of both, and whether this is subject to adjustment; 4) a tender offer (lasting 30 days) or requiring a shareholder vote (lasting four to six months); and 5) subject to certain conditions—due diligence, financing, anti-trust, or regulatory approval. The portfolio manager or analyst then analyzes the terms of the proposed transaction, assesses the likelihood of the proposed transaction being completed as agreed, and the spread that currently exists in the market between the shares of the acquirer and the target.

By purchasing shares immediately after a definite cash tender or exchange offer is established, a portfolio manager is able to earn the fixed spread that typically exists between the offer price and the post-announcement market price for the target firm. Of course, this price differential will only be earned if the merger ultimately occurs. When risk arbitrage funds go long and short two shares that may ultimately become part of the same corporation, they take the risk that the deal will "break," and the shares will then be subject to idiosyncratic and systematic market risk, in exchange for the chance of earning the deal spread.

The spread exists because there remains the likelihood that the deal will not be consummated—because of regulatory opposition, or the failure of the acquirer to gain approval for the acquisition from its shareholders, or a rejection of the offer from the shareholders of the target company. The deal spread often narrows as these deals near completion, with the share price of the target rising to its acquisition price. If the deal is not consummated and breaks, the stocks of the acquirer and the target will revert to being valued on their individual and prevailing market fundamentals. Typically, the stock of the target will fall and the stock of the acquirer may rise. Consequently, the deal spread is considered to be a risk premium that compensates an investor for the risk of the deal failing.

Suppose that a firm targeted for acquisition receives an offer equivalent to $33 for each of its outstanding shares. Assume further that prior to the announcement of the deal the stock of both the target and acquirer sold for $25 a share. Investors react to the announcement by bidding the price of the target firm's stock up to $30. At this time, the arbitrageur must judge whether the deal appears sufficiently likely to go through to justify purchasing the target firm's stock in order to capture the $3 price spread. If so, the exact strategy employed depends upon the nature of the acquiring company's offer. With a cash tender offer, the portfolio manager has only to purchase the stock of the target firm in order to lock in the price differential. When shares are exchanged, however, the post-announcement value of the exchange offer will vary with the price of the acquirer's stock. Thus, in order to lock in a particular spread, the stock of the acquirer will have to be sold short in appropriate quantities at the same time that the target firm's stock is purchased. In the present example, as $30 is spent for a share of the target firm, 1.2 shares of the acquirer will be shorted at the assumed price of $25.

The Risks of Risk Arbitrage Strategies

The hedge ratio is based on the deal being consummated and the shares exchanged. If the merger is consummated, the portfolio manager can cover

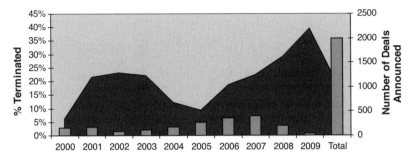

FIGURE 4.11   Analysis of Announced vs. Terminated Mergers (2000–2009)
Source: Bloomberg

the short sale with the exchanged value of the target share. The risk involved with such a position is that the hedge ratio is only valid if the deal is consummated. It has no reason to exist if the attempted merger breaks. If the deal falls through, it is likely that the target stock will return to its pre-announcement level or lower and the acquirer's shares may rally. In such a case, the portfolio manager will lose on the long position and the short position and potentially more than the $8 premium.[9]

This basis risk (that is, the hedge ratio having no validity in the event that the deal breaks) is the primary risk facing risk arbitrage funds.[10] The hedge typically becomes wholly ineffective and the long target stock position falls in value while the short acquirer stock position typically rises, actually compounding the fund's losses. Merger arbitrage managers may lose an amount considerably greater than the premium if the deal breaks.

Furthermore, as Figure 4.11 indicates, deals break fairly frequently. The figure shows 2,005 completed or terminated acquisitions between 2000 and 2009 where the deal size was greater than US$1 billion.[11] During that period, an average of 19 percent of the deals broke, although this varied significantly year-over-year. The rate of breaks rose significantly during the dot-com bubble, from a low of 6 percent to more than 22 percent, and then remained elevated through the September 11, 2001 period, before rising again in the credit crisis, when it approached 40 percent.

In addition, risk arbitrage funds are exposed to the idiosyncratic risks of each deal. The deal may be motivated by the specific financial motives of the acquirer. If the acquirer is dependent on substantial third-party financing, a change in the financial condition of the acquirer may cause a renegotiation or cancellation of the deal. Alternatively, the deal may be part of the acquirer's specific strategic goals. The deal may face anti-trust or other regulatory issues. In either case, the deal is exposed to

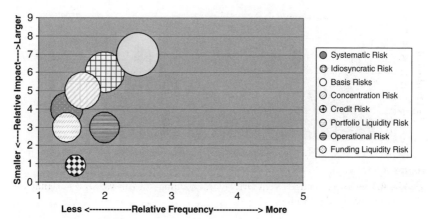

FIGURE 4.12 The risks of risk arbitrage strategies

the idiosyncratic risk of the acquirer. Furthermore, in the event the deal breaks, the fund is exposed to the idiosyncratic risk of both stocks. For these reasons, idiosyncratic risk is the second-most significant risk exposure for risk arbitrage funds.

Concentration risk is the third potentially significant risk but arises less frequently (see Figure 4.12). Given the potential for individual deals to break, the risk arbitrage portfolio manager will attempt to diversify across many deals to mitigate the risk of a significant loss. Most merger and acquisition deals appear to be uncorrelated with each other in normal markets. Consequently, the strategy is sometimes mis-categorized as a market neutral strategy. Though returns are often lowly correlated to market returns, severe market downturns can disrupt the outcome of multiple agreed deals and the strategy is, nevertheless, exposed if a significant number of deals fail to be consummated. This is more likely to occur when the equity market falls dramatically, making the value of the acquirer's stock to be swapped with the target worth significantly less. In such cases, either party may invoke a material adverse change clause in the documentation, scuttling the deal. Consequently, systematic risk is a significant exposure for risk arbitrage funds in that it can increase the correlation of deals breaking and have a negative impact on returns. In addition, the number of mergers announced during a period of market crisis drops significantly, eroding the opportunities available to funds to capture deal spreads and generate returns. Consequently, merger arbitrage funds frequently will invest in distressed securities to enhance their return during such periods and evidence a degree of style drift.

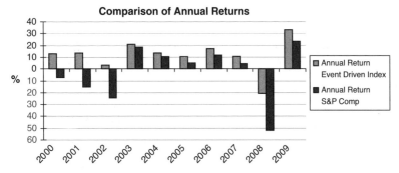

FIGURE 4.13   Eurekahedge Event Driven Index annual returns vs. S&P 500 Index
Source: Eureka Hedge, Shiller

Performance of Risk Arbitrage Strategies   The returns of risk arbitrage funds had been declining up to 2009 as the strategy is well-publicized and understood, resulting in announced deals quickly becoming crowded trades and a narrowing of deal spreads, lowering returns. However, returns in 2009 were exceptionally high. This was the result of recapitalization and merger events in the financial sector which created rich opportunities for event driven funds. As Figure 4.13 illustrates, risk arbitrage funds have outperformed the cumulative return of the S&P 500 over the past decade, primarily on the back of record returns in 2009 and the ability to preserve capital in most years (except 2008).

From January 2000 to January 2010, the Event Driven Index posted an average annualized return of 11.47 percent, with a high annualized standard deviation of 13.09 percent. The cumulative return of the Arbitrage Hedge Fund Index over the period was 114.7 percent, outperforming the cumulative return of the S&P 500 Index (−25.2 percent).

Risk arbitrage funds outperformed primarily because of their ability to deliver consistent returns and avoid significant drawdowns in nine out of 10 years. The fact that they delivered positive returns in three of the four years where the S&P 500 return was negative (indicating the loss-avoidance skills of risk arbitrage managers) significantly contributed to their cumulative outperformance of the S&P over the decade. Risk arbitrage funds delivered positive returns when the S&P 500 suffered drawdowns during the dot-com crash and in the aftermath of 9/11 but failed to do so during the credit crisis of 2008 (though their drawdown was less than half that of the S&P 500). Lastly, the returns generated by the S&P 500 index for the same period were 64 percent more volatile, with standard deviations of 13.9 and 22.9 respectively.

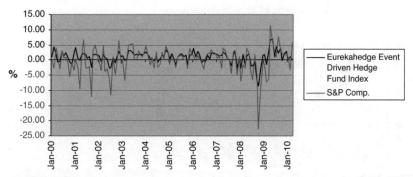

FIGURE 4.14 Eurekahedge Event Driven Index monthly returns vs. S&P 500 Index (January 2000–March 2010)

As Figure 4.14 indicates, risk arbitrage funds returns exhibited a moderate correlation to the S&P 500 monthly returns (0.74) and the overall equity market. Since 2000, these funds have returned a positive performance in nine out of the 10 years, while the S&P 500 index has posted negative returns in four of those years. The distribution of monthly returns is negatively skewed (−1.07) but is superior to that of the S&P 500 Index (−1.43) for the same period. Furthermore, the distribution of monthly returns is significantly less kurtotic than that of the S&P 500 for the same period (4.6 vs. 5.6), indicating a greater consistency of returns and a lesser presence of outliers in the monthly return distribution.

In conclusion, the risks to risk arbitrage are basis risk in the form of deal break risk, idiosyncratic risk, concentration risk and systematic risk. Deal break risk and idiosyncratic risk can be mitigated through diversification. However, risk arbitrage has systematic risk in the form of deals breaking more frequently and spreads widening in down markets.

Distressed Investing Strategies

These funds buy and typically hold equity, bond and other financial instruments of companies that are, or are perceived to be, in financial or operational distress or bankruptcy. These securities trade at substantial discounts to par or book value. The typical distressed fund is long sub-investment grade credit and low-investment grade credit. Such positions are typically put on when the company enters distress and institutional and private investors do not want to bear the risk of holding the company's securities. With the sellers motivated to get the company's securities out of their portfolios at distressed prices, this is a buyer's market for the distressed fund manager. The fund manager will buy securities of firms in distress but where the security trades below intrinsic value or where the underlying corporate entity is expected to improve financially. Some funds may even purchase a controlling interest in one class of company securities to benefit from restructuring decisions or to garner a control premium upon a later, carefully brokered, large block sale. Consequently, most distressed investment hedge funds are long biased and many are long only.

However, some distressed investments are relative value investments with a short component, rather than long only. A distressed fund manager who has fully analyzed the potential worth of a distressed company and the respective claims of holders of various security classes may conclude that selected senior securities may be overvalued, while more subordinated securities issued by the same company may be undervalued, or vice versa. In such cases, the fund manager will buy the undervalued security and short the overvalued security to extract an arbitrage profit if the securities are eventually fairly valued by the market.

Distressed debt funds are not a homogenous group. There is effectively a continuum of distressed investment styles illustrated by three archetypes which vary primarily in the degree of control the fund exerts over its investments:

1. Control. The fund independently, or in consort with other investors, takes control of the distressed large-to-medium-sized company by acquiring its debt (one-third minimum to block and one-half minimum to control). The fund takes operating control of the company during restructuring through a debt-for-equity swap and then restructures operations or purchases related business to generate cash flow. It exits the company via sale in two–three years, having targeted returns of 20 percent-plus. This is similar to private equity strategies.
2. Activist. The fund independently makes a significant investment (minimum one-third of senior secured or senior unsecured debt) of a distressed medium-to-large company. It plays an active role in the capital restructuring of the company. It exits late in the restructuring by selling senior debt or exchanging senior claims for equity, then selling equity upon relisting. The fund does not take operating control of the company and exits the investment via sale in one–two years. It targets returns of 15 percent-plus.
3. Passive. The fund independently makes investments in distressed securities, buying and holding senior secured, senior unsecured, busted convertibles, subordinated debt, equity, capital structure relative value. It plays a passive role in restructuring the company but may from to time hold greater than 5 percent of equity and be restricted. It trades out of positions when its price targets reached, typically over a period of six months to one year. Its target returns of 12 percent-plus.

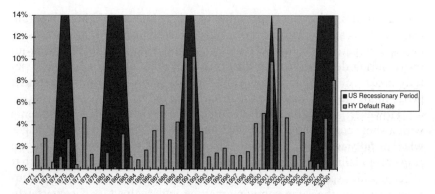

FIGURE 4.15 High yield bond default rates and U.S. recessionary periods (1971–3Q 2009)
Source: Edward Altman (New York University Salomon Center)

Passive distressed debt funds are significantly more common than their activist or control focused counterparts.

Opportunities for distressed investors are related to the high yield bond default rate and therefore countercyclical. Figure 4.15 illustrates historical high yield bond default rates and U.S. recessionary periods.[12] Distressed strategies are not viable in all markets at all times. The most disciplined of distressed fund managers intend to liquidate their portfolios and return money to investors when they do not expect the market to present them with opportunities for returns that meet their targets. This might be in periods where the economy is expanding and the default rate is low (as was the case in 1993–2000).

For the distressed investors, there are seeds of opportunity in economic crises. Default rates rose prior to the recessions of the 1970s and 1980s and peaked at approximately 10 percent and 12 percent in the two cycles of the early 1990s and 2000s. With a current notional amount of high yield debt outstanding of US$751 billion, at a 12 percent default rate the size of the opportunity presented by the current recession (2007–09) is approximately US$90 billion. In the previous two cycles, default rates have historically peaked (on average) four months after the peak of the recession, as struggling companies continue to grapple with problems that were exacerbated by the recession.

The number of investment opportunities (proxied by the default rate) peaked in 1991, 2002, and again in 2009. These are the same years that opportunities for risk arbitrage hedge funds dropped as a consequence of the decline in mergers and acquisition activity and the increase in frequency of deal break. In 2001–02 and again in 2009, many risk arbitrage funds departed from their usual field of expertise and became involved in investing in distressed securities, where there were greater opportunities. Similarly, multi-strategy funds allocate capital to these strategies depending on the economic cycle and opportunity set. Of course, the opportunities presented by economic crises cannot be monetized for between six months and three years until the economy turns.

Risks of Distressed Investment Strategies   Among the risks the strategy runs, credit risk is the most significant (see Figure 4.16). Though crises create medium-to-long-term opportunities, distressed funds perform poorly during recessionary years as they are fundamentally long credit: when spreads widen, their performance declines.

For distressed funds, credit risk is closely linked to systematic risk and idiosyncratic risk. The intrinsic value of distressed securities often deteriorates after the hedge fund managers make their purchase as economic crises deepen or as sector specific and/or company specific fundamentals deteriorate further. The timing and price of the purchase are critical. The entry price should be sufficiently below the intrinsic value of the securities as to create a value cushion that protects principal should fundamentals deteriorate further. Timing and choice of exit point are also critical to investment returns. One of the major decisions a portfolio manager must make and re-evaluate daily is the expected peak-to-trough pattern of recessions (whether they will be short and shallow, preludes to a depression, "V" shaped, or "W" shaped). Systematic risk factors that influence returns are a combination of high-yield credit spreads (B through CCC and below), the shape and

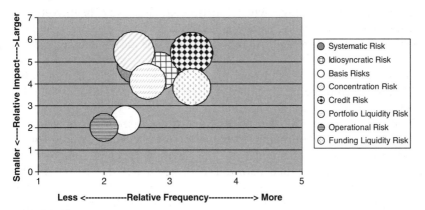

FIGURE 4.16   The risks of distressed investment strategies

level of the risk free curve, and conventional equity beta (often small cap beta). For funds investing outside of the U.S., systematic risk arises from exposure to assets similar to those outlined above but specific to the non-U.S. regions.

Concentration risk is another significant risk facing both the manager and investor of a distressed securities fund. Portfolios are often concentrated in the hands of 15–25 issuers, who tend to hold large block positions in a few, deeply analyzed deals. In addition, because the opportunity set is ephemeral and competition from other managers for access to deals is high, distressed fund managers often find optimal diversification of their portfolio difficult or expensive to create. When distressed securities come to market, control and activist investors must quickly accumulate their positions in sufficient size to influence the workout process. Large deals consume a disproportionately high percentage of some funds' assets under management, creating concentrated portfolios that are overly exposed to the outcome of certain deals. The problem is similar but less severe for passive investors, as they must compete with the control and activist investors for positions in attractive deals.

To mitigate the impact of concentration on returns, some portfolio managers seek to create a "barbell"-type portfolio. At one end of the portfolio are larger positions with moderate leverage in core deals the manager is highly confident will produce moderate returns with little downside risk. At the other end of the portfolio are numerous smaller positions in deals with greater uncertainty but higher potential upside.

As shorting to hedge deteriorating positions may be impossible and opportunities to increase positions further may be imprudent, the fund manager may use leverage tactically to reduce and increase market exposure. As confidence in the deals increases, the portfolio manager may seek to increase leverage when the time to monetize the investment draws closer. Conversely, if the manager's confidence decreases, he may seek to decrease leverage, thereby reducing the deal's impact on the fund's returns.

Managing leverage is critical to the distressed fund manager as his positions may not be highly liquid. Buyers for his positions may be relatively few and he may not be able to find a buyer for his positions at attractive valuations. Market prices for distressed securities may take a significant time to normalize around intrinsic values. Consequently, funds are typically structured with long investor lock-ups (one to three years) to provide the fund manager with adequate time to realize the investment thesis.

Portfolio liquidity risk is therefore a material risk for this strategy. Many distressed securities do not trade daily, or trade only "by appointment." Prices from brokers may be only indicative and only be representative for small lots, if they are available at all. In normal market conditions, a typical distressed hedge fund would be able to liquidate approximately 80 percent of its assets within 90 days without significant material impact on price. In a period of market crisis, however, this can very easily deteriorate to the point that only 50 percent or less of the fund's positions can be liquidated and with less certainty about a material impact on valuations.

As deteriorations in prices and liquidity typically accompany market crises, leverage provides the fund manager with a final means to control the impact of temporary deteriorations in the mark-to-market value of his positions on his overall fund performance. However, prime brokers tend to reduce or withdraw leverage and funding to distressed-fund managers as position liquidity declines. If a prime broker is unable to observe a frequent (minimum, weekly) transacted price on a security it has accepted as collateral to a loan, it will likely withdraw leverage provided to purchase that security and ask for the loan to be effectively repaid via a margin call on the hedge fund. Consequently, the risk of forced liquidation in a crisis to meet rising margin calls is the final major risk facing distressed funds. Prime brokers use their creditworthiness and fund assets pledged as collateral to generate low-cost secured financing from other financial institutions. They then use this cheap financing to fund the loans they extend to hedge funds as leverage, thus capturing an interest margin. This process is called "rehypothecation." In a financial crisis, financial institutions begin to doubt each other's creditworthiness and either demand greater amounts of assets from each other in order to finance the same amount or accept only higher quality securities for rehypothecation. If a security cannot be priced daily, it is immediately excluded, whether in good times or bad.

Consequently, in a crisis the first securities to become ineligible or inefficient for rehypothecation are securities which are already distressed. Thus, the distressed fund manager often has the leverage provided on his positions withdrawn or reduced and his funding withdrawn, which may force him to sell his positions at the trough of the market if he has does not have a margin lock-up. This problem can be compounded if his investors redeem and do not have longer-term investor lock-ups. For these reasons, distressed hedge funds typically have long-term lock-ups, use relatively low leverage, and seek margin lock-ups from their brokers.

Performance of Distressed Investment Strategies   The Distressed debt Hedge Fund Index returned 118.62 percent over the decade, while the S&P 500 delivered −25.20 percent and the J.P. Morgan Global Bond Index

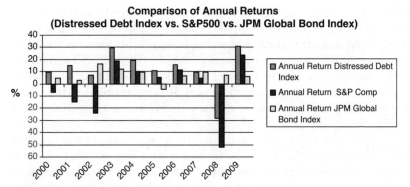

FIGURE 4.17 Eurekahedge Distressed Debt Index, annual returns
Source: Eureka Hedge, Shiller, Bloomberg

delivered 68.57 percent. As illustrated in Figure 4.17, from January 2000 to January 2010, the Distressed Debt Index posted an average annualized return of 11.86 percent, with a very high annualized standard deviation of 16.39 percent. Meanwhile, the S&P 500 and the J.P. Morgan Global Bond Index posted average annualized returns and standard deviations of $\mu = -2.52$ percent and $\sigma = 22.86$ percent; and $\mu = 6.86\%$ and $\sigma = 5.51$ percent, respectively.

Distressed investment funds outperformed primarily because of their ability to deliver consistent returns above the indices and avoid significant drawdowns in nine out of the 10 years. The fact that they delivered positive returns in three of the four years where the S&P 500 return was negative contributed significantly to their cumulative outperformance of the S&P over the decade. Distressed investment funds delivered positive returns when the S&P 500 suffered drawdowns during the dot-com crash and in the aftermath of 9/11 but failed to do so during the credit crisis of 2008, though their drawdown was slightly more than half that of the S&P 500. Lastly, the returns generated by the S&P 500 Index for the same period were 39 percent more volatile.

The monthly returns of distressed-investment funds (as shown in Figure 4.18) have been increasingly volatile but have significantly outperformed the cumulative return of the S&P 500 and the J.P. Morgan Global Bond Index over the past decade. The Distressed Debt Fund Index returned 118.62 percent over the decade, while the S&P 500 and the J.P. Morgan Global Bond Index delivered −25.20 percent and 68.57 percent, respectively.

Compared to other hedge fund strategies, the monthly returns of distressed investment funds exhibited a higher correlation to the S&P 500

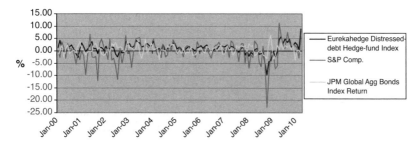

FIGURE 4.18 Eurekahedge Distressed Debt Hedge Fund Index, monthly returns
Source: Eureka Hedge, Shiller, Bloomberg

monthly returns (0.75) and the overall equity market but a low correlation to the J.P. Morgan Global Bond Index (.08). The distribution of monthly returns is negatively skewed (−0.92), indicating a slight downside skew. This, however, is substantially less than that of the S&P 500 index (−1.43) for the same time period but, as expected, not as high as that of the bond index (.08). Furthermore, the distribution of monthly returns exhibits kurtosis slightly higher that of the S&P 500 for the same period (5.7 vs. 5.6), indicating a slightly greater presence of outliers in the return distribution, while the kurtosis of the J.P. Morgan Global Bond Index is a stable 0.27.

In conclusion, the significant risks to distressed investment are credit and systematic risk in the form of long high yield credit risk exposure, short exposure to interest rates, and exposure to equity risk. Idiosyncratic risk is also present in all deals and is frequently not fully diversified, creating portfolio concentration risk. Liquidity risks, both position liquidity and funding liquidity, are material. Position liquidity is a risk due to the limited number of investors skilled in analyzing and permitted by regulators to invest in distressed securities. Funding liquidity risk is material because of the tendency of prime brokers to withdraw leverage for distressed securities in market crises because of the significantly lower liquidity risk of distressed securities in market crises and their decreased ability to be rehypothecated.

Activist Investment Strategies

Activist hedge funds accumulate large stakes in public companies and use their stakes to agitate for management actions that the fund managers conclude will create shareholder value and increase the price of their security investments in the company. Like value investors, activist funds typically target companies with a lower market value relative to book value, above mean return on assets (ROA) compared to their peers, average or superior cash flow compared to peers, lower payouts to shareholders compared to their peers, and more takeover defenses. The actions demanded by activist shareholders range from financial (increase of shareholder value through changes in corporate policy, financing structure, cost cutting, and so on) to non-financial (disinvestment from particular countries, the adoption of environmentally friendly policies, and so on). The mechanics of activism typically involve acquiring a 5–10 percent stake in the company (activists almost never acquire controlling blocks of stocks) and, once the position of influence is established, agitating for change via proxy battles, publicity campaigns, shareholder resolutions, litigation, and negotiations with management.[13] While activist funds never state their intended holding periods for investment in target companies, studies indicate that the median holding periods are in the range of one year or longer and can extend to over three years.[14]

While an activist strategy is fundamentally event driven, a pure activist hedge fund is a rarity. Even event driven and special situation funds that pursue activist strategies are in the minority. Most activist strategies are pursued within broader hedge fund mandates such as equity long only, equity long/short, and equity market neutral.

The returns of activist funds arise from the relative low cost of accumulating the fairly small stake (less than 10 percent of outstanding shares) necessary to launch a successful activist campaign. In comparison, a full takeover bid is a much more costly and difficult undertaking.[15] Section 13(d) of the Securities Exchange Act of 1934 requires that any investor, including a hedge fund, file a Schedule 13D with the U.S. SEC within 10 days of acquiring more than five percent of any class of securities of a publicly traded company if the investor has an interest in influencing the management of the company. Section 13(f) of the same Act requires that institutional investors that manage more than US$100 million must file a Form 13F each calendar quarter setting forth the number of shares they hold in exchange traded companies. Hedge fund activists with significant assets under management must make quarterly Form 13F filings to report their holdings. The analysis undertaken by Brav *et al.* (2008) indicated that, in the U.S., activist funds partially or completed achieved their strategic, operational, and financial plans for creating shareholder value in two-thirds of the cases. Furthermore, they observed that these security investments generated abnormally high stock returns, the majority of which occurred in the period 20 days before and after the filing of the regulatory disclosure.

The disclosure of an activist position in a company has a positive halo effect. The majority of the positive abnormal returns observed were from the market's favorable reaction to the announcement of activism and the expectation that the activism would create value. The filing of a Schedule 13D, revealing an activist fund's investment in a target company, resulted in large positive average abnormal returns, in the range of 7–8 percent, during the 20-day window around the announcement. Typically, the increase in both price and abnormal trading volume of target shares began about 10 days prior to the filing of the 13D. This may be due to the activist fund buying to build its position. The analysis also found that these positive returns at announcement were typically not reversed over time as two-thirds of the activist "interventions" were at least partially successful. Activism that targets the sale of the company or changes in business strategy, such as refocusing and spinning-off non-core assets, was associated with the largest positive abnormal partial effects. Within one year of the announced activism, target firms often increased cash and dividend payouts to shareholders, delivered improvements in operating performance, and replaced more members of the target firm's senior management.

The Risks of Activist Strategies   The risks of activist investing are significant and difficult to manage. Foremost is the concentrated nature of activist investing. In order to influence management and obtain valuable voting rights, activist hedge funds, and any investor for that matter, must accumulate a large long position in the stock. Activist hedge funds often hold undiversified portfolios consisting of large block holdings in individual companies and may use leverage and derivatives above and beyond their cash stock holdings. Given the size of these positions, it is often difficult and/or expensive to hedge the risk.

The concentration of the activist fund means that idiosyncratic risk cannot be optimally diversified. This leaves the fund's investors highly exposed to losses if one of the major activist investments fails. Idiosyncratic risk can and does manifest itself in the one-third of activist interventions that fail to achieve their stated objectives. Well-known activist investor Carl C. Icahn experienced significant losses from his non-diversified portfolio and was forced to abandon select activist investments. Icahn suffered with year-end losses in 2008 of 36 percent on his investments in Yahoo! and Motorola. He described the losses as being merely "temporary value declines" and called Motorola (which lost 38 percent of its value in the fourth quarter 2008) and Yahoo! (down 29 percent in the same period) as "well positioned to succeed in 2009." Nonetheless, rather than having to liquidate assets in order to pay investors who wanted their money back in a down market, Icahn had to invest US$500 million of his own cash in his hedge fund, Icahn Capital.

Within the context of idiosyncratic risk and activist investing, there is always the risk for a destructive conflict between the activist investors and the management of the target company and/or its board of directors. This can distract senior management from the day-to-day business of running the target company and can lead to both shortsighted, value destroying decisions and the loss of valuable management and director level expertise. While activist investing does tend to result in increased turnover of senior management and board members, it is not clear whether the new appointees are superior or whether there is a loss of key qualified people to serve on boards and run the company. In addition to heated battles with management, activist hedge funds can be proven wrong in the broader markets, resulting in significant losses.

In 2008, Christopher Hohn's fund, The Children's Investment Fund (TCI), prevailed in a bitter proxy battle with the railroad giant CSX Corporation, winning Hohn and three allies seats on the CSX board and beating back a CSX suit that accused TCI of securities violations. The victory was short-lived, however, as shares of CSX plummeted, contributing to a 43 percent loss in TCI's main fund in 2008. TCI could not sell the shares because TCI was in a "control" position as a result of its shareholdings and Hohn's seat on the board, making it subject to the "dribble out rule."[16] Hohn chose not to seek re-election to the CSX board, making it easier for him to sell off TCI's stake under U.S. regulations.

William A. Ackman, who runs Pershing Square Capital Management, struggled with a high-profile disaster in a fund (Pershing Square IV) he set up in 2006 to invest in the Target Corporation, the discount retailer. Target owns rather than leases the majority of its store properties. Among other value-creating activities, Ackman believed significant shareholder value could be created and redeemed if Target sold and then leased back some of the properties. Ackman fought a proxy fight to replace five directors on Target's board with his own candidates, hoping that the representation would persuade the company to buy back shares and turn some of its real estate into cash. The fund suffered a drawdown of more than 90 percent from its inception to 2008.

In addition, concentration and low portfolio liquidity result in an inability of activist funds to hedge and/or liquidate their large positions in a timely fashion, leaving them exposed to systematic risk. In their paper, Brav *et al.* calculated the average risk-factor loadings for the activist funds' returns. The market factor (beta) was the most correlated at 0.33, followed by target company-size factor at 0.27, followed by value factor at 0.17, and the momentum factor at .04. These factor loadings indicate that most activist hedge funds in the sample were exposed to systematic risk similar to small cap stock beta and value stock beta.

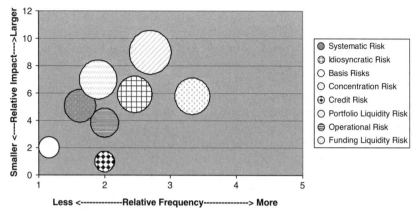

FIGURE 4.19 The risks of activist investment strategies

The relative impact and frequency of the risks facing activist strategies are summarized in Figure 4.19.

With respect to portfolio liquidity, not only is the size of positions (typically less than 5 percent of outstanding shares) problematic with respect to daily trading volume in the securities, there are regulatory impediments which often preclude rapid liquidation of an activist fund's position. The selling of such positions is often restricted by the fact that they make the fund an affiliate of the target company and thus subject to the affiliate restrictions under U.S. Securities and Exchange Commission Rule 144. Rule 144 defines an affiliate of an issuer "as a person that directly, or indirectly through one or more intermediaries, controls, or is controlled by, or is under common control with such issuer." Control is defined as "the possession, direct or indirect, of the power to direct or cause the direction of the management and policies of a corporate person." The ability to direct management is why activist hedge funds buy the shares in the first place. Even if the fund is ineffective in exerting its influence, it may still have difficulty liquidating as "it is the existence of the power to control rather than the exercise of the power to control that determine affiliate status."

To the extent that a fund trading in the U.S. acquires its stake in the form of restricted stock, it will face asset liquidity risk as a result of U.S. Securities and Exchange Commission Rule 144. To prevent a seller from purchasing unregistered securities with a view to resale in the public market, Rule 144 requires all unregistered securities to be held for at least one year, measured from the time the securities were purchased from the issuer or an affiliate, before any retail sale. This period is extended to two years for a fund with affiliate status (which is typically triggered by acquiring a seat on the board). After the initial holding period, unregistered securities can be sold only by complying with certain "dribble out," or volume limit, provisions set out in the Rule.

The provisions dramatically restrict a fund manager's ability to liquidate a position. According to these provisions, to qualify for the exemption, the total amount of securities sold in any three-month period cannot exceed more than one percent of the total number of the company's outstanding shares or the average weekly reported trading volume during the four weeks preceding such sale. Furthermore, the issuer has to have filed all reports (financial and otherwise) required by the SEC and the seller of the restricted stock has to comply with the manner of sale and notice requirements of the Rule.

If a stock is falling in value and an activist hedge fund holding it is considered an affiliate but wishes to liquidate its position prior to the end of the required holding period, it has limited and unappealing options for doing so. These include:

- An outright sale of the position to an institutional investor—in most cases, at a significant direct sale or block discount.
- A hedging transaction where an institution will first write a "collar" on the stock to remove most of the economic risk of the restricted stock position, and then lend aggressively against the hedged position. Purchasing a collar means purchasing a put option and writing a call option on the same security. This transaction has a cost to the investor similar to the discount taken in a direct sale.

Both the hedging and sales transactions described above are practicable mainly for highly liquid stocks, where publicly traded options are available and/or short selling is possible. Prime candidates for such transactions are companies with market capitalization in excess of US$500 million and those whose stock trades relatively actively—that is, in the range of 100,000–200,000 shares per day.

Consequently, portfolio liquidity is a significant and material risk for this strategy. In addition, the potential violation or non-compliance with Rule 144 makes this a legal/regulatory risk, increasing the fund's exposure to operational risk.

Lastly, funding liquidity is a material risk to this strategy. While most activist funds use relatively low leverage overall, specific positions or fund vehicles can be levered two to three times. The withdrawal of this leverage in a market crisis or a deterioration in the fund's performance is likely, as the prime broker providing the leverage risks inheriting the fund's restricted or affiliate Rule 144 status if the fund defaults. As the risk of a client fund defaulting increases, either due to poor performance or a market crisis, the prime broker will seek to withdraw the financing or require that non-restricted collateral be posted. To manage this risk, most activist funds negotiate margin lock-up agreements with their prime brokers that preclude the brokers from withdrawing financing or increasing margin requirements precipitously. In addition, to better match the tenor of their assets with their liabilities, most activist hedge funds require long-dated investor lock-ups, typically of at least two years or longer. This is consistent with the finding of Brav *et al.* that hedge funds with longer lock-up and redemption notice periods are more likely to engage in shareholder activism.[17]

Activist hedge fund investors should understand that, from quarter to quarter and year to year, their returns can be buffeted by the stock market, the idiosyncratic risks of each activist intervention the portfolio manager undertakes, and the portfolio liquidity. The current lack of a central database of activist hedge funds makes a statistical analysis of fund returns impossible at this time. The databases that are available include non-activist funds and exclude some of the larger activist funds. However, investors should also recognize that if more hedge-fund managers decide that they want to become activist investors, this will, in fact, reduce the opportunities for the discipline. If activist investing becomes a pervasive activity, under-valued and reformable companies will be harder to find because the gap between actual and potential values will shrink.

Performance of Activist Strategies   The performance of activist hedge funds is very heterogeneous. To date there is no standard index representing the performance of this strategy.

The most recent analysis of activist returns was conducted by Brav *et al.* in 2008.[18] They used a large hand-collected data set covering the self-reported returns of 236 select U.S. activist funds and constructed an equal-weighted index of returns covering the period from January 1995 to June 2007. This index should be interpreted cautiously as only surviving hedge funds contributed and those activist funds with positive performance were more likely to self-report than those with negative performance.

While the index does not cover the credit crisis, it does show that activist funds were able to avoid large drawdowns during the dot-com crash and in the aftermath of September 11, 2001. Compared to the returns of the S&P 500 index, their activism index tracks the S&P 500 index very closely up to mid-2000, and then exceeds the return of the S&P up to 2007. In addition, they find that their activist index outperformed the average equity-oriented hedge funds from 2003 to 2007.[19]

RELATIVE VALUE STRATEGIES

Relative value strategies seek to profit from mis-pricings of related securities. These mis-pricings may be identified based on a theoretical arbitrage free formula, statistical analysis of historical relationships, or fundamental analysis. These strategies are engineered to profit when a particular set of securities return or move to their historical or theoretically correct comparative value relationship. Relative value strategies seek to have little or no exposure to the underlying equity or bond markets. They tend to be market- or beta-neutral. Below we present analysis of a variety of such strategies.

Convertible Arbitrage Strategies

These funds manage positions in convertible instruments and their issuers' underlying equity to create portfolios that tend to be equity market neutral. Convertible instruments are typically convertible bonds, warrants or convertible preferred shares which are most often exchangeable into common stock of the issuer. The plain vanilla convertible arbitrage strategy involves taking a long position in a convertible bond and shorting the issuer's stock. It is possible to reverse this strategy (go long on the underlying and short on the bond), but this is less common. The latter is also often fairly expensive, even when the opportunity does arise to use it, because it is likely to have a negative carrying cost.

One goal of this strategy is neutralize the equity sensitivity inherent in the option that is embedded within this bond. Some convertible arbitrage funds also trade interest rate and credit default swaps to attempt to hedge all the market risk in the convertible bond. These swaps are used to mitigate that portion of the bond's inherent interest rate and credit risk which is not hedged out of the portfolio by shorting the stock.

The strategy is profitable when managers buy undervalued securities that are convertible into equity and then hedge out the market risks at a cost less than the difference between the purchase price and fair value. Fair value is based on the optionality in the convertible bond and the manager's assumptions primarily about future volatility of the underlying stock. Most managers view the cause of undervalued convertible securities to be the market underpricing future volatility. Convertible-arbitrage funds are consequently often long vega (long volatility) because of the optionality embedded in the convertible securities. An environment of slowly increasing market volatility will generally be positive for convertible arbitrage funds. A risk to performance, however, is that volatility will be lower than expected.

The strategy is also (though less materially) long gamma. The convertible's delta will rise as the price of the underlying rises. Both gamma and vega risk are difficult to hedge since the strike and maturity of the embedded options in the convertible are often uncertain, making the job of quantifying and maintaining the hedge imprecise and potentially costly.

Though the production of alpha seems somewhat formulaic, the experience and skill of the fund manager does come into play when determining the size of the hedge positions. For example, the short position in the underlying equity (the delta hedge) can be adjusted to over or under hedge the convertible, depending on the manager's view of the company and the market. In effect, the manager goes long or short idiosyncratic, volatility and beta exposure to amplify returns. As the manager's view of the market changes, these hedges can be re-adjusted. Such opportunities frequently arise from large fluctuations in the price of an issuer's underlying equity.

Opportunities for contributions to alpha also arise from deviations in the bond against a CDS. A credit default swap allows the holder of a bond to buy protection from default by entering into an agreement to swap a premium payment for a contingent payment that offsets the holder's losses on the underlying bond should the issuer default. The payment made by the premium receiver (the protection seller) in the event of a default is the par value of the bond minus the market price of the bond after default (that is, the recovery rate). The advantage of the CDS is that it is generally more liquid than its underlying bonds. Because of the different liquidity characteristics of the bond and CDS markets, the credit spreads implicit in CDS prices can vary from the credit spread of the underlying bonds. This is the bond vs. CDS basis. As a result, buying credit protection to neutralize the credit risk on a convertible bond may at times be cheaper than the credit risk of the bond. The manager of a convertible-arbitrage portfolio may use such market opportunities to hedge the credit risk of his bond positions but, conversely, may sell the protection when CDS prices are high, leaving the fund exposed to credit risk. In addition, there is basis risk as this strategy can swing against the manager and result in losses.

Lastly, because of the bond vs. CDS basis, CDSs are not always perfect hedges against credit spreads widening on convertible bonds. Credit spreads can widen and prices can fall by more than the value of any CDS protection may rise. This can be due to the greater liquidity of the CDS market compared to the convertible bond market and/or the fact that the convertible bond may not be deliverable into the CDS. Should the convertible bond actually default, the CDS protection will mitigate the loss but the portfolio manager may still be left with a defaulted bond that may fall further and cannot be hedged with equity since the option value of the portfolio is at or near zero.

As a result of these market opportunities, hedges on convertible-arbitrage positions are often managed dynamically. Dynamic management presents the fund manager with additional opportunities to capture profit. Dynamic hedging can add additional variability to the monthly return profile as the cost of hedging can change.

It takes considerable skill to manage idiosyncratic risks in complex convertible securities. Significant analysis and insight is needed to monetize the optionality embedded in more complex convertibles with various callable, puttable, mandatory conversions, contingent conversions, and conversion ratios based on future dividend payments, for example.

Risks of Convertible Arbitrage Strategies The above vega, gamma and basis risks, though material and perhaps frequent, are more often sources of alpha generation than of significant losses for a skilled manager. Portfolio liquidity, and systematic, credit and funding liquidity are the most significant risks (see Figure 4.20).

Position liquidity of the convertible securities themselves can also deteriorate rapidly, especially if a delta hedge is difficult to find or expensive. Convertible arbitrage funds are exposed to short squeezes in equities and low to intermittent liquidity for restricted, unrated, and sub-investment grade convertible bonds. A position in a certain convertible bond valued above par may become widely held by many hedge funds all seeking to hold it and hedge it. The position becomes a

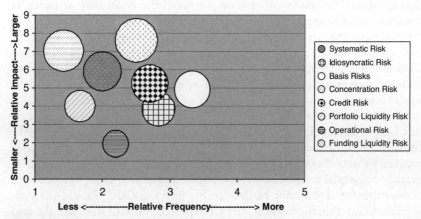

FIGURE 4.20   The risks of convertible arbitrage strategies

"crowded trade" and, in such cases, the stock can become hard to borrow and the cost of borrowing can go up above the expected arbitrage profit. In such cases, the convertible security may present a great undervalued opportunity but the difficulty finding stock to short in sufficient quantity and at a low cost, plus the risk that the short stock may be recalled (short squeeze) and leave the position unhedged, can make the capturing of that value highly risky. In addition, with little of the bond in circulation and potential buyers being aware of the difficulty or expense to hedge it, selling it near its theoretical value will be difficult and a fund manager will have to accept a lower price in order to exit the position.

Systematic and credit risk arises as a result of these funds being short credit spreads and particularly exposed to the high yield bonds and high yield credit spreads (to the extent that credit risk is not hedged). By being short credit spreads, convertible arbitrage funds are highly exposed to economic crises. In an economic crisis such as the recent credit crisis, credit spreads widen precipitously and investors who are short credit spreads lose money. In addition, convertible bond liquidity tends to decrease as the option value falls and investors do not want to call the bottom of the market and make significant investments. Both delta and CDS hedges, if they can be found, are very expensive and, in the case of a CDS, increasingly ineffective[20] because of the widening of the bonds vs. CDS basis. Because they are short credit spreads, convertible arbitrage and other relative value funds are effectively sellers of economic disaster insurance.

Funding liquidity risk, though infrequent, is also a significant risk to convertible arbitrage funds. Because convertible arbitrage is a widely known and understood strategy, mis-pricings of convertible securities are quickly recognized and exploited. Consequently, unlevered returns are typically a meager two or three percent. However, because of the hedged nature of convertible portfolios, prime brokers have been willing to provide significant leverage to hedge funds that practice this discipline. Convertible arbitrage managers eager to earn performance fees have also demanded extensive leverage in order to generate higher annual returns for themselves and their investors. As a result of this dynamic, convertible arbitrage funds tend to use extensive leverage (typically, 3x–10x gross leverage). Furthermore, as a result of inherently low unlevered returns, portfolio managers tend to deploy the majority of their investable funds and maintain relatively low cash reserves, to minimize the cash drag on their performance. Consequently, an increase in prime broker margin levels, though rare and tending to coincide with market shocks, can result in a need to liquidate convertible positions, sometimes at a significant loss.

The recent credit crisis provides a tremendous illustration of how the risks of convertible arbitrage strategies can combine and compound to create losses for investors. The market events and dislocations triggered by the Lehman bankruptcy in September 2008 resulted in severe losses for managers in this space, with index returns of −4.58 percent in September 2008 and −6.37 percent in October 2008.

Systematic and credit factors that contributed to losses in this period included widening credit spreads, volatile equities markets, the nationalization of the Fannie Mae and Freddie Mac agencies, as well as direct and indirect losses stemming from Lehman-issued shares. Yields on subinvestment grade convertibles rose from 5 percent in January 2008 to more than 22 percent in October 2008, according to Barclay's Capital Research. Most asset classes and hedge fund strategies struggled during this period as system-wide deleveraging caused their correlations to equity markets to increase and traditional arbitrage relationships to deteriorate.

Funding liquidity and portfolio liquidity factors that disadvantaged convertible arbitrage during this period included widespread hedge fund redemptions, global short selling bans, extensive de-leveraging, and higher funding and borrowing costs. In September 2008, the SEC temporarily suspended the short selling of financial stocks after Lehman Brothers collapsed and speculation grew that investors were purposely driving down the prices of large banks in an attempt to profit from their demise. With their downside protection severely hindered, convertible arbitrage managers were left vulnerable to the effects of the tumbling global market. With an increased share of their convertible bond collateral unhedged, many prime brokers became more risk averse following the Lehman bankruptcy and increased margin requirements at the same time that convertible valuations decreased. Most convertible arbitrage funds seek leverage of between three and 10 times their funds' AUM. Widening of the bid/ask spreads on convertible securities made their value as collateral decline quickly. Prior to the Lehman collapse, margin requirements were typically around 10 percent. As of December 2008, margin requirements increased to up to 30 percent. Funding liquidity concerns arose as funds had to liquidate holdings to meet margin calls. Unidirectional liquidity caused further widening of bid/ask spreads and mark-to-market losses became realized losses as the funds were forced to exit positions at a loss, even though the theoretical value was significantly higher.

This self-reinforcing spiral of systematic and funding factors resulted in a significant deterioration of value for the asset class. The period from September through November saw steep falls in prices, while the high trading volume was composed of mostly one-directional sell-offs. This was compounded by de-leveraging of the banks themselves, which sold their proprietary positions, including convertible securities.

A number of convertible arbitrage managers were consequently forced to continue selling, in many cases at reduced prices, in order to raise cash to meet the prime brokers' increasing margin demands. Because the market for lower-grade convertibles effectively disappeared, managers had little choice but to sell higher-quality assets, as well as their most liquid holdings, in order to generate cash. As a result, the securities that remained in many portfolios were holdings that managers could not readily sell.

While the market was crashing, new issuance of convertibles slowed to a trickle. New CB issuance in 2008 was only 10 percent of that in 2007. Meanwhile, redemptions by issuers of convertible bonds remained robust, with more convertibles taken out of circulation, reducing the investment opportunities for convertible arbitrage funds.

Performance of Convertible Arbitrage Strategies From January 2000 to January 2010, the Arbitrage Fund Index posted an average annualized return of 6.23 percent, with an annualized standard deviation of 14.7 percent (see Figure 4.21). The cumulative return of the Greenwich Alternative Investments International[21] Convertible Arbitrage Hedge Fund Index over the 10-year period was 62.3 percent, significantly outperforming the cumulative return of the S&P 500 Index (−25.2 percent).

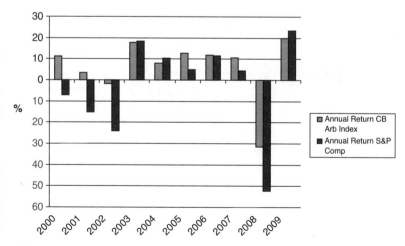

FIGURE 4.21 GAI International Index annual returns vs. S&P 500 Index
Source: Greenwich Alternative Investments LLC, Shiller

Convertible arbitrage funds outperformed primarily because of their ability to deliver consistent returns and avoid significant drawdowns in eight out of the 10 years. The fact that they delivered positive returns in two of the four years where the S&P 500 return was negative, and delivered significantly lower losses in the other two, contributed significantly to their cumulative outperformance of the S&P over the decade. By being long volatility, they delivered positive returns when the S&P 500 suffered drawdowns during the dot-com crash and in the aftermath of 9/11 but failed to do so during the credit crisis of 2008 when liquidity and a widening of credit spread outweighed the gains from higher volatility. Their drawdown during the credit crisis was 61 percent of that of the S&P 500.

As shown in Figure 4.22, the monthly returns of convertible arbitrage funds have been more volatile in the second half of the decade. Compared to those of other hedge fund strategies, they exhibited a moderate correlation to the S&P 500 monthly returns (0.63) and the overall equity market but this is surprising for an "arbitrage" strategy. Correlation with equities has been increasing compared to the previous decade, when correlation to the S&P 500 from 1990–2000 was only 0.31 and 0.35 for the period from 1995–2000.

Monthly returns were less volatile (at 2.55 percent) than those of the S&P 500 (4.35 percent). In comparison to the standard deviation of monthly returns, the large drawdowns in September and October 2008

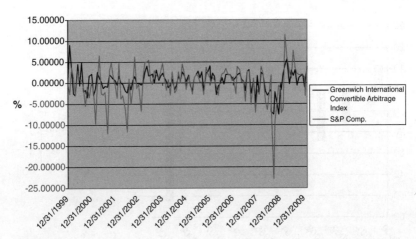

FIGURE 4.22 Greenwich International Convertible Arbitrage Hedge Fund Index monthly returns vs. S&P 500 Index (January 2000–March 2010)
Source: Greenwich Alternative Investments LLC, Shiller

(-6.9 and -7.5 percent respectively) were not Black Swan[22] events. Both returns were to have been expected given historical volatility and were not of significantly greater magnitude compared to earlier periods of negative returns (in fact, they were less than three standard deviation moves).

The distribution of monthly returns is significantly negatively skewed compared to other hedge fund strategies (-1.86), indicating material downside skew. This skew is larger than that of the S&P 500 index (-1.43) for the same period, indicating a greater potential for large monthly losses. Offsetting this greater negative skew is a narrower distribution of returns. The distribution of monthly returns exhibits significantly less kurtosis than that of the S&P 500 for the same period (2.3 vs. 5.6), indicating a significantly lesser presence of outliers in the return distribution.

In conclusion, the significant risks to convertible arbitrage funds are portfolio liquidity, systematic, credit and funding liquidity risk. Portfolio liquidity is a risk because of the impact of hedge availability on the demand for convertible securities and the concentrated convertible investor base. Systematic and credit risks are present as a result of short exposure to credit spreads. Funding liquidity risk is material, particularly for sub-investment grade, not-rated, restricted or contingent convertibles, because of the use of significant leverage, the risk aversion of prime brokers to less liquid or unhedgeable securities, and their decreased ability to be rehypothecated in market crises. Idiosyncratic risk is also present in more complex convertible securities, as well as basis risks due to the differing liquidity characteristics of bonds and CDSs.

Equity Market Neutral Strategies

In their most basic form, equity market neutral funds hold long and short positions in equal delta-adjusted dollar balance at all times. This approach is intended to eliminate net market exposure so that the returns generated are not affected by the direction of the overall market. Equity market neutral is also known as "pairs trading" and "equity relative value trading."

More sophisticated strategies minimize their overall net market exposure by constructing portfolios where neutrality is reinforced by balancing beta exposures in subsectors of the portfolio and neutralizing currency exposures. Hedging techniques involve neutralizing exposures across industries, market capitalization, investment styles (such as growth or value stocks) and fundamental risk factors. This is done while exploiting perceived market inefficiencies manifested by securities which deviate from their historical relative price relationships. The basic assumption behind such mean reverting investment strategies is that temporary anomalies will occur and, over time, correct themselves as the market processes information. By detecting "mispricing" opportunities early, the portfolio manager can capture a long/short spread as the anomaly is corrected.

Each individual "mis-pricing" opportunity is not certain to be profitable; some will be false positives while others will not be temporary but fundamentally driven and, effectively, permanent changes in price relationships. In other cases the transactions costs will exceed the actual profit. However, by following a disciplined investment strategy, over time, the odds are in the market neutral portfolio manager's favor. As with a croupier at a casino, not all market neutral trades will be profitable, but the winners tend to outnumber and be more profitable than the unprofitable trades and this return distribution tends to lead to positive and stable monthly gains.

Market neutral strategies can be defined along a continuum, with pure fundamental strategies at one end and quantitative strategies at the other.

Statistical Arbitrage Strategies

Statistical market neutral is the more complex form of pairs trading that involves the analysis and trading of a broader range of securities. Because "stat arb" managers trade long lists of securities, they are able to mitigate directional market risk and industry risk, and diversify idiosyncratic risk. Generally, they are less likely than fundamental managers to adopt directional biases.

Statistical arbitrage funds use quantitative algorithms to analyze the historical price relationship between large data sets of different securities, such as stocks, commodities, futures, and options; as well as analyzing fundamental corporate and accounting data. The traditional discipline involves hypothesizing a relative pricing relationship and then using statistical analysis to back-test and validate the relationship. If the relationship appears to be persistent and stable, trading rules are then developed to exploit the relationship.

Hypotheses are closely related to the research of financial academics. In many cases, the fund managers themselves were originally financial researchers, computer scientists and financial engineers. If the hypothesis is found to be historically robust, the portfolio manager then monitors market prices to detect periods where the price relationship deviates from its historical norm. Positions are then put on to exploit these statistical anomalies (that is, deviations from the historical relationship) with the expectation that the security's relationship will revert towards its historical mean. The strategy is implemented using the explicitly defined rules validated by the back-testing. The rules are only overruled by the subjective judgment of the portfolio manager in exceptional cases. Typically, the fund manager will go long the security trading below its historical relative value and short the security trading above that value. Mean reversion, residual reversal, earnings surprise and relative strength are popular statistical strategies that are based upon the application of reversal and momentum signals.

Stat arb funds use significant leverage to increase profits. Gross leverage can range from five to 20 times AUM. Since leverage can magnify losses, and can force the closing of positions when the value of the fund falls below its margin maintenance requirement, funding liquidity risk is a significant additional risk for these strategies.

Risks of Statistical Arbitrage Strategies   Because stat arb managers share a common academic lineage and tend to integrate the same academic insights from economics, finance, statistics, math, computer science, and engineering into their trading strategies, opportunities to profit from mis-pricings quickly become crowded trades where profits are fleeting and diminishing. Factor models and statistical arbitrage are no longer black boxes.[23] They are an increasingly crowded and transparent glass box.

Statistical arbitrage funds are estimated to represent 50 percent of the daily trading volume in the U.S. equities markets.[24] In addition, the flow of investment into these funds has been increasing to the point where they are growing to be some of the largest hedge funds in the industry.[25] Consequently, stat arb trades are increasingly becoming crowded trades, undermining their effectiveness and increasing the risks of self-inflicted Black Swan events. The relatively high leverage employed to increase profits amplifies the crowding effect. As the execution of trades is rules-driven, an errant buy or sell signal can trigger an unintended avalanche of compounding orders which temporarily destroy the funds' carefully built fundamental neutrality and cause violent prices swings in positions that are widely held by the funds.

Many statistical arbitrage funds have similar risk factor driven stock-ranking systems so an unwinding means popular shorts will go up while popular longs will go down. Convergence trades only work if there are reasons they should converge. When markets go through a regime change, "fundamentals" get overwhelmed by the shift from low volatility to high volatility. Historical relationships fail to apply to the present.

Since stat arb strategies use high leverage, a small loss can force large position reductions. For example, suppose a fund with $1 billion in net asset value holds $6 billion in long stock positions offset by $6 billion in short stock positions. If the long positions move down by 0.1 percent and the short positions move up by the same amount, the fund loses $12 million, or 1.2 percent of assets.

To maintain the original leverage ratio, this fund has to sell $72 million of long positions and buy to cover $72 million of short positions. So a move that would cost a $1 billion long-only equity manager $1 million, and would generate no trades, costs the stat arb equity manager $12 million and generates $144 million of trades. These trades add to the trades other quant equity funds are conducting, which might move the stocks more than 0.1 percent, generating a new larger wave of trades and creating a reinforcing wave of selling.

The Events of August 2007 The market events of August 2007 show clearly how crowded trades by statistical arbitrage funds can overwhelm market fundamentals, disrupting model driven trading strategies and creating dramatically large basis and portfolio liquidity risks in previously liquid and market neutral portfolios. Prior to August 2007, the success of statistical arbitrage had led many multi-strategy funds to develop copycat strategies and incorporate them into their overall fund. By mid-2007, stat arb strategies had, by some estimates, managed levered stock portfolios of about US$300–$400 billion long and short positions in equities.

In June 2007, the beginnings of the subprime crisis caused many banks and some hedge funds to experience significant losses from credit exposure. In July, some began to reduce risk and de-lever, raising cash by selling liquid instruments such as their stock positions, and hurting the returns of common stock selection strategies. Simultaneously, some hedge funds were experiencing redemptions. For instance, some funds of funds (hedge funds investing in other hedge funds) hit loss triggers and were forced to redeem from the hedge funds they were invested in.

The multi-strategy funds also had significant exposure to subprime-related fixed income assets. As the crisis spread, subprime securities lost significant value, and prime brokers lost faith not just in subprime but in other credit derivatives and increased their margin requirements and made certain forms of credit related securities ineligible as collateral. The multi-strategy funds had to raise cash to meet margin calls and, in some cases, redemptions. Consequently, they started selling more liquid securities such as the easily traded securities held in their stat arb equity portfolios, including the likes of Microsoft, IBM or General Electric. At first, the effects were largely hidden since the trades were spread over thousands of stocks, with some stock prices being pushed up and others pushed down.

But as the uncharacteristic market data accumulated, stat arb trading rules began to lose their effectiveness, and became a form of operational risk. To the funds' computer models which were scanning the market data, this change in market regime did not compute. When the dedicated stat arb portfolio managers realized that their statistical models were not working in this market environment, they began quickly to de-leverage to protect against even bigger losses but in so doing added to the downturn. Consequently, as the multi-strategy funds sold their liquid cash equity positions to meet their margin calls, it created a contagion effect, causing other funds to sell or face large losses. The funds were caught up in a ripple that began in a corner of the market that they had little to do with—namely, the sub-prime mortgage crisis.

On August 9 the S&P 500 ended down more than 380 points. When large stat arb funds like the AQR flagship fund opened for business the following day, it was down 13 percent for August. Renaissance Technologies Medallion fund, which had rarely had a down month, lost 8.7 percent in early August. By mid-August, the Goldman Sachs flagship, Global Alpha fund, was down 26 percent for the year.

While actual short-term returns are not public, Lasse Heje Pedersen[26] has simulated the minute-by-minute returns and industry-neutral long/short portfolio based on value and momentum signals during the August period. His analysis shows that by Monday, August 6, 2007, a major de-leveraging of stat-arb strategies had begun. His model portfolio incurred substantial losses from that Monday through Thursday, August 9, as stat arb and multi-strategy funds were unwinding, and then recovered much of its losses on Friday, August 10 and Monday, August 13, as the unwinding ended. The strategy lost about 25 percent in four days, about a four standard deviation move and more than a 30 standard deviation move based on the four-day volatility.

The high standard deviation move in volatility does not necessarily mean that this was an aberrant market event. It means that fundamentally driven volatility does not likely explain the event and its cause was more likely liquidity driven, and the subsequent recovery of the strategy indicates it was not based on stock fundamentals. Longer-term stock price fluctuations are driven primarily by economic news about fundamentals most of the time, but during a liquidity crisis, price pressure can have a large effect. Hence, the distribution of stock returns during this week in August 2007 can be better understood as a mixture of two distributions: shocks driven by fundamentals mixed with shocks driven by liquidity effects (that is, broad de-leveraging). Consequently, portfolio-liquidity risk is a significant risk to equity long/short strategies, and statistically driven equity long/short strategies moreover. It is the one-way liquidity effects which transmitted the sell-off from subprime to high-grade U.S. equities to markets around the world and caused the significant losses.

LIQUIDITY BLACK HOLES

It is not known exactly how much trading volume and liquidity in the markets is generated by computer-driven risk-neutral short-horizon trading strategies but the "flash crash" (on May 6, 2010, the financial markets experienced a brief but severe drop in prices, falling more than 5 percent in a matter of minutes, only to recover a short time later) was very likely compounded by these strategies. Numerous practitioners of high-velocity short-term strategies and, in particular, market making strategies, highlight the risk of "liquidity black holes." Liquidity holes occur when there is no bid (no-one is making a market) for a specific security or the bid price offered is significantly lower than the last executed price.

These trading strategies search exchange data for signals indicating that a technical pattern is developing or ending. One such computer-driven trading strategy is market making. These strategies are algorithmically driven and implemented via high-speed, very short-horizon trading strategies that are continuously in the market buying and selling very small lots of shares at prices based on the momentum patterns observed in microsecond-parsed exchange data. Risk-neutral short-term trading strategies such as market making decide whether to buy or sell shares or flash a bid or ask to the market depending on the direction and strength of the momentum signal in the market data. If the price drops slightly, the market making strategies will take this as a signal of selling momentum and will enter small orders to sell near the last selling price and orders to buy small lots below the last selling price. Larger lots will be sold and bought as the signal gets stronger and then decrease again if the signal gets weaker.

Multiple trading programs with similar short time horizons and unknown loss limits interact in the markets. For example, when a long-term investor decides to liquidate a large position, he enters a large sell order and drives down the price. This generates a strong downward-sloping residual demand curve or selling momentum to short-horizon program traders. The large sell order and fall in price generate losses for the short-horizon market makers and may pierce some of their loss limits, causing them to liquidate any remaining position in the shares. The selling of the risky asset by any short-term trader increases the incentives for other short-term traders to sell, and sales become mutually reinforcing. As the price continues to fall, any short-term program trader holding any of the shares in inventory has a strong incentive to sell that share at any price as he does not know the loss limits of other participants. In this way, risk-neutral short-term trading strategies amplify market trends, and a liquidity black hole develops.

Prices stop falling only when all the short-term traders have sold their holdings of the risky asset. The liquidity black hole is only fully extinguished, however, when prices drop far enough to provide an incentive to a risk-averse longer-term value-oriented investor to enter bids in the market. This reverses the momentum from sell to buy. Immediately afterwards, once the loss limits for the short-term traders have been adjusted down to the new price, there will be an immediate reversal of the trades until the price recovers to its fundamental long-term equilibrium. The price pattern that is generated by these reversals is typically V-shaped.

Evolution of Stat Arb   Given that they are dealing with ephemeral opportunities and rabid competition, stat arb funds seek to gain an edge over their peers through rapid, efficient, low-cost execution abilities to mitigate liquidity risk and stealth. Short-term stat arb is a growing discipline where funds use high frequency trading infrastructure, dark pools of liquidity, co-location of computer-automated electronic ordering at exchanges, and brokers' trading lines with exchanges to implement their trades speedily, opaquely and cheaply.

While mitigating portfolio liquidity risk, this automated trading strategy presents a significant operational risk. The "flash crash" on May 6, 2010 is another example of how high-speed automated execution and computer-driven trading decisions can have serious unintended consequences. May 6 started with unsettling political and economic news concerning the European debt crisis that led to growing uncertainty in the financial markets. Increased uncertainty during the day was corroborated by various market data: high volatility; a flight to quality among investors; and the increase in premiums for buying protection against default by the Greek government. This led to a significant, but not extraordinary, down day in early trading for the securities and futures markets.

However, shortly after 2:30 p.m., this overall decline in the financial markets suddenly accelerated. Within a matter of a few minutes, there was an additional decline of more than five percent in the overall U.S. equity and futures markets (see Figure 4.23). Most individual stocks declined by amounts that were generally consistent with the broader market decline. Approximately 86 percent of U.S.-listed securities reached lows for the

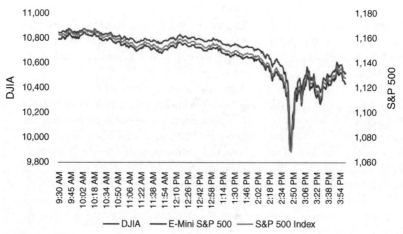

FIGURE 4.23   The "Flash Crash" May 6, 2010
Source: Bloomberg

day that were less than 10 percent away from the 2:40 p.m. price but by approximately 2:45 p.m. more than 200 individual securities (about 10 percent of all U.S.-listed securities) had fallen 50 percent or more from their 2:00 p.m. levels. Between 2:45 p.m. and 2:47p.m., the DJIA, S&P 500, and NASDAQ 100 all reached daily lows. During this same period, all 30 DJIA components reached their intra-day minima, representing a range from −4 percent to −36 percent from their opening levels. This rapid decline was followed by a similarly rapid recovery. The U.S. SEC and the Commodity Futures Trading Commission (CFTC) concluded that this extreme volatility in the markets suggested the occurrence of a temporary breakdown in the supply of liquidity across the markets.[27]

While investigation of the causes continues, the primary area of investigation is around arbitrage activity of the E-Mini S&P 500 futures contract, for which around 250 executing firms processed transactions for thousands of accounts during the hour from 2:00–3:00 p.m. Of these accounts, CFTC staff have more closely focused their examination to date on the top 10 largest longs and top 10 shorts. The vast majority of these traders traded on both sides of the market, meaning they both bought and sold during that period. One of these accounts was using the E-Mini S&P 500 contract to hedge and only entered orders to sell. That trader entered the market at around 2:32 p.m. and finished trading by around 2:51 p.m. The trader had a short futures position that represented on average nine percent of the volume traded during that period.

The SEC and CFTC tentatively conclude that based on data from the CME order book, trading volume in E-mini S&P 500 futures was very high on May 6, and there were many more sell orders than buy orders from 2:30 p.m. to 2:45 p.m. The data also indicate that the bid/ask spread widened significantly at or about 2:45 p.m. and that certain active traders partially withdrew from the market. Considerable selling pressure at this vulnerable period may have contributed to declining prices in the E-Mini S&P 500 and other equivalent products such as the SPY (an ETF that tracks the S&P 500). The question remains as to why liquidity was suddenly withdrawn.

High velocity stat arb trading algorithms cannot be programmed to evaluate all possible market conditions and properly interpret and react to all pricing and liquidity anomalies. Furthermore, the possible permutations of outcomes of a trading strategy are increased exponentially when actions of competitors are considered. The context in which a pricing anomaly presents itself is extremely nuanced and has been misinterpreted by trading algorithms despite rigorous back-testing. As a result, trades have been executed in magnitudes totally disproportionate to available liquidity and caused cascading automated same-way trades that result in violent price swings in the market. While operational risk is present even in the longer-term strategies, it is further heightened in the high-velocity direct market access versions of equity market neutral strategies, where computers are used to both identify and implement trades within milliseconds.

Figure 4.24 summarizes the relative significance and frequency of the risks of statistical arbitrage strategies. Basis, operational, and liquidity risks are the most likely to cause significant losses in this strategy.

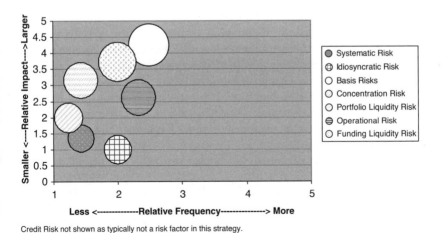

Credit Risk not shown as typically not a risk factor in this strategy.

FIGURE 4.24 The risks of market neutral statistical arbitrage strategies

Fundamental Arbitrage Strategies

In contrast, fundamental arbitrage strategies rely generally on in-depth company analyses of a more limited universe of stocks. While statistical arbitrage is to a large extent model-driven, with an overlay of judgment by the portfolio manager, fundamental arbitrage is essentially about picking over- and undervalued stock and constructing a portfolio that approaches market neutrality. The narrower focus of the fundamental style tends to limit the range of opportunities and reduce the potential return. Fundamental equity-market-neutral or pairs trading involves trading two or more fundamentally linked or related securities, such as Citigroup preferred vs. ordinary shares. Where there has been a temporary deviation from the normal price relationship of the two securities, the portfolio manager implements a position that will profit from the eventual convergence of prices of the two securities towards their fundamental price relationship. The portfolio manager buys the relatively undervalued security in the expectation that it will rise in price, and sells the relatively overvalued security in the expectation that it will fall in price. Once the shares are back in alignment, the trade would be reversed.

The fundamental strategy can also extend to securities of related companies or companies in the same industry, such as Hunt's vs. Heinz, or Coke vs. Pepsi shares. Trading decisions in fundamental market neutral strategies are driven by financial analysis and judgment while trading decisions for statistical arbitrage strategies are more quantitative and rules-driven. Fundamental market neutral analysts conduct fundamental financial analysis tracking the price-to-book value ratio (PBR), price-to-earnings ratio (PER), return on equity (ROE), return on assets (ROA), sales growth rate, profit growth rate, sales profit ratio, and sales cash-flow ratio to determine which securities to short and which to go long.

A popular value-based fundamental strategy employs signals derived from variations of the dividend discount model. For instance, "value" strategies seek to buy cheap securities (and short overvalued ones), and, since such securities often stay cheap for months, this is a low-frequency (that is, low-turnover) strategy. "Momentum" strategies buy securities that have recently performed relatively well, while shorting underperforming securities based on the idea that such recent performance has tended to continue more often than it has reversed.

Leverage in fundamental equity market neutral strategies tends to be less than that of statistical arbitrage (that is 5–10 times AUM). Consequently, while funding liquidity risk is still present; its impact is less severe (see Figure 4.25).

Systematic risk in this strategy results from the fact that these funds tend to invest in stocks which outperform (underperform) on a

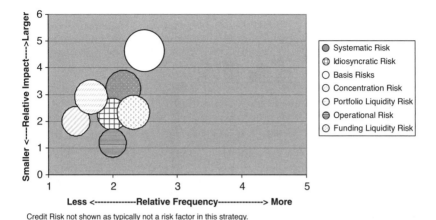

Credit Risk not shown as typically not a risk factor in this strategy.

FIGURE 4.25 The risks of equity market neutral fundamental arbitrage strategies

beta-adjusted basis and then subsequently tend to underperform (out-perform) on that same basis. Beta-neutrality of a portfolio is not static and individual stock betas can persistently deviate from their historical norms as a result of risk aversion on the part of investors (that is, flight to quality), market technicals (that is, limited and changing supply of stocks that fund managers are able to short) and regulatory changes (such as bans on selling short and tax policy). Idiosyncratic and basis risks are also present from instability in beta-controlled return to various risk factors such as earnings momentum, volatility, liquidity, value vs. growth stock, earnings yield, earnings variance, dividend timing, and dividend yield.

Performance of Market Neutral Strategies From January 2000 to January 2010, the Greenwich Alternative Investments International Equity Market Neutral Hedge Fund Index (see Figure 4.26) posted an average annualized return of 6.04 percent, with an annualized standard deviation of 4.78 percent. The cumulative return of the Relative Value Hedge Fund Index over the 10-year period was 60.4 percent, significantly outperforming the cumulative return of the S&P 500 Index (−25.2 percent).

Market-neutral funds outperformed, primarily because of their ability to deliver consistent returns and avoid significant drawdowns in nine out of the 10 years (see Figure 4.27). The fact that they delivered positive returns in three of the four years where the S&P 500 return was negative contributed significantly to their cumulative outperformance of the S&P over the decade. The funds delivered positive returns when the S&P 500 suffered drawdowns during the dot-com crash and after September 11, 2001, but

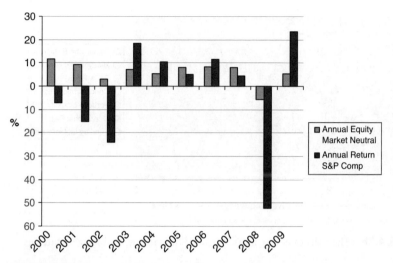

FIGURE 4.26 Greenwich Equity Market Neutral Hedge Fund Index annual returns vs. S&P 500 Index
Source: Greenwich Alternative Investments LLC, Shiller

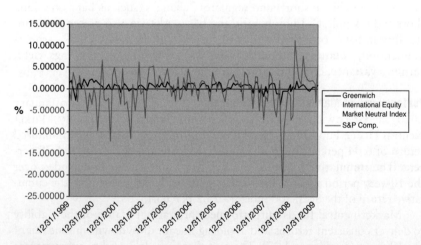

FIGURE 4.27 Greenwich Equity Market Neutral Hedge Fund Index monthly returns vs. S&P 500 Index (January 2000–March 2010)
Source: Greenwich Alternative Investments LLC, Shiller

failed to do so during the credit crisis of 2008, when liquidity effects overwhelmed fundamental price relationships, increasing the basis between positions that were intended to offset each other and creating residual beta exposure. Their drawdown during the credit crisis was only 11 percent of that of the S&P 500.

Compared to other hedge fund strategies, the monthly returns exhibited a relatively low correlation to the S&P 500 monthly returns (0.34) and the overall equity market for the overall period from 2000–10. While this is low by comparison with other hedge fund strategies, it is still surprisingly high for a market neutral strategy. In addition, the correlation with the overall equity market increased significantly in the latter half of the period. From 2000–05, correlation with the S&P 500 was a low 0.15, despite three periods of market crisis. During the period from 1995–2000, correlation increased to 0.47. For comparison, the correlation to the S&P 500 during the period 1995–2000 was 0.42.

Monthly returns were substantially less volatile than those of the S&P 500—0.97 percent vs. 4.35 percent, respectively. This means that the maximum monthly drawdown in October 2008 (−3.72 percent) was a 3.8 sigma event. The distribution of monthly returns was slightly negatively skewed compared to other strategies (−0.53), indicating slight downside skew. However, this was substantially less than the skew of the S&P 500 index (−1.43) for the same period. Furthermore, the distribution of monthly returns exhibited less kurtosis than that of the S&P 500 for the same period (4.1 vs. 5.6), indicating a modestly lower presence of outliers in the return distribution.

The market neutral approach is one of the most attractive strategies because of the generally stable returns it offers. However, the significant risks to such strategies are basis risks and portfolio liquidity. Basis risks arise in conjunction with liquidity risks during periods of market turbulence. Historical price relationships are undermined and the fund's previously most liquid positions may be subject to temporary one-way liquidity pressures due to de-leveraging of other market participants. Operational risk is significantly more pronounced for statistical arbitrage strategies while systematic risk is more pronounced for fundamental strategies.

Fixed Income Arbitrage Strategies

These funds seek to exploit price anomalies across a wide range of fixed income instruments, using high leverage to enhance returns. Fixed income arbitrage funds take offsetting positions in fixed income securities that are mathematically, fundamentally, or historically related. Substrategies include:

- Asset backed and mortgage backed securities vs. swaptions and other interest rate derivatives
- Asset swap spread vs. cash or CDS
- Forward yield curve arbitrages that profit from sovereign debt yield curve shifts and twists
- U.S.-dollar-denominated vs. non-U.S. bonds of the same issuer
- Physical bond vs. bond futures arbitrage
- On-the-run vs. off-the-run bond arbitrage
- Stripping and hedging option components from complex callable bonds or swaps
- Intermarket spread arbitrage, such as going long U.S. Treasury bill futures vs. Eurodollar futures (that is, TED spread).

Fixed income security values are driven by yield curves, volatility curves, expected cash flows, credit spreads, and bespoke option features. Given the complexity of fixed income securities, the alpha of the strategy is derived from the ability of the portfolio managers to more accurately model the value of complex securities, identify mis-pricings, and then structure portfolios to profit from the positive carry from numerous small mis-pricings in the market while being immune to broad market moves.

For example, a fixed income arbitrage hedge fund may purchase very high quality corporate or mortgage backed bonds using leverage. By doing this, they make an incremental return for each bond purchased with leverage, assuming the cost of the leverage is less than the interest received on those bonds. To hedge exposure to both interest rate and credit risk incurred by going long the bonds, the portfolio manager will also short sell bonds or buy CDSs for downside protection. In an efficient market, the cost of hedging these risks fully would cost as much as the expected return on the bonds. Consequently, the fund will seek to hedge only the tail risk by shorting bonds or buying CDSs of a lower credit quality than the long assets in the portfolio, assuming they will fall faster in value than high quality bonds if interest rates rise or credit markets deteriorate. This way, the portfolio manager can short fewer bonds than they are long, thereby producing a net positive rate of return, or a "positive carry." If structured properly, this trade creates a steady rate of return with relatively low volatility under most market conditions, but it is not a true arbitrage as it is not risk-free.

As the carry spreads to be earned tend to be small (2–15 bps), managers seek to leverage positions as much as possible. Leverage varies depending on the composition of the portfolio but tends to be 15–20 times AUM. Prime brokers are more willing to provide higher leverage for simple, stable, low-risk positions, such as carry trades, than for higher-risk trades that have directional yield curve or credit spread exposure. However, carry trades and the strategy as a whole are more prone to fat-tail return distributions, which have a greater likelihood of large losses than would be predicted by a normal distribution.

The risk of large losses arises from the fact that carry trades look, based on historical analysis, to be low-risk, and often work as planned for extended periods of time, but they can and do fail in market crises when liquidity preferences and market structure change. Generally, the identification and risk measurement of arbitrage strategies are based on the historical movement and behavior of the fixed income securities in question. However, effective risk management must include scenario analysis of the impact of unprecedented or unexpected market behavior on the portfolio, how potential losses are mitigated, and the amount of leverage employed compared to the expected liquidity of the portfolio. If markets move beyond and behave outside of historical norms, highly levered investments tend to incur significant losses, leverage is withdrawn and positions are liquidated, producing heavy losses over very short periods of time.

The implosion of two prominent Bear Stearns hedge funds, the Bear Stearns High Grade Structured Credit Fund and the Bear Stearns High Grade Structured Credit Enhanced Leveraged Fund, illustrate the risks of fixed income arbitrage.

KEY EVENTS IN THE FAILURE OF BEAR STEARNS' STRUCTURED CREDIT AND ENHANCED LEVERAGED FUNDS

October 2003: Ralph Cioffi moved to Bear Stearns Asset Management (BSAM) to set up the High Grade Structured Credit Fund. Cioffi told investors that the fund would invest in low-risk, high grade debt securities, such as tranches of CDOs, which the rating agencies had rated either AAA or AA. The fund took in about US$1.5 billion from investors. For 40 months, the fund never had a losing month and achieved a 50 percent cumulative return.

August 2006: Bear Stearns High Grade Structured Credit Enhanced Leveraged Fund opened, which used more leverage than the High-grade Fund.

Early 2007: The effects of a deterioration in the creditworthiness of subprime borrowers started to become apparent as subprime lenders and homebuilders were suffered defaults and evidence of a severely weakening housing market accumulated.

March 2007: Both funds lost—3.71 percent and 5.41 percent, respectively, in one month—causing investors to start redeeming their money and prime brokers to increase their margin requirements.

June 2007: Amid the losses, Barclays asked for its money back. Merrill Lynch, one of the prime brokers, seized and sold US$800 million of bonds that were put as collateral by the hedge funds. The Structured Credit Fund received a US$1.6 billion bailout from Bear Stearns, which helped it to meet margin calls and redemptions while it liquidated its positions.

July 17, 2007: In a letter sent to investors, BSAM reported that its Structured Credit Fund had lost more than 90 percent of its value, while the Enhanced Leveraged Fund had lost virtually all of its investor capital. Previously, the larger Structured Credit Fund had around US$1 billion, while the Enhanced Leveraged Fund had nearly US$600 million in investor capital.

July 31, 2007: The two funds filed for Chapter 15 bankruptcy. Bear Stearns effectively wound down the funds and liquidated all of its holdings. Several shareholder lawsuits were filed on the basis of Bear Stearns misleading investors on the extent of its risky holdings.

The core fixed income arbitrage strategy employed by the Bear Stearns funds was actually quite simple and is best classified as being a credit-based carry trade that was common to fixed income arbitrage funds at the time. The carry trades were implemented as follows:

1. Purchase collateralized debt obligations (CDOs) that pay an interest rate over and above the cost of borrowing. In Bear Stearns' case, AAA-rated tranches of subprime, mortgage backed CDOs were used. At the time, a senior CDO tranche (AAA) paid LIBOR + 80bps, while a Treasury bond (AAA) paid LIBOR + 15bps. CDOs themselves are levered securitizations of the underlying securities.

2. Given the high credit rating of the senior CDO tranches purchased by Bear Stearns funds, they were able to obtain further financing to buy these AAA tranches, often putting down as little as 5 percent margin. The fund focused on leverage to generate returns by borrowing from the low-cost, short-term repo market to buy higher-yielding, long-term CDOs. They then used this ability to leverage to buy more CDOs and enhance returns. Because the CDO tranches paid an interest rate over and above the cost of borrowing, every incremental unit of leverage added to the total expected return.

3. Some of the interest earned on the CDO tranches was used to hedge the credit risk by buying credit default swaps (CDSs) as insurance against movements in the overall credit market. This CDS protection mitigated the tail risk of the CDO portfolio.

4. When the cost of the leverage used to purchase the AAA-rated subprime debt, as well as the premium paid on the CDS protection, was netted out, the funds were left with a positive rate of return, a "positive carry."

The long positions in the CDO tranches were substantially less liquid than the CDS protection. In instances when credit markets (or the underlying bonds' prices) remain relatively stable, or even when they behave in line with historically based expectations, this strategy generates consistent, positive returns with very little deviation. The funds had high returns: 46.8 percent cumulative for the High Grade (11 percent only in 2006) and 6.3 percent for the Enhanced in less than six months in 2006. However, 70 percent of the net assets in the High Grade and 63 percent in the Enhanced fund were not quoted in the market and were valued using Bear Stearns' own models.

The Bear Stearns fund managers' first mistake was failing to predict how the subprime bond market would behave under extreme circumstances. In effect, the funds did not protect themselves adequately from basis-risk exposure in a market crisis where the effectiveness of their hedges eroded and exposed them to systematic risk.

Moreover, they failed to have ample unencumbered cash available to maintain their positions and ensure their funding liquidity. They were forced to unravel their positions in a down market as funding was withdrawn by the market. While maintaining this cash would have led to lower returns as a result of less leverage, it would have prevented the overall collapse and protected investors from millions in losses incurred by liquidating in a down market.

Scenario analysis was lacking in that the fund managers should have realized that, based on macroeconomic data and research, the subprime mortgage markets were overvalued and a correction was not only plausible but increasingly likely. Global liquidity growth over recent years had been tremendous, resulting not only in low interest rates and credit spreads, but also an unprecedented level of risk taking on the part of lenders to low-credit-quality borrowers. Since 2005, the U.S. economy had been slowing as a result of the peak in the housing markets, and subprime borrowers were particularly susceptible to economic slowdowns. Therefore, it would have been reasonable to plan for an economic correction and analyze their exposure under a scenario where subprime assets were likely to fall precipitously. They then could have made appropriate adjustments to their risk models and portfolio construction to hedge such an increasingly likely event or reposition the fund to profit from it.

Risks of Fixed Income Arbitrage Strategies

While fixed income arbitrage funds attempt to hedge away systematic risk, they retain residual directional exposures to sovereign yield curves and corporate credit spreads.[28] Figure 4.28 summarizes the relative significance and frequency of the risks facing most fixed income arbitrage strategies. Basis risks are always present in the hedging strategies but their potential impact increases significantly in periods of market crisis as traditional hedge relationships destabilize. The deterioration of hedge relationships creates other term structure exposures which can include exposure to U.S. agency curves, swap spreads, and to ratings and sector-specific credit curves. For example:

- By buying cheap fixed income securities and selling short expensive securities of different durations, fixed income arbitrage funds hedge against changes in interest rate levels. However, the mis-pricings opportunity often exists in part from the fact that the duration of the long and short positions are not the same. Consequently, the funds retain exposure to changes in the slope of the yield curve at different maturities.
- Where the fund buys credit-risky securities and hedges by shorting credit, the securities available to short tend to be limited to securities with high credit quality and low default risk. Consequently, the funds tend to be exposed to changes in the relative credit spread between low-grade and high-grade fixed income securities.

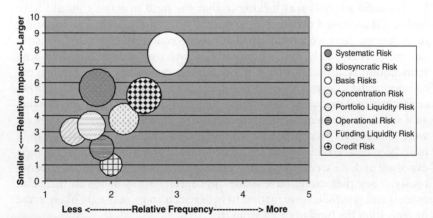

FIGURE 4.28   The risks of fixed income arbitrage strategies

■ The profitability of most fixed income arbitrage strategies is contingent upon low financing costs. Consequently, fixed income arbitrage funds are exposed to changes in the Fed Funds and LIBOR rates as well as the spreads over these rates demanded by their prime brokers. These rates themselves are determined as a function of interbank liquidity and central bank policy, which respond to systematic risk in the market.

To some extent, fixed income arbitrage funds sell crisis insurance to the market. Positive carry earns them a premium in most years but leaves them exposed to the occurrence of a crisis. In an economic crisis, liquidity deteriorates, particularly for lower-quality securities, which also fall the fastest. When credit spreads widen, investors who short the spread lose money. Fixed income arbitrage positions tend to be constructed by being long less-liquid securities and in shorting more-liquid securities. The funds are able to profit from the positive carry as long as the basis relationship remains stable. However, in a crisis where liquidity deteriorates and credit spreads widen, the long position loses value but may not be able to be liquidated, while the higher-grade short positions may not generate offsetting profits as investors may fly to quality, supporting higher-grade securities. The liquidity preferences of investors distort the historical basis relationship in a crisis, making fixed income arbitrage funds short liquidity or exposed to portfolio liquidity risk.

For funds investing outside the U.S., credit spread factors similar to those outlined above but specific to the region being invested in also contribute to systematic risks.

Performance of Fixed Income Arbitrage Strategies   From January 2000 to January 2010, the Fixed Income Hedge Fund Index posted an average annualized return of 8.36 percent, with an annualized standard deviation of 9.68 percent. The cumulative return of the Index over the 10-year period was 83.58 percent, outperforming the cumulative return of the J.P. Morgan Global Aggregate Bond Index (68.57 percent), as shown in Figure 4.29.

Fixed income arbitrage funds outperformed primarily because of their ability to outperform the JPM Global Bond Index in six of the 10 years. The fact that they delivered positive returns in 2005, the one year the index delivered negative returns, was offset by the substantial losses and underperformance compared to the index in 2008. The negative index returns in 2005 where driven by negative fixed income returns in Japan when the Bank of Japan (BOJ) announced an end to the policy of quantitative easing, thus increasing interest rate expectations, and in Europe, where the European Central Bank (ECB) increased its repo rate to counter the threat of inflation from high energy prices.

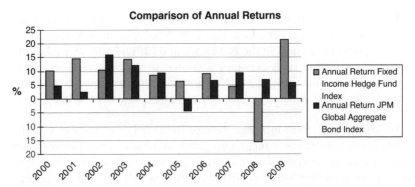

FIGURE 4.29 Eurekahedge Fixed Income Hedge Fund Index annual returns vs. JPM Global Bond Index
Source: Eureka Hedge, Bloomberg

The negative fixed income arbitrage returns in 2008 were to the result of negative returns from structured credit, ABS, MBS, and corporate bonds. The credit crisis caused a collapse in the interbank lending markets, dramatically decreased liquidity, and an inability to rephypothecate all but the highest-quality fixed income collateral.[29] Fixed income performance issues were compounded by the intense de-leveraging pressure this created as a result of the increased cost of, and reduction in, the quantity of funding from prime brokers. Managers experienced a consistent reduction of capital available for lending activities in the market, which resulted in an ongoing increase in funding costs.

Overall, the data do not provide any evidence of fixed income arbitrage managers collectively having the skill to avoid losses, despite their ability to go short. The funds delivered positive returns against the index in 2005 when the ECB and BOJ tightened monetary policy, but failed to do so during the credit crisis of 2008 when liquidity effects overwhelmed fundamental price relationships, increasing the basis between positions that were intended to offset each other.

The monthly returns (as shown in Figure 4.30) exhibited a relatively low correlation to the JPM Global Aggregate bond index monthly returns (0.26) but a surprisingly high correlation to those of the S&P 500 (0.67).

The monthly returns were substantially less volatile than those of the JPM Global Aggregate Bond Index; 1.26 percent vs. 1.82 percent, respectively. This means that the maximum monthly drawdown in October 2008 (−7.69 percent) was a six sigma event. The distribution of monthly returns is the most negatively skewed (−2.81) of any strategy evaluated in this book, indicating material downside risks. Furthermore, this negative skew

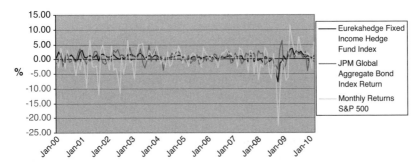

FIGURE 4.30   Eurekahedge Fixed Income Hedge Fund Index monthly returns vs. JPM Global Bonds Index monthly returns (January 2000–March 2010)
Source: Eureka Hedge, Shiller

is substantially worse than that of the JPM Global Aggregate Bond Index (0.06) for the same period. The distribution of monthly returns exhibits significantly greater kurtosis than that of the JPM Global Aggregate bond index for the same period (17.7 vs. 0.27), indicating a dramatically greater presence of outliers in the return distribution.

In conclusion, fixed income relative value strategies are primarily exposed to basis risk, which erodes the effectiveness of hedging in times of market stress and results in systematic and credit risk exposures. In addition, portfolio liquidity risk and funding liquidity risk are material risks to this strategy because of different investor liquidity preferences for the core assets and their hedges, together with the reliance on relatively high leverage from brokers to generate competitive returns. Despite this being a fixed income strategy, returns are highly correlated to the returns of the S&P 500 (0.67). The strategy also demonstrates the highest negative skew and greatest kurtosis of any of the strategies evaluated in this book.

CAPITAL STRUCTURE ARBITRAGE STRATEGIES

Capital structure arbitrage refers to trading strategies that take advantage of the relative mispricing across different security classes issued from the same company's capital structure. Typically, mispricing opportunities arise between equity-linked and debt-linked securities. These temporary mis-pricings arise because debt and equity markets have different participants and market structures that create different price discovery processes and speeds. For example, if a firm surprises the market and reports disappointing earnings, a company's stock may immediately fall 10 percent, but that same information may not be reflected in the company's bond price until several days later and may effect a drop in the bond's price of only 2 percent. In such a scenario, it may be possible to profit systematically from such mis-pricings and divergent intermarket dynamics.

These strategies usually can be implemented by, and require the management of, offsetting positions of an issuer's debt, CDSs, asset swaps, and equity and equity option securities. The central idea is to go long undervalued securities linked to one part of the company's capital structure while hedging by going short overvalued securities linked to another part of the capital structure. This is a relative value trade that utilizes only one company's securities. It is most similar to a convertible arbitrage strategy where the portfolio manager goes long the convertible bond but short the company's stock.

More sophisticated capital structure arbitrage strategies involve trading implied volatilities in the equity options market against default probabilities implied by credit spreads, effectively arbitraging the default probability predicted by the CDS market and the equity options market. As the equity value of a firm declines, its financial leverage increases, causing the distance to default to decline. The debt of the firm is therefore increasingly risky and the credit spread on its debt and CDS rate increases. Furthermore, as a consequence of the greater financial leverage, the returns to shareholders become more uncertain, the equity becomes increasingly risky, and its volatility increases. Conversely, as the equity value of the firm increases, the financial leverage decreases, and the credit spreads on its debt and CDS rates will tighten. Furthermore, as a consequence of the lower financial leverage, returns to shareholders become less uncertain and the equity volatility will tend to decrease. Equity volatility is a decreasing function of the equity price. Consequently, the equity market can provide a signal of some future change in a firm's credit quality (increased or decreased probability of default) and/or of the level of financial leverage of companies. In addition, the default probability of debt is positively related to the CDS rate and a logical consequence is that the information in the default rate should be reflected in the equity volatility skew.

The interrelationship between volatility skew, CDS rate (as a proxy to default probability) and credit spreads creates capital structure arbitrage opportunities. Whether an arbitrage opportunity exists depends on the rate at which these two different segments of the financial markets incorporate new information into the debt and equity prices. Empirical evidence indicates that the debt and equity markets are more co-integrated[30] than directly correlated.[31]

The theoretical foundation of capital structure arbitrage is mainly based on the contingent claim analysis (CCA) developed by Robert Merton.[32] CCA states that there is a direct link between a company's credit spread, and consequently its probability of default, and its asset value volatility, or its observable equity price and corresponding volatility. After the seminal work of Merton, various extensions and developments were proposed, in particular the KMV model and the web-based tool CreditGrades. All the CCA modeling proposed to date uses a closed-form structural model that relies on select closed-form assumptions to derive formula-linking credit spreads, the probability of default, and equity volatilities.

THE MERTON MODEL

The Merton model refers to a model proposed by Robert C. Merton in 1974 for assessing the credit risk of a company by characterizing the company's equity as a call option on its assets. The model assumes that a company has a certain amount of zero-coupon debt that will become due at a future time, T. The company defaults if the value of its assets is less than the promised debt repayment at time T. The equity of the company is analyzed as a European call option on the assets of the company with maturity T and a strike price equal to the face value of the company's outstanding debt. Put-call parity is then used to price the value of an equity put option and this is treated as an analogous representation of the firm's credit risk. The model can be used to estimate either the risk-neutral probability that the company will default or the credit spread on the debt, given the equity spot price, the equity volatility (which is transformed into asset volatility), and the debt per share, the default barrier, and the volatility of the default barrier. These inputs are used to specify a diffusion process for the asset values. The entity is deemed to have defaulted when the asset value drops below the default barrier. The Merton model simulates asset-value changes using a stochastic diffusion process and a fundamental purpose of the default barrier volatility is to provide a jump-like process which can capture short-term default probabilities. The Merton model has been shown to be empirically accurate for non-financial firms, especially manufacturing entities.

When searching for relative value opportunities, the portfolio managers use structural default models that assess default probabilities from information in the equity markets. They then use these models to gauge the richness and cheapness of the quoted CDS spread or bond credit spreads of the company being evaluated. Using the market value of equity, an associated volatility measure and the liability structure of the obligor, the portfolio manager compares the spread implied from the model with the market spread. When the market spread is substantially larger (or smaller) than the theoretical counterpart, there may be an arbitrage opportunity.[33]

When portfolio managers evaluate whether to implement a capital-structure arbitrage trade, they should have a fundamental economic view on the next stage of the business cycle and specifically the target firm's stage in the leverage cycle (whether financial leverage will increase or decrease going forward), and a deep knowledge of the company's capital structure and business strategy to enable them to anticipate financial problems that could disrupt the arbitrage. They should have analyzed the implied volatility surface of equity options traded to determine the default probability implied by the equity markets, and be tracking the company's credit spread. If it is confirmed that there is a significant divergence, then they should go short the overvalued securities and long the undervalued securities and wait for their convergence. The sizing of positions is model-driven and based on the expected change in the value of the CDS with respect to the equity price. The portfolio manager then sells (buys) a CDS and sells (buys) equity. If the CDS market and equity-implied spread from the model subsequently converge, he profits.

Risks of Capital Structure Arbitrage Strategies

Capital structure arbitrage is far from a textbook definition of an arbitrage. It is unclear whether the convergence trades implemented as part of this relative value strategy are less risky than an outright naked position in either market. The risks are manifold, with primary basis risks and concentration risks, potentially leading to significant systematic and funding-liquidity risks (see Figure 4.31). Lastly, model risk, a form of operational risk is also material.

Basis Risks Basis risk is evident in the weak statistical relationship between the CDS spread and the equity price. Currie and Morris (2002) and proprietary UBS analysis indicates that the average historical correlation between the CDS spread and the equity price on any single capital structure arbitrage trade is only of the order of 5–15 percent.[34] The lack of a close correlation between the two variables suggests that the debt and equity

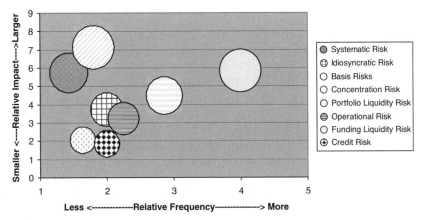

FIGURE 4.31 Risks of capital structure arbitrage strategies

markets can hold diverging views on an obligor for prolonged periods. If the strategy does not converge and the equity hedge works poorly, then the strategy can experience large losses during a general market correction or crash when marked to market, triggering margin calls and forcing an early liquidation of the positions.

The reasons for the weak and unstable price relationship are the nature of the price discovery process in the debt and equity markets and the fact that the relationship is not completely captured in a structural model. The best price discovery occurs in the markets where (informed) traders trade the most frequently. Although not knowing which market has more liquidity for a specific name, be it the equity market or the debt and CDS market, the equity market in general tends to be more liquid than the CDS market. In general, equities tend to react to new information faster than fixed-income instruments. First, it is known that options contracts have a lower contract size than CDS contracts, which could lead to more trading activities in the option market.

Secondly, the market participants in both markets have different objectives that drive different behaviors. Institutional investors and fixed income funds are often restricted by regulations or investor mandate to invest in only investment grade names. If a firm's debt is graded below investment grade, for example, these participants would have to liquidate their holdings, temporarily widening the bid/ask spread and blowing out the credit spread more than a structural model would rationally predict. Similarly, in the equity markets, if a company's equity value falls below a point where the stock becomes reclassified as a small cap stock, then institutional equity investors with mid and large cap mandates may have to sell the stock to remain compliant with their mandates, resulting in price movements and volatility unanticipated by a structural model.

Thirdly, basis risk is also driven by other factors driving the prices of both equity- and debt-linked instruments that are not captured in the structural model, such as asymmetric counterparty risks inherent to the CDS and equity option markets. A CDS is an over-the-counter security, while options are traded mainly on large exchanges. Keeping all other risks equal for debt and equity markets, a CDS security bears greater counterparty risk because the creditworthiness of the seller is typically lower than that of a mutualized exchange clearing house backing a listed option security. The greater counterparty risk does influence the price determination process in the CDS market and is not part of the structural models.[35] The impact of counterparty risk in the CDS market on the basis can be dramatic when a major broker-dealer or bank is thought to be impaired, as was seen during the credit crisis of 2007–08.

Lastly, company-specific events which impact the value of one security class and not the other do occur frequently. Corporate actions such as a change in dividend policy will have a greater effect on the value of equity than on debt. To the extent that a firm has issued debt in a foreign currency and equity in its home currency, foreign currency fluctuations will have a greater impact on the value of foreign currency denominated debt.

Individual positions can be very risky and most losses occur when the arbitrageur shorts CDSs but subsequently finds the market spread rapidly increasing and the equity hedge ineffective due to basis risk. The open question is whether such a strategy can be applied universally or is specific to particular companies at particular times.

Concentration Risk   Given the instability of the basis, it is important for a structural arbitrage fund to diversify its positions. Previous work on individual bonds (particularly Collin-Dufresne *et al.* 2001) has suggested that using the issuing firm's equity to hedge corporate debt was unlikely to be effective. Achieving optimal diversification, however, is difficult given the costs in time and research, and the transaction cost of finding and implementing structural arbitrage positions. That said, a more important reason to diversify is the idiosyncratic risks of unanticipated changes in the capital structure of individual firms. Both basis risk and idiosyncratic risk undermine the effectiveness of hedging debt with equity at the level of individual trades.

Mandalay Resort Group[36]   Capital structure arbitrage is very risky when based on individual obligors and not diversified. Bajlum and Larsen (2007) present the case of Mandalay Resort Group as an example of idiosyncratic risk in capital structure arbitrage, but there are many others cases.[37] Mandalay Resort Group was a hotel-casino operator based in Las Vegas, Nevada. Its major properties included Mandalay Bay, Luxor, Excalibur and Circus Circus, as well as half of the Monte Carlo casino. In market-capitalization terms, it was one of the largest casino operators in the world. Its stock traded on the New York Stock Exchange with the ticker symbol "MBG" and its debt (rated BB by S&P) and CDS were widely traded in the OTC markets. In 2003 and early 2004, the credit spreads based on historical volatilities diverged consistently and substantially from credit spreads imputed in CDS prices, creating a capital structure arbitrage opportunity. A portfolio manager sells protection on the debt via a CDS and sells the equity as a hedge, expecting the credit spreads implied in the two markets to converge over time.

However, on June 4, 2004, one of Mandalay Resort Group's largest competitors, MGM Mirage, announced a bid to acquire it for US$68 per share and to assume Mandalay's existing debt. Although the proposal was announced after the close of trading on June 4, the volume of trading in Mandalay Resort Group stock on that day was quadruple the normal, with the stock rising from US$54 to a closing price of US$60.27 per share. Moody's placed Mandalay's debt rating on review for a possible downgrade because of a high level of uncertainty regarding the level of debt employed by MGM Mirage to finance the takeover. However, as a result of the expected synergies realized from the expected takeover and the high confidence placed on the consummation of the deal, the equity price steadily increased from US$54 to US$69 over a short period. On June 15, 2004, both companies' boards approved a revised offer of US$71 per share. The agreement called for MGM Mirage to pay US$4.8 billion and to assume US$2.5 billion in debt. The transaction was completed on April 26, 2005, for US$7.9 billion. Over the May and June 2004 period, Mandalay stock's historical and implied volatility plunged, while the credit spread widened from 188 bps to 227 bps.

For the portfolio managers playing this deal, May and June 2004 were particularly painful as the difference between the credit spread implied by equity volatility and that of the CDS market reversed and stayed tight through the consummation of the deal. This opposite reaction in equity and credit gave the portfolio managers who were short in both markets a painful one-two punch. They lost on both the sold CDS protection position and the short equity position in Mandalay. These losses had to be realized when the deal was consummated and Mandalay stock and debt ceased to exist and had to be sold or converted to MGM Mirage securities.

At the portfolio level, it is important to diversify positions across firms and sectors to minimize the impact of basis risk and idiosyncratic risk. Various academic studies show that diversification is effective at reducing return variability, particularly for portfolios concentrated in sub-investment grade names. For capital structure arbitrage portfolios consisting of BB-rated bond positions, Schaefer and Strebulaev (2006) find that the strength of the hedge relationship between bonds and equity more than doubles, from 33 percent to 73 percent, when diversified and evaluated at the portfolio level.

Systematic Risks While capital structure arbitrage is very risky at the level of individual trades, idiosyncratic risk can be diversified. Basis risks, however, may lead to ineffective hedges and exposure to systematic risk. This exposure can lead to losses in market crises.

The exposure of capital structure arbitrage strategies to systematic-risk factors is confirmed by several academic studies. Schaefer and Strebulaev (2006), Elton et al. (2001) and Collin-Dufresne et al. (2001) confirm that capital structure arbitrage returns are significantly related to the small stock returns and value stock returns. In particular, Schaefer and Strebulaev show that the two Fama-French factors for small caps (Small minus Big, SMB) and value stocks (High [book/price] minus Low [book/price], HML) are correlated to the returns of capital structure arbitrage.[38] They find that this relationship holds over long periods and over sub-periods. Intuitively, these factors which measure the historic excess returns of small cap stocks and "value" stocks over the market as a whole would be correlated with the returns of fixed income-linked and equity-linked securities of small cap and value stocks independently. To the extent that capital structure arbitrage funds tend to invest in securities of firms where there are pricing inefficiencies arising from the fact that there is less analyst coverage (that is, small caps) and firms closer to the default barrier where the debt/equity correlation may be stronger (that is, value stocks), these results make sense because of the partial ineffectiveness of the debt/equity hedge.

Duarte et al. (2005) point out that exposure to such market factors also makes returns from capital structure arbitrage sensitive to major financial events such as a sudden flight-to-quality or flight-to-liquidity. In such scenarios, not only will the basis between debt and equity be in flux, but securities of small cap and value firms will be sold off in favor of higher-quality and less-risky securities. A systematic risk is a significant risk to capital-structure arbitrage funds.

Funding Liquidity Because of the instability of the basis and exposure to systematic risk, capital structure arbitrage positions are subject to having their financing reduced or withdrawn in periods of market turbulence.

Having said that, the impact of a withdrawal of funding is lower because prime brokerages tend not to provide capital structure arbitrage funds with significant leverage in light of the instability of the basis.

It is necessary to maintain low leverage and significant levels of reserve cash. A manager of a capital structure arbitrage portfolio should be cognizant that market spreads are much more volatile than model-predicted spreads and, consequently, convergence positions can lose money fast and margins can be increased. The portfolio manager must be able to stay liquid longer than the market can remain "irrational." In order to ride the convergence of the spreads to profitability, the portfolio manager must have substantial unencumbered cash reserves.

Yu (2006) shows that a longer holding period produces more converging trades, fewer trades with negative returns, and better average returns, but that the portfolio manager must be able to remain in his positions through periods of significant mark-to-market losses. Were a portfolio manager to employ levels of leverage common in fixed income arbitrage (5–20×), the arbitrageur could suffer a complete drawdown of capital and be forced to liquidate positions at a loss. Even at 2× leverage (that is, 50 percent average margin), the portfolio manager could suffer substantial losses at an alarming frequency.[39] This finding is ultimately related to the low correlation between CDS spreads and equity price changes, and stands in stark contrast to the favorable coverage that the strategy has received in the financial press.[40] As funding liquidity risk is high in this strategy, the key is to utilize a lower level of leverage to mitigate the impact of volatility in the basis, in order to increase the likelihood of being able to stay in the trade to convergence, and to accept a lower level of return as a result.

Model Risks Lastly, a form of operational risk, model risk, is a material risk in capital structure arbitrage. There is a material risk that as this is a model-driven trading strategy, positions may be initiated based on over-reliance on the model, model mis-specification or mis-measured inputs.

As discussed earlier, the structural models employed assume that market inputs, particularly equity option implied-volatility, incorporate all public information. Correct interpretation of these market inputs requires correct specification and measurement before analyzing them within a structural framework. Lastly, managers should be cognizant that their models can fail as a result of false information and exogenous events. Obviously, there have been numerous instances where critical information about a company's creditworthiness was not public or where public information was false. When that information became publicly known, credit spreads and equity volatilities jumped to default levels from previously low credit spreads. The losses sustained as a result of defaults ranging from Enron to WorldCom were not predicted in advance by the behavior of their security prices. Similarly, exogenous events such as the oil spill in the Gulf of Mexico cannot be structurally predicted from market inputs and can significantly change a company's creditworthiness after a trade is implemented.

Performance Performance information on capital structure arbitrage is not yet available. There is currently no index that exclusively represents the risk and performance of these strategies.

In conclusion, the risks of capital structure arbitrage strategies are significant, with primary basis risks and concentration risks potentially leading to significant systematic and funding liquidity risks. Model risk, a form of operational risk, is also material. At the theoretical level, the strategy should offer attractive Sharpe ratios and a positive average return with positive skewness. However, no representative data is available to evaluate the strategy's actual performance.

High-velocity Algorithmic Trading Strategies

High-velocity trading strategies produce alpha by rapidly executing highly cost-efficient strategies in liquid markets. The strategies employed are not new but they are blindingly accelerated and highly automated. The primary strategies tend to be equity, futures, and exchange traded option focused. They include electronic market making, statistical arbitrage, index arbitrage, index vs. exchange traded fund (ETF) arbitrage, ADR vs. local shares, spread trading, global macro, momentum strategies, trend-following strategies, and event driven strategies. These strategies are implemented at various turnover frequencies, from as fast as sub-millisecond to as slow as monthly. The unifying theme is that all make extensive use of algorithms in their trading and risk management decisions and of cutting-edge information technology to implement their trades at the lowest possible cost. High-velocity trading strategies are not the domain exclusively of hedge funds. Investment banks, proprietary trading shops and commodities trading advisors (CTAs) also implement such strategies.

The hedge fund industry produces one product, alpha, and has had an interesting evolution. The industry pioneer was Alfred Winslow Jones. Then it became a cottage industry practiced by a handful of innovative, elite money managers and investment banks that refined the ability to go short into discrete and unique alpha-generating investment processes (that is, convertible arbitrage or fixed income relative value). The industry spawned many imitators and, eventually, champions emerged, which combined strategies under one banner (multi-strategy funds) and gained operational economies of scale by concentrating assets. Now, it is becoming a mature industry where the alpha-production line is fully automated, systematized, highly efficient and accelerated. High-velocity trading/algorithmic portfolios are focused on building computerized decision and execution "engines" that rapidly assimilate data, identify mis-pricings, trends, or investing opportunities and then rapidly execute to harvest the most complex market inefficiencies. Typically, portfolio managers connect directly to exchanges, bypass sell-side brokers, utilize the most advanced equipment, and perpetually optimize their execution software in order to get an edge in speed and innovation on the rest of the market.

The nature of data has also enabled these strategies to flourish. From daily data, to minute-by-minute data to microsecond-by-microsecond parsed nano data, exchanges have been making more granular data available. The availability of copious, rapid, clean, granular, information-rich market data enables these inter-day, inter-hour, inter-minute, inter-second mis-pricings to be identified and arbitrage strategies to be implemented on a nano time scale.

Firms practicing high-velocity algorithmic strategies have several distinctive and core capabilities that enable them to implement these faster and more cheaply, including:

1. Ability to manipulate and analyze vast amounts of data. Firms maintain pristine historical data sets and have direct access to real-time nano data from exchanges.
2. Ability to rapidly identify opportunities by integrating diverse data sets, and back-test theories within an integrated quantitative research platform.
3. Ability to minimize execution costs using cutting-edge Execution and Order Management Systems.
4. Ability to execute trades within the minutest latency between order input and execution. This is enabled by latency-minimized infrastructure and co-location of servers at the exchanges.

These capabilities enable variants of equity market neutral and event arbitrage to be implemented, for example. Variants of the former include breaking equities and futures into fundamental risk factors and looking for mispriced factors to create an arbitrage. Trades include, for example, arbitrage between a basket of energy stocks representing energy and interest rate factors against oil and interest rate futures. More complex portfolios could incorporate a global agricultural, energy, and mining equity portfolio hedged with a portfolio of agricultural, energy, metals, and foreign exchange and interest rate futures. Event arbitrage strategies involve profiting from early event detection and positioning. High-velocity event arbitrage strategies parse words from machine-readable electronic newswire feeds regarding the economic data releases that historically cause volatility first in the futures markets and then in broader equity and fixed-income markets. Governments release economic data on a routine schedule. Historical market reaction to those releases has been studied and distilled into algorithmic trading rules based on binary outcomes or patterned changes in sentiment. Parsing these data feeds enables trading systems to know within a fraction of a second how to trade as soon as new data is released from the U.S. Treasury, for example.

Given the secrecy surrounding these strategies and their relatively low level of propagation through the hedge fund community, their risks are not entirely known, but operational, basis and funding liquidity risks are probably the most significant. Figure 4.32 shows the relative significance and frequency of the risks facing high-velocity algorithmic trading strategies.

Operational risk is significant because of the high dependency on accurate and computationally intensive algorithms and a highly efficient and robust infrastructure for continued access to markets. Computers make the trading decisions based on trading algorithms. While these algorithms are

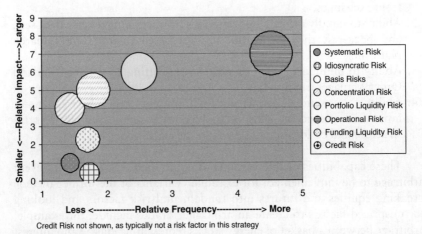

Credit Risk not shown, as typically not a risk factor in this strategy

FIGURE 4.32 The risks of high-velocity strategies

back-tested and refined with instructions on how to trade every conceivable market from benign (standard operating procedure) to crashing markets (go to cash and shut down), not every permutation of every scenario can be conceived and planned for. The future remains unpredictable and humans have cognitive limits. The algorithms can react in an unintended way to unanticipated market signals. This can have a serial compounding effect when multiple computers are trading against each other. The Flash Crash of 2009 and the Quant Meltdown of August 2007, when quantitative funds crashed together, are both examples of programmed trading strategies that went awry.

The dependency on continued access to markets is an operational risk as well, as these strategies, which must constantly rebalance their positions, put on and take off trades. A market discontinuity, such as when security trades limit up, close, and then re-open limit down, can cause material losses. Similarly, a loss of connectivity during a period of high volatility is a significant operational risk. The loss of connectivity to the Kospi[41] the moment after putting on one leg of an arbitrage could leave the fund exposed.[42] If the loss of access to markets is due to the firm's infrastructure and is total, rather than due to the failure of one exchange and limited to that exchange, this can be catastrophic.

Basis risks are also likely significant, as the relationships exploited by high-velocity strategies may exist only in specific market situations (phase specific) and for only a brief period. To the extent that these funds trade risk factors and not actual securities, they incur basis risk on those risk factors. The value of a unit of an interest rate risk factor embedded within an interest rate future may be pure and stable but the interest rate risk factor embedded in a bank stock or financial ETF will be polluted and unstable. Any intermarket relative value or convergence trade must be sized and levered conservatively to minimize the impact of a widening, intermittent, or volatile risk-factor basis.

The amount of alpha that can be captured from each trade and the fact that prime brokers call for margin on a daily basis creates an opportunity for excessive use of funding, and funding liquidity risk. To the extent that the fund is not a member of the exchange on which it is trading[43] and rents a broker's infrastructure for direct access to the exchange, it is only required to pay the daily margin to its broker based on the position held by the broker at the close of the previous day. This enables the fund to potentially put on and take off trades during the day without having to post margin, as long as it closes the day with relatively few positions or flat. Theoretically, high-velocity funds that make use of a broker's connectivity to the exchange can put on large positions limited only by the limit placed on the clearing broker by the exchange. That limit is based on the broker's equity. These positions dwarf the equity of the high-velocity funds.

The fact that individual high-velocity trades typically generate small amounts of alpha creates demand for leverage to amplify returns. Just as the funds have built the lowest-cost infrastructure to minimize execution costs to make capturing small amounts of alpha per trade a profitable endeavor, they want the highest possible leverage to maximize profits. The combination of motive and opportunity to abuse leverage creates a substantial risk to these funds. The reaction of brokers who detect abuse of leverage or excessive risk taking among funds to which they grant direct access to the exchange is to sever the connection to the exchange.

Performance   Performance information on high-velocity strategies is not yet available as currently there is no index that exclusively represents the risk and performance of these strategies.

In conclusion, the tools for an increasingly automated investment-management process are being used by high-velocity algorithmic-trading funds to create an automated alpha-production line that reaches across asset classes and markets. There are significant basis, operational and funding-liquidity risks in these strategies. Over time these risks will be increasingly well controlled. Hedge funds must join the low-cost/high-speed arms race or forge proprietary expertise for alpha discovery in existing or un-discovered strategies if they are to continue to produce alpha.

Commodity Trading Advisors/Managed Futures

A Commodity Trading Advisor (CTA) is an individual or a firm, registered with the Commodity Futures Trading Commission, which receives compensation for giving people advice on options, futures and the actual trading of managed futures accounts. Funds within this category are managed to accrue profits in global commodity futures and currency markets. Returns to these funds usually are uncorrelated with those of conventional equity and bond markets. CTAs frequently utilize formulaic trading strategies based on technical analysis. The primary CTA strategies are short-term systematic (or momentum), longer-term systematic (or trend-following) and discretionary long/short.

Systematic CTAs borrow many of their trading and risk management techniques from statistical arbitrage equity strategies. The value driver for this type of CTA is the portfolio construction and risk management. Individual trades are not as important as the behavior of the portfolio as a whole. Broadly, portfolio construction is based on risk factors that encompass portfolio risk, market risk, market direction, trend strength, liquidity and a variety of proprietary factors depending on the strategy and model. Risk is allocated to each sector and to each market and dynamically rebalanced on an intra-day, daily or weekly basis depending on the time horizon of the strategy, making adjustments to the market position to allow for trend strength, risk and liquidity.

The time-frames targeted by systematic CTAs vary widely—from minutes to hours to months to a year or more. Some CTAs specialize in one time-frame while others run models across multiple time-frames.

Short-term managers use models with greater sensitivity to short-term changes in underlying asset prices and volatility and thus enter and exit positions more quickly than their longer-term, less market-sensitive counterparts. Managers of short-term systematic portfolios attempt to trade according to market momentum or price patterns that are perceived to exist over time periods as short as intra-day to a week. Managers of long-term systematic portfolios seek to trade according to market trends or price patterns that are perceived to exist over periods of months.

Trends and momentum are phenomena that result from auto-correlation in prices whereby past prices influence future prices. This can be explained by the influence of crowd behavior and time delays for information to be absorbed into market prices, and the influences of different market participants all operating with different time horizons. This causes market segments to develop momentum and markets to trend with many different time horizons and frequency.

Systematic momentum and trend strategies use technical indicators such as moving averages, Bollinger bands, and breakouts to identify trading opportunities. CTAs that specialize in this strategy can profit from both rising markets (by being long), declining markets (by being short) and inflecting markets that are experiencing trend reversals.

Systematic traders use proprietary data filters, such as Kalman filters, to capture market behavior and predict future behavior over various time horizons based on observation of market data. Short-term, high-frequency data are best for identifying short-term momentum, while longer-term data are best for identifying longer-term trends. The key is to filter, isolate, and amplify the short-term or long-term trend from market data noise. The filters then isolate the dominant frequency to determine the strength and direction of the trend. Each model filters the market price to determine strength and direction for a given trading frequency. The filters detect signals of the start and end of trends. Depending on the strength of the signal and market volatility, positions will be sized and decisions to enter or exit and position will be made. The models that follow longer-term trends will tend to reduce positions as short-term volatility increases to smooth P&L and minimize drawdowns. In low-volatility environments, positions will be increased. A longer-term trend enables a more gradual entry and exit profile called a "pyramid," as the peak exposure occurs at the inflexion point of the scaling-in/out process.

While higher longer-term volatility enables these strategies to profit, these strategies often incur drawdowns in non-trending, low-volatility environments as drifting price action will result in weak entry signals that trigger the taking of larger long and short positions (as a result of low volatility) that subsequently drift up or down in price and get stopped out. Rapid, intra-session price reversals ("whipsaws") when prices oscillate around a stop level can cause the repeated initiation of trades followed by an immediate invocation of stop-loss limits. This results in a slow bleed of P&L from frequent, small trading losses and trading costs without profiting from any discernible trend.

Discretionary long/short CTA strategies seek to profit from fundamental and mean reversion strategies as well as from momentum and trend-following strategies. Fundamental trading strategies may speculate on volatility by selling options on futures contracts. Option selling is a strategy that focuses on writing options (and collecting their premiums) that are likely to expire worthless, similar to an insurance company selling property insurance. Within this strategy are naked option writers and spread option writers. The idea is that the CTA will benefit from the premium it collects from the buyer most of the time while the likelihood of having to pay a claim or hitting a strike is low. The associated risk is that its return profile has fat tails. The options may not expire out of the money and the contracts will go in the money, resulting in a substantial payout and cost to the option seller. Discretionary long/short CTAs may also seek to profit from relative value arbitrage strategies, of which there are a number of sub-strategies. The truest example of arbitrage is simultaneously buying gold on one exchange and selling it on another for a higher price. This strategy looks to profit from the price difference but is not a true arbitrage as it still retains a location-basis risk in that the price differential may rationally exist due to transport costs. Other relative-value strategies may be going long and short futures with different maturities on the same underlying asset (calendar basis trades). Discretionary long/short CTA managers may also take positions based on fundamentals similar to macro hedge funds but are based on more micro fundamentals such as crop reports and weather patterns.

Distinct Determinants of Leverage   Unlike other hedge fund strategies, CTAs derive their leverage from margins required by the exchanges where futures and options trade. Margins are determined under a different competitive dynamic. Futures clearing merchants (FCMs), who make up the membership of the exchange, clear futures and options for the CTAs and must post margin to the exchange for all contracts they clear while collecting margin from their clients. It is the FCMs who are responsible for posting margin for the trades they clear on behalf of their clients. The amount of margin required is determined by the exchange. FCMs are free to demand whatever margin they choose from their clients as long as they post the exchange minimum. While FCMs are free to charge higher than the exchange minimum, they typically do not, as competitive pressures between FCMs are high and the costs to customers of switching are comparatively low.

The same banks and brokerages that are the major prime brokers to hedge funds are also the major FCMs to CTAs. However, in general, the prime brokerages and futures clearing activities are separate business entities within the brokerages. Most of the revenue for an FCM is derived from fees on the execution and clearing of trades, not from interest charged on the financing of securities on margin. The business model for futures clearing is different from that of prime brokerage. Interest income from margin financing is not a significant source of income in the FCM business as exchange cleared futures and options cannot be rehypothecated to generate low-cost funding.

CTAs and managed futures strategies were the only ones covered in this book that were able to deliver positive returns in 2008. It is very likely that CTAs were only able to do this because financing for CTAs was not dramatically reduced in the credit crisis, and did not create a downward price spiral of liquidations. While the volatility of futures contracts did cause exchanges to increase the minimum margin requirements of numerous contracts, the impact was precise and well-targeted. The futures markets did not suffer from the wholesale collapse of the interbank rehypothecation markets when banks only lent to other banks against the most liquid and stable collateral. Unlike the prime brokers, FCMs did not suffer a dramatic erosion in profitability from increased funding costs. Consequently, they did not increase margins to reduce the amount of financing extended to CTAs (as prime brokers did to hedge funds), and there was no vicious circle of forced liquidations and de-leveraging. CTAs were thus able to deliver a positive performance in 2008, which was largely due to the fact that funding liquidity remained stable because of the distinct determinants of leverage in the futures markets.[44]

Risks of Managed Futures Strategies and CTAs   The primary risks of CTAs/ managed futures (as outlined in Figure 4.33) are systematic risk, basis risk, operational risk and funding-liquidity risk.

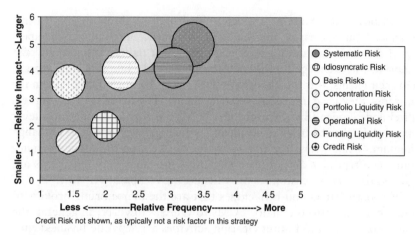

FIGURE 4.33   The risks of CTA and managed futures strategies

Systematic Risk   While CTAs are generally uncorrelated to the equity markets, systematic risk is still present but in the form of exposure to certain commodity indices and currencies—primarily the euro, the pound and the yen. Systematic events characterized by changes in Fed policy and by severe dislocations in markets that affect liquidity can overwhelm momentum and trend-following strategies in a given time period, leading to losses. Changes in monetary policy, whether expected or not, can affect trading in a variety of markets and the term structure of futures contracts. Periods when abnormally poor liquidity affects some markets and affects the correlations with a broader set of markets are those with which most trading strategies are least able to deal. These are considered the markets that offer the least opportunities and greatest risks for managers with long time horizons. CTA managers also do not have a good record of catching economic rebounds as many of the lowest monthly returns are those where recoveries followed major market events. However, managed futures strategies tend to perform well in years coinciding with market shocks once a positive or negative trend is identified. The Asian crisis in 1997, the Russian crisis (and LTCM failure) in 1998, the equity bear market in 2003 following the tech stock crash, and the credit crisis of 2007–08 were all examples of when managed futures did well when many other strategies were failing.

Basis Risks   Basis risks are present in the relative value and mean reversion trades implemented by discretionary CTA managers. Locational basis risk is the risk that arises from hedging with a contract that does not have the same or similar delivery point as the asset or cash flow that is being hedged.

For example, if a CTA is hedging an ICE natural gas future with NYMEX natural gas futures, they are still exposed to the basis risk between Henry Hub (the NYMEX natural gas delivery point in Erath, Louisiana) and the European grid delivery point (the Zeebruge Hub in Belgium). If the differential between supply and demand conditions on NYMEX and ICE change during the life of the trade, the price relationship between the two contracts will change, potentially exposing the CTA manager. Expanding on this example, the April NYMEX natural gas futures settled at $3.842/MMbtu while natural gas, for April, delivered to the European gas hub averaged $3.5610/MMbtu. In this case, the CTA is exposed to $0.2810/MMbtu of basis.

Product or quality basis risk is the risk that arises from hedging with an instrument that is not the same product or quality of product as that being produced, marketed or consumed. For example, jet fuel is often hedged with heating oil as the futures as it is much more liquid than the derivatives market for jet fuel. While jet fuel and heating oil are similar (in that both are distillates) and highly correlated, they are not the same and the basis relationship between the two is not always consistent.

Calendar basis risk, also known as calendar spread risk, is the risk that arises from hedging with an instrument that does not mature on the same date as the opposing future's contract. As an example, a CTA might seek to balance its one-month CME Eurodollar futures exposure using three-month CME Eurodollar futures. Here, the CTA is exposed to calendar basis risk as the three-month CME Eurodollar future does not expire until two months after the one-month CME Eurodollar contract expires. On the surface, it appears that the CTA is forced to accept the basis risk as part of its strategy. However, there are other instruments that will allow the CTA to mitigate its exposure to calendar risk: over-the-counter (OTC) swaps and options, but these are typically less liquid and not used in short-term systematic strategies.

Funding Liquidity While funding liquidity for the futures market as a whole was resilient in 2008, it remains a significant risk at the individual CTA level. CTAs are typically highly levered, as the futures trader need only deposit a margin rather than the full futures contract price. Because of the comparatively low exchange margins on futures and the competition between FCMs for clients, a CTA or futures trader can employ high amounts of leverage without having to resort to borrowing, as long as their FCM agrees. In the CTA world, leverage is measured using a margin-to-equity ratio that shows how much margin is being used relative to the funds being invested. CTAs typically have ratios ranging from 10 percent to 20 percent.

This high amount of leverage is possible because minimum margin requirements are determined by for-profit exchanges where revenues are a function of trading volume. Volume typically flows to the exchange with the lowest margin requirement. The exchange takes the credit risk of its member FCMs. The FCMs, which are typically also major prime brokers and provide CTAs with access to the exchange contracts, take the credit risk of their clients.

If a client is overleveraged or has deteriorating creditworthiness, it is prudent for the FCM to charge higher than the exchange's minimum margin. If a CTA defaults on its margin payment to an FCM, the FCM must still post the margin at the exchange and liquidate the client's position, potentially at a loss greater than the margin posted. In addition, when market volatility and/or liquidity changes, exchanges and FCMs can also change the margins required. Consequently, CTAs can be forced to liquidate positions at a loss in order to meet margin calls.

Funding liquidity risk and overleverage in part caused the failures of Motherock and Amaranth (see Appendix 2). These funds were very active in natural gas futures, incurred losses, and subsequently were forced to fully de-leverage when their FCMs increased margin because of their losses and deteriorating creditworthiness. They were forced to sell additional positions at a loss to meet margin calls and ultimately closed their funds.

Operational Risk As with the statistical arbitrage funds from which CTAs draw much of their model-driven strategy and trading techniques, operational risk can be significant in the systematic CTA strategies. Operational risk in the form of model risk exists as a consequence of the dependency on models for trading decisions. As with statistical arbitrage and high-velocity strategies, there is the risk of model mis-specification, data misinterpretation and, in the case of short-term systematic strategies, of loss of connectivity or trading disruptions.

Performance of Managed Futures Strategies From January 2000 to January 2010, the Greenwich Alternative Investments International Futures Index posted an average annualized return of 9.78 percent, with an annualized standard deviation of 6.82 percent (see Figure 4.34). The cumulative return of the Relative Value Hedge Fund Index over the 10-year period was 97.82 percent, significantly outperforming that of the S&P 500 Index (−25.2 percent).

Managed futures/CTAs outperformed primarily because of their ability to deliver consistent returns and avoid significant drawdowns in nine of the 10 years. The fact that they delivered positive returns in all of the four years where the S&P 500 return was negative indicates their low correlation with

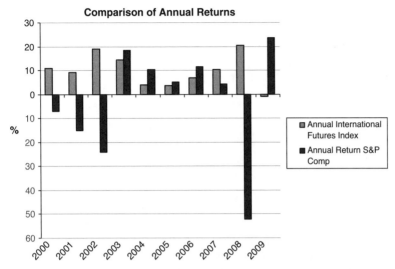

FIGURE 4.34 Greenwich International Futures Index annual returns vs. S&P 500 Index
Source: Greenwich Alternative Investments LLC, Shiller

equities and significantly contributed to their cumulative outperformance of the S&P over the decade. They delivered positive returns when the S&P 500 suffered drawdowns during the dot-com crash, in the aftermath of 9/11 and, most importantly, during the credit crisis of 2008. This is the only strategy evaluated in this book that delivered a positive performance in 2008 when systematic and liquidity effects overwhelmed fundamental price relationships for all other strategies. Managed futures/CTAs delivered an annual return of 20.5 percent during the credit crisis, where the S&P 500 delivered −52.2 percent.

Compared to other hedge fund strategies, managed futures/CTAs were the only strategy evaluated in this book where monthly returns exhibited *negative* correlation to the S&P 500 monthly returns (−0.196) and the overall equity market for the overall period from 2000 to 2010 (see Figure 4.35). While the negative correlation persisted through the period, it weakened in the latter half of the decade. From 2000–05, correlation with the S&P 500 was −0.34, despite three years of market crisis. From 2005 to 2010, negative correlation weakened to −0.029.

The monthly returns of managed futures/CTAs were substantially less volatile than those of the S&P 500; 2.92 percent vs. 4.35 percent, respectively. Unlike all other hedge fund strategies, which produced negative returns in October and November 2008, managed futures/CTAs generated

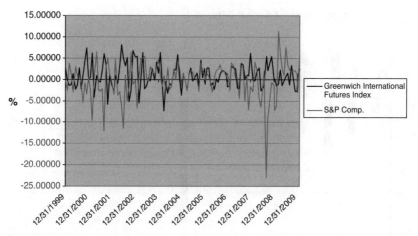

FIGURE 4.35 Greenwich International Futures Index monthly returns vs. S&P 500 Index (January 2000–March 2010)
Source: Greenwich Alternative Investments LLC, Shiller

positive returns of 5.44 percent and 2.12 percent, respectively. The maximum monthly drawdown for the strategy, however, was significant (−7.4 percent on April 30, 2004) but was not unexpected as it was only a 2.4 sigma event.

Overall, the distribution of monthly returns is positively skewed (0.147), a unique result compared to the negative skew observed for the other strategies in this book.[45] This positive skew is also in stark contrast to that of the S&P 500 index (−1.43) for the same period. Furthermore, the distribution of monthly returns exhibits less kurtosis than that of the S&P 500 for the same period (0.6 vs. 5.6), indicating a significantly lower presence of outliers in the return distribution.

In conclusion, the performance and risks of CTAs/managed-futures strategies are distinct from other strategies evaluated in this book. CTAs/managed futures are the only strategy to demonstrate a negative correlation of returns with the S&P 500 and to have generated positive returns during the credit crisis of 2008. Leverage for this strategy is high but sourced via exchanges and futures commission merchants. Leverage for exchange traded derivatives proved stable compared to that for cash securities and OTC derivatives provided via the prime brokerage model. The primary risks facing these strategies are systematic, basis, and operational risks, with funding liquidity risk being the most significant at the individual fund level.

Multi-strategy

By definition, multi-strategy funds engage in a variety of the strategies mentioned earlier. The investment objective of multi-strategy hedge funds is to deliver consistently positive returns regardless of the directional movement in equity, interest rate or currency markets. Sub-strategies adopted in a multi-strategy fund may include, but are not limited to, convertible bond arbitrage, equity long/short, statistical arbitrage and merger arbitrage.

Risks of Multi-Strategy Hedge Funds   The diversification benefits help to smooth the variability and reduce the volatility of returns at the multi-strategy level. In general, the risks facing multi-strategy funds (see Figure 4.36) include those risks facing their sub-strategies, with one significant addition.

Rarely will multi-strategy funds be the best- or worst-performing category of hedge funds over a short-term time horizon. The low correlation of sub-strategies will dilute the returns of any multi-strategy fund during a market rally. However, long-term investors value the consistency and low correlation of multi-strategy returns to the market and earn exceptional returns if the multi-strategy manager can consistently overweight outperforming strategies and underweight underperforming strategies through market cycles.

An example might be if convertible bond arbitrage performs exceptionally poorly during a 12-month period, while equity long/short delivers stellar returns. Dedicated equity long/short managers will outperform

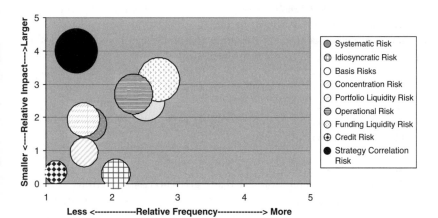

FIGURE 4.36   The risks of multi-strategy hedge funds

multi-strategy managers who engage in both disciplines. However, if the multi-strategy manager has allocated more of the risk budget to equity long/short strategies, he should do better than the average of equity long/short returns and convertible arbitrage returns. Over a longer time period, when equity long/short delivers mediocre returns and convertible bond arbitrage performs very well, then the opposite occurs; multi-strategy managers should outperform equity long/short funds and convertible bond funds because of their ability to dynamically allocate capital to winning strategies. In the long term, the consistency and performance of multi-strategy funds delivering low-volatility and high risk adjusted returns, both in absolute and relative terms, is what investors value.[46]

However, the additional risk is the risk of correlation of sub-strategy returns. Should the strategies employed under the multi-strategy umbrella become correlated, or exposed to a common set of risk factors, the primary benefit of multi-strategy funds (that is, the consistent positive returns regardless of movement in markets) evaporates. For the multi-strategy manager, ensuring the low correlation of sub-strategies and the diversified impact of broad systematic factors across the sub-strategy returns is essential to managing the risk of the multi-strategy fund and delivering its value proposition to investors. Detecting correlation in sub-strategy returns and cross-strategy exposures to "hidden risk factors" is essential to determine which strategies to include in the multi-strategy fund and their relative risk weighting. Furthermore, understanding the potential exposure of the fund to crisis-level systematic-risk factors is essential, as sub-strategies may be uncorrelated in normal market conditions but dramatically correlated in a crisis.

Correlation across Strategies   Correlation is the tendency of the returns on two or more strategies to move together.

The correlation coefficient measures the tendency of two strategies' returns to move together. This is written as:

$$\text{Corr}(R_A, R_B) \text{ or } \rho_{A,B}$$

where R_A is the return on strategy A and R_B is the return on strategy B.

The basics of correlation are:

- Can range from $-1.0 \leq \rho \leq +1.0$
- Perfect positive correlation: $+1.0$ and gives no risk reduction
- Perfect negative correlation: -1.0 and gives complete risk reduction
- Correlation between -1.0 and $+1.0$ gives some, but not all, risk reduction

For a multi-strategy fund with two strategies, the portfolio variance is:

$$\sigma_p^2 = X_A^2 \sigma_A^2 + X_B^2 \sigma_B^2 + 2 X_A X_B \, \sigma_A \sigma_B \, \text{Corr}(R_A, R_B)$$

Combining two strategies into the multi-strategy fund, and varying the percentages invested in each (X_A and X_B) from 0 percent to 100 percent, will result in a range of expected returns and standard deviations. Consequently, understanding the correlation between sub-strategy returns in a multi-strategy fund has a direct impact on the level and variability of returns of that multi-strategy fund.

A multi-strategy fund should constantly monitor the correlation of returns of its sub-strategies in order to a) deliver on its value proposition to investors that returns are not overly correlated to the market; b) deliver on its value proposition that returns are stable due to low correlation between sub-strategies and c) manage its downside risk. The variability of its returns dramatically increases, as does its downside risk, as sub-strategy returns become increasingly correlated. It is the job of the fund's risk manager to identify correlated returns across the sub-strategies, understand the cause of the shift in correlation and recommend hedging strategies or changes in capital allocation to correct for it.

Factor analysis and PCA of P&L   The analysis of sub-strategy return correlations should subsume the special statistical properties of alternative investment strategies: non-normality of the return series, serial correlation of consecutive return observations, as well as phase-locking behavior.[47] Additionally, the analysis should allow for the broad range of trading strategies employed in hedge funds: trading in illiquid securities, derivatives trading, short-selling of securities, and varying use of financial leverage.[48]

As a result, many risk management professionals recognize that mean-variance analysis is an inadequate framework for evaluating the impact of changes in correlation on the potential return distribution of multi-strategy hedge funds. Risk managers should consider the potential for extreme outcomes which are much higher in frequency and magnitude than predicted by models based on mean and variance alone. The higher moments (skewness and kurtosis) of the return distribution need to be understood. The hedge fund risk manager should seek the source of kurtosis in return distributions. One possibility is that returns are independent and identically distributed with a fat-tailed distribution. Another possibility is that while conditional distributions do not have fat tails, dependencies in conditional upper moments induce fat tails in unconditional distributions as in GARCH models. Yet another possibility is that returns may not be directly correlated but co-integrated.[49]

Sub-strategy returns can be expressed as a series of factors that drive these returns. Hypothesizing and then testing for the relevant factors requires a sound understanding of each strategy, its risks, and the likely persistence of a relationship. Factors come in many varieties—fundamental, technical, macroeconomic, and alternative. The factors searched for within sub-strategy returns should reflect sound economic/finance theory and the high likelihood of a persistent relationship to returns. Iterative data mining of returns can produce factors that appear to be highly correlated to sub-strategy returns but the relationship between those factors and returns is superficial. Causality cannot be determined. At a minimum, a multi-strategy fund seeking to deliver returns uncorrelated to the market should search for economic factors that affect most securities to some degree, such as GDP growth, yield curve slope, unemployment, and inflation. In addition, alternative factors such as analyst recommendations, corporate actions such as stock buybacks, and insider purchases should be considered. Lastly, technical factors such as market liquidity, volatility, movement in credit spread, and fund flows (for example, investment flows into and out of defensive industrial sectors) should be considered.

Factor Analysis   Once the factors to be searched for are specified, factor analysis of returns can be applied to identify which of the factors specified are underlying drivers of sub-strategy returns and disaggregate strategy performance into returns on factor exposures.[50] Factor analysis is a statistical method used to describe variability among observed variables such as sub-strategy returns in the form of a potentially lower number of unobserved variables called "factors." In other words, it is possible, for example, that two or three observed variables together represent another, unobserved variable, and factor analysis searches for these possible combinations or "hidden correlations." The observed variables are modeled as linear combinations of the potential factors, plus "error" terms. Principal component analysis (PCA) is the most common form of factor analysis. PCA seeks a linear combination of variables such that the maximum variance is extracted from the variables. It then removes this variance and iteratively seeks a second linear combination which explains the maximum proportion of the remaining variance, and so on.

The information gained from factor analysis and PCA regarding the commonality of factors influencing sub-strategy returns and the interdependencies between these returns can be used to change the construction of the portfolio and manage downside risk. Specifically, various AUM allocations and degrees of leverage employed in various sub-strategies can be evaluated for their degree of exposure to common factors and their potential to create downside return correlations. Effectively, the distribution of return drivers or return factors can be used to develop multi-factor return models to understand the potential distribution of fund returns under different sub-strategy allocations.

Liquidity Risks   Portfolio liquidity risk and funding liquidity risk in multi-strategy funds are not necessarily higher but their management is significantly more complex.

Portfolio liquidity risk is more complex due to the fact that common securities may be held across strategies and/or multiple securities of common issuers may be held across strategies. Assume, for example, that the metals and mining sector has very strong demand fundamentals. Because of the accelerating demand, mining giant Rio Tinto is issuing debt to finance an attempted takeover of another mining giant, BHP. Rio Tinto intends to merge and gain greater cost efficiencies, pricing power in the market, and economies of scale, and thereby create shareholder value. Rio Tinto has common shares listed in London, New York, and Australia. Because of expansion opportunities, BHP has issued debt in the form of convertible bonds that convert to equity if its equity price rises more than 25 percent. In such circumstances, it is likely that a multi-strategy fund will have exposure to Rio Tinto shares in its equity long/short sub-strategy, in its event arbitrage sub-strategy, and possibly in its capital-structure arbitrage sub-strategy. Tracking and knowing the overall size of the fund's position in Rio Tinto shares across sub-strategies and the time it would take to liquidate the aggregate positions is necessary but not terribly complex. The positions across sub-strategies in Rio Tinto equity need to be summed and compared to the average daily trading volume of Rio Tinto shares on the various exchanges on which they are listed. Conservative assumptions about trading volume in a crisis and the percentage of daily trading volume the fund could be on any given day without moving the market need to be made to evaluate the risk to the fund overall.

Liquidity issues become more complex when the overall exposure to Rio Tinto securities is evaluated. The capital structure arbitrage sub-strategy may be short Rio Tinto debt while long the equity, as the capital raising by Rio Tinto and the prospect of the merger may have created a mispricing between the debt and equity markets. The convertible-arbitrage fund may be long the BHP convertible that is becoming increasingly correlated with Rio Tinto equity as the market anticipates the merger will go through. Lastly, given the strong fundamentals for gold, the macro sub-strategy may be long gold and long BHP shares as BHP does not fully hedge its proven gold reserves. A rally in gold will increase BHP's stock price and gives the macro manager a cheap way to gain gold exposure. The multi-strategy fund could easily have more than 10 percent of its AUM exposed to Rio Tinto or BHP and the securities of both companies are becoming increasingly interrelated. This exposure could not be easily liquidated in a day and its risk to the performance of the fund must be evaluated. The complexity compounds even further if the Rio Tinto merger with BHP goes through.

A third source of complexity in liquidity risk management in a multi-strategy fund has an impact on both portfolio liquidity and funding liquidity. In the past several global market crises, shocks have occurred in specific geographic markets and asset classes that have gone on to create contagion and liquidity effects in other geographic markets and asset classes far from the epicenter. For example, the subprime crisis was initially felt in the mortgage-backed securities markets, which became illiquid. Investors active in this asset class were forced to de-lever as prices fell but, rather than sell because of what they thought was a correction in the market, they liquidated convertible bonds to generate the cash needed to meet margin calls. This caused one-way liquidity in the convertible-bond market and drove prices down. This then forced convertible-arbitrage funds to sell their liquid positions at a loss. Similar interactions were seen between the currency, debt and equity markets in the Asian crisis and Russian debt default. Such events make the management of portfolio liquidity and funding liquidity in a multi-strategy fund significantly more complex than in a single strategy fund. Incorporating cross market and cross asset class leverage and liquidity factors into stress testing for multi-strategy funds is necessary to ensure that the fund does not leverage itself excessively with respect to its worst-case liquidity and will always have the ability to exit losing positions and generate cash to meet margin calls in a crisis scenario.

Performance of Multi-Strategy Hedge Funds   Multi-strategy funds have arisen as a result of the maturation and consolidation of the hedge-fund industry and are a more recent phenomenon. Consequently, representative performance data have been available for a shorter time period. From January 2004 to January 2010, the Greenwich Alternative Investments International Multi-Strategy Hedge Fund Index (see Figure 4.37) posted an average annualized return of 6.18 percent, with an annualized standard deviation of 12.29 percent. The cumulative return of the Relative value Hedge Fund Index over the six-year period was 37.1 percent, significantly outperforming the cumulative return of the S&P 500 Index for the same period (2.7 percent).

Multi-strategy funds outperformed primarily because they incurred smaller losses in 2008. They outperformed the S&P 500 in four of the six

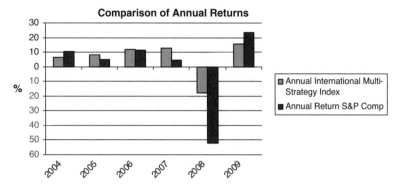

FIGURE 4.37 Greenwich International Multi-Strategy Hedge Fund Index annual returns vs. S&P 500 Index
Source: Greenwich Alternative Investments LLC, Shiller

years and incurred losses of only 18.0 percent in 2008 when S&P 500 suffered a drawdown of 52.2 percent. By contrast, the drawdown of the multi-strategy funds during the credit crisis was only 34 percent of that of the S&P 500.

Compared to other hedge fund strategies, the monthly returns of equity market-neutral funds exhibited a relatively high correlation to those of the S&P 500 (0.63) and the overall equity market for the period from 2004–10. This is surprisingly high, as it does not reflect a significant improvement or greater market neutrality compared to single-strategy hedge funds, despite the greater diversification of multi-strategy funds.

As indicated by Figure 4.38, the monthly returns of multi-strategy funds were less volatile than those of the S&P 500; 1.76 percent vs. 4.35 percent, respectively. In light of this standard deviation, the maximum monthly drawdown in September 2008 (−6.16 percent) was a 3.5 sigma event. The distribution of monthly returns is negatively skewed compared to other hedge-fund strategies (−1.25), indicating downside risk. However, this negative skew is less than that of the S&P 500 Index (−1.43) for the same period, indicating superior capital-preservation ability. Furthermore, the distribution of monthly returns exhibits less kurtosis than that of the S&P 500 for the same period (2.9 vs. 5.6), indicating a modestly lower presence of outliers in the return distribution.

In conclusion, as multi-strategy funds are blends of other hedge fund strategies, the risks depend on the allocation to each constituent strategy. The relative impacts of these strategy specific risks are reduced in the multi-strategy context, though their frequency of occurrence is not. In addition,

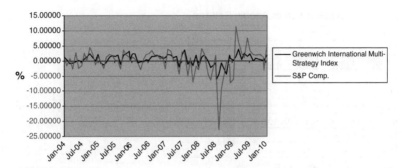

FIGURE 4.38   Greenwich International Multi-Strategy Hedge Fund Index monthly
returns vs. S&P 500 Index (January 2004–March 2010)
Source: Greenwich Alternative Investments LLC, Shiller

multi-strategy funds are exposed to the risk of correlation between hedge-
fund strategy returns and somewhat higher operational risk because of the
complexity of managing multiple strategies. Portfolio liquidity risk is in
some ways reduced compared to single-strategy funds because the multi-
strategy funds invest across a more diverse set of asset classes, which are
less likely to experience simultaneous liquidity problems. Performance data
are limited to six years and the events of 2008 are comparably over-
weighted in the data. That said, there does not appear to be any meaningful
reduction in volatility, skew or kurtosis of returns as a result of diversification of strategies and mean returns are not materially higher than those of
dedicated strategies.

ENDNOTES

1. Generally, macro traders look for unusual price fluctuations that can be referred
   to as far-from-equilibrium conditions. If prices are believed to fall on a bell
   curve, it is only when prices move more than one standard deviation away from
   the mean that macro traders deem that market to present an opportunity. This
   usually happens when market participants' perceptions differ widely from the
   actual state of underlying economic fundamentals, at which point a persistent
   price trend or spread move can develop. By correctly identifying when and
   where the market has swung furthest from equilibrium, a macro trader can
   profit by investing in that situation and then getting out once the imbalance has
   been corrected.
2. Eurekahedge is the world's largest independent data provider and research
   house dedicated to the collation, development and continuous improvement of
   alternative investment data. Eurekahedge was launched by financial

professionals in 2001 and maintains research data banks on over 23,236 alternative funds globally.

Eurekahedge's databases feature up-to-date return indices by hedge fund strategy. The index data are freely available for download at http://www .eurekahedge.com/indices/hedgefundindices.asp. The Eurekahedge Group is affiliated with the Alternative Investment Management Association (AIMA) and is registered with the Securities and Futures Commission (Hong Kong) and the Financial Services Authority (United Kingdom).

3. Excludes dividends.
4. L/S Equity has a variable beta and can be neutral to the market, long or short. In general, L/S equity managers tend to be more frequently long-biased than short or neutral.
5. When assets that are expected to move in conjunction instead diverge, this is called "basis risk."
6. Excludes dividends.
7. In addition to the risk already presented, emerging market funds which invest in corporate fixed income or money markets in emerging market countries face higher credit risk. The laws of many emerging market countries are skewed to defend the borrower, and lenders can often find themselves sued when seeking to collect from a defaulted borrower. In addition, accounting standards are more varied in developed markets, making credit risk assessment more difficult. Lastly, fraud by borrowers may be more prevalent and recourse by the lender may be frustrated by corruption in the local courts.
8. Excludes dividends.
9. If the deal breaks, the price to which the target firm's stock will fall is uncertain. If the pre-announcement price of $25 already incorporated market expectations about a merger, then the subsequent decline could be even more than the $8 premium. However, if due diligence during the takeover attempt revealed new and negative information about the target firm, $20 may be the higher end of the post-break price range.
10. This is often called an event risk (that is, the event that the deal breaks creates the risk). However, it is more accurate to say that the risk of loss to the fund is due to the change in the basis of the hedge ratio upon the deal-break event. This is a basis risk.
11. All pending deals, sovereign takeovers, affiliate mergers, divestitures and all other transactions which do not carry deal-break risk were excluded from the population.
12. See Edward I. Altman with Brenda J. Karlin, "Special Report on Defaults and Returns in the High-Yield Bond Market: Third-Quarter 2009 Review," New York University Salomon Center, Leonard N. Stern School of Business, November 2009.
13. Daniel Loeb, head of Third Point Management, is notable for his use of sharply written letters directed towards the CEOs of his target companies.
14. Brav, Alon, Wei Jiang, Frank Partnoy, and Randall S. Thomas 2008, "The Returns to Hedge Fund Activism," *Financial Analysts Journal* 64(6).
15. Ibid.

16. Per SEC Rule 144, restricted stock, shares owned by an affiliate and control positions may be subject to liquidation provisions referred to as "dribble out" rules which extend the required liquidation period. This is to prevent a seller from purchasing unregistered securities with a view to immediate resale. According to these liquidation provisions, the total amount of securities sold in any three-month period, to qualify for the exemption, cannot exceed more than 1 percent of the total number of the company's outstanding shares or the average weekly reported trading volume during the four weeks preceding such sale.
17. Christopher P. Clifford 2008, "Value Creation or Destruction? Hedge Funds as Shareholder Activists," *Journal of Corporate Finance* 14(4):323–36.
18. Brav *et al.* op. cit.
19. The authors use the HedgeFund.Net equal weight index to represent all equity-oriented hedge fund returns.
20. Except as a hedge against a bond default.
21. Greenwich Alternative Investments is a leading alternative investment firm providing hedge fund indices, industry research, and index-linked products and services to institutional investors worldwide. Founded in 1992, Greenwich Alternative Investments was the first to perform large-scale research on the hedge fund universe.
22. See Taleb, Nassim Nicholas 2007. *The Black Swan: The Impact of the Highly Improbable*, Random House. Based on the Taleb's criteria, a Black Swan event has the following characteristics:
1) The event is a surprise (to the observer), 2) has a major impact and, 3) after the fact, is rationalized by hindsight, as if it could have been expected (e.g., the relevant data were available but not accounted for).
23. In science and engineering, a black box is a device, system or object which can be viewed solely in terms of its input, output and transfer characteristics without any knowledge of its internal workings; that is, its implementation is "opaque" (black). Almost anything might be referred to as a black box: a transistor, an algorithm, or the human mind. The opposite of a black box is a system where the inner components or logic are available for inspection, which is sometimes known as a white box, a glass box, or a clear box.
24. Matthew Rothman, Global Head of Quantitative Equity Strategies, Barclay's Capital.
25. "Market-neutral funds—which buy some stocks while shorting others in an attempt to beat the market—control nearly $250 billion in AUM," in "Computerised crash" *The Sunday Times*, August 19, 2007.
26. Lasse Heje Pedersen, "When Everyone Runs for the Exit," *International Journal of Central Banking*, December 2009, New York University, CEPR, and NBER.
27. "Preliminary Findings Regarding the Market Events of May 6, 2010." Report of the Staffs of the CFTC and SEC to the Joint Advisory Committee on Emerging Regulatory Issues, May 18, 2010.
28. Fung and Hsieh (2002b) investigated funds within this category and found that the high yield credit spread explains a significant portion of the systematic return within the group.

29. The difference between LIBOR and the overnight index swap (OIS) rate, known as the LIBOR-OIS spread, widened to a new high for the year, signaling a decreased willingness to lend. Looking back over 2008, average spreads were less than 1 percent for most of the year; however, they began to increase sharply in mid-August and peaked around 3.6 percent on October 10.
30. Co-integrated variables are variables related by a dynamic long-run equilibrium with short-run divergence.
31. Currie and Morris (2002) quoted traders as saying that the average correlation between the CDS spread and the equity price is only on the order of 5–15 percent.
32. Merton, R. 1974, "On the Pricing of Corporate Debt: The Risk Structure of Interest Rates," *Journal of Finance* 29: 449–70.
33. Recent academic work has analyzed the information content of equity options for corporate bond and CDS pricing. It finds that the forward-looking option implied volatility dominates the historical volatility in explaining credit spreads, and the gain is particularly pronounced among firms with lower credit ratings. See Cremers, Driessen, Maenhout & Weinbaum (2006) and Cao, Yu and Zhong (2006)
34. Currie, A., and J. Morris 2002, "And Now for Capital Structure Arbitrage," *Euromoney* (December): 38–43.
35. This source of basis risk may reduce in the future if credit default swaps are required by regulation to be traded or cleared on exchanges such as the Chicago Mercantile Exchange (CME) or the Intercontinental Exchange (ICE).
36. Bajlum, C.and P. Tind Larsen, "Capital structure arbitrage: Model choice and volatility calibration," Centre for Analytical Finance Working Paper Series No. 230, September 2007.
37. These events are similar to the ones experienced by capital-structure arbitrage hedge funds in May 2005, when General Motors was downgraded while the equity price soared.
38. Schaefer, Stephen M. and Ilya A. Strebulaev, "Risk in Capital Structure Arbitrage." Graduate School of Business, Stanford University; First version: May 2006.
39. Fan Yu, "How Profitable Is Capital Structure Arbitrage?" *Financial Analysts Journal* 62(5) 2006, CFA Institute.
40. Currie and Morris, op cit.
41. The Kospi 200 Index future is the most widely traded futures contract in the world.
42. North Korean saboteurs seeking to disrupt the South Korean economy could potentially disrupt this electronic exchange.
43. Of the members of the CME, 19 are high-velocity proprietary firms or hedge funds. They include Citadel and GETCO.
44. Of course, a lack of confidence or the fear of failure of a major exchange would create similar instability in the funding markets for futures, as was seen in the cash markets during the credit crisis.
45. The negative skew for the other strategies analyzed in this book is significantly influenced by the large negative returns hedge funds experienced during the credit crisis.

46. In this aspect, a multi-strategy manager duplicates the role of a fund of funds manager, though the multi-strategy investor maintains a concentrated exposure to the operational risk of one fund group.

47. The subprime crisis affected alternative investments from July 2007 to March 2008, mainly through "hidden correlations" in hedge fund returns that caused massive drawdowns in hedge fund performance. This occurred though nothing was apparent in their historical returns prior to June 2007 that could have suggested such a potential high risk.

48. For example, the analysis should segregate risk-and-return measurements into those arising from equal weightings from those caused by the incremental effect of under- and overweighting.

49. Co-integration is an econometric property of time series variables. If two or more series are individually integrated (in the time-series sense) but some linear combination(s) of them has(/have) a lower order of integration then the series is said to be co-integrated. A common example is a stock market index and the price of its associated futures contract which both move through time, each roughly following a random walk. Testing the hypothesis that there is a statistically significant connection between the futures price and the spot price could now be done by testing for the existence of a co-integrated combination of the two series. (If such a combination has a low order of integration, this can signify an equilibrium relationship between the original series, which are said to be co-integrated.)

50. Alternatively, they can be ex-post factors which can be quantified but not intuitively defined.

CHAPTER **5**

Managing Funding Risk

The global financial system periodically undergoes periods of massive turbulence where funding stability and liquidity are essential to a fund's survival. The events which began in the summer of 2007 are an example. The increasing default rate in subprime mortgages triggered escalating losses on subprime mortgage backed securities, which then created enormous losses at various financial institutions. System-wide distrust in the creditworthiness of financial institutions led to a significant contraction in the tenor and amount of funding available in the interbank market. Brokers then faced funding pressure when global markets and market liquidity declined further. In particular, prime brokers such as Morgan Stanley, Goldman Sachs, Lehman Brothers, and Bear Stearns suffered from a maturity mismatch in their funding structure. All struggled, but Bear and Lehman failed to roll over their short-term liabilities. In such a situation of declining confidence in the interbank market, the banks' willingness and ability to continue extending credit to hedge funds was reduced. In addition, the worldwide decline in asset prices caused severe losses at hedge funds, causing investors to rush to redeem their investments and to put their money into cash. According to Albourne Partners databases, at the peak of the crisis approximately 25 percent of hedge fund assets were gated, locked or suspended. The end result was a dramatic funding crisis at many funds which caught many unprepared and forced the liquidation of assets at fire-sale prices.

As illustrated in Chapter 1, the investment risks of a hedge fund can be compounded by the actions of stakeholders in the fund. Ironically, because hedge funds use leverage, an investor run on the fund, like an old fashioned run on a bank, can bring to fruition the very fear that motivates investors to redeem their shares (that is, the fund collapses and they cannot redeem their shares). Countering this risk to the fund are the fund manager's varying rights to control the rate and nature of redemptions. Such rights may include the ability to invoke a gate, suspend redemptions, pay redemptions in the form of securities, or create a liquidating trust. Complicating matters is the prime broker's right to increase margins on existing positions, deny further trading by the fund, and cease providing finance.

The actions of investors and prime brokers have a direct impact on the fund's performance.

Ang and Bollen[1] found that funding liquidity risk arising from exceptionally large investor redemptions was negatively associated with subsequent fund performance but that the effect was less pronounced in funds with longer investor lock-up periods. A request for large capital withdrawals was correlated negatively with fund returns over subsequent consecutive months. While correlation is not causality, they did find that redemption restrictions such as longer lock-up, redemption notice and payout periods were associated with higher returns.

They further found that financial distress at a hedge fund's prime broker was also related to a significantly lower performance of the hedge fund in subsequent months. In addition, a hedge fund relying on more than one prime broker or bank has a significantly better performance than one with a single prime broker. This finding indicates that a potential funding-liquidity risk stemming from prime brokers or banks can be reduced through a diversification of funding sources.

Mitigating Funding Risk

The analysis of funding risk at a hedge fund requires an evaluation of the documents granting redemption rights to investors and rights to prime brokers to change margin financing. The *management* of this aspect of a fund's funding liquidity risk requires negotiation of these documents, with forethought given to the impact that the invoking of these rights in a market crisis may have on the performance of the fund.

Table 5.1 summarizes the various rights granted to investors and the fund in its constitutional documents; and those granted to the prime brokers and the fund in its prime brokerage documents. Some give the fund defensive options to help it manage investment and funding risk during a market crisis. Others give investors rights to redeem their fund shares for cash and force the fund to liquidate its investments. Prime brokerage documents give the prime broker the right to increase margin, which can also force the fund to liquidate its investments. Understanding these rights and planning risk-management strategies to deal with a rush of redemption requests while holding a portfolio of suddenly devalued and illiquid investments is essential for a fund if it is to weather a market crisis.

In negotiating these terms with investors and prime brokers, the fund's overarching objective is to embed options to manage its funding liquidity

TABLE 5.1 Stakeholders' rights and risk

Stakeholder	Rights	Incentives	Risks
Investors: Have an equity claim on the excess performance of the fund and a subordinated claim in the event of default.	Right to net returns of the fund right to redeem hedge fund shares.	*Upside:* Unlimited. Excess performance of the fund after management and performance fees. *Downside:* Total loss of principal.	■ Can force liquidation of assets, payment of liquidity premium and realization of mark to market losses.
Prime Broker: Custodian and provider of leverage. Receives interest payment on financing provided. Has a debtholder's senior claim on the assets of the fund in the event of default by the fund on a margin payment or securities contract.	Right to increase margin. Right to recall financing. Right to refuse trades. Right to liquidate collateral. Right to interest on funds lent to the fund.	*Upside:* Limited. Fees from provision of prime brokerage custody services and interest income from margin and securities lending. *Downside:* Partial loss of principal in the event of hedge fund default and insufficient proceeds from liquidation of hedge fund collateral.	■ Can force liquidation of assets, payment of liquidity premium and realization of mark to market losses by increasing margin. ■ Can restrict or stop hedging or risk taking by refusing trades. ■ Can seize collateral if margin is not paid and liquidate.
Hedge Fund Management & Staff: Have an equity claim on the excess performance of the fund and a subordinated claim in the event of default. Have information advantage over other stakeholders and financial and human capital invested in the fund.	Right to redeem. Right to leave. Right to gate the Fund. Right to management fee and performance fee.	*Upside:* Unlimited. Excess performance of the fund plus management and performance fees. *Downside:* Total loss of net worth, loss of reputation, loss of equity in management company, loss of job.	■ Can force liquidation of assets, payment of liquidity premium and realization of mark-to-market losses. ■ Can invoke the gate preventing investors from receiving redemptions. ■ Can leave creating both reputation and operational risk for the fund.

and minimize unexpected demands for large payments of cash on short notice. Such demands could force the fund to liquidate securities positions at a loss during a market crisis.

Fund Rights to Control Redemptions

In order to better manage its funding liquidity risk, the fund typically seeks the option to deny, delay, transform, or reduce the investor's ability to redeem for cash. The various rights vis-à-vis investors that a fund may negotiate prior to a market crisis and invoke during a crisis are primarily its ability to:

- enforce and rely on the investor lock-up period.
- alter provisions as to redemption notice periods, redemption dates, and frequency.
- suspend determination of its net asset value (NAV) and to suspend subscriptions and redemptions.
- suspend the date of payment of the redemption proceeds.
- impose a "gate" on redemptions.
- create side pockets or special purpose vehicles for illiquid investments.
- retain a percentage of any redemption proceeds as reserves against contingent or potential liabilities.
- pay redemptions in kind (that is, in the form of investment securities rather than cash).
- restructure to create a liquidating trust entity and an ongoing part that continues to implement the fund's strategy.
- liquidate itself voluntarily, as opposed to compulsorily, which gives it greater control over the timing of its liquidation.

The suitability of these risk management strategies depends on the prevailing market conditions. More importantly, the option to use these options depends on the terms by which these rights are granted to the managers of the fund in the fund's constitutional documents.

In addition, the granting of certain rights to investors can constrain the fund's ability to manage through a crisis and harm the interests of the staff and other investors. Chief among these types of rights are those that give certain investors preferred redemption and liquidity terms.

Rights of Prime Brokers over Margin

Prime brokers typically reserve the right in their prime brokerage agreement to stop accepting new trades, increase funding rates, and to call for additional margin at their discretion at any time. Subsequent to, or simultaneous with, opening a prime brokerage agreement, these rights can be negotiated by the fund vis-à-vis its prime brokers to give the fund more flexibility in risk managing a crisis and to reduce the prime broker's ability to deny trades and increase margin. The primary rights that a hedge fund can negotiate prior to a market crisis are primarily limitations on the prime broker's ability to:

■ deny future trades.
■ call for additional margin on OTC swap transactions.
■ call for additional margin on cash and derivatives positions.
■ increase interest rates on borrowed funds.

The importance of negotiating these aspects of the documentation depends on the reliance of the fund's strategy on leverage, the degree of leverage used, the expected volatility and liquidity of the fund's positions in a crisis, and the diversity of the fund's prime brokerage relationships.

CONSTITUTIONAL DOCUMENTS

An investor contributes to the limited partnership by subscribing for shares, usually under the terms of a limited partnership agreement, subscription agreement, offering document, and potentially a side letter. The fund in turn invests the capital raised from subscribers in the investments and market(s) described in the offering document. The rights and obligations of investors as shareholders in the fund, the terms of redemption and method of valuation are normally set out in the offering document and the company's articles. The shares for which investors subscribe are issued at a fixed price at launch. Thereafter, the fund may raise further capital by issuing new classes of shares at a fixed price, or additional shares of the same class at prices related to the net asset value of the investment portfolio relating to the initial class of shares.

Limited Partnership Agreement

The limited partnership agreement (LPA) is the governing legal document and sets out the rights of the investors and those of the manager and directors of the fund. When an investor becomes a "partner" in the fund, the investor is executing the limited partnership agreement.

Some LPAs address matters that raise few risk management concerns. Others, however, are of more concern to the risk manager and CFO of the fund as they may have significant funding implications in a time of market crisis.

Common items which are included in the LPA are:

- Rights and duties of the directors of the fund management company (regarding gates, suspensions, payment in kind, and side pockets)
- Rights and duties of the investors (lock-up periods[2] and notice period for redemptions)
- Definition of terms
- Information on formation (business office, registered agent, length of fund, and so on)
- Capitalization structure (initially and on a going-forward basis)
- Manner of allocation of profits and losses (including the various tax-allocation provisions)
- Manner of distributions and withdrawals
- Information on accounting, books and records
- Transfer rights
- Dissolution of the partnership; winding up
- Manner of final distributions
- Grant of power of attorney
- Miscellaneous provisions (headings, amendments, applicable law, and jurisdiction).

Subscription Documents

The subscription documents provide the manager with background information on the investor and may differ substantially from one fund to another. They include assurance and warranties that the potential investor is qualified to invest in the offering. Some firms have separate subscription documents for individual investors and for institutional investors.

Subscription documents typically include the following information:

- Certain legal disclaimers
- Directions on how to complete the subscription documents
- Subscription agreement (including certain acknowledgements, representations and warranties)
- Questions (which may be embedded in the subscription agreement) regarding the investor's suitability and status as a generally accredited investor, qualified client, or qualified purchaser
- The signature page to the LPA.

Offering Document

The offering document is typically a private placement memorandum (PPM), which comprises a wide range of information on the structural and business aspects of the fund that will enable a prospective limited partner to determine whether to invest. It includes conditions that are open to negotiation by an investor. In public capital investment offerings, the Securities and Exchange Commission regulates the document, but as a PPM is not regulated the material and specifics provided to the potential limited partners may vary by fund. As a PPM is primarily used for marketing the fund to investors, it describes the fund's strategy, investment process, track record, staff credentials, regulatory and legal set up, and key service providers.

While each fund's PPM is different, they have many common features. These include details of the investment program and the risk factors involved; a description of the management company, its managers and the management and performance fees; details of the prime brokerage arrangements and service providers; details of the LPA; ERISA disclosures;[3] and other notices pertinent to the fund's handling of privacy and disclosure matters.

Rights for redemption and liquidity are typically not granted in the PPM; these are usually found in the LPA or in side letters.

Side Letters

The side letter is one of the most important items for a hedge fund manager. The side letter is drafted by the fund's attorney and is signed by the investor at the signing of the subscription documents.

While the limited partnership agreement defines how the hedge fund will be run, a side letter is simply an agreement granting preferential terms to certain important investors. The letter gives these investors more favorable rights and privileges than other investors receive, typically in exchange for a large or seed investment in the fund.[4]

Seed Investors and Strategic Investors The side letter can be an important tool for raising assets. Typically, the letter will be used to entice early investors (known as "seed investors") to the fund. It can also be used to attract investors who will contribute a large amount of assets to the fund (that is, strategic investors). The side letter can also be used to entice a current investor to contribute more assets to the fund.

Some side letters address matters that raise few risk management concerns, such as the ability to make additional investments, to receive more favorable treatment, or to limit management fees and receive other incentives. Others, however, are of more concern to the risk manager and CFO of the fund as they may have significant funding implications and restrict the fund's risk-management options in a time of market crisis. They may grant rights to certain investors that can harm the interests of the fund's staff and other investors. Chief among these concerns are side letters that give certain investors preferred redemption and liquidity terms.

A side letter may be used for some of the following reasons:

- Lock-up and liquidity: The hedge fund manager may reduce or waive the investment lock-up for a specific investor or to allow for greater liquidity (that is, shorter waiting periods for withdrawals for seed or strategic investors). The manager may also reduce penalty fees for early redemption for a specific investor or agree to modification of gates and other restrictions on the ability to redeem. Lastly, the manager may allow the fund to be limited with regards to making in-kind distributions to a specific investor.
- Reduced fees: The hedge fund manager will reduce or waive the management fees or performance fees for certain important investors.
- Information: The manager may agree to provide an investor with greater informational rights, such as preferential or improved access to information on investment strategy or key investments of the fund, and the ability to request a description of the exact positions of the fund at any given time. Such information may also include advance notice of critical changes affecting the investment manager (for example, changes to key personnel).
- Jurisdiction: In the event of arbitration of disputes/choice of law, the manager may agree to be subject to the laws of a specific jurisdiction for certain investors (particularly pension funds).
- Most favored nation clause: This is usually reserved for very large or very early investors and gives them the best deal granted to any investor.

There are many different ways in which any of the above concepts can be implemented into the side letter and generally the rights granted will depend upon the priorities and bargaining power of the manager and the investor.

FUNDING LIQUIDITY RISK MANAGEMENT STRATEGIES: MANAGING INVESTOR REDEMPTIONS

A fund manager should have a number of alternatives available to him to ensure that sufficient capital stays in the hedge fund and ensure its funding liquidity at critical times. The extent to which a fund manager must be able to control the amounts, rate, and form of redemptions depends on the liquidity and volatility of the fund's investment portfolio, the amount and stability of leverage provided by his prime brokers, and the level of cash maintained by the fund. Options for managing investor redemptions are discussed below in order of increasing effectiveness and potentially negative impact on investors.

Fund's Ability to Enforce Investor Lock-up Period

Investors can request redemption of their shares at any time. The fund manager has the option, but not the obligation, to honor that request immediately if the fund has sufficient liquid assets on hand. The fund manager is not obliged to make immediate payment because lock-up and redemption notice periods are generally in place to help manage the fund's liquidity risk. Investor lock-up terms define the minimum amount of time an investor must be invested in the fund before redeeming his shares and the amount of notice the investor must give before enacting this right. These terms give the fund manager the right to delay payment until he is legally obliged to do so.

The length of the lock-up is really a business and risk decision that the fund manager makes when launching the fund and seeking seed investors. Factors to consider are 1) the gestation period of investment ideas; 2) the liquidity of underlying assets in a market crisis; and 3) how potential investors may react to an overly long lock-up period.

Since 2008, there has been a clear trend towards greater investor power in negotiating lock-ups. While initial lock-up periods for new investors continue to be one year or more, once that initial period is over, investors expect to be able to demand that their shares be redeemed at relatively short notice. A recent Credit Suisse survey reported that investors are increasingly expecting redemption terms to be tied to underlying portfolios: only 25 percent are open to investing with a 90-day redemption-notice period for "higher liquidity" strategies, whereas 72 percent are comfortable with 90-day notice for "lower liquidity" funds. In addition, two-thirds of investors believe that they should have to pay a lower management or performance fee if they agree to a lock-up of their capital for longer. In addition, two-thirds of the fund managers surveyed agreed.[5]

Investors are right that the notice period should vary depending on the hedge fund's investment strategy. There are funds that offer quarterly liquidity with 30 days' notice but most hedge funds have at least one-year lock-ups and at least 30–90-day notice periods. This means that investors must notify hedge funds of their intention to redeem 30–90 days before the quarter end. The two-year lock-up period used to be popular because of a now-defunct SEC registration rule that required hedge fund managers to register with the SEC as investment advisors unless the hedge fund instituted a two-year lock-up period. In response, many managers changed their lock-up period to two years. After the registration rule was overturned by the courts,[6] the two-year lock-up became less popular and lock-up periods longer than two years are now extremely rare.

The investor notice period should be at least as long as the average period of time needed for the typical fund investment to bear fruit. For example, for a hedge fund following a distressed investment strategy, where it typically takes six months to a year or more to see any results, the initial lock-up should be at least two years, as it takes time to find investment opportunities and to deploy the necessary cash. The notice period should be 180 days or more to match the average maturity and liquidity profile of the investments. If the investment strategy is more short-term in nature, such as a managed futures or high-velocity strategy, then the lock-up period can be 30 days or shorter.

A new fund requiring a lock-up greater than 90 days may find that investors react negatively and be forced to sign side letters granting shorter periods to seed or strategic investors. In such cases, the percentage of AUM from seed or strategic investors who negotiate shorter lock-ups or no lock-up periods should be kept to a minimum to reduce the risk of having to liquidate part of the fund when liquidity is at a premium and thus crystallizing mark-to-market losses.

The lock-up terms in the LPA give the hedge fund manager the right to enforce the minimum investment and notice periods before having to pay redeeming investors. From a funding risk management perspective, the longer the investor lock-up, the more flexibility the fund manager has to manage periods of market crisis. However, determination of the minimum lock-up terms is a business decision that should balance potential investor demands for liquidity and the risk this can present against the business need to attract seed and strategic investors until the fund reaches the optimal size.

Altering Redemption Notice Periods, Redemption Dates, and Frequency

The fund manager can negotiate additional means of managing the funding-liquidity risk presented by potentially high redemptions. These include negotiating flexibility in the required redemption notice period, redemption dates and redemption frequency. While such rights may temporarily mitigate the effects of a funding event, they typically are limited in scope and consequently of limited effectiveness in a market crisis.

Ex-ante negotiation of the fund's ability to temporarily extend the redemption notice period and defer redemption payments allows for tactical management of a cash shortfall. Such agreements are rare, as investors typically do not like the uncertainty this can create in their own cash flow management. When they are conferred, the latitude given is often limited to one month or less.

Likewise, the ability to alter the frequency of an investor's redemptions is of limited value. Funds argue that the credit crunch demonstrated "the ATM effect," where fund of funds and other investors in need of cash redeemed their investments more frequently and significantly in funds with the most generous investor lock-ups. This in turn caused negative performance of these funds since they had to maintain greater cash positions in anticipation of redemptions, even though their performance to that point and their underlying portfolio was sound. Consequently, some funds require that investors can redeem with 30 days' notice, for example, but the fund can limit redemptions to six times per year. This option is of limited risk management value as the right to limit redemptions in this way is likely to result only in the redemption amounts being larger, with the sixth being the remaining value of the investment in the fund.

Lastly, the ability of the fund to change redemption dates is significantly restricted by investors and only allowed in cases where the redemption date falls on a weekend or public holiday. Consequently, it is of limited value for managing funding risk.

Charging Redemption Fees

Some funds charge investors an early redemption fee if they seek to withdraw money from the fund before the end of the lock-up period. Where a redemption fee exists, it is often charged only during a certain period of time (typically between six months and two years) following the investment, or to withdrawals representing a specified portion of an investment.

The early-redemption fees generally range from 1–5 percent. The purpose of the fee is to discourage short-term investment in the fund, thereby reducing turnover and allowing the fund to use more complex, illiquid or long-term strategies. To a degree, it will also dissuade or limit investors from withdrawing funds during a market crisis or after periods of modest performance. Obviously, the higher the fee, the greater the disincentive, as it has a direct impact on the investor's net returns. In defending the early redemption fee, fund managers point out that honoring the redemption of an investor who redeems early or often can impose a cost on the remaining investors: it can force the fund to underperform if it must stay in highly liquid assets in order to honor frequent redemptions and it can leave other investors exposed to greater liquidity risk if the liquid portion of the fund must be sold to honor early redemptions. Consequently, unlike management and performance fees, redemption fees are usually retained by the fund to offset such redemption costs and thereby directly benefit the remaining investors rather than the manager.

Imposing a Gate on Redemptions

A "gate" provision is a right of a fund manager to limit the amount of withdrawals on any withdrawal date to not more than a stated percentage of the fund's net assets—often 10–25 percent, depending on how frequently investors have a right to withdraw capital. For example, if the fund has a gate of 15 percent and investors request redemptions equal to 20 percent of the fund's NAV, then all redemption requests will be reduced pro rata until only 15 percent of the redemption requests are met.

Redemption gates are often imposed at the discretion of the fund manager, while other gates are drafted as a non-discretionary mechanism exercisable only in specified circumstances. For example, redemptions may be prohibited if the exchange on which any significant portions of the fund's investments are trading is closed, or trades are restricted or suspended. Offering documents should provide substantial disclosure regarding the circumstances for triggering redemption gates and describe when standard redemptions will resume.

This is a less-severe withdrawal restriction than an all-out redemption suspension, which doesn't allow for withdrawals at all. Gates are a very common feature in hedge funds of almost all strategies. The purpose of the provision is to prevent a run on the fund, which could cripple its operations, as a large number of withdrawals would force the manager to sell off a large number of positions. Imposing a gate slows a potential run on the fund by forcing investors to wait until the next regular withdrawal date to receive the unfulfilled balance of their withdrawal requests.

But there is concern in the industry that some funds could be dragging their feet on returning money to keep their businesses going, enabling them to continue to charge often hefty fees. Many funds charge management fees of about 2 percent and take 20 percent or more of any gains.

A gate provision mitigates demands for cash to fund redemptions and aids a fund to weather a market crisis by capping the amount of cash needed in any one redemption period. In so doing, it reduces the need to liquidate a large percentage of assets at any one time. Gates, like suspending redemptions, are acts which are criticized by the investment community as not always being in investors' best interests because they ensure a minimum management-fee income to the fund. Consequently, they can be seen as protecting fund franchises, and the livelihoods of fund employees over the best interests of investors.

Such moves by the funds are legal if the terms are included in its constitutional documents and demonstrably in the best interest of all investors. A fund manager who invokes a gate should, and typically does, write to the investors explaining the expected amount of the redemption reduction.

Major hedge funds that are known to have raised their gates in 2008 include Citadel Investment Group, D. E. Shaw, Farallon Capital Management and Magnetar Capital. The long-term fallout of such decisions for these franchises appears to be muted as these firms continue to be among the Top 100 hedge funds in the world.

Stacked vs. Investor-level Gates   An investor-level gate independently limits redemptions for each of a fund's underlying investors to an equal percentage across all investors. In addition to promoting the orderly unwinding of positions and alleviating the pressure of en-masse redemptions, investor-level gates also help reduce legal risks faced by managers as they balance competing interests of redeeming investors and those remaining in a fund.

An inferior alternative to investor-level gates are stacked gates (also referred to as "fund-level gates"). A stacked gate permits gated investors to be given priority over investors subsequently seeking to redeem on the next redemption date. Where a fund has a stacked gate, any unpaid redemptions from a given redemption date are rolled forward and assume priority on the next redemption date.

However, investors who do not put in redemption requests can find themselves at the back of the line for withdrawals, as people who were not paid in full in the previous quarter have priority with the common stacked-gate structure. Stacked gates are inferior because they provide an incentive to investors to submit "defensive redemptions" as soon as possible to get in line for liquidity, which is particularly evident during periods of market stress. Consequently, redemptions stack up and investors who may not ultimately redeem still submit requests in order not to be at the back of the queue if they ultimately decide to cash out.

During the credit crisis, when many funds were experiencing redemption pressure and seriously contemplating invoking their gates, the ramifications of the difference between investor and stacked gates was stark. For example, Polygon Investment Partners had seen an increase in exit notices at its US$8-billion Polygon Global Opportunities Fund. Polygon Global Opportunities had established a stacked-gate system which would allow only a limited number of investors out at any one time. However, Polygon changed its policy when it realized that this system would simply encourage investors to put their requests in early. Consequently, Polygon took a different course and moved investors into a new share class that would have a more-favorable investor-level gate on redemptions, rather than the first-come, first-served stacked-gate system. This reassured investors that the fund would not be forced into liquidation and that they need not submit redemption requests simply to secure a place in line or to beat other investors to the exits.

Suspension of Redemptions

Further options available to a fund manager to manage funding liquidity risk become more draconian. The constitutional documents of most hedge funds anticipate that money may be invested in assets that may be or become (i) illiquid or (ii) incapable of being valued in a market crisis. Consequently, fund managers seek to include provisions that give the fund and its directors the power to (a) restrict the proportion of assets under management that can be redeemed on a given redemption date or (b) suspend redemptions altogether. Redemptions may also be refused if the manager reasonably believes that the net asset value of the fund's investments cannot be fairly ascertained, the redemption or realization of the fund's investments cannot, in the manager's opinion, be effected at normal prices or normal rates of exchange, if certain adverse regulatory conditions emerge, or if there are negative tax consequences to the redemption.

The right to suspend redemptions was invoked by a large number of funds in the wake of the bankruptcy filing of Lehman Brothers and the dramatic increase in redemption requests by investors. Among the global hedge-fund names suspending redemptions during the credit crisis were the US$10-billion Tudor BVI Fund, D. E. Shaw Group, Farallon Capital Management, RAB Capital, Legg Mason's Permal Group, Centaurus Capital, Gottex Fund Management, Highbridge Capital Management, and Goldman Sachs/JB Were Managed Funds Limited. While, in retrospect, most of these funds continue to have thriving businesses in 2010, invoking this right must be balanced against the likely temporary alienation of the investor community and potential legal challenges.

Securing the Right to Suspend Redemptions In order to secure this right, the terms of a fund's constitutional documents, taken together, should be drafted in a manner that gives its manager and directors wide powers to act in the fund's best interest and the right to exercise the power of suspension.

The decision to suspend redemptions must be exercised before the date on which redemptions are to be paid. Legal precedence makes clear that a suspension of redemptions cannot be applied retroactively and that nonpayment of eligible redemptions prior to the invocation of the right to suspend can be an event of default by the fund and give investors the right to force the liquidation of the fund.[7]

It is crucial that the fund have evidence that it is acting in the best interest of investors. If the power to authorize suspension of redemptions is exercised in bad faith, such action can be challenged by investors and rendered invalid.[8]

Exercising the right to suspend redemptions should be done with extreme caution. While it is highly effective in solving a fund's immediate funding crisis and avoiding liquidation of assets in a distressed market, the reputational fallout from suspensions may destroy any goodwill a fund may have among the investment community. Future investors are not likely to invest in those funds that have exercised their right to suspend redemptions.

Suspending Determination of the Fund's Net Asset Value As an escalating alternative to suspending redemptions, it may be possible to suspend the determination of the NAV (and therefore the redemption of shares) in certain situations if the power has been included in the fund's offering and constitutional documents. Most commonly, a fund may suspend NAV calculations if, in the reasonable good faith discretion of its directors, the liquidation of assets to fund redemption requests would result in unreasonable losses to the fund and its investors.

The clear downside of this approach is that it has the additional impact of precluding all subscriptions to the fund. Subscriptions cannot be accepted because the subscription price cannot be determined as the fund has suspended its NAV calculation.

Suspension of the fund's NAV calculation is typically not the best strategy as it precludes subscriptions. In addition, management fees are not paid in such circumstances. Obviously, this may aggravate the fund manager's cash-flow needs.

Creating Side Pockets or Special Purpose Vehicles for Illiquid Investments A significant factor contributing to the funding risk of a hedge fund is the mismatch and tension between the short-term funding that it obtains from investors with short lock-ups, and the long-term investments it may make. In a market crisis, funds may then be left in a situation where they cannot easily divest themselves from illiquid positions without incurring large losses for those investors wishing to redeem and a collateral loss for the investors that remain in the fund. The best solution is to match the tenor of funding with the liquidity profile of fund investments whereby funds that provide for redemption at short notice invest in liquid assets, while funds that invest in illiquid or "hard to sell" assets have lock-up provisions that keep investors in the fund for a given number of years. This would be easy to do in an ideal world where the liquidity profile of investments is known with certainty and is static. However, in the real world, where the liquidity profile of investments changes and deteriorates rapidly in a market crisis, the ability to change the profile of investor redemptions to better match the liquidity of investments can provide the fund with the time needed to ride out the market crisis.

Side pockets allow for the segregation of illiquid or hard-to-value investments from a fund's portfolio of liquid investments. Side pockets can be used to manage the funding risk by allowing investors to continue to subscribe and redeem shares in the liquid assets of the fund while preserving the "potential" value of the illiquid assets for investors by placing them in the side pocket.

Side pockets are not only used during liquidity crises. Typically, a side pocket is created for an illiquid investment at the discretion of the investment manager—either for a newly created opportunity or from an existing investment that has become illiquid. The types of investments often side-pocketed in the normal course of business include real estate, private equity, bankruptcies, re-organizations, liquidations and other distressed securities. Investors in a side-pocketed investment are locked-up indefinitely and their investment cannot be redeemed until the investment is realized or otherwise becomes readily marketable (on the sale of the side-pocket investment or on the occurrence of an event whereby the investment becomes liquid or is deemed to be realized).

Side pockets may be used when an existing investment becomes illiquid for idiosyncratic reasons such as a de-listing, suspension, or pending litigation. However, they have proved particularly useful in recent systematic-liquidity crises.

During a liquidity crisis, a fund manager may choose to establish a side pocket or move additional illiquid assets into a side pocket to bifurcate the liquid and illiquid assets of the fund. In doing so, only the liquid assets of the fund are then available to be liquidated to fund redemptions. A decision to move an asset or assets to a side pocket may be necessary to achieve both fairness amongst investors and accurate calculations of net asset value and performance fees. Separating out the special investments from the general portfolio of the fund into side pockets may be fair and appropriate for all investors in the following specific cases:

1. If the illiquid investment or special investment would distort the fund's net asset value if it were included in the general portfolio, as it can only be valued at the base acquisition cost or the fair value as assessed by the investment manager, rather than at a quoted market price.
2. If some investors were to redeem their interests in a fund which includes an illiquid asset in its general portfolio, causing the remaining investors

to hold a disproportionately large interest in the illiquid investment(s) held by the fund.
3. If charging a performance fee on the theoretical value of the illiquid investment would be improper as the true liquidation value is unknown until the investment is actually sold.

Upon the creation of a side pocket or the movement of a position from the liquid portion of the portfolio to the side pocket, a portion of each investor's equity interest is converted to a new class or series of non-redeemable equity interests, representing the fund's investment in the illiquid side-pocketed investment. Generally, only those investors actually invested in the fund at the time the side pocket is established are able to participate in the profits and losses of the particular investment allocated to the side pocket. Any follow-on investment or value realized, or the asset itself, will only be available for participation by those investors participating in the original side-pocket investment.

The advantages of side pockets for funds are that investors do not have their interests in a special investment diluted when additional investors subscribe to the fund, nor are they left with a disproportionately large interest in illiquid investments if other investors decide to redeem out of the fund. In addition, the net asset value of the fund and the performance fee payable to the investment manager are not based on unrealized gains on investments valued other than at a quoted market price.

Moving Illiquid Investments to Side Pockets   In practice, upon the fund's acquisition (or designation) of an illiquid investment, a portion of every investor's holding in the liquid portfolio of the fund (the "liquid shares") is exchanged for a newly issued class of shares representing the fund's investment in the special investment ("special investment shares"). This exchange is affected by a redemption of the relevant number of investor shares in the liquid portion of the fund equal in value to the amount determined for that investor to purchase a pro-rata share of the illiquid portion of the fund. As the transaction is equal and common to all other investors in the fund at the relevant time, it is not dilutive or prejudicial against any one investor. A separate series of special investment shares is often issued to represent each illiquid or special investment.

Funding liquidity management is enhanced from the fund's perspective as no voluntary redemption of special investment shares is permitted. Shares of side-pocketed investments may only be exchanged into liquid shares when the underlying illiquid investments are sold (that is, in a liquidity event). The timing of the sale is determined by the fund manager. Upon the occurrence of a liquidity event, each investor will have its special-investment shares redeemed, followed by an immediate subscription by the investor of an equivalent value of liquid shares (usually of the original class from which they were converted), less any fees payable. Investors, of course, may continue to redeem their interests in the liquid portion of the fund's portfolio. If an investor has already redeemed all of its liquid shares, the special investment shares are redeemed for cash, less any fees. Thus, the forced sale of illiquid assets at distressed prices as a result of high redemptions of liquid shares is avoided.

A fund manager's flexibility in using side pockets to manage a liquidity crisis may be constrained in the fund's constitutional documents. For example, at the inception of the fund investors may require that the value of side-pocketed investments be limited in size, either by reference to the fund's assets or a shareholder's investment in the fund (typically, between 10–30 percent of the fund's assets or a shareholder's investment). In addition, investors may require the fund to give them opt-in/opt-out rights for side pocketed investments, allowing them the option to participate or not in a fund's special investments. Both of these provisions, either in the fund's constitutional documents or in side letters with investors, can significantly reduce the ability of a hedge fund to manage funding liquidity risk.

Partial Suspension of Redemptions or Retaining a Portion of Redemption Proceeds

An alternative mechanism for managing funding liquidity risk arising from redemptions is to hold back a portion of the payment of redemption proceeds as valuation reserves or reserves for contingent liabilities.[9] This right may be negotiated by the fund in either the constitutional documents or in a side letter. The latitude granted to the fund manager may vary from absolute reserving of 100 percent of payments on redemptions to as little as a five percent reserve. The range of suspension provisions and their effectiveness may be pre-specified in a schedule defining the percentage of redemptions that can be withheld as a function of the amount of illiquid assets over the total assets of the fund. The downside of this solution is that it makes the determination of the subscription price for any new investor complex as the new subscription price could be over- or understated, depending on the interpretation of the portion held as a reserve.

Paying Redemptions in Kind

A final alternative mechanism for managing funding liquidity risk from redemptions is to honor redemption requests but pay these redemptions partly in cash by liquidating liquid investments and partly in illiquid securities. This mechanism puts the liquidation decision in the hands of the investor rather than the fund manager. This solution has generally been used by funds in wind-down mode and need not be negotiated by the fund in advance.

Liquidating Trusts

When a fund faces a high level of redemptions and a portfolio of cash and illiquid investments, distributing cash only to redeeming investors has the effect of concentrating the fund's investment portfolio, and the interests of its non-withdrawing investors, in the remaining illiquid assets. Distributing a substantial share of its cash to the redeeming investors limits the liquidity of the fund and its flexibility to take advantage of new investments at a time when there could be severe market dislocations and excellent investment opportunities. In addition, the liquidity characteristics of the resulting portfolio would not be in line with the fund's previously agreed investment program, leaving the fund with no alternative but to rebalance its risk profile by selling substantial quantities of illiquid assets at potentially fire-sale prices. The end result is that the remaining investors take a loss, as the fund manager liquidates less-liquid investments, and are left with shares in a fund with little remaining upside. Consequently, the only equitable course of action may be to restructure the fund to create a liquidating trust to finance eventual redemptions; and an ongoing fund to allow continuing investors the opportunity to profit from new investment opportunities.

Given the possibility of such circumstances, it may be prudent for a fund manager to include a liquidating trust provision in the LPA as a last means of managing funding liquidity risk from high investor redemptions. Liquidating trust provisions establish that if investors elect to withdraw more than a set percentage of the fund's capital (typically 25 percent or more) on any withdrawal date, the "General Partner" (that is, the hedge fund manager) may, in his sole discretion, elect to make such distribution by distributing to a liquidating trust, instead of directly to investors. The liquidating trust is then administered exclusively by the fund manager, who acts as a trustee on behalf of the withdrawing investors who are beneficiaries of the trust. Assets and liabilities equal in net value to the amount investors seek to redeem are placed in the trust.

If a redeeming investor has requested a full withdrawal from the fund, for example, he will become a beneficiary of the trust and will receive an undivided proportionate interest in the trust based on the value of his interest in the overall fund at the withdrawal date. The fund manager, in his role as administrator of the trust, should then use all reasonable efforts to reduce the assets transferred to the trust to cash and to promptly distribute the cash to the beneficiaries. Typically, there is no commitment as to the timing of completing the liquidation. In addition, the fund manager will likely retain some cash in the trust even after full liquidation of the positions as a reserve for future liabilities (such as lawsuits brought by investors). In addition to distributions in cash, the trust may also make distributions in kind, at the sole discretion of the fund manager. Beneficiaries of the trust may or may not receive any transferable interest in the trust that they could redeem in a secondary market and consequently may have no choice but to wait for distributions from the trust in order to exit. Lastly, management and incentive fees may be payable to the fund manager for his services.

Obviously, a fund manager will have to evaluate carefully whether to invoke this right and create a liquidating trust. This option is extreme, but it gives the manager tremendous flexibility in managing funding risk arising from high redemptions. Invoking this right should only occur after the fund manager has given careful consideration to the alternatives and concluded that this is the best way to balance the interests of the redeeming investors with those of the remaining investors.

From an investor's perspective, the concerns relating to agreeing to a liquidating trust provision are the total loss of control over their investment if the fund manager invokes this right. Investors have effectively no recourse. Liquidating trust provisions give the fund manager complete discretion in paying redemptions in kind into the trust, which satisfies the legal requirement to meet redemptions but results in positions being placed in the trust for an unlimited time. Furthermore, for some funds, redemptions can be met with a disproportionate share of hard-to-value, illiquid securities being placed in a liquidating trust outside the investor's control. In addition, the fund manager may continue to earn full fees. Lastly, in some instances, there is no way for investors to exit the trust, even if they only want possession of their fair share of securities in the fund as there is no obligation for a fund manager to make a redemption in kind to investors who want to exit the fund and the trust.

Legal Implications

The choice to exercise a right granted a fund manager in the fund's constitutional documents to manage funding risk arising from redemptions must be made with the awareness that it can be challenged in court. The implications can be serious: if the court rules in the investor's favor, it can lead to the forced liquidation of the fund.

An investor that is locked into a fund when it exercises its right to suspend redemptions could institute a petition to wind up the fund on just and equitable grounds. Subject to a review of the fund's constitutional documents, the court may judge that the investor has legitimate grounds to expect to be able to redeem its shares in accordance with those documents. Furthermore, a court may conclude that in exercising its right to suspend redemptions, the fund acted solely in its own best interests and inequitably in that it has exposed the investor to additional risk that the assets of the fund may decline further, beyond the point where the investor could be repaid in full, and without any likelihood the investor will benefit from an increase in asset values. If the court were to draw such a conclusion, it may force the liquidation of the fund in order to benefit investors.

FUNDING LIQUIDITY RISK MANAGEMENT STRATEGIES: PRIME BROKERS

A hedge fund's relationship with its prime broker is, in the best of times, a symbiotic partnership. The hedge fund receives leverage, which can magnify investment returns, along with a variety of valuable services; while the broker receives interest income and security collateral it can use to generate low-cost funding and additional fees. This relationship is one of trust but also of co-dependency. Consequently, the relationship breaks down when confidence in the stability of either party falters, as the failure of one can cause losses for the other. The relationship is typically governed by several documents including the Prime Brokerage Agreement (also called a "Client-Account Agreement") and an International Swaps Dealers Association Agreement (ISDA Agreement).

These documents grant rights to both parties which can be used to insulate each from the failure of the other. The most significant rights granted to the prime broker in relation to funding liquidity risk are the right to call for additional collateral and the right to terminate the relationship, withdraw all funding, and call for the close-out amounts to be paid.

Prime Brokerage Agreements

The Prime Brokerage Agreement is a unilateral service agreement offered by the prime broker to the fund. It covers an infinite number of trades by the fund with the broker across most security types and contains credit, business, collateral, operational and legal terms. Negotiation of the Agreement prior to 2007 was limited, as prime brokers were not receptive to negotiating the terms by which they would provide services to hedge funds. However, since 2007, when the failure of several prime brokers to provide adequate services had a negative impact on the performance of their hedge fund clients, the agreement is increasingly subject to negotiation, with hedge funds focusing on several key areas relating to funding liquidity risk and the ability to recall collateral quickly.

Credit Terms   The primary credit terms in the Prime Brokerage Agreement establish the prime broker's ability to:

- Perfect a security interest in the collateral pledged by the fund to secure the financing provided by the prime broker
- Rehypothecate the collateral and to determine the extent to which this is required
- Net credit exposures across transactions and legal entities
- Be indemnified for losses arising from the actions of the hedge fund
- Declare the hedge fund in default and immediately recall all financing extended to the fund
- Increase margin levels and demand cash payment by the fund at any time for any reason.

Events of default under the Prime Brokerage Agreement allow the prime broker to terminate the relationship and immediately withdraw all funding extended to the fund. Events of default by the fund include:

- Where the fund is legally dissolved
- Failure to pay or deliver required collateral
- A breach of the prime brokerage agreement due to failure of the fund to continue to perform any obligations under the agreement
- Discovery of misrepresentation by the fund
- The "cross default provision"—default on any obligation owed to any legal entity relating to the prime broker such as an affiliate or foreign entity of the financial institution housing the prime brokerage entity.
- The "third party cross default provision—default to any third party
- Voluntary or involuntary bankruptcy.

The most commonly negotiated points under a Prime Brokerage Agreement are:

- Ringfencing: This is an attempt by the funds to weaken the cross-default provision by limiting the obligations which can trigger default to the specific prime brokerage entity alone. This prevents the prime broker from terminating its financing unless the fund specifically defaults on an obligation owed to that specific prime brokerage entity.
- Third Party Cross Default: Hedge funds also seek to have the third party cross default provision removed. This allows the fund to default to a third party, such as a second prime broker, without giving

other prime brokers the right to withdraw financing. This reduces the risk that funding provided by all prime brokers is withdrawn simultaneously.

- Cure Periods: Hedge funds often seek time to fix events that could trigger a default. By negotiating a cure period for potential events of default, they can force the prime broker to delay declaring a default and withdrawing funding from the fund.

- Margin Timing: Standard terms are that margin is payable to the prime broker on demand. Hedge funds often negotiate terms such that margin is only due by the end of the business day if a margin call is made before 10 a.m. If not, margin is payable the following day. This extends the time a hedge fund can have to find cash and have it delivered to its prime broker to meet a margin call.

- Rehypothecation Limit: Funds often negotiate that the prime broker cannot rehypothecate securities greater in value than 140 percent of the fund's indebtedness to the prime broker. This provision protects the fund from an inability to access collateral from a given prime broker as a result of financial difficulties being experienced by that broker. In the Lehman case for example, when Lehman became cash constrained, it ceased providing funding to funds but could not return their collateral, which it had rehypothecated to generate funding for itself. While many funds fearful of Lehman's collapse, sought to move their collateral away from Lehman so that it could be used it to generate funding with their more creditworthy prime brokers, they could not get it, which caused funding constraints and forced liquidation of other positions. By limiting the ability of a prime broker to rehypothecate their collateral to a regulatory limit of 140 percent, hedge funds can limit their exposure to the risk of being unable to access their collateral with a prime broker that is experiencing funding difficulties itself.

- Return of Excess Collateral: In addition, after Lehman, funds increasingly desire that any collateral in the prime brokerage account greater than the amount required as margin be returned on demand. Prime brokers resist this since, in an interbank funding crisis, excess collateral may have been rehypothecated and be difficult to get back from other financial institutions. To enforce rehypothecation limits, some funds request the ability to put the prime broker in default if collateral is not returned within a certain time. This is a very significant threat to a financial institution, which is also subject to cross default provisions in its funding arrangements. If its prime brokerage entity is in default, then the institution can be put in default on all of its funding agreements, resulting in a withdrawal of funding to the institution as a whole. Consequently, prime brokers very rarely agree to such requests.

- Recall of Securities Collateral for a Shareholder Vote: Activist funds in particular require that shares be returned to them in time for them to vote on critical corporate actions.
- Lock-up Terms in Prime Brokerage Agreement: Some funds will ask for clauses to be added to the agreement to limit the prime broker's ability to call for additional margin without notice. This is typically resisted by the brokers as a separate document is usually drafted to govern margin lock-ups. (Lock-ups are covered in greater detail later in the chapter.) If it is agreed to, it is extremely rare for the waiting period to be more than five business days.

ISDA

The ISDA is a bilateral trading agreement covering most derivative securities (that is, all swaps but also options, commodities, foreign exchange and structured products). It recognizes the two-way nature of the relationship between the prime broker and the fund in that it establishes rights and obligations of *both* counterparties. Like the Prime Brokerage Agreement, it is an umbrella agreement covering an infinite number of derivative transactions, each containing an element of leverage and funding. Each individual derivative transaction is documented by an individual confirmation containing the economics of the specific trade.

The key benefits of an ISDA to both counterparties are:

- It is a "bankruptcy protected" document in that it ensures creditors can be paid by the bankrupt counterparty.
- It establishes the terms of payment between counterparties.
- It establishes the tax status of the transactions. This is important to funds as derivative transactions can be more tax efficient than cash transactions while delivering the same upside potential.
- It sets out the documents required to be produced and delivered between counterparties to monitor the ongoing creditworthiness of each counterparty (including hedge fund financials, constitutional documents, NAV statements, periodic performance statements, and so on).
- It sets out mechanisms for resolving trade disputes (appointing the calculation agent and establishing valuation dispute resolution procedures, and so on).
- It sets out the rights of each counterparty in the event of a breach (Events of Default, Termination Events, Termination Procedures, and Calculations of payments owed in the event of termination).
- It establishes the rights to set off collateral to minimize counterparty exposures in the event of a default by the other.

The ISDA is a modular document in that it is made up of many different supporting documents. The ISDA Master Agreement contains standard terms and negotiated bespoke schedules pertinent to the specific dealing relationship. The Credit Support Annex (CSA) contains standard terms plus additional credit terms specific to the relationship. The Master Confirmation may contain product specific terms, guarantees, and unique definitions. Individual confirmations contain the economic terms of individual trades.

Like the Prime Brokerage Agreement, the ISDA documents contain important credit, business, collateral, operational, and legal terms. The credit and collateral terms are the most important for managing funding liquidity risk.

Credit and Collateral Terms The core credit concept of the ISDA agreement is that it establishes the ability of both counterparties to terminate the relationship in the event of a default by either, net the offsetting obligations, and settle the portfolio of obligations with one net payment. It is the timing of payment and the amount of this close-out amount that can create funding liquidity risk to a hedge fund in the event of a termination of the ISDA.

Netting down of exposure has benefits for both counterparties in that it can reduce the close-out amount. The netting of obligations under an ISDA has the effect of:

- Reducing credit exposures, as the portfolio's true exposure is the net exposure across transactions.
- Increasing trading capacity under credit exposure limits, since exposure is measured as net exposure. Consequently, limits are not hit as quickly, increasing trading capacity while minimizing potential credit exposures.
- Minimizing the collateral required, as parties post collateral based on net margin requirements, freeing up capital and increasing effective portfolio leverage to the hedge fund.

ISDA Master Agreement

The most commonly negotiated points under an ISDA Master Agreement are the Events of Default, the Termination Events, and the Calculation of Close-Out Amount provisions. Each of these areas can have a direct impact on the speed by which the relationship can be cancelled and the prime broker can withdraw funding and call for the close-out amount to be paid. Consequently, they have a direct impact on the funding risk of the hedge fund.

Events of Default   With regards to Events of Default, the most heavily negotiated points by hedge funds are:

- Failure to Pay/Deliver: Hedge funds typically negotiate a cure period in the event of a failure to pay or deliver in order to limit the prime broker's ability to declare the fund in default. The cure period is typically one–three days after the broker delivers notice of non-payment by the hedge fund. This gives the fund time to fix the incident that could lead to termination of the ISDA and delays the broker's ability to demand payment of the close-out amount.
- Breach of Agreement: The failure of the fund to provide the agreed documentation (financials, NAV statements, and so on) to enable the prime broker to monitor the fund's creditworthiness is an event of default under the ISDA. Hedge funds typically negotiate up to a 30-day cure period, which begins after the prime broker has given notice that it has not received the required documentation, in order to buy additional time to prepare and deliver the documentation. This is extremely useful as, during a crisis, the hedge fund's financial position may be shifting from day to day, assets may become difficult to value, and standard reporting may become time-consuming and delayed.
- Credit Support Default: This is a failure to comply with obligations under the Credit Support Annex (see below); specifically, the payment of margin. Hedge funds typically seek to negotiate a cure period before the prime broker can declare a default.
- Default under Specified Transactions: This provision defines the scope of transactions where any default allows termination of the ISDA relationship. As a default on a transaction may be a sign of hedge fund distress, prime brokers prefer to define the scope of transactions as broadly as possible to include failure to perform on any transaction with any related legal entity on any transactions not governed by the ISDA (such as the non-return of securities under repo transactions and other securities lending activities to any legal entity within the financial group). Hedge funds seek to narrow the scope and to "ringfence" legal entities. Typically, the funds will seek to embed minimum amount thresholds ("carve-outs") from the definition of non-return of collateral under repo transactions if the repo is recalled, and cure periods for administrative error to ensure that trivial non-payments cannot trigger default.
  - Threshold amounts are typically set at the lesser of $10 million or 2–3 percent of the fund's net asset value and 2–3 percent of the broker's market capitalization or shareholders' equity.
  - For administrative error carve-outs to be used generally requires that the defaulting party demonstrate that the non-performance or

non-payment was the result of an administrative error, rather than an inability to pay.

- The cure period for administrative errors is typically three days or less, requiring the error to be rectified and payment made within three business days.

These terms helps to ensure that the ISDA is not terminated and does not create a funding risk for the wrong reasons.

- **Cross Acceleration:** Hedge funds also seek to delay the ability of the prime broker to declare a default if there is a default on a non-ISDA transaction or a third party transaction by requesting that the defaulting non-ISDA or third party transaction be accelerated and closed out before the ISDA can be closed out. This forces the prime broker to wait to terminate the ISDA and delays the call for the close-out amount payment until the third party has accelerated its claim. Lastly, hedge funds seek that ISDA transactions be accelerated before a default can be declared under the ISDA. All these steps buy the Fund more time before the close-out amount must be paid and helps mitigate the potential funding risk a default can create.

- **Cross Default:** Hedge funds seek to carve out from the default events failures to perform obligations between the hedge fund and a third party. In addition, if the third party obligations cannot be carved out, the funds seek to create cure periods which allow time to fix the default and delay the prime broker's ability to call for the close-out amount.

Termination Events Termination Events are terms that give the non-defaulting party the right, but not the obligation, to terminate the relationship.[10] These events can be waived by the non-defaulting party and can be used to get the defaulting party to renegotiate more preferential terms, chief of which are requirements for additional collateral to protect the non-defaulting party in return for continuing the relationship. Termination events are typically "no-fault" events in that they are not entirely within the hedge fund's control. These are typically less punitive than the Events of Default in that they trigger a mutual and controlled unwinding of the ISDA relationship where both parties calculate the necessary close-out payment amounts to be delivered. In contrast, the Events of Default are fault events that are within the hedge fund's control and where the non-defaulting party becomes the calculation agent determining the close-out payment amounts. Typical termination events include:

- Illegality: it becomes illegal for a counterparty to continue its ISDA obligations
- Tax Event: tax laws change, causing a party to withhold taxes on ISDA payments

■ Credit Event Upon Merger: as a result of a merger, a counterparty's creditworthiness becomes "materially weaker."

Importantly for a hedge fund, prime brokers seek to embed additional termination events to cover additional "fault" events which are specific to the hedge fund's risk profile. These additional events can be used to end the ISDA relationship and force the payment of the close-out amount, creating a funding risk to the fund. Such events include:

■ NAV Triggers: As a decline in the fund's net asset value is typically the result of negative performance and/or redemptions by investors, it can be indicative of increasing liquidity problems at the fund and a decline in the fund's creditworthiness. Consequently, prime brokers establish monthly, quarterly, and annual NAV triggers where the ISDA can be terminated if the NAV falls below a preset level. Brokers seek to set low trigger levels and include the impact of investor redemptions on the NAV of the fund as well as performance, while hedge funds seek to set high triggers and exclude the impact of redemptions.
  – The mechanism for measuring declines in NAV is also heavily negotiated, with hedge funds seeking to define the calculation as being from any the end of any month or quarter to the end of another month or quarter. Prime brokers, on the other hand, seek to be able to measure the decline from the end of a month or quarter to any point within the month or quarter. The difference is that under the hedge fund's preferred mechanism, if the NAV drops below the trigger level during a month or quarter but recovers by the period end, it does not trigger a termination event, while under the broker's method it does.
  – Supercollateralization: As a compromise, the parties may agree that performance only should be counted in the NAV trigger, but that a separate set of triggers be agreed that include performance and redemptions but which allow for the prime broker to call only for a preset amount of additional collateral without the ability to terminate the ISDA. While not as severe as withdrawing all funding provided under the ISDA, supercollateralization triggers can require that the hedge fund post additional cash with the prime broker.
■ Minimum NAV Floor: As a decline in NAV can be indicative of a slow trend of poor performance and redemptions which, over time, diminishes the fund's NAV and creditworthiness but is not fast enough to trip any monthly, quarterly or annual trigger, a "slow drip" provision is often included that sets an absolute minimum NAV in dollar terms for the fund. If this level is breached, the ISDA can be terminated and renegotiated with stricter terms.

■ Failure to Deliver Agreed Transparency: As prime brokers seek to understand and monitor the fund's creditworthiness, they typically require the fund to deliver information regarding its risk profile on a monthly basis. Without this, the broker is not able to monitor the fund's changing creditworthiness. Consequently, failure to deliver "transparency" such as NAV statements, oral estimates of inter-month NAV, overall asset allocations, levels of unencumbered cash, the liquidity profile of fund assets, risk reports and/or results of stress tests is grounds for termination of the ISDA relationship. Hedge funds typically request time to prepare this information after the month-end close, often 15–30 business days and additional grace periods of, typically, five days. This delays the prime broker's ability to terminate the ISDA and, consequently, defers the payment of the close-out amount.

■ Key Man Provision: Changes in the management of the fund can be a sign of potential credit problems and a prelude to high redemptions at the fund. Consequently, prime brokers require that if a key individual, such as a founder of the fund or key portfolio manager, departs, they have the right to terminate, call for a close-out payment, and then renegotiate the ISDA.

As the ISDA is a two-way agreement and hedge funds are concerned about the return of collateral if the prime broker's creditworthiness deteriorates, hedge funds may also negotiate provisions to allow them to terminate the ISDA. One such provision is the Credit Downgrade Trigger, which allows a fund to terminate the ISDA relationship if the prime broker's credit rating drops below a threshold level (typically BBB), and to call for posted collateral to be returned and close-out payments to be made.

Calculation of Close-out Amount   In the event of termination of the ISDA, calculation of the close-out payment can be highly complex and there is potential in illiquid products for the valuation to be somewhat subjective. There is no market consensus as to how this is to be done. Consequently, the mechanics of the calculation are highly negotiated at the inception of the ISDA, with hedge funds seeking to ensure they can influence the calculation where it is objective and opaque.

Market Quote Method   The standard ISDA mechanism is the market-quote method where the non-defaulting or non-affected party obtains market quotes on the replacement value of the swaps and derivative transactions. While objective for liquid transactions, it may be impossible to get quotes for illiquid transactions. In addition, by requesting quotes from market participants, this method also has the disadvantage of communicating to the market details of a large portfolio that may soon be sold, prompting market participants to quote lower market prices.

Loss Method   However, prime brokers prefer that the close-out amount be based on the non-defaulting party's calculation of its "losses," which can include the cost of liquidation of the prime broker's hedge put on at the inception of each swap transaction in addition to the liquidation value of the swap, and the use of internal models to value illiquid swap transactions. Consequently, the loss method can potentially result in close-out amounts higher than the market quote method and a present a higher funding risk to the hedge fund. The loss method also creates the possibility for greater subjectivity in the determination of the close-out amount and consequently is resisted by hedge funds in ISDA negotiations.

Credit Support Annex of the ISDA

The Credit Support Annex (CSA) further establishes the secured party's (the prime broker) valid and perfected security interest in all collateral posted to it by its counterparty (the hedge fund). It specifies how collateral calls are determined, the timing required for making margin calls and their form of payment, any collateral substitution requirements, dispute-resolution procedures, and the standard of use and care of the hedge fund's collateral by the prime broker. It may also contain additional CSA-specific events of default.

The primary negotiated points in a CSA are:

- Unilateral or Bilateral Agreement: Whether the CSA applies one way (that is, only to the hedge fund) or two ways (that is, applies equally to the hedge fund and the prime broker). Typically, the requirement to post collateral is born by the hedge fund. However, since the collapse of Lehman Brothers larger funds may be able to negotiate that lower-rated prime brokers also post collateral. Close-out amounts may be reduced to the extent that CSAs are bilateral, reducing potential funding risk for the hedge fund.
- Eligible Collateral and Collateral Haircuts: Whether securities are acceptable collateral in addition to cash and, if so, the type of securities. Being able to post securities as collateral can reduce the cash requirements on the fund and mitigates potential funding risk. Haircut levels are also heavily negotiated, with hedge funds seeking to select prime brokers that will provide them the greatest funding against their security collateral. This leaves the fund in control of the resulting freed-up

cash which it can hold in reserve in an account away from the prime broker and use to meet cash requirements with any counterparty or investor. (Haircut and margin levels will be discussed in more detail later in this chapter.)

■ Collateral Thresholds (or "unsecured amount"): The point at which it is necessary for the fund to post additional collateral to cover its collateral shortfall. The higher the threshold, the greater flexibility provided to the fund before it must source cash or securities to meet a margin call.

■ Minimum Transfer Amounts: The amount below which collateral owed need not be posted. This is often a low threshold for smaller funds but can be large for the top funds. It serves to decrease the operational burdens of an ISDA relationship and the frequency of collateral transfers by both parties. Collateral does not need to be transferred until the exposure reaches a material amount.

■ Notification Time and Transfer Time: The time of day by which a counterparty must notify the other of a margin call in order to be owed payment by a transfer of cash or security collateral by the end of the business day. Typically, notification is required by 10 a.m. or noon for payment to be owed by 5 p.m. the same day. If a counterparty is notified after the notification time cut-off, the transfer can be effected the following business day. Having time after notification to trade out of security positions or source cash from elsewhere is important to avoid technically defaulting on a collateral payment and causing a close-out of the ISDA.

■ Grace Periods for Non-payment of a Margin Call: Typically one business day's grace is negotiated to accommodate holiday schedules and operational delays to avoid technical defaults and closing out of the ISDA.

■ Supercollateralization Amounts: The extent to which a counterparty may increase its required margin amounts because of a violation of a supercollateralization threshold. Typically this is defined by a negotiated schedule of margins for each security type or set as twice the initial schedule.

Lock-ups and Term Commitments

If ISDA agreements are like speed dating, and a prime brokerage agreement is like going steady, then the aptly named "lock-up" is like a marriage between the hedge fund and the prime broker. While an ISDA may specify margin terms for individual swaps and derivative transactions, the prime brokerage agreement specifies the margin terms for a portfolio of securities and a prime brokerage lock-up fixes those portfolio margin terms for a set period of time.

In the most basic terms, a lock-up or a "term commitment" is a credit facility extended by a prime broker to a hedge fund. Lock-ups prevent the prime broker from changing margin rates and methodologies that determine collateral requirements. For a hedge fund, certainty, stability and predictability of margin requirements can serve as a sea anchor in a maelstrom and a tremendous asset in a funding crisis.

In addition, prime brokers may extend the lock-up to cover financing rates on margin financing and limit the broker's ability to decline to clear the hedge fund's trades during the term of the lock-up. For large managers, lock-up tenors are often 60 to 180 days and perhaps even longer for the largest hedge funds. The way the arrangement works in practice is that if a prime broker wants to make a change to an aspect of its financial relationship with the hedge fund that is covered by the lock-up, it must provide the manager with the requisite notice before doing so.

After the credit crisis, the problems affecting major banks also had an impact on their prime brokerage units. This resulted in less appetite to extend credit to hedge funds and to a demand for higher quality collateral when doing so. However, as the banking industry recovers, the appetite is increasing. That said, there is little appetite in most prime brokerages to finance illiquid securities or any position for which the prime broker cannot continually source objective prices daily.

Negotiating Lock-up and Prime Brokerage Agreements A margin lock-up is negotiated separately from a prime-brokerage agreement. Hedge funds have significant negotiating power when they are first looking to select a prime broker and the threat of their switching brokers gives them considerable leverage throughout the relationship. Furthermore, a broker may be most receptive to the idea of favorable lock-up terms once a fund has been with him for at least six months and he has had time to observe the fund's trading habits and risk profile. After several months of proven profitability, the prime broker may well be inclined to offer favorable terms.

There are five significant areas to negotiate in a margin lock-up: (1) the Covered Terms (2) Excluded Positions, (3) the Termination Events, (4) the Transparency Requirements, and (5) the Margin rules.

Covered Terms The scope of the commitment is defined by the "Covered Terms," and the prime broker cannot change any of these without giving notice and then waiting for the lock-up period to expire before effecting the change.

Covered Terms typically include:

- The methods used by the prime broker to determine the margin or collateral requirements or financing charges applicable to the hedge fund's accounts.
- The format or substance of the information exchanged between the broker and the hedge fund in connection with executing, financing, reconciling or reporting activity in the fund's accounts.
- The applicability of the lock-up and margin rules to both financed cash securities positions and derivatives such as swaps.

In addition, funds may seek to include the prime broker's commitment to continue clearing trades. A prime brokerage agreement is a demand facility and, consequently, the broker can normally decide to stop clearing a fund's trades at any time and for any reason. This could be highly disruptive, and could result in significant losses for a fund if it cannot implement a hedge or stop losses on a losing position by selling it. If the commitment to continue clearing trades is included in the covered terms, the broker will have to provide the requisite notice before refusing to do so, which will allow the fund time to open new accounts with other brokers.

Conditions and Exclusions   The condition terms specify the types of collateral portfolios to which the locked-up margin rules will apply. Prime brokers are more comfortable agreeing to lock-up margins on liquid, diversified, and low volatility portfolios because of their more stable risk profile. The following are typical conditions terms:

- Minimum number of positions: A prime broker typically will require that the collateral portfolio consist of at least 15–25 different security positions. This provides the broker with increased certainty that the value of the portfolio will not be affected by idiosyncratic risk. As long as all other criteria are met, this requirement may be waived or reduced during the ramp-up period of a new relationship as the fund builds its balances incrementally.
- Maximum asset class exposures: Just as diversification across positions is important to ensure stability in the value of the collateral, so too is diversification across asset classes. While the amount of the portfolio that can be in liquid equities and high grade sovereign bonds is generally unlimited, other limits may apply. For example, a broker may not want to agree a lock-up margin on a portfolio of more than 50 percent in corporate bonds or more than 10–25 percent in commodities, for example. This is as much for risk reasons as it is for funding reasons.

Equities and sovereign bonds are readily rehypothecated and can generate low cost funding for the broker. However, low grade corporate bonds and commodities are not as easily rehypothecated and are more costly for the broker to finance, all other things being equal.

The exclusions specify the types of positions to which the locked-up margin rules will not apply. Prime brokers will seek to preserve the ability to change margin on higher risk positions. Consequently, they will seek to exclude from the lock-up segments of the hedge fund's portfolio which are considered excessively risky and will want to be able to change margin on these positions. The following are typical types of exclusion terms:

- Concentration: Prime brokers want the ability to charge higher margin on positions which present higher risks because they represent a risk concentration in the securities collateral pledge to the broker. Typical concentration exclusions are, for example, positions in a single emerging market with a combined market value greater than 20–30 percent of the portfolio's gross market value or positions in the securities (including equities, derivatives, bonds etc.) of a single issuer greater than 5–10 percent of the gross market value of the portfolio.[11]
- Liquidity: Prime brokers want the ability to charge higher margin for positions that they may not be able to liquidate at their quoted market value due to potential illiquidity. Typical liquidity exclusions are, for example, positions in securities greater than 10–15 percent of the issue size of that security or positions in debt securities greater than 5–10 percent in the total outstanding debt of the issuer. Other liquidity exclusions might relate to restricted trading securities such as 144a issues, control positions, or private securities.
- Other Risky Positions:
  - Small cap stocks: Small cap stocks can be highly volatile and institutional buyers may not exist for securities of such small companies. Consequently, liquidity can be low. Prime brokers seek to exclude excessive portions of the locked-up balances consisting of positions in companies of less than US$300–500 million in aggregate market cap and typically seek to limit small caps to 10 percent of the gross market value of the locked-up portfolio.
  - Penny stocks: Similar to small cap stocks, stocks valued at less than $1 have riskier liquidity and volatility characteristics than stocks priced at over $1. This is both a function of the securities lending market and the institutional investor appetite for such stocks. Prime brokers seek to exclude excessive portions of the locked-up balances consisting of stocks with a price less than $1 in aggregate and

typically seek to limit penny stocks to 10 percent of the gross market value of the locked-up portfolio.

- Sub-investment grade debt: The risk of sudden default in sub-investment grade corporate debt (below BBB+) is materially higher than in investment-grade and sovereign debt. Consequently, prime brokers seek to be free to change margin on these types of securities and to exclude portions of the hedge fund's balances from the lock-up if they consist of sub-investment grade corporate debt and are typically greater than 10–15 percent of the portfolio. Furthermore, brokers may seek to exclude any debt securities rated below B– entirely.
- Unrated debt: As with sub-investment grade debt, prime brokers do not want to lock up margin rates on debt securities where the risk is not measurable and will seek to exclude portions of the hedge fund's balances from the lock-up if they entirely consist of unrated corporate debt or limit it to a small percentage of the collateral portfolio's gross market value.

■ Emerging Markets:
- Given the history of emerging market crises and contagions, prime brokers seek to exclude from the lock-up excessive amounts of emerging market exposure. With the continued stability and robust growth in emerging markets, however, the appetite for emerging market collateral is increasing. Nonetheless, brokers seek to be free to change margin on these types of securities and to exclude excessive portions of the hedge fund's balances from the lock-up if they are typically greater than 50 percent of the portfolio.
- Prime brokers rely on the legal right to liquidate a hedge fund's positions in the event of default in order to retrieve their financing. In certain less sophisticated emerging market countries, this legal right is unclear. Consequently, the prime brokers will seek to exclude securities from these countries from being financed and their margins being locked up.

In negotiating the conditions and exclusions, the prime broker should customize these terms to fit the strategy of the hedge fund. A hedge fund should expect the prime broker to decrease the restrictiveness of certain conditions and exclusions to better fit the fund's investment strategy while increasing others so that the hedge fund is comfortable that the lock-up serves its need for stable financing of its investment portfolio. With respect to exclusions, where percentage of portfolio limits are established, it is important to specify that only the excess positions above these thresholds will be excluded from the lock-up, and not the entire position.

Termination Events   The termination events in a margin lock-up give the prime broker the right to terminate the lock-up if a certain event occurs. Termination events can be very contentious in a margin lock-up negotiation. Hedge funds tend to see them as "if . . . then" statements, as in "if this event occurs, then the prime broker will terminate the lock-up." For the broker, however, having these terms as options is useful, though they hope never to have to use them.

Prime brokers typically seek to have termination events that protect them in all cases where the fund encounters difficulties. Termination events that allow the broker to unilaterally terminate the relationship immediately and increase margins based on subjective assessments could make the margin lock-up worthless in a funding or market crisis. For example, some prime brokers will try to include a provision that allows termination if the they determine that they may suffer reputational risk if they continue to do business with the fund. Fund managers should be wary of subjective termination events, and such provisions should be negotiated out of the agreement. Typical objective termination events include:

- Default/Cross Default: A default by the fund on any of its agreements with the prime broker or related entity is grounds for termination of the lock-up. Hedge funds may seek to limit this to default by the fund to the broker alone and to exclude defaults to other financial institutions as a trigger for the broker's right to terminate the lock-up. Generally, this is not acceptable to the brokers.
- NAV triggers: To the extent that a decline in net asset value indicates either negative performance and/or investor redemptions, it is a potential indicator of a fund's deteriorating creditworthiness. The speed and persistence of a decline is another indicator. Prime brokers seek to be able to terminate the lock-up when the fund's own monthly NAV report indicates such a decline.

Monthly, quarterly and annual NAV change triggers allow the lock-up to be terminated if the change exceeds a predetermined threshold. This is one of the most heavily negotiated lock-up terms. Hedge funds prefer these thresholds to be as high as possible and to exclude the impact of investor redemptions so that the lock-up will hold in a market crisis or a funding crisis caused by high redemptions. Prime brokers prefer the opposite. Typically, NAV triggers are set at a 15 percent decline over a month, 25 percent over a quarter, and 35 percent over a year, and include the full impact of redemptions.

The ultimate agreement of NAV triggers, and the amount of flexibility a prime broker and hedge fund will have, depends on the volatility of the fund's strategy and the aggressiveness of the margin demanded by the hedge fund. If the fund follows a low volatility strategy, provides the broker with detailed, frequent and up-to-date information about its funding position and unencumbered cash, and the margins demanded are comparatively conservative from the broker's perspective, then the broker may be agreeable to setting high NAV triggers.

- NAV Floor: A slow decline in the fund's NAV can occur that does not trigger any of the NAV triggers but which, over time, changes the creditworthiness of the fund. Prime brokers view such a change as a commercially acceptable reason to terminate the existing lock-up and renegotiate it. Typically, the NAV floor is set at the greater of 50 percent of NAV at the start of the lock-up agreement and 50 percent of each subsequent year-end.
- Key Person Provision: The departure from a fund of its founder, fund manager, star trader, or other significant contributor may cause a significant number of investors to redeem in the expectation of poor performance. At the extreme, it may signal malfeasance at the fund. For these reasons, prime brokers seek the right to name key persons in the lock-up and to terminate the lock-up if one or more quit the fund. Hedge funds typically seek to amend this termination event to require more than one key person to quit the fund and for suitable replacements not to be found within 30 days before the lock-up can be terminated.
- Regulatory: A regulatory investigation can be an indication of a fund's declining creditworthiness. Consequently, prime brokers seek to be able to terminate a lock-up in the event of such an investigation. However, hedge funds seek to restrict the provision such that brokers can only terminate if an objective sanction is imposed by regulators on the fund, its manager or principals after an investigation concludes that a regulatory violation did indeed occur.
- Failure to Provide Transparency: As further discussed below, a prime broker will require periodic, timely and detailed monthly information regarding the hedge fund's overall risk profile in order to monitor its ongoing creditworthiness. If the fund does not provide this information, the broker can only rely on the balances in its custody by which to evaluate the riskiness of the fund. If a fund has multiple prime brokers, then any one broker is only seeing part of the picture. Consequently, if the fund fails to provide the pre-agreed transparency on a timely basis, then the broker may terminate the lock-up. The most commonly negotiated points are the content of the transparency disclosure and the amount of time after month-end that the fund has to deliver and whether there are any days of grace. Typically, transparency is required on a monthly basis and within 15 days of the month-end.

Transparency and Disclosure Typical transparency requirements include:

- Net asset value: The fund's monthly NAV, net subscriptions and redemptions, and performance
- Leverage reporting: Including off-balance-sheet position long and short market value
- Percent of book: The broker's financing as a percentage of the hedge fund's overall portfolio
- Funding liquidity: Unencumbered cash amount or percentage of NAV
- Portfolio liquidity: Liquidity profile of the total hedge fund portfolio broken into tenor based liquidity buckets showing the percentage of the portfolio that can be sold for cash over various time horizons.
- Risk reporting: VaR reports, VaR/NAV; results of stress scenarios, stress loss/NAV
- Portfolio asset class exposures: Portfolio breakdown by percentage of gross market value or risk factor sensitivity in a given asset class, country, industry, rating bucket, etc.

These transparency requirements may place an operational burden on the hedge fund. To reduce this burden, the fund may seek to have the prime broker accept the same level of transparency that the fund provides to its investors on a monthly basis. Prime brokers often find this level of transparency insufficient and feel they are entitled to superior information since they are senior creditors of the fund.

Margin Rules Hedge funds may view a lock-up as fixing margin rates on all securities they seek to trade with a prime broker. This is rarely the case. In reality, lock-ups typically only fix the method by which margin rates are calculated. The lock-up removes the prime broker's ability to change the method but that may not result in fixing a flat rate in all market environments.

This is because brokers' margin methodologies are increasingly sophisticated and market-driven. Most prime brokers have a menu of methodologies available to them. Margins may be determined based on the stress testing of the hedge fund's portfolio (stress-based margin); by a VaR-type analysis (VaR margin); or based on a complex series of rules or algorithms (rules-based margin).

A lock-up of a VaR-margin methodology will actually be pro-cyclical. As the market enters a crisis, volatility and correlation will likely increase for most securities. Consequently, the VaR of the balances at the prime broker will increase and with it the margin. This will come just at the time the fund needs to maximize its funding flexibility.

A stress-based margin may be based on the worst outcome of a mix of historical scenarios and potential future scenarios that can be defined by the prime broker depending on their market outlook. Obviously, a more severe scenario can result in an increase in margin without a change in methodology. Alternatively, the stress scenarios may be defined as three, four, or five standard deviation moves of relevant risk factors. These standard deviations are drawn from recent historical time series. In market crises, these too will be pro-cyclical, as the standard deviation of most risk factors will increase as volatility increases.

Rules-based margins typically consist of base margin rates that determine the margin in normal markets but which contain mathematical functions that increase margin above the base rates as liquidity, volatility, and/or concentration hits preset thresholds. These additional charges begin to increase margins in a crisis.

Locking up rules-based margins provides the greatest predictability of margin and best sets bounds on the amount margin can increase under a lock-up. The methodology also has the advantage of being able to be replicated by the hedge fund once the prime broker provides the rules. This enables the fund to conduct a "what if?" analysis of potential trades and their margin impact. It also enables it to simulate its margin changes under adverse market scenarios and plan its funding-liquidity management.

In the lock-up negotiations, the margin methodology is fair game. A fund can evaluate all of the prime broker's methodologies by providing a sample portfolio and evaluating the margin under each available method. Once a method is chosen, hedge funds can ask for specific parameters in the calculation to be changed to produce lower margins or margins that step up at a slower pace in times of market turbulence. The result will be a bespoke methodology for the fund. The prime broker's receptiveness to this will depend on how much profit it expects to make from the fund, the broker's assessment of the riskiness of the fund, and the aggressiveness of the other terms in the lock-up.

Secondary Considerations

Financing Rates and Fees Hedge funds can also lock up their fees and financing rates. This is typically of secondary importance to margin levels, as the funding impact on the fund of a change in fees is several orders of magnitude smaller than the impact of a change in margin levels.

This can be part of the margin lock-up negotiation. The prime broker will typically provide the fund with a schedule of financing rates by currency and by type of collateral. Rates will be quoted as a spread over LIBOR or Fed Funds rates and vary depending on the ability of the broker to secure funding via rehypothecation of the fund's collateral.

Collateral that can't be rehypothecated will generally be charged a higher unsecured funding rate.

Bilateral Termination Provisions   Because of the events of the credit crisis, where brokers collapsed as a result of creditworthiness and funding issues, some hedge fund managers and CFOs feel that margin lock-ups should not be completely unilateral. For example, a fund may request that a downgrade in the credit rating of the prime broker to below investment grade should be a termination event. This is very much a secondary consideration, though, as the fund can simply choose to not use that broker and move its balances elsewhere if it is concerned about the broker's creditworthiness. The lock-up does not need to be terminated in order for this risk to be avoided.

Substitution Rights   Substitution rights may be an additional option available to a hedge fund within a lock-up. Substitution rights allow that after the prime broker has served notice on the lock-up, the broker must continue to accept trades that meet certain requirements and provide the same level of financing to the fund until the end of the notice period. This effectively allows the fund to continue trading and substitute new positions for old positions as it trades and continue to have the new positions qualify for locked-up margin treatment. For example, the hedge fund will be able to do this so long as it satisfies the following conditions:

- Substitution of the new position for the old must be within the same day
- The risk profile of the collateral pool must not deteriorate in aggregate. This is typically measured objectively on a predefined set of tests such as:
  - The number of positions with more than five percent of the gross market value of the portfolio may not increase
  - The percentage of the collateral portfolio in securities positions representing more than two days' trading volume may not increase.
  - The percentage of the collateral portfolio in non-investment-grade debt may not increase.
  - The percentage of the collateral portfolio in potentially illiquid large blocks of bonds may not increase. A large block position may be measured as any bond position which is more than 10 percent of the total issue size of the bond.
  - The collateral portfolio may not become concentrated. The percentage of the portfolio in any one country or industry sector may not increase to be more than 20 percent of gross market value of the portfolio.

– The average credit spread of the bonds in the collateral portfolio may not increase on a market value weighted basis and the average credit rating of the bond portfolio may not decrease on a market value weighted basis.

All of the above terms are presented to the fund in a "term sheet." The term sheet is a summary of the broker's proposed terms for the lock-up agreement in plain English. The hedge fund's CFO or portfolio manager then considers the operational implications of those terms on the fund and responds to that proposal. Once agreement on the terms is reached, the final term sheet is given the broker's lawyers and the agreed terms are written into the formal lock-up letter. A sample term sheet is shown in Figure 5.1 (with explanatory comments in italics).

Icarus Capital LP

Proposed Lock-up Terms (Indication only)

(Subject to satisfactory documentation)

Term	5–180 calendar days
Description	Broker can change margins on demand but under this agreement Covered Terms cannot be changed for a period of XX days (subject to termination events and exclusions outlined below).
	Broker retains the right to refuse additional trades and to designate assets as excluded from this lock-up.
Covered Terms	(i) the methods used by broker XYZ to determine the margin or collateral requirements or financing charges applicable to Fund's accounts; and (ii) the format or substance of the information exchanged between broker XYZ and Fund in connection with executing, financing, reconciling or reporting activity in Fund's accounts.
Margin Terms	See Margin Schedule
Conditions:	Minimum number of positions must be at least 25 positions. *(This condition may be reduced to 15 positions for the first 30 days of the lock-up as long as all other criteria are met.)*
	No more than 50 percent of market value of margined portfolio may be in corporate bonds *(as distinct from more liquid sovereign bonds).*

FIGURE 5.1 *(Continued)*

Excluded Positions: Concentrated positions:

1. Single Country Exposures greater than 20 percent of gross market value of the portfolio.
2. Positions of Single Issuer greater than 10 percent of gross market value of the portfolio excluding National Governments in OECD countries.
3. Position(s) in securities greater than 10 percent of the issue size of that security.
4. Position(s) in debt securities greater than 20 percent in the total outstanding debt of the issuer.
5. Position(s) in companies < $500 million market cap in aggregate shall be limited to 10 percent of Gross Market Value of the portfolio
6. Position(s) in straight debt investments rated below BB- shall be limited to 15 percent of Gross Market Value of portfolio.

Restricted Securities: Positions(s) relating to restricted or private securities

Non Priceable Securities: Broker XYZ must be able to continually value the position by sourcing a fair market price on a daily basis. *(Securities which cease to be priced will be excluded, irrespective of whether they were initially included in the lock-up.)*

Unrated Securities: Securities not rated by either S&P or Moody's.

Domestic Currency: Aggregate non US$, Euro, and JPY exposure greater than 20 percent of Gross Market Value of the portfolio. *(This serves to limit the exposure to more exotic currencies.)*

Agency Rating: No securities rated below B- by S&P or Moody's equivalent. *(This serves to ensure the credit quality of the bonds in the portfolio remain mostly of investment grade. When split rating, lower prevails.)*

(For the above, excess positions outside these criteria will be typically excluded from the lock-up.)

Termination Events: Cross Default: breach or default under any other agreement with any entities related to the broker.

Bankruptcy: bankruptcy, insolvency or appointment of receiver for the fund.

Decline in Net Assets of Fund: 10 percent monthly (performance only), 12 percent quarterly (performance only) or 20 percent quarterly (inclusive of redemptions); 30 percent annually (inclusive of redemptions).

NAV Floor: The greater of 50 percent of NAV at start of agreement and 50 percent of each subsequent year-end.

FIGURE 5.1 *(Continued)*

Change of Manager: The existing hedge fund manager ceases to run the fund.

Failure to Provide Transparency: Monthly within 15 days of month-end. *(Broker specifies what transparency information is required.)*

Regulatory Sanction: Regulators impose sanctions on fund, manager or named principals.

Substitution Rights: Should the portfolio be in violation of the Excluded Positions or Other Limits, the client will be allowed to substitute collateral that satisfies the following:

(a) Substitution notice must be within the same day that any position is removed from the portfolio.

(b) Percentage of the portfolio in the following may not increase:

- Positions with >5 percent of the Gross Market Value of the portfolio

- Securities with >two days' trading volume

- Non-investment-grade debt

- Bonds > 10 percent of Issue

- Bonds in any country or industry sector > than 20 percent of Gross Market Value.

(c) Average credit spread of the bond portfolio may not increase on a Market Value weighted basis and average credit rating of the bond portfolio may not decrease on a Market Value weighted basis.

Transparency Requirements *(Typical information required by brokers)*

Monthly NAV and Performance of Fund

Leverage Reporting: including off-balance-sheet positions (LMV, SMV, GMV, and NAV)

Percent of Book Reporting: broker XYZ financing as a percentage of Fund's overall portfolio

Unencumbered cash/NAV

Balance sheet liquidity by liquidity bucket

Risk Reporting (VAR/NAV; Stress Risk/NAV)

Country Breakdown, Ratings Breakdown, Corporate vs. Sovereign breakdown

FIGURE 5.1 Representative Lock-up Term Sheet

Managing Margin Requirements Whether locked up or not, margin requirements vary by fund and by the type of asset being financed. The primary determinants of the amount of margin required and, therefore, the leverage a prime broker will provide to a hedge fund are:

1. The broker's assessment of the fund's creditworthiness
2. The quality of collateral provided by the fund.

Hedge Fund Creditworthiness At the initiation of a prime broker's relationship with a hedge fund, the broker will conduct a credit assessment of the fund. The assessment is intended to rank the fund's relative default probability and will be monitored monthly and formally reassessed annually. The primary factors for assessing creditworthiness are:

1. The risks of the fund's primary strategy or strategies
2. The historical volatility of the performance of the fund
3. The diversity of investors and the length of investor lock-up periods
4. The demonstrated risk management capabilities and discipline of the fund
5. The portfolio manager's appetite and control of leverage
6. The fund's cash flow and funding-liquidity management
7. Back office capabilities, pricing procedures, and operational risk exposures.

On the basis of this assessment, the broker will determine the types of transactions it will undertake with the fund: cash securities, exchange-traded derivatives, OTC derivatives, commodities, convertible bonds, credit derivatives, and so on. Typically, this credit assessment is qualitative in that it relies on the experience and judgment of the credit officer making the assessment. Increasingly, the larger brokers and investment banks are institutionalizing this credit skill through the application of scorecards which evaluate hedge funds on a consistent but relative basis across the seven areas shown above. In the future, a quantitative assessment of a hedge fund's creditworthiness may be possible using structural default models but significant amounts of potentially sensitive data from hedge funds. (See Appendix 3 for a discussion of a structural framework for evaluating hedge-fund default probability. The objective of this appendix is to present a conceptual framework for quantifying hedge fund failure that may serve as a useful mental model for CFOs and CROs to frame strategic decisions relating to their minimal level unencumbered cash.)

The fund's creditworthiness will also be factored into the aggressiveness of the terms in the legal documents governing the trading. It will also determine whether the broker will intermediate transactions executed by the fund with other firms and then given up to and financed by the broker. These eligible transactions will also typically define the security types that will be accepted as collateral.

Collateral Quality While credit assessment is a relative indication of the potential of the fund to default, the collateral quality is used to control the prime broker's exposure in the event of default. The amount of financing extended to the fund is a function of the collateral's potential value in a market crisis (that is, its market risk).

Brokers evaluate the quality of a hedge fund's collateral based on its:

1. Market Neutrality: Is the collateral portfolio truly an arbitrage portfolio and well hedged or is it directionally biased and exposed to systematic market moves? How close is it to being beta-neutral, delta-neutral, gamma-neutral, DV01, CSO1 and convexity-neutral?
2. Concentration: Is the collateral portfolio concentrated in specific names, industries, countries, currencies, or regions that make its value vulnerable to specific risk?
3. Crowded Trades: Does the portfolio consist of substantial positions similar to or related to positions held by other hedge funds that could be subject to dramatic changes in price and liquidity if hedge fund sentiment changed?
4. Liquidity: Can the positions be sold in the market within one trading day without moving the market?
5. Priceability: Can each of the positions be objectively valued using executed prices daily so that the broker can be confident of the amount of cash it would receive if the fund were to default and the broker was forced to liquidate the collateral to recover its loan to the fund?

Other broker specific factors that may influence the assessment of the quality of collateral include:

1. The broker's ability to generate secured funding by rehypothecating the collateral pledged. This can vary according to the broker's regulatory regime and its institutional abilities.
2. The broker's ability to generate high-margin short-sale revenues by lending out long positions within the collateral that are "hard to borrow" and therefore can demand a high premium.
3. The amount of similar collateral pledged by other hedge funds to the broker. Generally, prime brokers seek to maintain diversified collateral across hedge funds as well as within specific collateral pools.

This assessment of the quality of collateral is a continual process evaluated by stress testing the collateral daily, at a minimum, and intraday for high-velocity funds with intraday trading.

Margin requirements are linked to the quality of individual security positions pledged as collateral but also to the quality of the portfolio construction within the collateral portfolio. Margin requirements are determined by:

1. Static algorithms or "rules": These are liquidity, concentration, volatility, hedge stability, and market neutrality tests applied to the portfolio, which increase or reduce margin requirements around a base margin amount.
2. VaR analysis: For select highly liquid markets, such as G-10 foreign exchange and government rates markets with historically low kurtosis in their return distributions, margin based on VaR with a 5–10 day liquidation horizon and 99 percent confidence interval may be an acceptable basis on which a broker will determine margin. However, the extreme 6 and 7 sigma market moves of 2007 and 2008 (as discussed in Chapter 1) undermine the prudence of VaR-type margin methodologies and, instead, favor stress testing methodologies.
3. Stress analysis: Margin may be determined based on predefined stress algorithms such as 3–4 sigma market moves with conservative correlation assumptions that are periodically updated by the broker.
4. Scenario analysis: Margin may be determined based on a predefined set of scenarios defined by the broker. These may be agreed in advance between the fund and the broker based on their joint assessment of the relevant risk in the fund's investment portfolio. The broker will typically retain the ability to change the scenarios if the risks of the portfolio change and the fund's investment style drifts.

Each of these methodologies can contain multipliers which gross up or down the margin requirement from the output of each methodology. The broker's assessment of the fund's creditworthiness will also determine the multiplier applied to the result and consequently the level of margin that will need to be posted by the fund.

Other Determinants of Margin Though rarely explicitly discussed between the prime broker and the fund, the total amount of risk the broker (and the financial institution housing the broker) take to the fund is a factor governing the size of the overall relationship. Margin levels charged to the fund and the risk taken by the broker are typically inversely related. All brokers measure the amount of potential loss they face if a fund defaults and the margin posted is insufficient. Typically, this potential loss is the stress-loss exposure. Stress loss is the worst-case decline in value of a fund's collateral portfolio before it can be liquidated in a market crisis. Stress loss exposure is measured as follows:

$$\text{Stress Loss Exposure} = \text{Max}\,(0,\ \text{Stress Loss} - \text{Margin})$$

where Stress Loss = Drop in value of collateral in an extreme market crisis.[12]

The broker will take a loss if the fund defaults and the realized stress loss exceeds the margin posted. Potential stress loss exposure occurs when the margin posted is less than the potential drop in value of the collateral in a market crisis.

Brokers seek to maximize the ratio of client revenues to client-driven stress loss exposure. They have risk appetite for stress loss exposure to funds they view as more creditworthy. They also have risk appetite for taking stress loss exposure to funds that generate significant revenue streams. They have little appetite for exposure to those they view as less creditworthy or which do not generate significant revenue streams.

Regardless of the total revenue a hedge may generate for a broker or the fund's creditworthiness, there are limits to the amount of acceptable stress-loss exposure a broker should bear to any single fund. These are potential exposures where if the client fund were to default, the potential loss to the broker would threaten the viability of the brokerage by the reducing earnings of the broker or damaging its creditworthiness and ability to fund itself in the market.

Optimizing Capital Efficiency: Characteristics of Low Margin Portfolios   True arbitrage portfolios that are market neutral, highly liquid, highly diversified, and contain little basis or tail risk typically receive the highest leverage from brokers. The characteristics of such portfolios differ by asset class.

Foreign Exchange   Macro funds taking positions in foreign exchange markets will get the greatest leverage if their collateral portfolio meets the following criteria:

1. Market neutral long and short spot and forward positions within G-3, G-7, and G-10 currencies.[13]
2. Offsetting long and short forward positions well-matched in tenor and amount.
3. Offsetting long and short foreign exchange option positions well-matched in delta, gamma, rho, vega and theta terms.
4. No more than 20 percent of delta of the portfolio in any single currency.

Fixed Income   Fixed income relative value funds taking positions in the interest rate markets will get the greatest leverage if their collateral portfolio meets the following criteria:

1. Duration neutral swap, government bond, and rates futures positions across and within G-3, G-7, and G-10 rates curves.[14]
2. Limited inflation linked or emerging market rates exposures as these tend to attract higher margin because of the lower liquidity in these instruments compared to G-10 markets.
3. Limited offsetting exposure across curves of differently rated governments, as such positions tend to attract higher margin from basis risk under flight-to-quality stress scenarios.
4. Offsetting long and short swaption, cap and floor positions well-matched in interest rate delta and sensitivity to the level of interest rate volatility.
5. No more than 20 percent of duration weighted exposure in any sovereign curve.

Credit relative value funds taking positions in the credit markets will get the greatest leverage if their collateral portfolio meets the following criteria:

1. Interest rate duration and credit spread duration-neutral CDS, corporate bond, and CDS index positions across and within investment-grade, high yield, non-investment grade credit curves, and specific issuer curves.[15] The more credit spread and interest rate duration neutral within distinct maturity buckets (<1 month, 1–3 months, 3–6 months, 6–12 months, 1–3 years, etc), rather than across the curves overall, the lower the sensitivity to non-parallel curve shifts and the lower the margin.
2. Limited exposures to bond issues with no credit rating, in default, or in emerging markets, as these tend to attract higher margin from the lower liquidity in these instruments compared to rated issues and performing issuers in G-10 markets.
3. Limited offsetting exposure across curves of different credit quality (that is, investment grade vs. high yield, and so on) as such positions tend to attract higher margin from basis risk under flight-to-quality stress scenarios.
4. Offsetting long and short CDO, Itraxx or CDX tranche positions well-matched in credit spread duration, underlying obligations, and sensitivity to volatility of correlation of default probability.
5. No more than 5 percent of credit spread duration weighted exposure to any individual issuer.

Equities Equity-focused funds will get the greatest leverage if their collateral portfolio meets the following criteria:

1. Beta-neutral cash equity, equity index, equity swap and contracts for difference across and within countries, regions and industrial sectors.[16]
2. Limited small cap, emerging market, or restricted equity exposures, as these tend to attract higher margin because of their lower liquidity compared to unrestricted large cap stocks in developed markets.
3. Limited high-volatility stock exposures as these tend to attract higher margin because of the greater potential change in liquidation value.
4. Offsetting long and short equity option positions well-matched in delta, gamma and vega sensitivity at the issuer level.
5. No more than 7 percent of net delta exposure in any individual issuer.

Convertible Bonds Convertible arbitrage funds will get the greatest leverage if their collateral portfolio meets the following criteria:

1. Beta-neutral CB, warrant, preferred stock, common stock, and option exposure across and within countries, regions and industrial sectors.
2. Interest rate duration and credit spread duration neutral positions across and within investment grade, high yield, non-investment grade credit curves, and specific issuer curves.
3. Limited small cap, emerging-market, non-rated, restricted, or highly structured convertible bond exposures, as these tend to attract higher margin because of their lower liquidity.
4. Limited high volatility stock exposures, as these tend to attract higher margin because of the greater potential change in liquidation value.
5. Limit portion of portfolio in high premium convertible bonds because of their sensitivity to equity volatility. Convertible bonds trading near bond value floor have lower equity delta and more stable valuations.
6. Offsetting long and short convertible bond and equity option positions well-matched in delta, gamma and vega sensitivity at the issuer level.
7. No more than 7 percent of net delta exposure in any individual issuer.

Commodities CTAs will be charged no more than the exchange required margin by their brokers if their collateral portfolio consists of exchange traded commodity futures and options that meet the following criteria:

1. Basis risk is minimized by investing in a portfolio of commodity specific, delta-neutral futures across and within commodity sectors, exchange specific commodity curves, and time buckets.

2. Limited exposure to comparatively low volume commodity sectors (freight, weather, carbon, exotic metals, for example) and long-dated futures greater than six months to one year, as these tend to have low trading volume and attract higher margin because of their lower liquidity.
3. Limited short volatility positions such as naked short options on futures positions as these tend to attract higher margin because of the significant potential for large increases in volatility in commodity markets.
4. Limited positions that represent a large share of the open interest or volume in any one contract, as these positions can be difficult to roll and less liquid, consequently attracting higher margin.

Responding to Calls for Increased Margin from Prime Brokers   Prime brokers provide leverage and earn revenues on the financing extended to hedge funds. Since this is a symbiotic relationship, why do brokers sometimes decrease the amount of leverage they are willing to extend, or take it away entirely by increasing margin? The answers lie in the quality of the collateral as measured by the potential stress exposure brokers run, the credit quality of the hedge fund, and the relationship of stress loss exposure to the revenue and profits earned by the broker.

Collateral Quality and Stress Loss Exposure   Brokers measure their risk exposure to a fund based on stress loss exposure. The methods for measuring stress loss exposure incorporate dynamic market variables. A broker's stress scenarios typically incorporate at least 4 sigma daily price and volatility shocks; with widening of bid/ask spreads, and widening of historically stable basis relationships to their worst-case historic levels; increasing of correlation across asset classes approaching 1; a substantial decline in liquidity and then the extension of the one-day impact of these shocks to a minimum of five days because of an assumed inability to liquidate the collateral portfolio quickly after a hedge fund technically defaults.

When stress loss exposure increases above a threshold set by the broker, one way to reduce it back below the threshold is to call for additional margin. Stress loss exposure can increase as a result of changes in the composition of the portfolio that do not result in equal changes in both margin and stress loss, changes in market-driven variables such as volatility and liquidity used in the estimation of stress loss, or changes made by the broker in its stress loss methodology.

Changes in Composition of Collateral Portfolio   Changes in a collateral portfolio's composition often result in an increase in stress loss exposure and calls for additional margin. Changes can occur without any action on the part of the hedge fund and be as simple as an increase in market value of a position such that the position becomes an increasing concentration in the collateral portfolio. More often, however, compositional changes come about from active decisions made by funds. For example, stress loss can increase from a fund simply lifting a hedge on a position, making it more directional and resulting in an increase in stress loss under a 4 sigma market move. Alternatively, the fund may decide to increasingly scale into a high-conviction position, resulting in an increasing concentration in the portfolio and resulting in higher stress loss. When the portfolio composition changes and results in higher stress loss, additional margin is required to keep the broker's exposure to stress loss within limits.

Rising Volatility of the Collateral Portfolio Several components of the stress loss calculations are market-driven. Changes in market conditions can result in increased stress loss and calls for more margin. For example, as stress loss is calculated in part by using 4 sigma price moves, an increase in market-wide volatility or stock specific volatility can increase the 4 sigma price move shock used in the stress loss calculation.

Deteriorating Liquidity of the Collateral Portfolio Similar to volatility, liquidity is a market-driven input in the calculation. If trading volume in a stock or open interest in a futures position decreases, the relative liquidity of an existing position in the collateral portfolio can decrease. This can increase the number of days the broker assumes it will take to liquidate the portfolio and, consequently, the number of days the portfolio could be subject to consecutive negative market moves. The result is an increase in the stress loss.

Increasing Concentration of the Collateral Portfolio Another market-driven variable is the change in value of securities in the portfolio, which can result in concentrations developing in what was previously a diversified portfolio. Consider a portfolio consisting of 20 stocks each with equal market value on day one. If on day two, half the positions appreciate 2 percent while the other half depreciate 2 percent, the overall portfolio value is still the same but the appreciating positions are an increasing proportion of the portfolio. If this continues for 37 trading days, each of the first 10 positions will represent more than 10 percent of the value of the portfolio and each is a concentrated position. Concentrated positions contribute disproportionately more to the stress loss calculation.

Decreasing Market Neutrality of the Collateral Portfolio Similar to the changing price effects on a diversified portfolio, market neutrality can be difficult to maintain because of price patterns over time and because individual stock beta is not stable. Additionally, if ETFs on stock indices or index swaps are used to hedge the systematic risk of an individual stock portfolio, the index can change, both in the relative weighting of index constituents and the constituents themselves. To the extent that market neutrality decays because of changes in the portfolio construction, changes in the market value weightings of securities in the portfolio, or beta drift of individual stocks, the stress loss will increase.

Additional Reasons for Increasing Margin Requirements   The amount of leverage a prime broker is willing to provide is not just a function of the quality of collateral. The probability of default of the fund, as indicated by its creditworthiness, is also a major factor.

Deteriorating Creditworthiness   Indications of deteriorations in a hedge fund's credit quality may also trigger increased margin calls. Such indications include:

1. Repeated failure to meet margin calls in a timely fashion may indicate liquidity problems or operational weaknesses at the fund.
2. Monthly returns of lower than −10 percent, quarterly returns of lower than −15 percent or annual returns of lower than −30 percent are indications that a fund's investment strategy is not working as intended. This is why most brokers implement NAV triggers in their ISDAs and margin lock-up agreements which allow them to terminate the agreements in the event of negative performance.
3. A declining trend in the levels of unencumbered cash that reaches less than 20 percent of AUM for funds trading equity and fixed income relative value, less than 40 percent for funds trading distressed debt or other less liquid strategies, and less than 50 percent for funds trading options and futures exclusively may indicate that the fund's ability to remain solvent in the event of severely adverse market moves is decreasing.
4. Significant increases in redemption requests when evaluated against the available unencumbered cash at the fund or the liquid assets of the investment portfolio increase the likelihood of a run on the fund and the likelihood that the fund may need to impose a gate on redemptions.
5. A gradual decline in the fund's AUM over time may cause the prime broker to reassess its creditworthiness.
6. Performance of the fund that is widely inconsistent with the returns of funds following a similar strategy may be indications of style drift and cause a reassessment by the broker of the appropriate margin level.
7. Regulatory sanctions or rumors of impropriety, such as insider trading or fraud, at the fund may also prompt brokers to increase margins.

8. The resignation of key staff at the fund.
9. Failure or extended delays in providing agreed periodic disclosure of fund performance, redemptions, high-level portfolio composition, levels of unencumbered cash, or failure to respond to the broker's queries may increase the uncertainty regarding the fund's creditworthiness and result in higher margins.

Finally, margin increases may be made to improve the profitability of the fund's business for the broker.

Increasing Broker's Costs The profitability of a hedge fund to a prime broker is primarily based on:

1. The interest margin the broker is able to earn between the interest income earned on the financing extended to the fund and the interest paid by the broker to fund the financing extended to the hedge fund.

    The profitability of the relationship to the broker can become negative if the broker is unable to maintain a positive interest margin on the financing extended to the fund. This may occur because the securities pledged by the fund are not easily rehypothecated because of their poor quality or because the fund has precluded the broker from rehypothecating a sufficient portion of the collateral portfolio to generate adequate low cost funding to match the amount lent to the fund.

2. The income a broker can earn from selling stock short to the fund.

    To short a stock, the fund must pay a fixed rate to the broker for the right to do so. If the fund does not do so or does not include in its collateral pledged to the broker long stock positions that the broker can profitably lend out, the profitability of the relationship to the broker can be low or negative.

3. The operational cost the broker must bear to service the specific needs of the hedge fund. These include costs to maintain legal, risk management, sales, account management, operations and IT staff to service the fund.

The fund can impose uncompensated operational costs on the broker by requiring bespoke services, such as unique margining methodologies, custom reporting, specialized research, protracted negotiation over legal documentation, special consulting services, or by simply being repeatedly late in meeting margin calls.

If the profitability of the overall relationship to the broker is decreasing or negative, the broker will seek to reduce the costs of the relationship by eliminating aspects which are less profitable. This may mean downsizing the scope of activities included in the relationship. Selective increases in margin may be used to prompt the fund to take unprofitable business elsewhere.

Potential Stress Exposure vs. Profitability Lastly, assuming the relationship is adequately profitable, margin may be used to improve the risk profile of the relationship overall. Prime brokers periodically evaluate the profits earned from a relationship with a fund against the stress loss exposure created by that relationship.

If a relationship is only marginally profitable but generates a high stress loss exposure for the broker, margins may be increased selectively to decrease that exposure without further eroding profitability.

Managing Increasing Margins: Funding Liquidity Risk and Potential Strategies

If a broker seeks to increase margins and thus decrease the leverage available to a fund, there are a numerous strategies the fund's CFO or COO can employ to manage the potential funding liquidity risk.

Responses to Margin Increases due to Deteriorating Collateral Quality
Reversing or avoiding margin increases imposed because of deteriorating quality of a fund's collateral is generally the easiest to deal with. True hedge funds following low-risk arbitrage strategies typically have positions in their overall investment portfolio which mitigate the concentration, liquidity, directionality or volatility concerns of a given broker. Those positions are, however, simply held at another broker and need to be moved. The hedge fund needs to divide its investment portfolio into *pari passu* collateral portfolios among its prime brokers so that each broker holds an equally risky collateral portfolio. If the portfolio cannot be efficiently divided in this way, the fund should consider obtaining the majority of its financing from one broker, which will receive the majority of its collateral, while keeping an account open at another broker as a back-up.

Tactically, increasing the quality of the collateral pool to avoid or reduce potential margin increases involves the following:

1. Offsetting trades: Reduce the directionality of the collateral portfolio with a given broker by moving offsetting positions to a second broker.
2. Diversifying positions: Reduce concentration in the collateral portfolio at a given broker by moving additional uncorrelated positions to a second broker.
3. Improving liquidity: The overall liquidity profile of a collateral pool can be improved by moving additional, highly liquid positions, which improve the overall liquidity of the collateral pool, or reducing the size of

less-liquid positions held at any given broker by dividing the position amongst several brokers.

4. Reducing volatility: The overall volatility profile of a collateral pool at a given broker can be improved by moving additional less volatile positions which improve the overall volatility profile of the collateral pool.

5. Moving high margin positions: Not all brokers have the same risk appetite. If offsetting, diversifying or more liquid positions are not available, it may be possible to move the positions that attract higher margin to another broker which has greater risk appetite and will not increase margin as significantly.

Of course, if a hedge fund is not truly following a diversified arbitrage strategy, it may not have positions to mitigate the risks the broker may see in its collateral portfolio. In this case, a commercial discussion needs to be had with the broker about increasing its risk appetite to the fund in light of the profitability of the relationship.[17]

Responses to Margin Increases due to Deteriorating Creditworthiness
Reversing or avoiding margin increases that arise from a broker's assessment of a deterioration in a fund's creditworthiness is more difficult to manage as it is more subjective. Such assessments can be the result of a real deterioration, or of a misperception by the broker. The latter are more easily managed.

If the broker's request for additional margin is based on a misperception born of having incomplete information regarding the fund's true position, this can be corrected if the fund is willing to make available additional information to the broker. The fund's CFO should take the following steps to correct any erroneous credit assessment:

1. Request a meeting with the broker's staff to answer any questions they may have. Be prepared to provide written information regarding the following:
   a. Unencumbered cash levels maintained by the fund
   b. A breakdown of the fund's AUM by asset class
   c. A general description of the fund's 10 largest positions, including aggregate size and type of positions
   d. Details as to the diversification of the overall investment portfolio
   e. Portfolio level sensitivities to primary-market risk factors (beta sensitivity to primary equity indices, duration, credit spread duration, convexity, fx, and so on)
   f. A liquidity profile of assets in the investment portfolio, including percentage of the fund which could be liquidated in one

day, five days, and so on, under current and stressed market conditions.

    g. A stress analysis of the market value of the total investment portfolio and an assessment of the adequacy of unencumbered cash to maintain fund solvency in a crisis

    h. The amount of expected investor redemptions/subscriptions in the next redemption/subscription window.

2. Offer to improve ongoing disclosure of information to improve insight into the fund's creditworthiness and increase the broker's risk appetite.

If a the fund is in the unfortunate situation of experiencing a real deterioration in its creditworthiness, it may consider taking the following steps to help ensure that this does necessarily result in increased margins:

1. Improve quality of collateral: As discussed previously, improving the quality of collateral can result in lower margin, reduce the broker's stress-loss exposure, and offset any need to increase margin.
2. Increase transparency on the fund's unencumbered cash: A broker need not call immediately for more margin to protect itself from a deterioration in the fund's creditworthiness if the fund can show that it has the ability to post additional margin at a later date if its creditworthiness deteriorates further.[18] Providing the broker with frequent updates on the level of unencumbered cash held by the fund will reduce the broker's uncertainty in this regard. If the fund's creditworthiness, as indicated by its level of unencumbered cash, improves then no increase in margin should be required.
3. Maintain excess equity in the broker's account: Maintaining excess equity or cash in its account at the broker shows the broker that the fund has the ability to post additional margin without liquidating positions if needed. If the fund's creditworthiness improves, as indicated by a stable or growing level of excess equity in the account, then no increase in margin will ultimately be required. This approach has the advantage of not requiring additional reporting by the fund to the broker.

The first of these options effectively reduces the broker's exposure to the fund in the event of default by the fund. The second and third options effectively improve the broker's ability to determine the probability of default by reducing uncertainty, and buy the fund time to improve its creditworthiness.

Responses to Margin Increases due to Deteriorating Profitability Reversing or avoiding margin increases due to a deterioration in the profitability of the relationship between fund and broker is easily managed in the short term and should not contribute to a funding crisis at a hedge fund. However, the longer-term implications may be more intractable.

Components of the relationship may be profitable when the rehypothecation markets are stable and interbank lending is high. However, when interbank credit risk increases, as it did during the European sovereign-debt crisis in 2010, the ability to rehypothecate certain forms of security collateral can evaporate.

For example, assume a prime broker is providing five times leverage on a portfolio of European investment grade convertible bonds by charging 20 percent average margin on the collateral portfolio and has agreed previously to charge 3 Month LIBOR +50bps on the 80 percent of market value of the collateral portfolio being financed. This pricing was agreed when the market for rehypothecation was strong in 2006. However, following the credit crisis and the European sovereign debt crisis, the rehypothecation market for European sub-investment grade convertible bonds has shrunk. The broker is not able to generate enough secured funding from the convertible-bond collateral to fund the loan and is having to fund the rest of the loan at the broker's unsecured commercial paper rate, resulting in the broker earning a *negative* interest margin. If the broker decides to eliminate this, and consequently withdraws the financing by increasing the margin to 100 percent on the convertible bonds, this will cause the hedge fund to have to de-lever and liquidate some of its positions in order to pay back the financing to the broker. In this situation, the margin increase can be avoided or mitigated in the short term by making the financing profitable to the broker. To do this, the hedge fund should pay a higher financing rate in order to restore the positive interest margin for the broker. Accepting a higher financing rate may be preferable in the short run if it prevents a forced liquidation of the fund's portfolio.

In the longer term, this situation may erode the fund's performance. Effectively, the broker has reduced the carry and eliminated the fund's ability to earn a liquidity premium on the convertible bond positions by increasing the financing rate. To continue with its strategy and to meet its investors' return expectations, the fund may need to find alternative sources of cheap funding for its activities.

CONCLUSION

In conclusion, it is clear that hedge funds can establish many mechanisms in their constitutional documents, trading agreements, and prime brokerage documents to mitigate and manage funding risk arising from both investor redemptions and increased collateral requirements by prime brokers. These rights and mechanisms can ensure the fund's continued solvency and protect all investors from the consequences of a fire sale of fund positions in a distressed market.

While a variety of options to manage the funding risk from a high level of redemptions can be established in the fund's constitutional documents, there are legal and reputational risks involved in exercising those rights. The biggest potential risk is legal. Faced with the inability to immediately monetize their hedge fund shares, investors may seek legal recourse. The case law is still evolving. A court could decide that the fund acted unjustly and inequitably in exercising its rights to control redemptions and that involuntary liquidation of the fund is, in fact, the most equitable course of action for investors.

With respect to prime-brokerage agreements, the biggest potential risk is that the fund fails to meet a margin call and the broker liquidates the fund's assets in order to recover its financing, leaving little or nothing for investors.

While documentation can establish rights and mitigate funding risk, the foremost way to avoid losses from funding risk is for funds to actively manage their liquidity profile and to structure their investment portfolios in a way that aligns the liquidity of their investments with expected long- or short-term redemption levels and notice periods. The 2008 crisis and the failure of Lehman Brothers should be a cautionary lesson to fund managers to stress-test their offering and constitutional documents to ensure that sufficient provisions are included to manage and weather any run on the fund by investors or the failure of a broker. Funding-liquidity stress tests, as described in earlier chapters, are essential for avoiding such potential losses.

ENDNOTES

1. Ang, Andrew and Nicolas P. B. Bollen, "Locked Up by a Lockup: Valuing Liquidity as a Real Option." NBER Papers in Asset Pricing, April 2010.
2. The lock-up provision says that, during a certain initial period, an investor may not make a withdrawal from the fund. This is known as the "actual lock-up period."
3. The Employee Retirement Income Security Act of 1974 (ERISA) is a U.S. federal law that sets minimum standards for pension plans in private industry. ERISA requires pension plans to regularly provide participants with information about the plan, its features and funding. It sets minimum standards for participation, vesting, benefit accrual and funding; requires accountability of plan fiduciaries; and gives participants the right to sue for benefits and breaches of fiduciary duty. Since the trustees of the plan are accountable and must make these periodic disclosures to the beneficiaries, they require the hedge funds in which they

invest to meet ERISA standards and to disclose the necessary ERISA-defined information to trustees. For a hedge fund to attract U.S. pension plans as investors, they must meet ERISA standards.

4. As an alternative to an investment and side letter arrangement, an investor may simply enter into an arrangement for a separately managed account (SMA) with the fund manager.

5. "2010 Hedge Fund Investor Survey," Credit Suisse AG.

6. Phillip Goldstein, *et al.*, Petitioners v. Securities and Exchange Commission, United States Court of Appeals, District of Columbia Circuit. Argued December 9, 2005. Decided June 23, 2006.

7. The Turnaround case upheld the power of the directors to suspend the redemption payments because the resolution to suspend payment was made prior to the date on which the Constitutional Documents required the redemption proceeds be paid. See "In the Matter of Strategic Turnaround Master Partnership," 12 December 2008, Cayman Islands Court of Appeal.

8. In the Turnaround case, the court reinforced the position that it would not "assume that the powers of the directors had been exercised otherwise than bona fide without clear evidence to that effect."

9. Investors will be entitled to return of the retention should the value of the Lehman assets increase.

10. As prime brokers may have the right to terminate an ISDA but may delay doing so, causing significant uncertainty regarding cash requirements at a hedge fund, funds feel that brokers should not be able to subject them to an infinite period of limbo. As this can create a liquidity squeeze, exacerbate funding risk, complicate the management of the fund and potentially lead to a self-fulfilling downward spiral, hedge funds often require a "Fish or Cut Bait" clause be included whereby the right to terminate expires within, say, 30 days if not exercised.

11. Sovereign bonds of G-12 countries are typically not included in the concentration exclusion because of their high liquidity and relatively low risk.

12. Brokers' stress scenarios typically incorporate at least 4 sigma daily price and volatility shocks; with widening of bid/ask spreads, and historically stable basis relationships to their worst-case historic levels; increasing of correlation across asset classes approaching 1; and inability to liquidate the collateral portfolio for a minimum of five days.

13. Margin will increase from G-3 to G-10 and then increase further for currencies outside the G-10. Margin is typically based on the historical volatility of each currency. For controlled-currency regimes, margin is based on the expected change in currency level in the event of a regime change. Given the depth of the G-10 FX markets, size of position is most often immaterial to the risk but this is not so outside the G-10 and with controlled currencies.

14. As most rates' margining methods are stress based, for the greatest margin reduction, duration neutrality should extend to narrow time buckets along each respective curve so as to minimize risk from non-parallel curve movements such as curve steepening or flattening, twisting, etc. Most brokers' margin

methodologies incorporate non-parallel stress scenarios which will increase margin requirements for portfolios that are not duration neutral within and across time buckets.

15. Prime brokers use both rules-based algorithms and stress-based methodologies to margin credit portfolios. In both methodologies, credit-spread duration-neutrality must extend to specific time buckets along issuer specific curves to get the minimum margin.

16. Brokers typically use rules-based algorithms for margining equity portfolios. These algorithms assign base margin by capitalization and country of risk of the issuer. They then adjust margin up for the highly volatile stocks. In addition, depending on the size of the position and its relative value in the context of the portfolio as a whole, margin will be increased further for concentration and liquidity risk. Margin will then be reduced depending on the matching long and short positions in the portfolio and the overall market neutrality of the portfolio.

17. Of course, if the relationship is not sufficiently profitable to warrant a higher risk appetite by the prime broker, a discussion about paying higher financing rates or the fund taking its business elsewhere is logical.

18. The prime broker does not want to precipitate a funding crisis and force the hedge fund to liquidate any more than the hedge fund does, but the prime broker does not have the same level of information as the fund.

CHAPTER 6

Managing Counterparty Risk

The global financial markets operate through a series of interconnected contracts among counterparties in the market, ranging from global commercial and investment banks, to corporate end-users, asset managers, insurance companies and individual investors. The smooth functioning of the global financial markets relies on each of these counterparties fulfilling its contractual obligations. Counterparty risk is the risk that a party to a transaction or contract will fail to fulfill its contractual obligations.

In the context of hedge funds, the most significant counterparty risk arises under contracts between the hedge fund and its most common trading counterparties, specifically investment banks and prime brokerages. The simplest form of counterparty risk facing the typical hedge fund is non-payment or non-performance by a prime broker or investment bank under a swap agreement or other OTC derivatives contract. If the contract is in the money and the counterparty fails to pay at maturity, the hedge fund will incur a loss. If the counterparty defaults before maturity, the hedge fund may have to replace the swap with a more costly one at a new counterparty that may be more costly. In addition, under a typical swap, a hedge fund is required to post collateral at the inception of the swap (this is called initial margin) and then periodically increase or decrease that collateral throughout the life of the swap as the swap value rises and falls (this is called variation margin). If an investment bank or a prime broker fails during the life of the swap, the hedge fund also faces the risk of non-return of collateral exchanged under the swap agreement.

While an individual swap is a self-contained collateralized transaction, a prime brokerage agreement is a collateralized trading facility. Trading under such an agreement also requires collateral to be posted and exposes the fund to the non-return of collateral pledged to the counterparty. Lastly, hedge funds rely on prime brokers for custodial services. The failure of a broker to fulfill its contractual obligations regarding the custody and safekeeping of securities is a major counterparty risk for hedge funds.

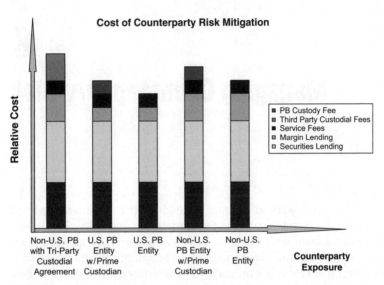

FIGURE 6.1 The costs of mitigating prime brokerage counterparty exposures

Fortunately, there are many strategies and institutional alternatives for hedge funds to manage and mitigate their counterparty exposures. These are summarized in Figure 6.1 and, as it illustrates, some strategies may incur no additional costs; some incur direct and indirect financial costs; while others incur both financial and operational costs. The financial costs are primarily driven by the fact that the solutions take collateral out of the prime broker's control. The broker is unable to rehypothecate the collateral and is thus subject to a higher funding cost. Whether this cost is passed on to the hedge fund depends in large part on the fund's sophistication and negotiating power. Operational costs from the various alternatives result primarily from the hedge fund having to manage its excess collateral more actively, moving it to and from one institution or account to another as margin requirements dictate, rather than keeping it at the prime broker and allowing it to debit and credit the excess collateral account as margin requirements change.

The alternatives also vary in their effectiveness at mitigating counterparty risk. To some extent, costs increase as counterparty risk diminishes but this is not true in every case or for every hedge fund. Tri-party custodial arrangements are the most effective but also the most costly, financially and operationally. U.S. regulatory rules provide greater certainty that a hedge fund's assets will be segregated in the event of a broker defaulting and typically incur lower margin lending fees, but they also constrain the amount of leverage a fund can ultimately obtain.

Using a non-U.S. prime broker's legally separate and bankruptcy remote custody vehicle can segregate assets if the broker defaults, but is potentially less effective at mitigating counterparty risk due to the hedge fund's dependency on access to the broker's systems to move the collateral out of the vehicle. Using a non-U.S. vehicle typically incurs an additional fee and higher margin-lending costs.

As we will see, the optimal choice will depend on the hedge fund's specific priorities, risk tolerance, demand for leverage, and strategy.

HEDGE FUND EXPOSURES TO PRIME BROKERS

Hedge funds, through their business model and operations, take counterparty exposure to their prime brokers, which can result in losses in the event that the broker fails. As hedge funds maintain cash and financed-security positions in their brokerage accounts and maintain additional fully paid-for securities in custody with their broker, a failure of the broker can result in loss of access to those assets. Historically and today, approximately 80 percent of derivative trading and collateralization by hedge funds and institutional managers occurs with less than 20 percent of the brokerage community. The risks of this type of concentrated counterparty exposure were clearly demonstrated in the failures of Bear Stearns and Lehman Brothers, which caused havoc in collateral-management departments within hedge funds as they scrambled to gather data on positions, collateral balances and contract agreements to assess their potential losses (see Chapter 2).

The defining features of the brokerage relationship (and the most important brokerage services) are: (1) clearing and settlement; (2) financing; and (3) custody. Clearing and settlement services enable transactions to be executed with multiple executing brokers, with centralized clearing and settlement through a single prime broker. Prime brokers typically provide financing through margin loans, securities loans (for example, for short sales), repurchase agreements and OTC derivatives (via intermediation and embedded leverage). For convenience, and to support access to financing, hedge funds often place assets in the custody of a broker.

Utilizing brokerage services exposes the fund to the risk that the broker may become insolvent—generally, in the amount of its assets held, and available for rehypothecation, by the broker (actual exposure can exceed this amount), which grows commensurate with use of brokerage services.

For example, to provide financing, the broker typically requires a security interest in all of the fund's assets that the broker holds; and in the case of some OTC derivatives and repurchase agreements, it will require the outright transfer of collateral. The degree to which a fund's assets can be caught in insolvency is commensurate with the amount of those funds held by the broker.

Prime brokers also typically demand the right to rehypothecate all assets, although some jurisdictions (including the U.S.) impose limits. Rehypothecation exacerbates the risk of insolvency by increasing the likelihood that the broker will have insufficient assets to satisfy customers' claims. Hedge funds also face the risk of trades not being properly executed or credited immediately preceding and during an insolvency due to the chaos created by a sudden insolvency.

The risks posed by a particular broker's insolvency will vary based on: (1) the terms of the brokerage documentation; (2) the broker's legal structure, including the applicable regulatory and insolvency regimes, and the involvement of unregulated affiliates; (3) where, how and in whose name assets are registered and held; (4) the extent to which rehypothecation is permissible and (5) the nature of the business conducted between the broker and the fund.

In August 2008, the Counterparty Risk Management Policy Group III (CRMPG III) noted, in a report entitled *Containing Systemic Risk: The Road to Reform*, the manner in which funding-constrained brokers and investment banks can adversely affect counterparties when seeking to maximize their cash and near-cash securities. These effects include:

- Requesting that a hedge fund counterparty close out derivative transactions, especially those that are in-the-money to the fund and thus require the return of high-quality collateral to the broker.
- Withdrawing funding lines to the hedge fund to maximize the broker's cash.
- Where the booking of trades consumes funding and balance sheet for the broker, requesting assignments or novations of trades away from the broker and not accepting assignment or novations of trades to the broker.

Collateral management practices have always had to balance risk mitigation against portfolio liquidity and cost, and the sell-side community has historically led the way on the development of collateral management expertise, capabilities, and systems to actively manage exposure and collateral. However, as a direct result of the collapse of Bear Stearns and Lehman Brothers, historical collateral management concepts, such as the rehypothecation of collateral to increase liquidity and reduce funding costs, are being re-evaluated by hedge funds owing to the difficulties they experienced in recalling their collateral and securities during the crisis. To protect access to their collateral in the event of a failure by a broker or investment bank, funds are experimenting with tri-party arrangements whereby collateral and securities are held by a third-party custodian rather than the broker.

COUNTERPARTY RISK MITIGATION STRATEGIES

Obviously, clearly documenting contracts, selecting high-quality counterparties and diversifying brokers reduces the likelihood and magnitude of a failure by a broker.

Timely, Detailed and Enforceable Documentation

Although written documents per se may not be necessary to establish a contract, they are the best evidence of the terms of a contract and the best means of ensuring that parties agree on the specific terms of a transaction. Failure to document a transaction appropriately or expeditiously, therefore, creates unnecessary counterparty risk.

Delays in documentation are surprisingly common. Lapses between the time a transaction is entered into and the execution of documents evidencing the transaction can give rise to the risk that one of the parties could walk away from the trade or dispute its terms. In much the same way, inaccurate or incomplete documents could lead to litigation when parties misunderstand their obligations and, as a result, fail to perform as expected. Equally significant, hedge funds can confront unexpected market and credit risk as a result of misunderstandings about how documents work, particularly in disrupted markets. Close-outs of transactions in which funds experience unanticipated market and credit losses during contractual grace and notice periods provide a good example of this risk. In addition, in litigation, documents are frequently put under a microscope and any flaw is magnified and used as an excuse for non-performance.

Counterparty risk can be controlled with adequate staffing and strong practices but hedge funds often outsource the negotiation and documentation of key contracts to third-party law firms, with limited involvement from the fund's CFO or COO. More active participation by dedicated fund staff has several benefits. First, it can effectively reduce the time between the date of the trade and its codification in writing. Second, it permits the hedge fund, as the most vested party in the contract, to address, upfront, issues that may seem distant or irrelevant at the time of negotiation, but could become material in the event of a dispute. Third, the process provides a forum for the fund and the counterparty to agree upon numerous issues in a non-litigious setting. Finally, it permits the discussion and codification of the legal nature of the relationship between the parties relationship before problems arise.

Negotiating and maintaining signed agreements governing the terms of the transactions or relationship (for example, derivative contracts, account opening documents, brokerage agreements, stock lending agreements, ISDA, collateral-support agreements and give-up agreements) is essential. Lawyers should review the terms of the agreements to make sure the hedge fund's interests are protected. Critical issues to be considered include:

1. Rights of set-off: The parties to, and the terms of, each document greatly affect the scope of a fund's exposure to a broker's insolvency. The fund should evaluate whether the agreement adequately allows it to set off losses against amounts owed as a result of different transactions. How will set-off amounts be valued and handled? Will there be universal set-off rights across all relationships and transactions between the parties? Will the rights be unilateral or asymmetrical? In the event that the fund and its counterparties have entered into a Master Netting Agreement, then the actual exposure on the default of a counterparty is not the loss on each individual securities contract but the net value of all contracts covered by the netting agreement. Without a netting agreement, the fund would receive recovery on each contract with a positive value while still owing the full market value of contracts with negative market values. With a netting agreement in place, contracts with a negative market value will be subtracted from the value of contracts with a positive market value, thus reducing the overall exposure. The specific forms of agreed set-off will depend greatly on the nature of the fund's business with the broker. It is also extremely important to note that enforceability of set-off rights varies by jurisdiction.

2. Rights of cross default: What constitutes a default? Is non-return of collateral an agreed event of default? How will default be determined objectively? Will one or both parties seek to have a portion of the relationship "ringfenced" so that a default by one entity for one transaction does not result in termination and unwinding of all contracts between the entities?

3. Termination provisions: Under what conditions can the contract be terminated? How much notice must be given if one party seeks to terminate the relationship and how soon must collateral be returned? Including mutual "adequate assurances" clauses and termination events based on shareholder equity, book value or rating downgrades in the ISDA schedule can provide early warning signs and termination rights (under the Master Agreement) before an insolvency.

4. Segregation of assets: Requiring assets and collateral to be segregated (with a third party custodian or, at least, on the broker's books) and/or registered in the hedge fund's name (which is rare) rather than in "street" name (which is common) can provide additional protection.

These are key issues which have a direct bearing on a fund's ability to reduce its exposure to a counterparty with deteriorating creditworthiness and should be addressed in agreements before any risks actually materialize. However, while this may serve to reduce uncertainty, it may lead to protracted and difficult negotiations with brokers who may, in return, demand cross default provisions with no cure periods or prior notice and significantly increased initial margin requirements, while imposing zero thresholds and low minimum transfer amounts. Negotiating such terms is not always in the fund's best interests as they can also increase exposure in some instances depending on the overall mark-to-market value of the portfolio.

Individual hedge funds will, of course, make different determinations regarding the provisions to be contained in their Master ISDA and prime-brokerage agreements depending on the nature of their business and risk appetite. Understanding the options and implications of various negotiated provisions will enable better management of counterparty risk.

Counterparty Selection

The first step in addressing counterparty risk is to have controls concerning the selection of counterparties. When selecting counterparties, hedge funds should consider:

1. The creditworthiness, reputation, experience and identity of the specific entity.
2. The counterparty's ability to provide an appropriate level of service in light of the fund's business needs (including complexity of products and frequency of trading), such as:
   a. Efficient and timely processing, reporting, clearing and settlement of transactions;
   b. Financial capabilities necessary to support the fund's business;
   c. Competent staff to service the fund's needs, including the support and reporting of information to prepare books and records; and
   d. Terms and conditions for movements of margin and cash required by transactions.
3. The regulatory environment in which the counterparty operates.

4. The stability of terms on which the counterparty is willing to enter a transaction or to provide service to the fund (such as term funding lock-ups for brokers).

Careful evaluation and selection of high quality counterparties is one leg of an effective counterparty risk management strategy. One important take-away from the fall of Bear Stearns, as in any major event which demonstrates counterparty risk, is the need to continually reassess a counterparty's creditworthiness while recognizing that hedge funds will never have timely access to all the information necessary to ensure the ongoing creditworthiness of selected counterparties. Consequently, diversification of counterparty exposures is an essential second leg of an effective risk management strategy.

Diversify Counterparty Risks

In the cases of Bear Stearns and Lehman Brothers, the market was deprived of key information as the firms spiraled downward. This information asymmetry, where clients will likely always have less-complete and less-timely information about a counterparty's creditworthiness than the counterparty itself, will persist. One primary means of mitigating this risk is to diversify counterparties. This lesson has now been taken to heart by investors and fund managers in the light of recent failures. It is very rare today to see even a small new hedge fund go to launch without at least two prime brokerage relationships in place.

In addition, many hedge funds are also exploring other means of diversifying their risk. Many with sufficient scale are building proprietary clearing and settlement systems or outsourcing those services to niche (non-prime broker) providers, while others continue to explore alternative sources of funding. Repurchase agreements executed directly with "cash providers" (for example, large pension plans) in the market are a good example of an alternative funding source, which benefits hedge funds through counterparty diversification, increased liquidity, lower financing rates, lower margins, the potential to escrow margin as well as providing potential access to government liquidity programs.

Limiting Rehypothecation

In addition to the risk of property being tied up in protracted bankruptcy proceedings, the Lehman Brothers case also demonstrates the risk of (1) the lack of clarity regarding the priority given to counterparty claims in transactions such as derivative transactions with an insolvent entity, and (2) using an insolvent entity as prime broker—in essence, a form of counterparty risk as a broker is on the other side of lending transactions with its customers.

One form of broker risk relates to the rehypothecation of a fund's assets, which involves the pledging of the asset without delivery of title. Under a traditional brokerage arrangement, when the client enters into an agreement with the broker, the latter generally takes security over all of the client's assets to secure the client's obligations under the agreement. The broker may then rehypothecate the securities in order to obtain a low-cost secured loan for itself, which it typically uses to fund the loan extended to the hedge fund as leverage. The difference between the rate the broker charges the hedge fund on its loan and the rate the broker must pay to secure funding via the rehypothecation markets is the broker's interest margin. In instances in which the broker defaults on its loan and the rehypothecated assets are sold to satisfy the loan, the owner of the securities is without recourse other than to proceed against the broker.

In the U.S., the extent to which a broker can rehypothecate a client's assets is limited by the Securities Exchange Act of 1934 and subsequent amendments. A broker can rehypothecate assets to the value of 140 percent of a client's liability to the broker. Further, brokers cannot use those assets to raise more money than they lend to their customers. This is different from the U.K., where there are no such statutory limits. Because rehypothecation is so profitable for brokers, some agreements allow for a U.S. client's assets to be transferred to the broker's U.K. subsidiary to circumvent these limits. Under U.K. law, when the broker exercises its right to rehypothecate an asset, the title to that asset transfers to the broker. For these reasons, U.S. agreements are often structured to permit such transfers. Although U.S.-regulated brokers are more limited than their European counterparts in the amount of assets they may rehypothecate, hedge funds can still face problems in the event that their brokers file for bankruptcy.[1]

To reduce the risks involved, many hedge funds now seek to prohibit or at least limit the rehypothecation of their collateral by amending their CSA or Prime Broker Agreement. Since the Lehman collapse, the practice of seeking to impose limits in this way has become much more common, even in the U.K. where there are still no statutory limits. The 140 percent level is increasingly accepted as a commercially balanced amount to request even non-U.S. prime brokers to limit their rehypothecation. In addition, hedge funds may require varying limits on the value of securities that may be rehypothecated across various asset classes. At the extreme, hedge funds may refuse to consent to rehypothecation altogether. Some funds try to restrict rehypothecation only to brokers that maintain a specified credit rating (although this would have had no effect in the Lehman Brothers case since Lehman maintained its credit rating right up until the collapse). All these options may result in higher funding charges from their brokers.

An additional problem on both sides of the Atlantic in the wake of Lehman's bankruptcy was the lack of transparency regarding which assets had been rehypothecated. Many clients, including hedge funds, now request that their prime brokers increase their reporting on these activities. Some hedge funds are even insisting on daily reports on where their assets are being held.

While limiting rehypothecation decreases counterparty risk, it inevitably results in higher funding costs for the broker, which may translate into higher service fees for the hedge funds. Hedge funds dispute the claim that limits on a broker's ability to rehypothecate decreases the broker's interest margin and resist paying additional costs and higher financing rates on securities positions they buy on margin.

Evaluate Differences in National Legal and Regulatory Regimes

With non-U.S. prime brokers, there can be even more widespread disruptions for clients. In the specific case of Lehman Brothers International (Europe) (LBIE), the London-based Lehman Brothers subsidiary filed administration proceedings (British insolvency proceedings) on the same day that Lehman Brothers Holdings, Inc. filed for bankruptcy in the United States. Hedge fund clients of LBIE have been dragged into protracted administration proceedings in London to recover assets held with LBIE as prime broker. The British system treats rehypothecated assets as assets of the insolvency estate, which gives clients the status of unsecured creditors. Furthermore, even client assets held at LBIE which were not rehypothecated have been tied up in the administration process.

Pricewaterhouse Coopers UK, which is acting as the Administrator for LBIE, has cited confusion with records and complexity of transactions as reasons it could take years for LBIE clients even to receive their assets. For rehypothecated assets, the issues are even more unclear; the administration process could take many years and recoveries could be small fractions of the original value. Many hedge funds have sharply criticized the LBIE administration process for tying up fund assets.

A prime broker's legal structure greatly affects the risk its insolvency poses to its customers. U.S. brokers have a statutory obligation to register as broker-dealers and to join, and comply with the rules of, self-regulatory organizations. Segregation of customer assets, rehypothecation, securities possession/control and minimum net equity are all regulated under the 1934 Securities Exchange Act. Customers of U.S. prime brokers holding assets in the U.S. may be protected by the Securities Investor Protection Act of 1979, as amended (SIPA), which established the Securities Investor Protection Corporation (SIPC).

Generally, in an SIPC proceeding, customers of the insolvent party take priority over general unsecured creditors to recover from the pool of customer property on a pro rata basis. A hedge fund customer would be an unsecured creditor to the extent of any shortfall. Subject to certain restrictions, SIPC covers shortfalls up to US$500,000 per customer. Some brokers maintained additional insurance with the Customer Asset Protection Company (CAPCO) to cover excess shortfalls prior to 2009, but because of the expiration of all outstanding CAPCO surety bonds in February 2009, only former customers of Lehman Brothers Inc. and Lehman Brothers International (Europe) are currently eligible for Excess SIPC protection from CAPCO.

The regulatory protections afforded to U.S. prime brokers do not generally apply to their non-U.S. affiliates, to non-U.S. brokers or to assets held outside the United States. U.S. brokers commonly rely on such unregulated affiliates for margin lending or securities lending and/or to act as custodians in non-U.S. jurisdictions.

In such instances, the relevant jurisdiction's laws may provide less protection and impose fewer restrictions (many jurisdictions permit rehypothecation in full, for example) than would be the case in the United States.

Ideally, a hedge fund whose major concern is counterparty risk should choose prime brokers that hold assets in the U.S., do not use unregulated affiliates and that have legal structures that subject them to the U.S. regulatory regime. Of course, counterparty risk is not the only consideration in choosing a prime broker. If there are business reasons for involving unregulated brokerage affiliates, a cost-benefit analysis should be performed to ensure proper compensation for the additional risk.

As the LBIE example amply demonstrates, as an aspect of counterparty risk, firms need to give careful consideration to the regulatory framework that will be applied in the event of a dispute with, or the insolvency of, the counterparty. Here, the following issues come into play:

- Choice of law: What legal regime will take precedence and govern in the event of a dispute with a counterparty?
- Choice of forum: Where will such a dispute be adjudicated (in court or through arbitration?) and in what jurisdiction?
- Choice of regulation: What regulations take precedence and govern the counterparty, particularly its related foreign entities?

Arbitration has not proven to be an avenue for recourse for most funds facing losses from Bear Stearns or LBIE. Most firms have turned to the courts to establish their rights and to recover their assets.

Sweeping of Excess Equity

A straightforward way to mitigate a hedge fund's exposure to a potential default by a prime broker is to maintain that exposure at the minimum level necessary to conduct successful investing. This entails maintaining excess value (equity) in the broker's account sufficient to cover expected day-to-day changes in required margin but "sweeping up" any excess equity resulting from accumulated profits, dividends and interest payments on securities owned, or from the liquidation of positions, and transferring it to a third-party custodian.

The primary difficulty in determining the optimum excess value to maintain is the unpredictability of margin requirements. A hedge fund does not want the operational burden of having to transfer cash into the account daily for small changes in margin as the late payment of margin is an event of default under most brokerage agreements and can give the broker legal grounds for terminating all agreements with the fund. This can result in a withdrawal of all funding and be highly disruptive to the hedge fund's performance. Consequently, a fund should seek to maintain some excess equity in the account which can be debited to pay margin calls quickly. In addition, the fund and its prime broker can agree a minimum transfer amount such that immaterial changes in margin need not be paid immediately. Low initial unadjusted margin requirements and high thresholds for daily exposure adjusted variation margin in the CSA[2] can reduce exposure by minimizing unnecessary posting. This reduces the number of margin calls that must be paid immediately and enables the fund to periodically top up its excess with one significant transfer rather than numerous small daily transfers.

When excess equity is withdrawn from the brokerage account, it is typically deposited in an account at a third party or custodian bank thereby reducing the fund's exposure to a potential prime broker default. Depending on the deposit taking institution, this account may or may not be interest bearing.

Bankruptcy Remote Custody Arrangements

As noted previously, investors were unable to recoup collateral assets that were caught up in the LBIE bankruptcy proceedings.[3] Consequently, hedge funds began to actively demand that their remaining prime brokers provide options to shift any assets not being directly utilized to support margin indebtedness or cover short selling into a segregated and bankruptcy remote account.

Prime brokers have responded with offerings which follow one of two basic models. In one approach, a special purpose custody vehicle or trust is set up as a distinct legal entity and excess assets can be moved out of prime brokerage accounts and into these custody vehicles. This model allows for funds to continue to monitor and manage both their broker and custody accounts through their existing service relationship and allows for an effective and easy exchange of data and reporting across the two accounts. The collateral remains with the broker and only excess assets are moved to the custody vehicle. The collateral and any excess assets remain within the same broker-dealer infrastructure, however, eliciting questions as to whether the collateral and assets are sufficiently remote to ensure rapid access by the hedge fund in the event of the broker's bankruptcy.

A second model moves excess assets and collateral completely out of the broker-dealer entity and its infrastructure and into a third-party custodian. This arrangement is perceived as offering greater bankruptcy protections, but increases operational complexity through having to move assets across unrelated entities. But as the model has evolved and brokers and custodians have improved the interface between their respective systems, the operational complexity has reduced.

The use of a third party custodian usually allows collateral to be traced more readily, thereby affording certain statutory protections in a number of jurisdictions in the event of a default. However, where a third party custodian is used and the collateral is then rehypothecated, it is likely that such statutory protections will not apply and the outcome would be similar to that where the broker holds the collateral. Another drawback to this model is that while the broker keeps collateral with a third party custodian, it may still have rehypothecation rights. Because the hedge fund will not have been involved in negotiating the contract with the custodian, it will not be able to preclude rehypothecation and has no contractual right to require the custodian to return collateral in the event of insolvency of the prime broker, despite having a clear lien and segregated account.

Tri-Party Agreements As a result of this remaining counterparty risk, many fund managers seek to negotiate agreements with the broker and a third-party custodian. This three-way contract ensures the hedge fund's right to require the return of collateral as long as specific conditions are met, and to restrict the rehypothecation of any securities in the custody account. This model places both the excess assets and initial margin posted on derivatives transactions in a custody account at an independent custodian. If the hedge fund, as the borrower, fails, the prime broker gets the collateral in the account. If the prime broker fails, its relationship with the hedge fund remains and, together, they can execute an orderly unwinding of the business. Once settlement amounts are agreed, any shortfall owed to the broker is deducted from the collateral held at the custodian and the hedge fund receives the remaining collateral. Both prime broker and hedge fund have a measure of protection from the collapse of the other.

Because securities cannot typically be rehypothecated, prime brokers and custodians have required higher fees for agreeing to tri-party arrangements. The higher costs involved in such arrangement have made them less popular to date with small and mid-size funds that do not have the ability to absorb the costs nor the profit potential to bring prime brokers to the negotiating table. Only the largest hedge funds have been successful in negotiating tri-party arrangements. Small and medium-sized funds are increasingly looking to the other alternatives because of the additional protections they provide without substantial costs.

CONCLUSION

Hedge fund managers can greatly reduce their credit exposure to counterparties by negotiating contracts that anticipate the potential default of a prime broker. In negotiating such contracts, appreciation of the implications of the governing legal and regulatory regime is essential. In addition, limiting the extent to which a broker may rehypothecate a hedge fund's collateral, negotiating netting, set-off and collateral provisions in ISDAs and Credit Support Annexes, setting minimum transfer amounts, and negotiating bankruptcy remote custodial arrangements which ensure that excess assets and/or collateral posted is held in accounts maintained by a third party can significantly reduce counterparty exposure to the prime broker. As negotiated contracts with high quality counterparties cannot limit counterparty risk, diversification of counterparties can further reduce the likelihood of a loss. While these actions can significantly reduce a hedge fund's counterparty risk, they can be directly and indirectly costly. Operational and financial costs incurred by the fund should be balanced against the potential losses avoided through these actions.

ENDNOTES

1. In the case of LBIE, the safe and timely return of client assets was hindered because U.S. prime brokerage clients lost their proprietary interests in the assets, and consequently lost money and asset protections under the U.K. Financial Services Authority's Client Assets Sourcebook (CASS).
2. A CSA requires that when either party to a security contract owes the other during the life of the contract, collateral be posted. The two counterparties

maintain an account with collateral consisting of cash and/or securities which mitigate the amount of loss incurred should either counterparty default on the net value of all the contracts under the netting agreement. When the difference between the net value of the contracts and the amount of collateral posted exceeds the margin requirements, additional collateral must be posted to make up the difference. This limits the exposure to the size of the market moves before additional posting is demanded, plus the size of the margin requirement.

3. Adding insult to injury was the fact that hedge funds that had put on short positions by putting up cash to borrow stock from Lehman found themselves still required to return the stock to the bankrupt prime broker's estate, even though their own collateral at the broker had not been returned.

CHAPTER 7

Risk Management for Hedge Fund Investors

Many investors are eager to make a hedge fund investment and assets under management at hedge funds continue to grow. The opportunity to improve returns and reduce risk is enticing. However, there are many issues relating to risk and risk management that an investor needs to be aware of before committing to such an investment. Mastery of these issues or engaging a skilled advisor or fund of funds manager greatly increases the odds of long-term success.

A partial allocation to hedge funds as an asset class can improve the risk-return profile of most investment portfolios. Specifically, specially constructed hedge fund exposures can complement a traditional investment portfolio. For example, an investor wanting to reduce his directional exposure to changes in interest rates without reducing income may lower the duration of his fixed income allocation but add a specific lower-volatility hedge fund or a fund of hedge funds heavily or exclusively weighted towards non-directional arbitrage strategies as a partial replacement for a portion of his fixed income exposure. Similarly, a more sophisticated investor seeking greater short-term equity exposure may choose to keep overall allocations of equity and fixed income risk factors fairly stable, but replace some his directional equity exposure with long/short equity hedge fund exposure. This would serve as a partial equity beta hedge to protect on the downside. An investor seeking primarily to reduce risk without reducing returns could allocate part of his exposure to a diversified fund of funds focusing significantly on risk factors which are not currently present in most traditional portfolios, such as commodities, currencies, credit strategies, managed futures, short sellers, or natural catastrophe or weather exposures.

While the above examples have strong intuitive appeal, there are several complexities and potential pitfalls to be aware of. For example, as discussed in Chapter 4, fitting fixed income arbitrage strategies into a hedge fund allocation to reduce duration and volatility while maintaining return is a seemingly failsafe move, until it is remembered that most of the fixed income arbitrage strategies have fat left tail distributions and during market breakdowns can exhibit strong short option-like features. Fixed income arbitrage managers are often generating their alpha by being leveraged sellers of liquidity and structure trades to pick up a premium for holding illiquid securities. These trades generate modest returns most of the time, but not in a crisis. Other "arbitrage" trades in the portfolio may be basis trades, which can occasionally blow out dramatically against the fund. Recall that when markets go into crisis, credit spreads and traditionally stable basis relationships blow out, and liquidity dries up. Drawdowns for fixed income arbitrage funds will be unavoidable and simultaneous. In such exceptional cases, the portfolio benefits that the hedge fund allocation was intended to deliver will evaporate and test the investor's resolve.

With the risks discussed in this book in mind, investors with a defined risk tolerance can establish an overall risk budget and determine an appropriate allocation to hedge funds as part of their overall asset allocation plan. Through risk budgeting, core satellite portfolios can be constructed that improve the risk-return profile of traditional portfolios.

DETERMINING THE ASSET ALLOCATION TO HEDGE FUNDS

Investing in hedge funds involves non-traditional risk taking due to the complex, sometime illiquid or opaque nature of hedge fund investment strategies. Furthermore hedge funds receive comparatively little regulatory oversight. Investing in hedge funds is suitable only for sophisticated investors who are able to identify, analyze and bear the associated risks, and follow appropriate practices to evaluate, select, monitor, and exit these investments. If a sophisticated investor is comfortable taking such risks and has the skills or can outsource the work required to dynamically manage these investments, then the question becomes how much an investor should invest in hedge funds. An institution or high-net-worth individual may benefit from an intermediary partner (for example, a fund of hedge funds) that possesses the necessary qualifications and skills to filter through the many thousands of hedge funds and understands how the different hedge fund strategies can be optimally combined to generate consistent absolute returns.

Hedge funds emerged as an important alternative asset class during the last decade. Their non-normal risk-return characteristics and attractive absolute returns apparently helped institutional investors such as US university endowments to achieve a significant outperformance over traditional asset allocations for many years leading up to the financial crisis.[1] The substantial outperformance prior to the crisis suggests that, in particular, hedge funds offer investors significant portfolio benefits by enhancing the risk-return trade-off of their portfolios. Hedge fund allocations generated returns that appeared to be rather lowly correlated with returns of conventional asset classes such as stocks and bonds. However, recent studies indicate that diversification benefits of hedge funds have continuously declined due to a slow but persistent upward trend in the co-movement of hedge fund returns with conventional asset classes.[2] This decline is thought to be due to the time-varying correlation of hedge fund returns with that of traditional asset classes. This point is illustrated *in extremis* by the recent financial crisis, where the investment performance of hedge funds deteriorated substantially and coincidentally with equities and bonds. This time-varying and potentially phase-locking behavior weakens the diversification benefits of a static hedge fund allocation and argues in favor of a more dynamic allocation to hedge funds.

Andrew Lo provides empirical evidence of hedge fund asymmetric correlations with conventional asset classes and that correlations increase substantially during periods of financial turmoil.[3] Similarly, Mila Getmansky, Igor Makarov and Lo document different hedge fund return regimes, suggesting that portfolio benefits of hedge funds decrease exactly during those market regimes when they would be most valuable.[4] Therefore, time variation in expected returns, variances, and correlations of hedge funds with other asset classes might affect their diversification benefits in different market environments.

This time variation of expected returns, variances, and correlations significantly complicates the analysis needed to determine the asset-class allocations needed to maximize expected returns and minimize expected volatility of a portfolio of traditional and alternative asset classes. Clearly, mean-variance optimization is insufficient.

While mean-variance optimization is not sufficient,[5] no best-practice methodology has yet emerged that is widely adopted and is clearly superior. Promising rival methods include the regime-switching dynamic correlations model (RSDC model), the full-factor multivariate GARCH model (FFMG model)[6] and, to a lesser extent, Bayesian Asset Allocation Frameworks.[7]

Giamouridisa and Vrontos found that a regime-switching dynamic correlations model reduced portfolio risk and improved sample risk-adjusted realized returns. In particular, they found that tail risk, as measured by conditional value at risk, was lowest under the RSDC model. This suggests that the RSDC covariance model represents a more accurate tool for tail risk measurement. In their analysis, the FFMG model ranks second, with significant differences. When they studied the cost of rebalancing portfolios under each method, they found that the RSDC imposes substantially higher transaction costs than the FFMG. This indicates a trade-off between tail risk reduction and transaction costs. Reducing tail risk under the RSDC model incurred greater transaction costs.

Bessler, Holler and Kurmann also analyzed the portfolio diversification benefits of hedge funds when they are combined with traditional and other alternative asset classes. In their study, they incorporated realistic forward-looking estimates of return and risk with historical observation. Their Bayesian Asset Allocation Framework incorporated investors' prior expectations regarding the ability of hedge funds to provide positive risk adjusted returns and incorporated that input into the mean-variance portfolio construction process. Much like a generalized Black-Litterman approach, the Bayesian approach allows investors to incorporate current views regarding return and risk and adjust portfolio allocation around equilibrium allocations. This allowed the study to reflect the differing expectations of heterogeneous institutional-investor clienteles such as university endowment funds and pension funds in the asset-allocation process. The empirical results showed that the portfolio benefits of hedge fund investments crucially depended on the market environment, because of the substantial time-variation in the risk-return offered by hedge funds. While the analysis over the full sample period suggests a positive shift of the efficient frontier irrespective of investors' level of optimism, the results for different sub-periods indicate that upward shifts of the efficient frontier seem to be more likely in time periods of rising stock markets. Based on this evidence, they concluded that hedge funds are an attractive asset class at relatively low levels of volatility.

Some practitioners also attempt to reallocate within hedge fund strategies as their expectations change and the Bayesian inputs in the asset-allocation process are updated. However, investor lock-up restrictions complicate the rebalancing and reallocation process significantly. Also, with increasing allocations to hedge funds, investors might increase the illiquidity risk of their portfolios overall as a result of these lock-up restrictions without significantly increasing overall expected returns. Lock-up restrictions can be monthly, quarterly and annual (or longer) and may come with lengthy redemption-notice periods. Given these real-world liquidity constraints, individual investors have minimal flexibility when it comes to reallocating across strategies. Funds of funds typically seek preferential liquidity terms and may have somewhat greater ability to dynamically allocate across funds.

INVESTMENT APPROACH

Assuming an allocation to hedge funds is consistent with the investor's objectives and has been quantified, the investing approach needs to be determined. What is the optimal way for investors to start a hedge fund investment program? Should an investor invest in single-strategy funds, multi-strategy funds where allocations are made across the spectrum of strategies through a single firm, or an allocation to a reputable fund of funds? Each approach has its pros and cons and the correct choice depends on the investor's sophistication, institutional investment capabilities and investment goals.

Single Strategy Investments

Some investors forgo the fund of funds or multi-strategy approach by building their own portfolio of single strategy funds. Managers of single funds have actual or perceived expertise in a specific strategy or similar strategies. These investments are typically offered in a commingled vehicle.

Considerable and effective due diligence is required for selecting top managers in the hedge fund space. Accordingly, the investor will need to have significant expertise to evaluate a series of different strategies. Extensive knowledge of this space is also required to implement an asset allocation across strategies in order to achieve the correct risk-return profile for the investor. Finally, expertise is vital to perform the ongoing due diligence necessary for the manager program.

If an appropriate level of in-house proficiency exists, investing in several single-strategy funds can be a viable alternative to the fund of funds or multi-strategy models. This approach has the potential for higher return, albeit at a higher level of risk. Investors may also be able to implement a more customized program. Fees are also typically lower than when using other types of investment vehicles.

As with the other approaches discussed, there are definite drawbacks to single-strategy investing. Due diligence is time-consuming and usually expensive. Why spend 50 percent of your staff's time and resources to oversee a small (typically 5–10 percent) allocation? Access to the top managers in each category can be very difficult due to the "word of mouth" nature of the business as well as high account minimums. It may also be difficult for the average investor to access the network of "star" and up-and-coming managers. Investor liquidity and transparency requirements may also reduce the universe of managers that can be hired. Building the appropriate asset allocation can also be difficult if the required expertise and experience are not present in the internal group.

Multi-strategy Investments

For investors who cannot accept the additional fees or the other issues associated with a fund of funds, multi-strategy vehicles may be an attractive alternative. Their objective is to deliver consistently positive returns regardless of the directional movement in the equity, fixed income or currency markets. Multi-strategy funds consist of different hedge fund investments offered in a single portfolio structure by one firm. Such an approach may be appropriate for clients who have strong convictions about the investment acumen of a particular firm across different strategies. Similar to fund of funds complexes, multi-strategy firms can offer portfolios with more generic risk-return characteristics, as well as funds customized to meet the investor's specific requirements.

One obvious advantage of multi-strategy funds that is similar to the fund of funds model is the diversification benefits of allocating your investment across different hedge fund sectors. However, unlike funds of funds, there is no additional layer of performance-based fees. Managers in a multi-strategy vehicle net performance fees so the investor does not pay for poor performance.

Since they are not subject to restrictions placed upon them by outside managers, multi-strategy funds can offer the investor increased liquidity and transparency when compared to most funds of funds. An additional advantage to using the multi-strategy approach is institutional-quality client service and reporting, which is not always available from smaller, boutique organizations.

Single-strategy funds, which we will discuss below, are limited in the scope of their investment opportunities. When their investment "advantage" disappears, managers may have to reduce exposure by shifting to cash or remaining in underperforming investments. In contrast to single-strategy funds, running multiple strategies in-house allows for the quick movement of capital to whatever investments are working well across any asset class. There are also capacity constraints associated with single-strategy funds that are less of a consideration for multi-strategy products.

The most convincing argument against the multi-strategy approach is the risk of being exposed to the possible operational difficulties of a single firm. Funds of funds tend to moderate this risk through sheer numbers of underlying managers. Studies have shown that the majority of fund failures can be attributed to operational problems.

Another shortcoming associated with multi-strategy funds is the difficulty in attracting and retaining talented investment professionals across different strategies. The best managers have traditionally concentrated on a single or narrow group of strategies. Also, while multi-strategy funds offer a broad degree of portfolio diversification, these benefits may be lower than those available through a fund of funds structure. If investment teams are closely aligned or composed of similarly trained personnel across different individual funds, there can be a decrease of independent ideas and an increase in concentration risk.

Fund of Funds Investments

Many investors who are starting an allocation to hedge funds find that the fund of funds route is the smoothest road to successful implementation of a hedge fund program. This approach is especially advantageous for investors who have had limited exposure to alternative assets in general and who lack the necessary expertise.

In a fund of funds investment, a third party provider constructs a portfolio of various single strategy funds to achieve a particular risk-return profile. The fund of funds manager is responsible for all research, which results in the hiring and termination of managers in the underlying portfolio, as well as program construction and fee negotiation. One significant responsibility of the provider is a thorough due-diligence review of the fund manager's capabilities and ongoing monitoring of the investment.

Most fund of funds providers usually develop one or more core portfolios that they feel offer a well-diversified exposure to the hedge fund marketplace, while meeting the objectives and risk profiles of a large percentage of investors. A well-diversified portfolio of investments can protect the investor from experiencing large losses arising from the underperformance or failure of a single strategy. Many also customize their portfolios based on an investor's unique circumstances and requirements.

There are obvious advantages to the choice of a fund of funds program. The first is the expertise the provider brings to the asset-allocation, selection, termination and due-diligence processes. As an example, most funds of funds require a minimum degree of portfolio transparency before they will hire a manager. The average investor facing the hedge fund directly may not be given access to this information. Given the amount of assets the fund of funds provider can direct, they also have access to a wide selection of funds, some of which are closed to outside investors. Many funds of funds are expert at sourcing talented undiscovered managers who are usually "under the radar" or not available to the broader investment community. Third-party providers can also use scale to negotiate reduced lock-up periods, thereby lessening liquidity risk.

The greatest perceived disadvantage of investing with a fund of funds complex is the additional layer of fees charged to the investor. Typically, providers charge a management fee plus a performance fee. Accordingly, costs can be a significant issue for investors.

All told, funds of funds offer the investor the best combination of knowledge, due diligence, quantitative expertise, diversification, risk management and access to top performing hedge fund managers. However, the number of funds included in one fund of funds portfolio can also cause problems for the investor. If a large group of single-strategy funds is assembled, the possibility of duplicate holdings can increase the concentration risk of the overall portfolio. This is one reason why risk management at the fund of funds level is important.

SELECTING STRATEGIES AND SCREENING FUNDS

Once an investor concludes that an allocation to hedge funds is desirable and chooses an approach, the selection of the specific hedge funds to invest in is the logical next step. If working through an investment advisor, the investor should evaluate the advisor's capabilities in the hedge fund space. Specifically:

- Is there a qualified individual or team that evaluates hedge funds for the financial advisor?
- What specific issues are assessed in the due diligence process? What is the depth and quality of the assessment?
- How often is the fund assessed?
- Has the product been suitably screened following a best practice screening process?
- What relevant experience does the fund of funds manager have?
- What other experience, qualifications and registration does the manager have?

If working through a multi-strategy fund, the investors should assess the above but also focus on the manager's ability to allocate across strategies and the idiosyncratic risk of the multi-strategy fund. Operational due diligence is essential as the entire allocation will be in the hands of one firm.

If not working through a fund of funds or advisor, investors should have the necessary skills and experience themselves to allocate among strategies and compute the optimal allocations by strategy and manager.

Determining Appropriate Sub-allocation to Strategies and Managers

Investing in hedge funds requires a diversified and well-constructed portfolio of strategies to ensure that risks at the individual fund manager level are diversified and the systemic risks are minimized. In addition, dynamic management of hedge fund allocations can theoretically be a source of alpha.

One interesting question in this area is the relative importance of the ability to pick the best managers versus the ability to dynamically overweight and underweight various strategies. The answer could inform fund of funds managers about where they should focus their efforts. Liew and French provide empirical evidence that manager selection is somewhat more important than strategy allocation over time but that both are critical components of outperformance. Manager selection is thought to have greater ability to generate excess returns than dynamic strategy allocation due to the greater dispersion of performance among managers within the same strategies than between the strategies themselves.[8] Consistently picking the winning managers produces higher returns than picking the winning strategies but both are important sources of return. Furthermore, it is undeniable that picking the wrong manager or being overexposed to the wrong strategy at the wrong time can create losses.

Whether seeking alternative asset exposure directly or through funds of hedge funds, the universe of eligible outperforming funds can be narrowed somewhat by first screening for funds which represent a match to an investor's investment objectives and the investment mandate. The investment mandate should specify the client's targeted risk reward profile and include a clear definition of risk from the investor's perspective. Is risk the risk of losing money or is it of not achieving a certain minimum return? Does "risk" mean not having money available (that is, liquidity) when and if needed? What is the investor's ability to tolerate large drawdowns and mark to market losses? Are there securities or investments, such as mortgage-backed securities, private placements, small-cap stocks, or tech stocks that are out of bounds based on the mandate? What is the maximum acceptable expected tail loss (ETL)? The answers to these questions can eliminate a large number of potential managers immediately if, for example, their lock-up periods are too long or the securities they trade are unacceptable to the investor.

Accounting for Dynamic Risk and Return Profiles

As discussed in Chapter 4, different hedge fund strategies are persistently exposed to different risk types but the dynamic macro environment, changing leverage, and positioning by the fund manager will dynamically change the risk profile of the fund through time. For example, a long/short manager with past high volatility typically will continue to employ a similar trading style in the future, and thus exhibit high future volatility. Similarly, a high-velocity statistical arbitrage manager or a CTA with low past volatility tends to have low future volatility, as tight risk controls and trading rules incorporated into the process persist over time. In practice, risk exposures tend to persist over the short term (that is, one–three months for most funds) but amplify or diminish over longer periods. Analyzing risk exposures and modeling their potential impact is a critical component of portfolio construction in hedge fund portfolios.

On the return side, academic research provides mixed evidence about performance persistence in the hedge fund industry. In a controversial study, Malkiel and Saha found that a small majority of top performers in any given year repeat their performance in the subsequent year.[9] Agarwal and Naik find evidence of performance persistence in quarterly returns, and Edwards and Caglayan find evidence of performance persistence at one-year and two-year horizons.[10]

For a fund of funds manager, the different and time-varying risk-return profiles of various hedge fund strategies and hedge funds provide almost endless possibilities for creating value through active portfolio allocation, where strategies and managers interplay to minimize risk and generate consistent absolute returns.

A prerequisite for adding alpha via strategy and manager allocation is developing as thorough an understanding of the different risk-return drivers in each strategy and fund as possible. A hedge fund's returns and risks come through exposure to the different underlying security instruments but also through the strategy the fund employs and the extent of use of leverage. Many hedge fund strategies invest in more than one asset class, thereby diversifying the return generation, but this does not necessarily reduce the total risk exposure. Regression and factor analysis of strategy and hedge fund returns enables insights to be made into the historical sources of risk and return. From these inevitably incomplete risk analyses, projections of future performance and a maximally informed allocation can be made.

Factor Analysis of Returns

Multi-factor models can be a useful starting place for analyzing past returns and estimating future returns.

Factor analysis assumes that hedge fund returns consist of an unexplained source of return called "manager's alpha" and risk premiums earned from exposures to various common hedge fund factors.

Hedge fund return = Manager's alpha
+ Risk premiums from hedge fund factors

Or, more formulaically:

$$\text{Hedge fund return} = \text{Alpha} + \sum (\beta i \times \text{factor } i)$$

where βi is the return on hedge fund factor i.

Some researchers use hedge fund indices as factors; some use market factors, some use macroeconomic factors and others derive strategy-specific or style factors using principal components analysis.[11] All have their pros and cons.

For the purposes of exposition, market factors tend to be the most intuitive. Hedge fund return streams can be decomposed based on groups of market factors such as 1) bond factors, 2) equity factors, 3) volatility factors, and 4) credit factors. Sophisticated institutional investors or their advisor should be able to fine-tune these factors and apply them appropriately based on the investment strategy of the fund under investigation to explain a greater proportion of the return variability. For example, if the hedge fund under consideration is an equity long/short fund, the factors used could be a subset of the equity factors group (that is, small-minus-big cap, high P/E-minus-low P/E/, previous one-year returns, equity volatility, and so on).[12]

Whatever factors are used, they should be consistently applied across the funds being analyzed. Once the identification of common factors across funds is as complete as possible, understanding the correlation of the risk drivers behind each hedge fund allocation is essential. This is necessary not only to construct an efficiently diversified portfolio but, importantly from a risk perspective, to enable stress testing.

Decomposing candidate hedge funds' returns into their factor components allows for explicit recognition of common risk factors in different strategies. Common factors between two hedge funds will be indicative of converging risk profiles and potential factor concentration, whereas discrete sets of factors driving the two funds' returns can be interpreted as the two funds having diversifying risk profiles.

Furthermore, by observing the long-term relationship between hedge fund factors and conventional asset-class indices likes bonds and equities, a fund of funds manager can integrate hedge fund selection into the overall asset-allocation process.[13] Quite often, expectations on the future performance of conventional assets will have an impact on the expected return from hedge fund factors. This will in turn impact the expected return from hedge funds exposed to those factors via their particular strategy. This can provide insight into the long-term return sensitivity of a portfolio of bonds, equities, and hedge funds to common market-risk factors such as a change in interest-rate levels, credit spreads, or stock-market levels.

By construction, hedge fund factors are supposed to be discrete factors but a risk manager must consider the potential for co-movement, correlation and co-integration of factors and their impact on the overall portfolio. As hedge fund returns and correlations are time-varying and tend to increase in crises, it is important to assume that some future extreme market conditions will cause future cross-correlations to be higher than they were in the past. Estimating the hypothetical loss of diversification and the consequent worst-case performance of the proposed allocation in a time of stress can further help to identify unacceptable or sub-optimal portfolios. Similarly, running the various portfolios through historical stress events shows the magnitude of losses due to actual events.

Just as factors can be applied to refine the investor's stress-test estimates, it can also be used to identify diversifying styles during stressful markets. Factor exposures can be identified that can be expected to mitigate losses in extreme market events and provide a tail-risk hedge. For example, Fung and Hsieh (1997) noted the inverse performance characteristics of trend-following funds to global equity markets.[14] Subsequently, this empirical regularity was modeled and verified in Fung and Hsieh (2002).[15] They showed, for example, that the trend-following factor can be used to generate large positive returns during periods of large equity-market declines. Their results indicate that factors can be used to identify hedge fund exposures that can provide large, positive returns during periods when conventional equity markets are under stress.

Lastly, analysis of potential correlations of different hedge funds and fund strategies in a time of stress can provide a framework for constructing a core satellite fund of funds portfolio. Strategies and funds which demonstrate consistent low correlations or provide tail risk hedges should be part of the core portfolio and where the fund of funds manager can monitor the risk-return parameters continuously, and dynamically allocate to different hedge fund strategies as market conditions change, these allocations would be part of the satellite portfolio. For less-sophisticated investors or investors without such capabilities, the hedge fund portfolio should be kept at a core strategy level consistent with the client's long-term investment objective.

Quantitative Screening

Once the investor has developed an investment mandate and set out a core-strategy allocation, then individual funds must be identified for investment. Hedge fund databases containing detailed statistical data are often used to screen potential funds.[16] The factor analysis described above can be used to initially screen out funds that are ill-suited to the investor's mandate. The quality of returns can be evaluated based on auto or serial correlation of returns, percentage of profitable months, and so on. In addition to screening for pure risk criteria, risk-adjusted performance metrics—including downside deviation, Sharpe ratio, Calmar ratio, Sterling ratio, Sortino ratio, and maximum drawdown—can form the basis for screening. The critical statistics used may vary but should be directly or closely linked to the investment mandate and the expected returns and risk appetite defined therein.

From a risk perspective, it is important to set thresholds for volatility, skew and kurtosis in the screening process. It is true that within each major hedge fund strategy, the average historical volatility of funds that tended to subsequently fail was typically greater than the average volatility of surviving funds. Funds which subsequently failed also tended to have lower positive skew than surviving funds. This result is particularly strong for event-driven strategies, where the average active fund had positive skew while the average dead fund had negative skew. Funds which subsequently failed also tended to have higher estimated kurtosis, indicating that return distributions of the riskier funds tend to have fatter tails. It is also important to evaluate auto and serial correlation of returns as a potential indication of return-smoothing or fraud.

Lastly, statistical performance data should never be evaluated as of one point in time or for one manager in isolation but always on a rolling basis relative to a peer set. Doing so accelerates the search process by screening out managers who fail to consistently outperform their peers over time. The screening should result in a shortlist of eligible funds.

Qualitative Screening

Everything covered above will help the investor or advisor get to a shortlist of managers on whom the investor intends to perform due diligence. One of the first steps in this process is to develop a full statistical profile on each of the managers on the list. If a complete quantitative profile is generated on a potential investment before the qualitative analysis has begun, one can formulate better due diligence questions which are specific to the manager's history and strategy. In addition, one can identify issues such as capacity or lack of risk control that could have an adverse impact on the investment in the future.

For example, a very strong annualized return versus the fund's benchmarks could hide a strategy shift by the fund. A small-cap equity long/short manager's 25.39 percent compound annualized return since inception may outperform both the Russell 2000 and the HFR Long Short Equity Index. However, if the rolling returns indicate that the manager's return outperformed the Russell 2000 by an increasing margin through time and that his returns became more correlated with the HFR Long Short Equity Index, then the manager should certainly be questioned as to whether he has increasingly drifted out of his small-cap focus and more into mid and large caps. It is up to the investor or his advisor to determine if the manager's strategy or risk control has fundamentally changed. If an investor were to rely too heavily on just the annualized statistics since inception, he may miss these important questions.

Investor Due Diligence

Investors should directly undertake or engage professional advisors to conduct rigorous due diligence on prospective hedge fund managers. This should in no way be considered a mere formality by investors. Prospective fund managers may initially offer little more than the due-diligence information available in the fund's offering documents but investors must ensure all relevant questions are answered and be prepared to probe beyond the standard material.

Experience is critical when assessing investment potential and risk. No two managers are the same, and funds cannot simply be reviewed using a mechanical checklist or a simple "one size fits all" approach. Quantitative analysis of the fund prior to the due diligence can indicate areas where further qualitative investigation is needed. A careful, experienced perspective is needed to assess the relative strengths and weaknesses of each fund structure, probing deeper in relevant areas, prioritizing the risks of the fund strategy and operations, and evaluating those risks against existing controls and evolving best practices.

Due Diligence Process

While due diligence should be customized by strategy and fund, there are many common areas of investigation for all funds. This part of the process can be accelerated by submitting a due diligence questionnaire to the fund's management in advance of the face-to-face meeting, requesting information covering major aspects of the fund such as the investment terms of the fund; the nature of the fund's business and investment strategy, including its management, workforce, creditors, customers, assets, liabilities, revenues, competition, and other business risks; and the regulatory schemes applicable to the fund. Investors or their advisors should review the documents submitted to ensure satisfactory compliance with the request and to determine what additional information is required. Potential investors or their advisors should then seek meetings with the officers of the fund and other persons significantly involved in the fund's business, risk management and investing to probe bespoke areas relevant to the fund and the investor.

In addition to the due diligence outlined in earlier chapters, investors should look in the areas set out in Table 7.1 and address any warning signs before committing to an investment in a hedge fund.

In addition, potential investors should evaluate the character of the key staff at the fund. Investors may prepare and distribute questionnaires to directors, officers, and principals of the fund management company asking for their background and experience, including any involvement in bankruptcy, criminal, civil, or administrative proceedings; ownership of the fund's securities; business transactions with the fund; and other information related to their knowledge and participation in the fund's business. This information may also then be cross-referenced against a third-party background investigation on key fund individuals.

TABLE 7.1 Additional due diligence considerations

Description/Area	Key Areas to Probe/Warning Signs
Organizational Documents	
What is the fund's mailing address? Is it the same as the physical address?	If there are multiple addresses for the fund, or if the fund shares an address or office space with another fund or another business or company, require an explanation and obtain document (written contract) that enables sharing or co-location. Beware of soft dollar[17] arrangements where investors inadvertently subsidize costs of investment activities in which they do not benefit.
Is the fund domestic or offshore?	If offshore, determine whether the manager and/or fund are regulated by any regulator and, if so, obtain regulatory filings. While neither legal location—domestic nor offshore—is a warning sign, investors must understand the regulatory framework or lack thereof governing the fund.
Ask about lawyer, accountant, administrator and prime broker.	Are the lawyer, accountant, administrator and prime broker reputable? Inquire about the lawyers and the accountants: use of professionals who are not well known raises concerns and there is a limited universe of professionals in each offshore jurisdiction. Request letters of engagement to prove relationship with the fund. If any professional service providers are unknown to the investor, references on each should be obtained. If references are not forthcoming, this is a warning sign.
Where are the funds and securities custodied?	If the answer is not New York, London, or some other major financial center, this is a warning sign.
If the fund is domiciled in the US, is the fund registered with the SEC?	Request a copy of Form D, as filed with the SEC and relevant states. Verify the Form D or state regulatory equivalent

(continued)

TABLE 7.1   (*Continued*)

Description/Area	Key Areas to Probe/Warning Signs
	filings in all states. If Form D is not forthcoming, this is a warning sign.
What state is the fund organized in?	Most domestic funds are organized in Delaware, although some are organized in Nevada, and, occasionally, in another state. Obtain fund formation documents (e.g., Articles of Organization or Articles of Association). If Articles are not forthcoming, this is a warning sign.
Request State Certificate of Good Standing from fund.	This can be obtained from the State of formation. Contact State to verify certificate status or request that certificate is mailed directly to you. If State Certificate of Good Standing is not forthcoming, this is a warning sign.
Fees and Expenses	
What is the management fee?	Does the manager have the right to more than 2 percent of assets under management? If so, is the investment strategy sufficiently operationally intensive to justify this high operational load? Gross returns may not be high enough to leave investors with sufficient net return to warrant the risk. If not, this is a warning sign.
What is the performance fee?	Does the manager have the right to more than 20 percent of the profits? If so, this is a warning sign as even if the fund is profitable, returns to investors may be insufficient to justify the risk. Is the expected return likely to be sufficient net of fees? If not, think twice about investing as net returns may be insufficient to justify the risk. Does the agreement have a "high water mark" (i.e., where an investor has had profits, and the manager has taken a share of profits, manager can only take profits in a later year if the losses are made up first)? If not, this indicates unfairness on the part of the manager and it is probably inadvisable to invest.

What are the Withdrawal Terms? Does the agreement permit an investor to withdraw all or part of its capital? If so, on what conditions must the investor give written notice (such as 90 days or 180 days) and how often in each year can an investor withdraw? Industry standards vary.

The ability to partially withdraw funds is important in that it enables an investor to rebalance their portfolio or execute a change in strategy without losing the opportunity to invest in the fund entirely. Long notice and liquidation periods increase the risk of loss to investors due to illiquidity of their investments. If the agreement contains very restrictive withdrawal rights that are inconsistent with the purported liquidity of the underlying fund assets, this is a warning sign.

Financial Statements & Performance

Obtain copies of the last three years' audited financial statements directly from the auditor.

Review them to see whether they agree with what the manager has represented to be the fund's results. Do not accept copies provided by the fund. Failure of the auditor to provide true copies is a warning sign, as are any inconsistencies between the audited and reported results. Unsatisfactory opinions are also warning signs.

Obtain copies of filed tax returns for last three years directly from the fund's accounting firm. Compare results to audited financials, and reconcile tax results with financials (through unrealized gain/loss).

Do not accept copies provided by the fund. Tax returns should include schedules and statements (except Schedule K-1, which discloses each investor's position in the fund). Determine whether for tax purposes the fund is treated as a trader in securities or as an investor. If the fund is treated as an investor, this is a warning sign as the taxes on investors are typically less favorable.

Obtain Performance Reports since inception net of fees. If Performance Presentation Material (PPM) gives statistical history, review this and compare to audited financials. If manager supplies historical results, ask if these results are presented in compliance with AIMR (industry association) guidelines for presentation of results.

Have the manager explain any volatility in monthly performance history, or dramatic changes in the size of the fund. What were the largest withdrawals from the fund since inception? If the manager cannot fully explain significant volatility in performance or significant changes in AUM, then this is a warning sign. If the performance results are not AIMR compliant, then this is a warning sign.

(continued)

TABLE 7.1 (*Continued*)

Description/Area	Key Areas to Probe/Warning Signs
Examine the investment manager's past performance at other funds (if applicable).	If performance reports are AIMR compliant, perform autocorrelation[18] and Omega ratio[19] evaluation of returns to detect return manipulation or smoothing. Ask manager to explain substantial deviation in either measure from his peers. Inability to adequately do so is a warning sign.
Does the fund report far superior results to other funds in its investment strategy group?	If so, ask for an explanation since there have been a number of frauds involving purportedly excellent results that ran counter to prevailing trends.
Method for valuing portfolio holdings, including illiquid holdings. Discuss the valuation process and the sources used for pricing. If there are any illiquid securities, find out what percentage of the portfolio they make up and the guidelines that are used for pricing. Additionally, verify how they measure illiquidity risk.	If the manager determines or overly influences the valuation of certain assets or types of assets, this is a warning sign.
Investment Terms	
Fund manager's level of investment in the fund	The fund manager should have a material portion of his personal net worth invested in the fund in order to align his interests with those of investors. Failure to do so is a warning sign.
Types of clients and investors in the fund (e.g., institutional, high net worth, etc.)	Ideally, clients would be diversified by type and liquidity preference, but this is not always possible. A concentration of investors with high liquidity preferences and short redemption terms could be a warning sign but it also depends on the underlying liquidity of the fund assets if there is no early-redemption fee.
Investor lock-up and withdrawal periods	Investors with side letters allowing preferential or early withdrawal from the fund is a warning sign.

Integrity of Manager and Staff

What are the employment histories of the personnel? Were they employed at other hedge funds?	If so, verify employment and review the history of those funds. What was the fate of the previous funds? Histories of funds that failed dramatically, gated themselves, or were forced to be liquidated are a warning sign. Were they employed at major financial institutions, and, if so, in what capacity? Any misrepresentation of employment is a warning sign.
Obtain photo identification from the manager (driver's license, passport, etc.). Be sure to obtain permission from each individual to run a background check.	Denial of a request to conduct a background check is a warning sign.
Check on court decisions against the manager and its principals.	All litigation or regulatory proceedings against the fund, manager or staff should be reviewed. The investor should decide whether the events were duly resolved and whether any investor suffered as a result. A fund manager that exhibits a pattern of investigations and proceedings should be avoided even if those events were dismissed. Court decisions against the manager and its principals are a warning sign.
Get at least three references from the manager: inquire as to who the referees are and conduct due diligence.	Refusal of the manager to provide references is a warning sign.
Is there a compliance manual and code of ethics? What are the personal trading policies? Are any portfolio managers located outside of the office that cannot be monitored?	Lack of a code of ethics and compliance manual can indicate a weak compliance culture. Similarly, lack of a personal trading policy can indicate a weak compliance culture. Both are potential warning signs.
What has the employee turnover been like (departures and new hires) for the last three years?	Sudden, multiple, unexplained departures can be a sign of employees leaving the firm due to discomfort with unethical business practices. This can be a warning sign.

(continued)

TABLE 7.1   *(Continued)*

Description/Area	Key Areas to Probe/Warning Signs
Portfolio Construction	
Request details of portfolio characteristics (e.g., typical number of long and short positions, breakdown of industries held long and short, average holding period, days to liquidate, turnover, volatility, etc.)	What is the manager's approach to diversification (e.g., a possible limit might be no more than five percent in any particular holding and no more than 10 percent in any particular industry)? Excessively diversified portfolios can dilute alpha. Insufficiently diversified portfolios can increase idiosyncratic risk without providing proportionate return. Does portfolio liquidity match potential investors' redemption terms? Excessively concentrated or illiquid portfolios are a warning sign.
Average holding period for investments	Excessively long holding periods may indicate illiquid positions and may be a warning sign.
Leverage information for the fund and aggregate leverage limitations	Historical periods of very high leverage and large gains or losses may indicate lack of discipline or gambling type of behavior and is a warning sign. An inability to articulate concrete limitations on leverage may indicate lack of trading discipline and is a warning sign.
Manager's risk management processes	Risk management processes should focus on primary risks of the specific strategy and include not only investment risks but funding, operational, and counterparty credit risks. An inability to articulate a risk management process may indicate lack of risk management discipline and is a warning sign.
Operational Capabilities	
Who is (are) the fund's brokerage firm(s)?	Are they reputable? What is their creditworthiness? Has the fund diversified its prime brokers? What procedures does the fund follow to mitigate counterparty risk of the prime broker? Do they allow securities to be

	rehypothecated? If so, is it greater than 140 percent of indebtedness? Do they routinely sweep out excess equity in their prime brokerage? Do they have a margin lock-up? Do they have a tri-party margin agreement? If prime brokers are not diversified and these issues collectively expose the fund to counterparty and/or funding risk, this is a warning sign.
Contingency and business continuity plans	A BCP plan that enables the fund to quickly recommence operations after an operational disruption is critical to avoiding potentially major losses. Lack of a BCP plan is a significant oversight and such funds should be avoided.
Description of trade-allocation process	For a manager managing multiple funds and managed accounts, a written trade-allocation process should be requested. Such a process should be consistent with AIMR principles. Lack of a written policy should be considered a warning sign as it can lead to unfair allocation of trades and manipulation of performance.
Historical monthly net asset values frequency and detail of information given to investors	A hedge fund that cannot provide monthly performance results within two weeks of the end of the month may indicate either a) illiquid assets or b) insufficient operational capability, and should be avoided.

DETECTING ABNORMAL RETURN PATTERNS

One of the main reasons why performance and risk measures fail to adequately expose certain risks such as fraud in hedge funds is the uniqueness of hedge fund strategies and related operational issues in executing these strategies. Hedge fund returns are not as easily decomposed and attributable to explicit risk factors as long-only funds.

That said, quantitative analysis can provide a clue to potential return manipulation and fraud. A number of authors, including Getmansky *et al.*, have argued that the presence of autocorrelations in hedge fund returns is an indication of fraud, while others have argued that it is simply an indication of the illiquidity of the underlying assets held by hedge funds.[20] Bollen and Krepely have claimed that the presence of positive autocorrelation can be an indication of return-smoothing, though Asness, Krail and Liew consider it evidence of stale pricing which can be benignly incidental or malignantly intentional.[21]

Any quantitative assessment of an individual fund's returns must be evaluated with respect to its strategy peers. This is because certain strategies display higher positive autocorrelation than others. Autocorrelation estimates are higher for convertible arbitrage, distressed securities and fixed income arbitrage and very low for equity and global-macro strategies mainly because of the differentials in liquidity of the underlying securities used in each strategy.

As autocorrelation alone is not evidence of return manipulation or fraud, there is the danger that applying an autocorrelation test would result in false positives. To reduce the likelihood of false positives, an additional filter for abnormal outperformance of peers coincident with autocorrelation is recommended.[22]

Autocorrelation

Autocorrelation exists if performance today will have an effect on performance next month. Formally, autocorrelation can be measured as

$$r_{t+1} = \rho_0 + \sum_{k=1}^{q} \rho_k r_{t-k} + \varepsilon_{t+1}$$

where: q = number of lagged returns
ρ_k = the partial autocorrelation of returns at the kth lag
ε = residuals.

A test for autocorrelation is the Box-Ljung Test (or Q-Statistic)[23]

$$Q = T(T+2) \sum_{k=1}^{q} \frac{\rho_k^2}{T-k}$$

where the null hypothesis is that the time series is independently distributed and is not autocorrelated and the alternative hypothesis is that the time series of returns is autocorrelated. Using six-month lagged returns for autocorrelation, the level of p-value of the Q-statistic indicates whether the null hypothesis can be rejected. The smaller the p-value the stronger evidence against the null hypothesis and the greater the likelihood that autocorrelation is present.

As many hedge fund strategies indicate autocorrelation, for an individual fund to be suspect, it should significantly exceed the autocorrelation level for its strategy and be significantly outperforming its peers. It is unlikely that a manager would manipulate his returns to underperform his peers.

Outperformance

One method available to detect outperformance that does not assume a normal return distribution is Omega.[24] Informally, Omega is the ratio of probability-weighted gains and losses over a predefined return threshold. Formally, it is:

$$\Omega_X(\tau) = \frac{\int_\tau^\infty (1 - F_X(x))dx}{\int_{-\infty}^\tau F_X(x)dx} = \frac{Gains}{Losses}$$

where τ is a predefined return threshold or minimal accepted return.

The advantages of Omega over other return metrics are that it does not assume normality of returns and uses the exact empirical distribution of returns in its calculation. For example, the Sharpe ratio assumes returns are Gaussian, which is too strong an assumption for hedge funds.

Application

Autocorrelation and Omega can be used to rank potential hedge funds with respect to their peers and representative indices. Individual fund results for Omega and p can be indexed to the Omega and p levels for the HFR index that matches their strategy where the HFR index values are the divisors. Funds can then be ranked according to their indexed Omega and p values. A high-indexed Omega value and low-indexed p value may be a signal of elevated fraud risk. For example, Bernie Madoff's fund, Greenwich Fairfield Sentry, would have had an Omega Index Ratio equal to 42 with a p value approaching 0, indicating strong outperformance of peers and high autocorrelation of returns relative to peers. An investment advisor or fund of funds manager could formalize a rule where the top 10 percent of funds in each distribution could be filtered out and require further investigation for fraud if it were to remain a viable investment candidate.

HEDGE FUND MONITORING

When the target allocation has been determined and the investor allocates capital to the chosen hedge funds, the work is by no means done. From this point on, it is essential to monitor the investment to ensure that it meets expectations. The managers in the portfolio must be continually evaluated to determine if they remain the best choices. Do they still meet the investor's minimum acceptable return and risk standards? Do they have peers that are now performing better in one or more categories? Are the managers still doing what they were hired to do? In comparison to their peers, are these investments still the best the investor can do? The investor, his advisor, or fund of funds manager will typically visit the manager every few months to ensure that the provisions of the investment agreement are still followed. Between regular visits to the office, the investor has to rely on reported fund returns to determine if the fund is following the agreed guidelines. These then need to be combined to evaluate whether the fund of funds portfolio is acting as expected.

In general, it is a good idea to run a full quantitative analysis on the invested funds at least monthly. This enables tracking of the evolution of hedge fund factors, confirmation that expected correlations continue to be realized and rolling volatility remains within expectations, monitoring of downside risk and the ongoing risk analysis of the combined portfolio. In addition, it is advisable to have a mini due diligence session quarterly or semi-annually to go over the portfolio, markets, and strategy with the manager. The quantitative analysis is also useful in generating relevant questions for discussion with the fund manager. Finally, it is important to continue with regulatory and reference checks at least once a year.

Again, factor analysis has a valuable role to play in the monitoring process. Updating the factor analysis of hedge fund returns after investment allows investors and fund of funds managers to have a better view of the changing fund profiles within their portfolios (for example, increasing or decreasing alpha, beta, and correlations). It can guide also questioning of the fund manager regarding changes in performance or strategy. Lastly, significant and sustained changes in the relative power of various factors to explain returns can indicate a change in the risk profile of the fund and motivate adjustments to allocations to various managers.

Many investors and FOF managers, in an attempt to build a diversified portfolio, select funds with low, no or negative correlations with one another or to a benchmark. To check that the correlations between funds and the benchmark remain low on a continuing basis, the investor or FOF manager may run consistent correlation calculations on a monthly basis. Because of the likely lengthy return time series before investment and the fact that hedge funds report returns monthly, updating the correlation calculations monthly may not necessarily demonstrate developing trends in the portfolio until it is too late. Tracking the rolling correlation of the underlying funds of a rather short time window introduces greater volatility and less precision in the correlation statistic but makes it more responsive to a change. The investor or fund of funds manager can then enquire about the change with the fund. Why is the correlation of the fund increasing? Have there been significant changes to the strategy? Is the fund investing excess cash in indexes? What does the manager plan to do, if anything, in the future to ensure that the fund does not become excessively and permanently correlated to a particular index? If the correlation change is spurious, the fund will have no explanation. If it is due to a change of strategy or exogenous market phenomenon, the fund will say so. The shorter time window increases the likelihood that the investor can make adjustments before a potential loss is incurred but creates a greater possibility for false alarms.

Similarly, factor analysis can be run on hedge fund returns. The key is to examine factors over rolling time periods for changes that might have a negative impact on the portfolio, and not just look at snapshots in time. While this shorter time window increases the uncertainty of the results, by the time you are certain, it may be too late to avoid losses.

A sound process to monitor a regression relationship known to be stable for a given historical period in light of new incoming data was proposed by Hornik *et al.*[25] This process is then adapted to hedge fund factor monitoring by Gupta and Kazemi, who show that it would have been effective in detecting style drift before three notable hedge fund failures (Bayou Fund, Marque Partners I, and V-Tek Capital).[26]

Essentially, the monitoring process proposed compares the factor loadings estimated based on data received up to the last due-diligence visit with the factor loading estimated based on the data after and including the last due diligence visit. The difference in the estimated factors is scaled based on the volatility of the data and the standard errors of the estimates. The scaled difference measure fits a Brownian bridge distribution and the empirical scaled difference is evaluated against that distribution to see if it is statistically significant within a given confidence interval. If factor exposures change over time and violate the 95 percent confidence interval, it is indicative of style drift.

Briefly, suppose the rate of return on a fund's strategy can be expressed by a linear factor model of the following form:

$$r_t = \beta_0 + \sum \beta_j\, f_{jt} + \varepsilon_t$$

In this expression r_t is the return on the fund at time t, β_j for j=1, . . . , F are factor exposures of the fund, f_{it} is the return to factor i and ε_t is the error term or unexplained manager's alpha.

The manager's return up to the last due-diligence visit, t=n, was generated by the above model. Therefore, the objective of the analysis is to use returns observed at time t, where t=n+1, . . . , T, with T being the time for next visit, to see if there have been material changes in factor exposures. The monitoring test proposed by Hornik *et al.* uses the following test statistic:

$$Y(t) = \Lambda(t) \times (\beta^{\Lambda(t)} - \beta^{\Lambda(n)})$$

where $\beta^{\Lambda(n)}$ is the estimated value of the vector of the coefficients of the linear factor model using data up to period n (that is, the date of the last due-diligence visit), $\beta^{\Lambda(t)}$ is the estimated value of the vector of the coefficients of the factor based on the most recent return data, and $\Lambda(t)$ is a scaling factor related to the volatility of the data and the standard errors of the estimates. To decide if there has been a structural change in the linear factor model, the value of $Y(t)$ is compared to $\pm b(t)$, where

$$b(\tau) = \sqrt{\tau(\tau - 1)}[\lambda^2 + \log(\tau/\tau - 1)]$$
$$\tau = t/n$$

If $Y(t)$, for t=n+1, . . . ,T, crosses the two boundaries, then the null hypothesis of no change is rejected. The value of λ^2 is selected to reflect the level of confidence (for example, at 95 percent confidence level $\lambda^2 = 7.78$). If factor exposures change over time and violate the 95 percent confidence interval, it is indicative of style drift.

Other types of strategy drift can be detected through qualitative monitoring. It seems likely that asset size is a very important performance factor in evaluating and monitoring hedge funds. Many managers tend to post their best returns when their funds are small and nimble. The best close their funds to new investors rather than let performance suffer; but others, enticed by larger management fees and confidence that their performance will not suffer, continue to gather assets. Depending on the strategy, performance could suffer as assets increase if there are insufficient opportunities to deploy capital. In such circumstance, managers may deviate from the strategy that made them initially successful and may resort to one of the following tactics to keep capital in play:

1. Look outside the manager's area of expertise for additional investment opportunities. Some outgrowths are logical and can prove profitable (merger arbitrage managers looking at other event-driven opportunities,

convertible managers looking into Reg. D, and so on.). However, there is always a risk when a manager deviates from his or her tried and true strategy.

2. Concentrate more money into top-tier investment ideas, thus increasing the risk that one particular investment could seriously impact the entire fund. This can be detected by tracking largest positions through time as a percentage of assets under management (AUM).

3. Move from top investment ideas to second, third or fourth-tier opportunities, thereby compromising the performance of the fund. This will be detected through deteriorating performance.

4. Keep large amounts of the fund in cash, thereby lowering returns. This can be detected by tracking the fund's unencumbered cash positions monthly as a percentage of AUM.

5. Farm portions of the investment management process out to other sub-advisors who may not have the manager's level of experience, credentials or back office infrastructure. This should not occur without advance notice to the investors and can be enquired into in periodic due diligence updates.

6. Spend more time managing the organization and less time managing the fund, leaving the day-to-day operations in the hands of more junior personnel. This should not occur without advance notice to the investors and can be enquired into in periodic due diligence updates.

If performance has trailed off as assets have grown, the investor should ask if the manager reached the limit of his capacity. Does he have ample staff to handle the additional capital or is he spending more time on back office duties and less on the actual money management? Does the manager believe he has reached his maximum capacity?

What has caused the spikes and dips in performance and how did the manager react to each? Are there other funds in his stable that continue to grow which require more of the manager's attention? If the manager believes assets have not affected performance, what is the explanation for current performance? There are a host of issues that can be detected from a simple time-series graph of performance vs. assets under management.

CONCLUSION

Empirical evidence indicates that investing in hedge funds, when done well, can provide higher portfolio returns, lower portfolio investment correlations, and partial protection against losses in down markets. But hedge fund investing comes with challenges that the typical long-only investor may not have faced previously.

Determining how much of a traditional portfolio to allocate to hedge funds requires a sophisticated assessment of the risk tolerance and targeted return expectations of the investor or as defined in the investment mandate. Creating an allocation that meets those requirements is complicated by the paucity of transparent data and the non-normal return distributions of hedge funds. Investors need to arm themselves with more sophisticated analytical techniques such as factor analysis, risk adjusted performance statistics that are appropriate for non-normal return distributions, and in-depth knowledge of hedge fund strategies to enable value-added due diligence. All this quantitative and qualitative analysis must then be brought together to screen and rank hedge funds. The screening and portfolio construction process must include advanced stress and scenario analysis for uncovering downside and ways to mitigate tail risk.

After the commitment has been made to a defined hedge fund allocation, those investments must be monitored to see if expectations are being, and are likely to continue to be, met. Tracking of factor exposures, correlations, and periodic qualitative assessments of hedge fund returns is necessary to detect style drift and potential in fund performance before losses are incurred. If executed well, these processes can increase the probability that investors will achieve higher upside and avoid many of the downside risks of hedge fund investing.

ENDNOTES

1. Bessler, W., and W. Drobetz 2008, "Editorial Special Issue: New Asset Classes," *Financial Markets & Portfolio Management* 22: 95–9.
2. Bessler, W., J. Holler and P. Kurmann 2010, "Hedge Funds and Optimal Asset Allocation: Bayesian Expectations, Time-Varying Investment Opportunities and Mean-Variance Spanning," Center for Finance and Banking, Justus-Liebig-University Giessen: 3.
3. Lo, Andrew W. 2001, "Risk Management for Hedge Funds: Introduction and Overview" in *Financial Analysts Journal* 57: 16–33.
4. Getmansky, Mila, Andrew W. Lo and Igor Makarov 2004, "An Econometric Model of Serial Correlation and Illiquidity in Hedge Fund Returns" in *Journal of Financial Economics* 74: 529–609.
5. Markowitz's mean-variance optimization technique is commonly used in portfolio construction. Unfortunately, this technique can introduce errors, both because the future tends not to resemble the past and because the technique generally takes historical point estimates for the vector of mean returns and the variance-covariance matrix as inputs. To the extent that high past returns and

low correlations do not persist over time, mean-variance optimization may produce misleading results.

6. Giamouridis, D., and I. Vrontos 2006, "Hedge fund portfolio construction: A comparison of static and dynamic approaches" in *Journal of Banking and Finance*: 23.

7. Bessler, Holler and Kurmann, op. cit.

8. French, Craig W., and Jimmy Kyung Soo Liew 2005, "Quantitative Topics in Hedge Fund Investing," *Journal of Portfolio Management* 31(4): 21–32.

9. Malkiel, Burton G. G., and Atanu Saha 2005, "Hedge Funds: Risk and Return," *Financial Analysts Journal* 61(6): 80–8. This study is criticized for not fully understanding the hedge fund index provider's methodology and erroneously concluding index returns are overstated.

10. Agarwal. V., and N. Naik 2000, "Multi-Period Performance Persistence Analysis of Hedge Funds," *Journal of Financial and Quantitative Analysis* 35(3).

11. Using PCA, Fung and Hsieh (1997) identified five return-based style factors. Since then Brown and Goetzmann (2003) extended that study using an updated data set applying different statistical techniques and found eight style factors. They interpreted these factors to be Global Macro (similar to Fung and Hsieh (1997)); Pure Leveraged Currency (similar to the trend-following factor of Fung and Hsieh (1997)); two equity factors—a US and a non-US factor (similar to the Value factor of Fung and Hsieh (1997)); an Event-Driven factor (similar to the Distressed Factor of Fung and Hsieh (1997)); and two sector-specific factors—Emerging Markets and Pure Property (both excluded from the Fung and Hsieh (1997) study). Like Brown and Goetzmann (2003) other studies on return-based style factors have generally identified additional factors that help to better explain returns. It is satisfying to note that, like the Brown and Goetzmann (2003) study, they have mostly concluded consistent findings to Fung and Hsieh (1997). This adds credence to the proposition that there are only a limited number of systematic hedge fund risk factors that persist over time.

12. Edwards, F. R., and M. O. Caglayan 2001, "Hedge Fund Performance and Manager Skill," *Journal of Futures Markets* 21: 1003–28.

13. While the short-term relationships can be quantified as well, the dynamic nature of hedge fund exposures makes generalizing about short-term sensitivities prone to error. Long-term relationships are more reliable but admittedly less useful for dynamic manager or strategy-allocation purposes.

14. Fung, W., and D. Hsieh 1997, "Empirical Characteristics of Dynamic Trading Strategies: The Case of Hedge Funds," *Review of Financial Studies* 10(2).

15. Fung W., and D. Hsieh 2002, "Asset-based Style Factors for Hedge Funds," *Financial Analyst Journal* 58: 16–27.

16. Not all funds of funds use databases in their screening. Among the reasons for this is that the very best managers often do need to contribute to these databases to source investors and consequently do not do so.

17. "Soft dollars" is a term used in finance to describe the commission generated from a trade or other financial transaction between a client and an investment manager. A soft-dollar arrangement is one in which the investment manager

directs the commission generated by the transaction towards a third party or in-house party in exchange for services that are for the benefit of the client but are not client directed.

18. Autocorrelation is the cross-correlation of a signal with itself. Informally, it is the similarity between observations as a function of the time separation between them. It is a mathematical tool for finding repeating patterns that could be created by a hedge fund manager manipulating returns month on month to either exaggerate returns or understate volatility. Lo (2002) documents that the positive autocorrelation in hedge fund returns can overstate the Sharpe ratio.

19. The Omega ratio is a measure of risk of an investment asset, portfolio or strategy. It involves partitioning returns into loss and gain above and below a given threshold; the Ω ratio is then the ratio of the probability of having a gain by the probability of having a loss. The Omega ratio takes into account all the moments of the distribution (mean return, volatility, skewness, kurtosis and higher moments). As a consequence, it is valid for non-normal returns and suitable for the asymmetric nature of hedge fund returns, for instance.

20. Getmansky, M., A. W. Lo, and I. Makarov 2004, "An Econometric Model of Serial Correlation and Illiquidity in Hedge Fund Returns," *Journal of Financial Economics* 74: 529–609.

21. Bollen, Nicolas P. B., and Veronika Krepely Pool, "Conditional Return Smoothing in the Hedge Fund Industry," *Journal of Financial and Quantitative Analysis* (JFQA), Forthcoming. Available at SSRN: http://ssrn.com/abstract=937990

22. Regardless of cause, if the monthly return series suffers from positive autocorrelation and the quantitative analyst fails to make the appropriate adjustments, true annualized volatilities will be underestimated and true diversification benefits will be overestimated. Some funds of hedge funds may allocate to managers using risk budgeting. Frequently this approach is accompanied by marginal value at risk analysis or maximum risk limits across strategies and managers. To the extent that the underlying hedge fund return streams suffer from positive serial correlation, allocating to risk buckets without any adjustments to estimated risks will bias the overall portfolio and unduly overweight those managers.

23. Ljung, G. M., and G. E. P. Box 1978, "On a Measure of a Lack of Fit in Time Series Models," *Biometrika* 65: 297–303. doi:10.1093/biomet/65.2.297.

24. Barreto, S. 2006, "'From Omega to Alpha' A New Ratio Arises," *Inside Edge*, Hedgeworld.

25. Hornik, Kurt, Friedrich Leisch, Christian Kleiber and Achim Zeileis 2005. "Monitoring structural change in dynamic econometric models," *Journal of Applied Econometrics* 20(1): 99–121.

26. Gupta, Bhaswar (with Raj Gupta) 2009, "Abnormal Return Patterns and Hedge Fund Failures," *Risk Management of Financial Institutions*, Spring.

CHAPTER 8

Conclusion

The recent credit crisis triggered market events that were unprecedented. As the crisis swept through the financial markets, it demonstrated the fragility of the hedge fund business model and, in particular, the need for hedge funds to balance their risk taking and leverage with stable liquidity and funding. The art of generating sustainable alpha requires that gyrating market forces, funding, leverage and risk taking be kept in continual equilibrium. There is no quantifiable formula for doing so as the behavior of fund managers, investors and creditors, and the frequency and magnitude of extreme market movements cannot be predicted with a high degree of certainty. There is significant potential—but often little room—for error.

While hedge funds and their investors have learned many lessons from direct experience during the financial crisis, these have been learned in isolation and have often been hidden to minimize the potential damage to the reputation of the funds. This book has attempted to bring those lessons together and distill them so that the investment and financial community need not repeat the mistakes of the past.

In summary, these lessons include:

1. Hedge funds should practice comprehensive risk management and in many cases employ a full time risk manager. Given the risk-management capabilities required (as outlined in Chapter 2), there is a need for risk management staff at hedge funds. The dominance of investment and funding risks in the risk profiles of most hedge fund strategies (as shown in Chapters 3 and 4) makes it imperative that the individuals responsible for risk management and chief financial officer should work closely together. Alternatively, these positions should be combined.
2. Risk management should consider the fund's total business risk, rather than simply focusing on the risks of the investment portfolio in isolation. The investment risks of the portfolio are typically evaluated solely with respect to the intrinsic risks of the securities in the investment

portfolio, and not in the context of the funding, counterparty and operational risks embedded in the fund's business model. This focus on investment risk implicitly assumes that the significant risks in the hedge fund all emanate from the investment portfolio and that the portfolio manager has sole and exclusive rights over the assets of the fund under all circumstances. This is an incorrect and potentially disastrous assumption.

3. Forward-looking scenario analysis should be employed that explicitly anticipates the potential actions of various stakeholders in the fund. Demands for cash to fund redemptions and meet potential margin calls should be evaluated in light of the rights of stakeholders, as defined in the fund's constitutional documents and prime-brokerage contracts. Analysis of potential extreme requirements for cash should be evaluated against the worst-case ability to generate cash from the investment portfolio, and appropriate contingency plans should be developed. The liquidity implications for the fund of the failure of a major counterparty should be part of this scenario analysis.

4. The ability to manage funding risk may be limited by the rights granted investors and creditors in the fund's constitutional documents and in its financing and collateral agreements with prime brokers. As discussed in Chapter 5, strategies for managing funding risk should be evaluated in light of worst-case funding scenario tests where the test results show potential asset/liability mismatches and funding gaps. The structuring of a fund's constitutional documents and its arrangements with prime brokers should aim to minimize these potential funding gaps.

5. As part of their funding risk management, funds should value stability and predictability in their margin requirements over market-driven margining methodologies that may provide high leverage in a calm market but increase margin unpredictably in market crises. The likely stability in funding from prime brokers can be increased by ensuring that the relationship remains profitable for the broker even in times of market disruption and a decline in the liquidity of the rehypothecation markets.

6. The hedge fund business model outsources many services to gain operational efficiency but in doing so creates operational and financial dependency on its counterparties. The failure of a counterparty can have a significant negative impact on a fund's performance and can be highly disruptive to its operations. Management of counterparty and operational risk, as discussed in Chapters 2 and 6, requires rigorous due diligence in the selection and diversification of counterparties and in ongoing monitoring. Minimizing exposures to counterparties comes at an economic cost. Limiting a broker's ability to rehypothecate

collateral, or placing initial margin in tri-party arrangements, minimizes counterparty exposure but also imposes a cost on the broker that diminishes the attractiveness of providing financing unless duly compensated.

THE IMPORTANCE OF CHANGE

The silver lining in the most recent crisis is that the painfully negative returns which accrued to relative-return investors means that absolute-return investing is here to stay. The increasing sophistication of investors and the accelerating competition amongst hedge funds for opportunities and for investors means that absolute-return investing on a large scale will become increasingly institutionalized.

The future of the hedge fund industry is primarily driven by the discriminating demands of its investors. The losses experience by investors in the credit crisis, the unsatisfactory correlated performance of most strategies (other than CTAs) to the market, and the unsatisfactory reaction of many high-profile hedge funds to large redemption demands have put fund managers under pressure. Investors will continue to allocate capital to funds which demonstrate risk adjusted performance superior to their peers. These funds will be allowed by investors to leverage off the mistakes of their peers and extend their proven investing and risk management discipline into new strategies and geographic regions.

Alpha generation will become more difficult as a result of a widening understanding of hedge fund strategies and the progressive emergence of high-velocity versions of traditional arbitrage strategies. Competition will diminish returns. While rewards for performance will remain high, expenses will increase because of the technology and personnel investments required to maintain an edge. Increasing demands from investors for greater transparency in their investing practices, risk profile, and risk management will also increase costs for hedge funds. Requests for separately managed accounts will continue to grow in light of redemption risks. Investors will continue to be more focused on the potential pitfalls of hedge funds and the expertise required to run and manage a fund successfully. Existing players will need to maintain and improve economies of scale and new entrants will face increasing barriers to entry. Consolidation is likely, with larger institutionalized firms built on core investing and risk management capabilities rather than on individual star managers.[1]

Given the shifts in economic and political power occurring between developed and developing nations, and the difficult political choices emanating from demographic shifts (declining fertility and rising longevity), developed-nation debt levels (rising taxation and low real interest rates), globalization and immigration, limited supply and growing global demand for commodities, clashing religious beliefs, widening income differentials, and global warming, uncertainty is also here to stay. Risk management cannot eliminate uncertainty but it can reduce risk by avoiding risks that are unnecessary, diversifying and quantifying those that are unavoidable and ensuring that investment decisions are made with a full knowledge of the potential consequences should those decisions prove to be wrong.

Rewards to industry participants are not, and will not be, evenly distributed. Payoffs amongst hedge funds are increasingly skewed, depending on their risk profiles and risk management capabilities. The ability of the top hedge funds to measure, budget and control the amount of risk they take is a strategic and competitive advantage. This book has endeavored to analyze those abilities and to share the knowledge so that the mistakes made by the investment and financial community during the recent credit crisis need not be repeated.

ENDNOTE

1. Over the past three years many successful firms have returned capital and shut down, either due to poor performance or client redemptions. The most recent high-profile closure to be announced was that of Stanley Druckenmiller's Duquesne Capital Management LLC, which oversees US$12 billion and has never had a losing year, but which is down five percent in 2010. Druckenmiller stated that he was frustrated by his failure in the past three years to match returns that had averaged 30 percent annually since 1986 and would be closing the fund.

Topics for Due Diligence

HISTORY OF FIRM

Founded when, by whom and with what amount of seed AUM?

Background of key decision makers?

Organizational structure (management/decision making)?

Is there an investment committee and what is its role in overall asset allocation decisions?

Which individuals cover which markets?

What is the NAV (total and breakdown by fund)?

What is the legal structure of the fund?

Are there any cross shareholdings between legal entities? If so, to what extent?

Is the fund incorporated in any unusual offshore jurisdictions? If so, why chosen?

Any apparent conflicts of interest?

INVESTORS

What is the minimum investment in each fund (typically found in the offering memo)?

What is the history of fund raising (may be obvious in financials)?

How much capital raised (initially and in recent periods)?

What has been the withdrawal history (obtain history of capital in/out-flows and fees)?

What is the capital raising and marketing strategy?

What is the background of the major investors?

What is the redemption policy?

What percentage of the AUM is invested by high-net-worth individuals?

What percentage of the AUM is invested by institutions (examples)?

What percentage of the AUM is invested by Funds of Funds?

Amount of principals' money invested and in which funds?

Are there any concentrations of AUM held by certain investors or investor types?

Percentage of AUM held by the largest investor?

Percentage of total AUM owned by the top five/10 investors by fund?

How long have largest investors been with the fund?

INVESTMENT STRATEGY

Description of each strategy used.

Securities instruments used?

Major sources of financing/leverage?

What hedging techniques are used?

Examples of trades they like, trades they don't and why.

Time horizon of trades. Does it fit with the investment strategy and redemption terms?

Redemption rights? How are mismatches managed?

Any new strategies? If so, how have they added expertise for new market/risks?

Are all funds run in parallel? If not, the differences should be explained.

PERFORMANCE

What were the worst trading periods? Reasons for the poor performance? What lessons were learned and what remedial action was taken?

Detailed historical data of returns? Request updated reports as frequently as they are provided to limited partners.

How has performance tracked hedge fund indices and the fund's defined benchmark (e.g. CSFB/Tremont)?

RISK MANAGEMENT

How does the fund quantify risk by position, for entire fund(s)?

Request VaR, preferably by sub-component of the fund.

Is asset liquidity incorporated in VaR?

Request results of stress test (scenario description, financial results).

How does the fund monitor correlations between assets, funds, etc?

Review risk measurement methodology and procedures.

What are the stop-loss limits and procedures for individual trades?

Does the fund habitually implement stop-loss orders when putting on positions?

What is the tendency of the fund to override stop-loss and other limits? When and who makes these decisions?

What are the fund's concentration limits: typical and maximum size vs. NAV? Are there concentration limits by trade idea or investment theme? By security? By market? By geography?

Liquidity risk management: Liquidity of positions, manager's definitions and policy limits related to NAV.

Are there security-related liquidity limits (i.e. percentage of given security outstanding, trading volume)?

Overall policy limitation on "illiquid" positions as defined by management.

Operational risk measurement: internal control and organization.

Request copies of all risk reports.

TOLERANCE FOR LEVERAGE

How is leverage measured by management?

Are off-balance-sheet positions included? If so, how?

What factors change management's tolerance for leverage (e.g. asset/ market risk, volatility)?

What is the effect of leverage on market risk, funding risk and asset-liquidity risk?

What are the risk-based leverage measures (e.g. VaR/Equity or Stress Loss/Equity)?

CASH FLOW & MANAGEMENT OF FUNDING LIQUIDITY RISK

What measures are employed (e.g. cash/equity or VaR/Cash + Borrowing capacity)?

How many prime brokers? Who are they? What is the breakdown of business by broker?

How much cash is available to meet margin calls, meet redemptions (review redemption rights)?

Liquidity planning process/contingency planning.

PRICING PROCEDURES

What are stated procedures in audited reports? What percentage of AUM in Level 1, 2, and 3 assets?

What are the pricing procedures described in the offering memo? Do they match the audited financials?

Mark-to-market policies.

Valuation procedures for listed products.

Check dealers for unlisted investments (number of dealers providing prices? Who in the fund determines valuation of unlisted investments?)

How frequent is the use of manager/trader marks (percentage of total)?

Daily P&L availability.

Valuation procedures relating to side pockets.

Valuation procedures relating to private or restricted securities or private equity stakes.

BACK OFFICE

Internal: How many people involved and what responsibilities do they have?

External: Who are the service providers?

Hedge Fund Failures

AMARANTH ADVISORS LLC (2006)

Amaranth Advisors lost roughly US$6 billion in the natural gas futures market in September 2006. Amaranth had a concentrated, undiversified position in its natural gas strategy. Employing significant leverage, its positions were staggeringly large, representing around 10 percent of the global market in natural gas futures. Amaranth failed to factor in the size of its positions in comparison to the quoted value for small daily transactions and to set aside a sufficient liquidity reserve. Given its concentration in the security, it failed to correctly assess and reserve for its inability to sell its futures contracts at or near the latest quoted price. Hedge funds need to manage asset liquidity risk explicitly.

In Amaranth's case, the concentration was far too high and there were no natural counterparties when it needed to unwind the positions. Part of the loss Amaranth incurred was due to asset illiquidity. Regression analysis on the three-week return on natural gas futures contracts from August 31, 2006 to September 21, 2006 against the excess open interest suggested that contracts whose open interest on August 31 was much higher than the historical normalized value experienced larger negative returns.[1]

LTCM (1998)

Long-Term Capital Management (LTCM) was bailed out by a consortium of 14 banks in 1998 after being caught in a cash flow crisis when economic shocks resulted in excessive mark-to-market losses and margin calls. The fund suffered from a combination of funding and asset liquidity. Asset liquidity arose from LTCM's failure to account for liquidity becoming more valuable (as it did following the crisis). Since much of its balance sheet was exposed to liquidity risk premium, its short positions increased in price relative to its long positions. This was essentially a massive, unhedged exposure to a single risk factor. LTCM had been aware of funding liquidity risk. Indeed, it estimated that in times of severe stress, haircuts on AAA-rated commercial mortgages would increase from 2 percent to 10 percent, and similarly for other securities. In response to this, it had negotiated long-term financing with margins fixed for several weeks on many of its collateralized loans. Because of an escalating liquidity spiral, however, LTCM could ultimately not fund its positions, in spite of the numerous measures it took to control funding risk.

ENDNOTE

1. Ludwig Chincarini, "The Amaranth Debacle: A Failure of Risk Measures or a Failure of Risk Management?" *The Journal of Alternative Investments*, Winter 2007: 91.

Cash Management and the Probability of Failure

Hedge funds are a new business model for which data for quantifying forward-looking and even historical default probabilities remain scant. Creating exposures to alternative risk factors and generating alpha entails undertaking less conventional trading activities compared to long-only funds. In addition, hedge funds seek to produce asymmetrical expected-return profiles with non-linear risk exposures compared to long-only funds. To do so, they make use of margin financing and high leverage; invest in illiquid instruments; and quickly seize and then exit market opportunities, which results in high portfolio turnover. These strategies for alpha generation originated in the proprietary trading groups of investment banks, which were supported by the large balance sheets and robust operational infrastructure of those banks. Such is not the case for hedge funds, however, which may carry a level of funding and operational risk for which the investor receives no premium.

The objective of this appendix is to present a conceptual framework for quantifying hedge fund failure that may serve as a useful mental model for CFOs and CROs to frame strategic decisions relating to their minimal-level unencumbered cash. Formal quantification of the variables described below and of failure probabilities requires significantly more data than are publicly available and is beyond the scope of this book.

RETURN PROFILES

Hedge fund return profiles show non-Gaussian[1] characteristics. As shown in earlier chapters, an analysis of hedge fund-style specific-return indices showed that fund strategies have exhibited non-zero monthly returns and

TABLE A.1 Monthly Hedge Fund Index Returns Ranked By Kurtosis

Monthly Returns (January 2000–March 2010)

Hedge Fund Strategy	Mean	Standard Deviation	Skew	Kurtosis	Min Return	Max Return	Correlation to S&P
Fixed Income Relative Value	0.70	1.26	−2.81	17.72	−7.70	3.70	0.67
Distressed Debt	1.06	2.18	−0.93	5.73	−9.81	8.74	0.75
S&P 500	−0.17	4.37	−1.43	5.59	−22.80	11.35	1.00
Event Arb	0.94	2.07	−1.07	4.64	−8.58	6.86	0.75
Market Neutral	0.53	0.95	−0.53	4.12	−3.72	4.40	0.34
Multistrat	0.52	3.10	−1.25	2.90	−6.16	3.91	0.63
Convertible Arb	0.60	6.50	−0.19	2.33	−7.53	9.10	0.63
Equity L-S	0.84	2.28	−0.28	2.09	−7.04	9.21	0.67
Emerging Markets	1.33	2.62	−0.87	1.53	−8.81	7.91	0.90
Global Macro	0.89	1.31	0.58	1.21	−1.97	5.96	0.25
JPM Global Bonds	0.55	1.81	0.06	0.27	−3.91	6.35	0.03
CTA/ Managed Futures	0.81	8.53	0.15	0.06	−7.30	8.10	−0.20

Sources: Greenwich Alternative Investments, EurekaHedge, J.P. Morgan, Dr. Robert Shiller (Yale University)

varying degrees of kurtosis, all greater than zero (see Table A.1). A financial model that is able to fit this observed fat-tailed behavior is required.

STRUCTURAL DEFAULT MODEL

Structural-default models, such as the Merton Model, have been shown to be empirically accurate for non-financial firms, especially manufacturing entities. However, for highly leveraged financial firms, structural models predict credit spreads which are significantly higher than those observed in the market because of the high volatility of their assets and liabilities compared to those of less-levered non-financial firms. While not directly applicable to the measurement of the default probability of hedge funds, structural default models can provide a useful framework for considering that probability.

Structural models take three specific inputs: net asset value, the volatility of net asset value, and the value of liabilities/equity. The model also takes two inputs: the default barrier, and the volatility of the default barrier. These inputs are used to specify a diffusion process for the asset value. An entity is deemed to have defaulted when the asset value drops below the barrier. The barrier itself is stochastic, which has the effect of incorporating jump-to-default risk into the model. Structural default models evolve asset-value movements through a diffusion process and a fundamental purpose of the default barrier volatility is to provide a jump-like process which can capture short-term default probabilities.

Hedge funds have assets and liabilities. Liabilities are primarily debits owed to prime brokers to repay margin loans. Equity is contributed by investors in exchange for shares in the hedge fund. Assets are primarily unencumbered cash and the net liquidation value of the securities in the investment portfolio.

The challenge in applying a structural default model to hedge funds is that the value of the fund's assets and liabilities is highly stochastic but not normally distributed (i.e. non-Gaussian).[2] The value of the investment portfolio varies depending on market returns, as hedge fund returns (as shown in Table A.1) are to varying degrees correlated with the returns of the S&P 500, but it also varies as a result of other unobservable factors. Similarly, the value of the fund's liabilities vary primarily as a result of changes in the value of debits owed to prime brokers which are driven by market variables embodied in the broker's margin rules, the quality of the collateral portfolio at the broker, and the broker's assessment of the fund's creditworthiness. The fact that the hedge fund investment portfolio, level of liabilities, and quality of the collateral portfolio can change radically and daily as the portfolio manager makes trading and leverage decisions based on his constantly updated market view and opportunity set, only adds to the complexity.

FUNDING-BASED FAILURE MODEL

As the experience of the credit crisis showed, the hedge fund business model collapses when funds are unable to fund themselves on an ongoing basis. This may be due to a run on the fund by investors seeking to redeem their shares in a magnitude that exceeds the cash on hand and the cash that can be generated by liquidating the investment portfolio in the short term. It can also be due to increasing margin calls by prime brokers that require immediate posting of cash greater than the cash on hand and the cash that can be generated by liquidating the investment portfolio. Consequently, a simpler and more conservative conceptual framework for modeling hedge fund failure could be one where the failure rule is set at when the hedge fund's unencumbered cash and potential cash from immediate liquidation of its investments is less than the cash required to fund net redemptions and margin. Conceptually, the fund's net cash distribution replaces the net asset value distribution used in the structural model.

Formally, a framework determining the probability of failure over any investor redemption window would be:

$$P(A \cap B \cap C) < 0$$

where   A = Distribution of Potential Cash Generated by Liquidation of the Investment Portfolio between T_0 and R
        B = Distribution of Potential Cash Required due to Net Redemptions payable on R
        C = Distribution of Potential Cash Required due to Change in Margin Requirement between T_0 and R
    and R = Redemption Payable Date.

In other words, what is the likelihood of the value drawn from the joint distribution of Cash from Liquidations (A), Cash from Redemptions and Subscriptions (B), and Cash from Changes in Margin (C) on the redemption payable date being less than $0? Note that B and C can be net positive or negative.

Estimating the Distribution of A, B, and C

The shape of the distribution of A (Potential Cash Generated by Liquidation of the Investment Portfolio between T_0 and R) will vary depending on each hedge fund's strategy and the unique contents of each hedge fund's investment portfolio. However, all fund CFOs or risk managers can estimate the expected and worst-case potential amounts of cash that can be generated over any time horizon for their specific portfolios by conducting liquidity stress testing as described in Chapter 3.[3]

The shape of the distribution of B (Distribution of Potential Cash Required due to Net Redemptions payable on R) will be different for each fund because of the variations in the composition of its investor base. However, all fund CFOs and risk managers can estimate the expected and worst-case level of redemptions for their respective funds. These points in the distribution of B can be estimated based on historical analysis of investor redemption behavior. If the fund's constitutional documents prescribe the conditions under which the fund manager may gate the fund (for example, if redemptions are greater than 20 percent of the fund's AUM), then the worst-case value of B is known.

The shape of the distribution of C (Distribution of Potential Cash Required due to Change in Margin Requirement between T_0 and R) will also vary for each fund because of variations in their creditworthiness, strategy, and margin terms provided by their prime brokers. However, all fund CFOs and risk managers can estimate the expected and worst-case level of margin required for their funds. These points in the distribution of B can be estimated based on modeling of the prime broker's margin methodologies (VaR, stress and rules-based margin methodologies should be made transparent to the fund by the prime broker and can all be replicated internally by hedge funds) and applied to varying quality of collateral portfolios and under different market scenarios. In addition, if margin methodologies are not transparent, then historical analysis of margin requirements made on the fund's portfolios can give significant insight into the distribution and variability of margin required. Regression can provide insight into the drivers of margin. If the funds have margin lock-ups, then the worst-case level of margin required for a given portfolio during the notice period of the lock-up can be estimated with significant precision and confidence.

Potential Applications

The funding-based failure model outlined above can be a useful framework for analyzing various strategic decisions. These include:

- The optimal investor lock-up tenors, redemptions terms, margin lock-up tenors, and margin levels a hedge fund should have, given the volatility of the investment portfolio, the liquidity of the investment portfolio, and long-term targeted returns.
- The optimal level of unencumbered cash a fund should maintain in light of the variability of investment returns, the variability of liquidity of the investment portfolio, the variability of margin requirements, and the variability of investor redemptions, given required leverage and targeted returns.
- The optimal level of liquidity of the investment portfolio in light of the variability of investment returns, the variability of margin requirements, and the variability of investor redemptions, given required leverage and targeted returns.

■ The minimum level of unencumbered cash a fund should maintain in light of the variability of investment returns, the variability of liquidity of the investment portfolio, the variability of margin requirements, and the variability of investor redemptions, given an acceptable probability of fund failure.

■ The minimum level of liquidity of the investment portfolio in light of the variability of investment returns, the variability of margin requirements, and the variability of investor redemptions, given required leverage and targeted returns.

ENDNOTES

1. In probability theory and statistics, the normal distribution or Gaussian distribution is a continuous probability distribution that often gives a good description of data that cluster around the mean. The graph of the associated probability density function is bell-shaped, with a peak at the mean, and is known as the Gaussian function or bell curve.

2. "Stochastic" means "random." The value of a hedge fund's assets and liabilities is stochastic because it is non-deterministic, in that the value of assets and liabilities is determined both by some predictable elements and by a random element, specifically the market.

3. The estimation of cash that can be generated by liquidation should be overlaid with a simulation of the net asset value of the investment portfolio and incorporate a severe market decline in order to best estimate the worst-case cash-liquidation value.

Index